Quantitative Methods in Archaeology Using R

Quantitative Methods in Archaeology Using R is the first hands-on guide to using the R Statistical Computing System written specifically for archaeologists. It shows how to use the system to analyze many types of archaeological data.

Part I includes tutorials on R with applications to real archaeological data showing how to compute descriptive statistics, create tables, and produce a wide variety of charts and graphs. Data transformation and missing values are also covered. A chapter on confidence intervals and hypothesis testing introduces these statistical concepts and provides examples of several approaches including bootstrapping. Associations between variables including Chi-square tests, and simple linear regression completes the section on basic statistics. Part II addresses the major multivariate approaches used by archaeologists including multiple regression (and the generalized linear model); multiple analysis of variance and discriminant analysis; principal components analysis; correspondence analysis; distances and scaling; and cluster analysis. Part III covers specialized topics in archaeology including intra-site spatial analysis, seriation, and assemblage diversity.

David L. Carlson is a Professor of Anthropology at Texas A&M University where he has been teaching quantitative methods and the R statistical system to anthropology graduate students for eight years. His research focuses on the application of quantitative methods to discover and understand patterning in the distribution of artifacts on archaeological sites. He is a co-author of *Clovis Lithic Technology* (2011).

Cambridge Manuals in Archaeology

General Editor

Graeme Barker, *University of Cambridge*

Advisory Editors

Elizabeth Slater, *University of Liverpool*
Peter Bogucki, *Princeton University*

Cambridge Manuals in Archaeology is a series of reference handbooks designed for an international audience of upper-level undergraduate and graduate students and professional archaeologists and archaeological scientists in universities, museums, research laboratories and field units. Each book includes a survey of current archaeological practice alongside essential reference material on contemporary techniques and methodology.

Books in the series

Vertebrate Taphonomy, R. LEE LYMAN
Photography in Archaeology and Conservation, 2nd edition, PETER G. DORRELL
Alluvial Geoarchaeology, A. G. BROWN
Shells, CHERYL CLAASEN
Sampling in Archaeology, CLIVE ORTON
Excavation, STEVE ROSKAMS
Teeth, 2nd edition, SIMON HILLSON
Lithics, 2nd edition, WILLIAM ANDREFSKY, JR.
Geographical Information Systems in Archaeology, JAMES CONOLLY and MARK LAKE
Demography in Archaeology, ANDREW CHAMBERLAIN
Analytical Chemistry in Archaeology, A. M. POLLARD, C.M. BATT, B. STERN and
    S. M. M. YOUNG
Zooarchaeology, 2nd edition, ELIZABETH J. REITZ and ELIZABETH S. WING
Quantitative Paleozoology, R. LEE LYMAN
Paleopathology, TONY WALDRON
Fishes, ALWYNE WHEELER and ANDREW K. G. JONES
Archaeological Illustrations, LESLEY ADKINS and ROY ADKINS
Birds, DALE SERJEANTSON
Pottery in Archaeology, 2nd Edition, CLIVE ORTON and MICHAEL HUGHES
Applied Soils and Micromorphology in Archaeology, RICHARD I. MACPHAIL and PAUL
    GOLDBERG

Quantitative Methods in Archaeology Using R

David L. Carlson *Texas A & M University*

CAMBRIDGE
UNIVERSITY PRESS

CAMBRIDGE
UNIVERSITY PRESS

University Printing House, Cambridge CB2 8BS, United Kingdom

One Liberty Plaza, 20th Floor, New York, NY 10006, USA

477 Williamstown Road, Port Melbourne, VIC 3207, Australia

4843/24, 2nd Floor, Ansari Road, Daryaganj, Delhi – 110002, India

79 Anson Road, #06-04/06, Singapore 079906

Cambridge University Press is part of the University of Cambridge.

It furthers the University's mission by disseminating knowledge in the pursuit of education, learning, and research at the highest international levels of excellence.

www.cambridge.org
Information on this title: www.cambridge.org/9781107040212
DOI: 10.1017/9781139628730

First published 2017

Printed in Great Britain by Clays Ltd, St Ives plc

A catalogue record for this publication is available from the British Library.

ISBN 978-1-107-04021-2 Hardback
ISBN 978-1-107-65557-7 Paperback

CONTENTS

FIGURES

TABLES

BOXES

ACKNOWLEDGMENTS

I first began teaching anthropology students how to use the R statistical computing system in my graduate quantitative methods class in 2008, having used SAS, SPSS, and various other programs before. As open source and freely available worldwide for Windows, MacOS, and Linux, R was an obvious alternative. It is also the only software that readily accomplishes all of the quantitative analyses that archaeologists routinely employ. Anything that is not included in the base R system is covered in one of several thousand packages.

My interest in quantitative methods spans several decades beginning in a seminar taught by J. Ned Woodall at Wake Forest University. We were required to read a minimum number of articles or book chapters each week and I ran across a large book in the library that I thought would keep me occupied for several weeks. *Analytical Archaeology* by David L. Clarke did exactly that and illustrated many ways that quantitative approaches could facilitate the analysis of archaeological data. Later at Northwestern University, I studied with Bob Vierra, James A. Brown, and Stuart Struever and began applying quantitative methods to the Koster site for my dissertation research along with fellow students including John Hewitt, Sarah Neusius, and Mike Wiant.

At Illinois State University, I worked with Ed Jelks and Fred Lange learning to apply quantitative approaches to historic and prehistoric sites investigated during cultural resources investigations. That research continued at Texas A&M with Harry Shafer, Vaughn Bryant, Jr., and D. Bruce Dickson. It also involved a wide range of projects ranging from reservoir surveys and excavations in Texas (in collaboration with Kate Mueller Wille, Joe Saunders, and Alston Thoms) to a nineteenth-century sugar plantation in Mexico (with students Alan Meyers and Sam Sweitz). With Ron Bishop, W. Dennis James, M James Blackman, and Shawn Carlson, I was able to learn more about the analysis of ceramic compositions.

More recently, I collaborated with Michael Waters and Charlotte Pevny in analyzing the Clovis component in an excavation at the Gault Site in *Clovis Lithic Technology*. I am currently working with Michael Alvard on Domenican fishing activities using R to identify different fishing techniques from global positioning system (GPS) locational data.

While applying R to archaeological problems in my research, I also began to develop teaching materials for other archaeologists in the form of companion guides for introductory statistics texts for archaeologists, including Stephen Shennan's *Quantifying Archaeology* and Robert Drennan's *Statistics for Archaeologists*. I also began pulling data sets included in Michael Baxter's *Exploratory Multivariate Analysis in Archaeology* and *Statistics in Archaeology* to make them more easily available to my students. Those data sets and others are incorporated into the R package, `archdata`, that is used throughout the book. I have also benefited by participating in the r-help mailing list where an amazing range of people ask and answer questions about how to use R in their research.

I am indebted to all of these people for stimulating my interest in quantitative methods and suggesting interesting ways to apply them to archaeological data. I also appreciate the patience of my wife, Shawn, over the last several years that this book has been in development and my repeated promises that it was "almost" done.

The anonymous reviewers of the original manuscript lead to substantial improvements in the final product and the staff at Cambridge University Press, including Beatrice Rehl, Asya Graf, and Edgar Mendez, have been patient and supportive during the process.

My thanks also to Marion Coe who created Figures 5, 6, 9, and 41.

Introduction

Archaeology is the study of human culture and behavior through its material evidence. Although archaeology sometimes works with the material evidence of contemporary societies (ethnoarchaeology) or historical societies (historical archaeology and classical archaeology), for most of our past, the archaeological record is the only source of information. What we can learn about that past must come from surviving artifacts and modifications of the earth's surface produced by human activity. Fortunately, people tend to be messy.

Our basic sources of evidence consist of artifacts, waste products produced during the manufacture of artifacts or their use, food waste, ground disturbances including pits and mounds, constructions that enclose spaces such as buildings and walls, and the physical remains of people themselves. Study of this evidence includes identification of the raw materials used, what modifications occurred to make the object useful, and the physical shape and dimensions of the final product. Wear and breakage of the object and its repair are also examined.

In addition to its life history, each object has a context. It was discovered in a particular part of a site, in a particular site in a region, occupied by humans at a particular time. Together these make up the three dimensions that Albert Spaulding referred to as the "dimensions of archaeology" (Spaulding 1960).

Our discovery and analysis of archaeological evidence is directed toward the broad goal of understanding our past. The range of questions archaeologists are attempting to answer about the past is substantial. Broadly they could be grouped into a number of big questions:

1. How did our ancestors come to develop a radically new way of living that involved changes in locomotion (bipedalism), increasing use of tools, the formation of social groups unlike any other living primate, and increases in cranial capacity? Quantitative methods are used to identify sources of raw material

for stone tools to determine how far they were transported. They are also used to classify stone tools, to compare the kinds of tools and the kinds of animals found at different sites, and to look for correlations between the distributions of stone tools and animal bones.

2. Human culture involves the transmission of information across generations without depending on genetic inheritance. Part of that transmission involves the use of a flexible communication system and language, but culture includes the use of other symbolic forms of communication embedded in objects and artwork. Culture also includes the construction of different kinds of social groups and networks. How did culture emerge initially and how did its role in our survival increase? How did culture facilitate the migrations of our ancestors across the globe? Quantitative methods are used to study the distribution of artifact types, their composition, and the sources of the raw materials used to construct them. They are also used on plant and animal remains to identify changes in diet. The spatial distribution of artifacts, structures, and hearths can provide information on how societies subdivided space for various purposes.

3. How did cultures around the world begin to depend on domesticated resources after the end of the last Ice Age? How did this require the construction of new kinds of social groups and networks? What role did artifacts, art, and structures play in communicating those new social arrangements? Quantitative methods are used to trace dietary changes, including the introduction of domesticated plants and animals. Stable isotopes in human bone provide evidence of diet and to determine how much people moved from their birthplace during their lifetime. Differences in ceramic design and house construction can help to identify the sizes and geographic range of social groups.

4. Changes in social complexity and the division of labor emerge in many parts of the world after the establishment of farming communities. How does differential access to resources in some farming communities allow the development of power differentials that result in social stratification? How are power differences communicated though artifacts, art, and structures? Quantitative methods allow for the comparison of site sizes and locations to identify hierarchical settlement patterns and to document differences in wealth and social rank through comparisons of domestic house size and complexity, mortuary customs, and the construction of public spaces and buildings. Shifts toward craft specialization often reflect the production of standardized artifact forms with less variation and the production of objects produced from non-local materials and exhibiting a high degree of craftsmanship.

5. Beginning about 2,500 years ago, transcultural ideologies (Buddhism, Christianity, Islam) began to spread outside their areas of origin, creating networks of people who share a common religion, but not a common culture or language. The last 500 years has seen the emergence of capitalist economies and colonial empires that extended power differentials across cultural and geographic boundaries. In the last 250 years, the Industrial Revolution has transformed artifact production, agriculture, and transportation. While historical records provide many details, archaeology can contribute by focusing on the local impacts of these changes. Most of the approaches mentioned above are relevant here as well. Standardization of artifact types continues and evidence of trade networks such as ships, port facilities, and roads reflects greater transportation and human migration.

The big questions involve major transformations in the ways our ancestors lived, but they were gradual and our understanding of the changes will necessarily involve looking at quantitative differences as well as qualitative ones.

Quantifying archaeological materials is as old as archaeology itself. While archaeologists have developed a few of their own quantitative methods (e.g., seriation), they have also actively borrowed methods from related disciplines, especially ecology and geography. The present volume attempts to provide archaeologists with some of the tools they need in order to make some headway toward answering the big questions.

Archaeological data consist of measurements of objects, pits, and structures. Usually there are multiple measurements and they are made on different scales. Dichotomies measure the presence or absence of a characteristic. Categorical (or nominal) measures increase the number of categories beyond two to include a variety of qualitative differences such as cord-marked, incised, or plain. Rank (or ordinal) measures allow comparison between two objects to indicate that one is more or less than the other for some characteristic (e.g. older or younger), but the exact amount of the difference cannot be expressed. Numeric measures express the amount of the difference. Important distinctions for numeric measures include interval versus ratio and discrete versus continuous. Interval measures lack an absolute zero (Fahrenheit, Celsius, BCE/CE dates, and years BP). Ratio measures have an absolute zero (Kelvin, length, weight, volume). Discrete measures can only take positive integer values (e.g., the number of sites, flakes, or tools) while continuous measures can take any real value (e.g., length, width, thickness). Some quantitative methods are appropriate only for certain kinds of measurements. For example, if the raw material of stone tools is measured as rhyolite, flint, or quartz, then average raw material is a meaningless concept (but the mode is not).

Quantitative archaeological data can be divided into four broad classes: shape, composition, age, and location. Compositional data can be further divided between object composition (e.g., elemental or isotopic composition) and assemblage composition (counts of particular types of artifacts from a site, grave, level, or grid square). Quantitative methods that are applicable to these classes of data fall into four broad areas:

1. Descriptive statistics include ways of visualizing data using simple numeric summaries, tables, or graph including many methods described as exploratory data analysis.
2. Classical inferential statistics (aka frequentist inference) involves confidence interval estimation and statistical hypothesis testing. The data consist of a sample of a larger population (e.g., measurements of 25 passage graves thought to be representative of all of the passage graves in England). Classical inferential statistics provide methods to estimate the dimensions of the population (all passage graves) using the sample and to place confidence intervals around that estimate. Classical inferential statistics also provides a method for testing the hypothesis that two samples were drawn from a population with the same parameters (e.g., that the dimensions of passage graves from England are identical to those from Ireland). These estimates can be made assuming that the underlying population has a normal distribution (parametric statistics), or not (non-parametric statistics).
3. Bayesian inference incorporates prior knowledge into the inferential process whereas the classical approach does not. In archaeology, Bayesian statistics has had its greatest impact in radiocarbon dating where stratigraphic relationships and closed depositional contexts provide some prior knowledge about the ages. Bayesian statistics has become more important since the widespread availability of computing since the models quickly become too complex to compute by hand.
4. Statistical learning (aka data mining or data science) is a relatively new approach to quantitative methods that has been stimulated by the availability of massive computing power and massive data sets although most of the methods were developed in the first half of the twentieth century. Statistical learning involves efforts to make a prediction about something based on a large number of variables. Supervised methods use a sample of data with known characteristics. Using discriminant analysis on samples of obsidian flakes from known sources to predict the source of obsidian artifacts found in site is an example. Unsupervised methods attempt to find groups in the data using only the data

itself. Using cluster analysis to divide graves into groups based on their contents would be an example.

All of these approaches are used in archaeology. Basic descriptions of data form an important part of the research process and the reporting of results. Those descriptions consist of tables of statistical summaries as well as graphs and charts depicting the distribution of the data. If we can treat the data as a sample (or a set of samples), statistical hypothesis testing may let us identify differences between samples or construct a confidence interval for a particular estimate. Finally, we may need ways to simplify the mass of data to identify patterns that provide insight into past culture and behavior.

One barrier to the wider use of quantitative methods in archaeology has been the availability of computer programs that provide the access to traditional and more recent methods. Spreadsheet programs such as Microsoft Excel® and LibreOffice Calc® provide basic data handling and graphics functionalities, with the ability to add an increasing number of statistical methods. Commercial software such as SPSS®, SAS®, Systat®, Stata®, Statgraphics®, and JMP®, each provide most of the necessary functionality, but can be expensive to license. Further, these comprehensive packages can be slow to add new methods, especially those for a narrow market such as archaeology.

No single text can hope to cover every method of interest to archaeologists. The goal of this book is to provide a resource that provides more hands-on guidance than is currently available. One way to provide that guidance is to standardize on software that is readily available and that provides access to all of the quantitative methods typically used by archaeologists. That software is The R Project for Statistical Computing, which has emerged over the last 20 years.

The R Project for Statistical Computing is the only comprehensive statistical analysis system that is open-source and freely available worldwide without licensing fees. It is available for Windows®, Apple®, and Linux operating systems (R Core Team 2016). R provides the same functionality as commercial programs and it includes a powerful programming language for manipulating data and coding new methods. New procedures for specialized purposes are readily added. The basic R package provides a great deal of functionality that can be extended by the availability of over 8,890 packages of specialized functions on the Comprehensive R Archive Network (CRAN) and 1,211 packages specialized for bioinformatics on Bioconductor (August 2016).

Quantitative methods in archaeology are not something that happens briefly toward the end of the long process of archaeological research from location to excavation to analysis and finally publication of the results. Just as excavation can involve long periods of tedium interrupted by discovery, so do quantitative analyses. There are blind alleys and methods that seem to provide no useful insights for a particular data set. We should not be just hunting for the occasional significant hypothesis test in order to publish and move on to the next project. Quantitative methods are a way of interacting with the data that is less tangible than handling the artifacts, but just as valuable. Our overall guide should be that a good quantitative analysis tells us something new and useful about the data, a bad one tells us something we already know, and an ugly one sends us in the wrong direction (with apologies to D. H. Thomas, 1978).

1.1 ORGANIZATION OF THE BOOK

This book consists of three parts. Part I introduces the R statistical system, reviews basic descriptive statistics (both numeric and graphical summaries), confidence intervals, and hypothesis testing. Part II expands to include multivariate methods for pattern recognition that have proven useful in archaeology. Finally, Part III provides examples of specific methods often used by archaeologists. You will learn more if you work through the book interactively, running the commands as they are listed in the book. The figures in the book show you what to expect, but they are black and white where the figures you produce may include color. Also figure titles have sometimes been eliminated from the published versions to save space.

Part I, R and Basic Statistics, provides a basic introduction to R. R allows you to create data sets, transform variables, and conduct a dizzying number of statistical analyses, but it has its own way of doing things that can be intimidating at first. Chapter 2 is a basic introduction to installing and using R. Chapters 3–9 each include a brief introduction of an important topic in R and then show how to use R to compute descriptive statistics, tabulate data, and produce charts and graphs. Often it is necessary to transform data distributions or deal with missing data and these topics are addressed next. From there, we move on to constructing confidence intervals and comparing two or more groups and to methods for measuring the association between two or more variables.

Part II, Multivariate Methods, explores statistical methods that operate on many variables simultaneously. Broadly they fall into two categories depending on the nature of the variables we are using. In Chapters 10 and 11 multiple regression and discriminant analysis assume that the variables can be divided into two groups. Explanatory (or independent) variables are used to make a prediction about the values of the response (or dependent) variable (or variables). These methods use some of the variables to predict the value of another variable or variables. Unsupervised multivariate techniques do not divide the variables into groups. The variables may be ways of measuring the size and shape of an artifact or the composition of an assemblage. These techniques try to find ways of displaying the data to reveal interesting patterns that we would not have seen otherwise or to combine artifacts or assemblages into groups. Principal components analysis (Chapter 12), correspondence analysis (Chapter 13), multidimensional scaling (Chapter 14), and cluster analysis (Chapter 15) are examples.

Part III, Archaeological Approaches to Data, provides introductions to specialized topics in quantitative methods as they are used in archaeology. Chapter 16 describes ways of using R to analyze the spatial distribution of sites, features, or artifacts. Chapter 17 illustrates quantitative approaches to the seriation of archaeological data, and Chapter 18 describes approaches to assemblage diversity.

I

R and Basic Statistics

2

Introduction to R

R is an open source programming language that includes functions for managing and analyzing data (R Core Team, 2016). It includes extensive graphical and statistical capabilities that are continually being expanded. In addition to the basic installation, there are numerous packages contributed by R users worldwide that provide additional functions. R is freely available worldwide and compiled versions are available for Windows®, Mac OS X®, and several versions of Linux (Debian®, Redhat®, Suse®, and Ubuntu®). In this chapter, you will learn how to install R, type commands, and get help.

2.1 FIRST STEPS USING R

The main R Project website is www.r-project.org/ (Figure 1) . The main page provides access to information about R and to extensive documentation. Select CRAN under "Download" on the left side of the page. At the top of the page, labeled 0-Cloud, click on https://cloud.r-project.org/. That will take you a secure server near your location to download R. Download the version for your computer's operating system (Windows, OS X, or Linux). The download link for Windows is straightforward. The link for Linux requires you to select which flavor of Linux you are using and then provides instructions for installing the software. The link for Mac OS X is a bit more complicated. Assuming you have a recent version of OS X (10.9 or later), follow the instructions and install XQuartz first and then download the.pkg file to install R.

You interact with R by typing commands and executing them. There are several ways to do this. We will start with the basic interface and then describe some other options at the end of the chapter. When you start R by clicking on the icon, you will see the R Console window (Figure 2). The window includes information on what

The R Project for Statistical Computing

Getting Started

R is a free software environment for statistical computing and graphics. It compiles and runs on a wide variety of UNIX platforms, Windows and MacOS. To download R, please choose your preferred CRAN mirror.

If you have questions about R like how to download and install the software, or what the license terms are, please read our answers to frequently asked questions before you send an email.

News

- The useR! 2017 conference will take place in Brussels, July 4 - 7, 2017, and details will be appear here in due course.
- R version 3.3.1 (Bug in Your Hair) has been released on Tuesday 2016-06-21.
- R version 3.2.5 (Very, Very Secure Dishes) has been released on 2016-04-14. This is a rebadging of the quick-fix release 3.2.4-revised.

[Home]

Download

CRAN

R Project

About R
Logo
Contributors
What's New?
Reporting Bugs
Development Site
Conferences
Search

FIGURE 1 The R project website.

version of R you are using, how to get help, how to quit, and some basic instructions on how to cite R in publications. Below that is a line beginning with ">" which is R's way of saying it is waiting for you to type a command. The menu bar at the top of the window includes File, Edit, Misc, Packages, Windows, and Help tabs (in Windows®, the OS X® menus are slightly different and the tabs do not appear in the Linux terminal window). In Windows, the default is to use the multiple document interface (MDI) so the R Console window is within a larger window. As you open additional windows, they will appear within the larger window. If you prefer to have the windows separate so that you can see your desktop underneath, switch to the single document interface (SDI) by clicking on the Edit menu tab and selecting graphic user interface (GUI) preferences. Then click SDI, Save, and OK. R will warn you that you cannot switch without restarting the program (just R, not the computer). Quit and restart R.

First, use the menus at the top of the window to open a new R Editor window ("File | New script"). This opens a blank window labeled "Untitled - R Editor." In Linux, you will need to run a separate text editor such as Gedit. You can type commands directly into the R Console window, but it is helpful to save your commands in an Editor window so that you can easily run them again later. You can also copy/cut/paste in the editor window and search and replace text to change your commands. To send the commands to the Console window, keep the cursor on the line you want to submit (or select multiple lines) and select "Edit | Run line or selection" from the menu at the top of the R Editor window or just press Ctrl + R. Use Copy/Paste from the editor to the terminal in Linux. Later we will save both windows. First, we need to see what directory we are in when R starts and create a subdirectory to store the files we create while using R. In the R Editor window, type each

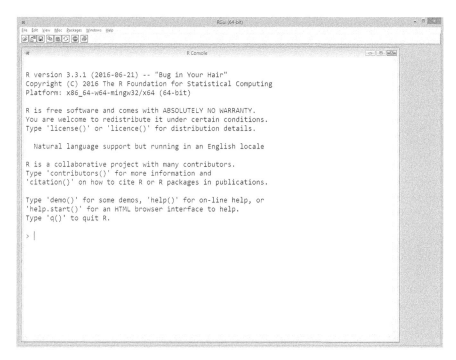

FIGURE 2 R Console window in Windows® using multiple document interface (MDI).

command on the left and then run it. The output in the R Console should match the right side except that "xxxxxx" will be replaced with your user name:

Type this into the R Editor:	Output in the R Console:
getwd()	> getwd()
	[1] "C:/Users/xxxxxx/
	Documents"
dir.create("LearnR")	> dir.create("LearnR")
setwd("LearnR")	> setwd("LearnR")
getwd()	> getwd()
	[1] "C:/Users/xxxxxx/
	Documents/LearnR"

In the R Console each command is shown in red type preceded by ">" and any results are shown underneath in blue. The first command, getwd(), tells you what directory R starts up in. We want to save the results as we go, so we create a directory called "LearnR" using the dir.create() function, and then move into that directory with the setwd() function. Finally we use getwd() again to make sure we are in the correct directory. You should get in the habit of doing this whenever you use R. Create a directory for the project you are working on so that all the files relating to that project are in one place and do not get mixed up with other projects. When you start R, use setwd() to move into the correct directory and then getwd() to list the current directory in the R Console window. Before continuing, use the top menu on the script window to save your work so far ("File | Save") and give the file a name (e.g. Chapter02). R will automatically add .R so the complete file name is Chapter02.R. Save the file regularly as we are going along.

Type the following commands into the script window and then execute them:

Type this into the R Editor	Output in the R Console
A <- 1:8	> A <- 1:8
B <- A/10	> B <- A/10
C <- letters [A]	> C <- letters[A]
D <- A > 4	> D <- A > 4
A	> A
	[1] 1 2 3 4 5 6 7 8
A[3:5]	> A[3:5]
	[1] 3 4 5
A[-(3:5)]	> A[-(3:5)]
	[1] 1 2 6 7 8
A[c(3, 5, 7)]	> A[c(3, 5, 7)]
	[1] 3 5 7
B	> B
	[1] 0.1 0.2 0.3 0.4 0.5 0.6 0.7 0.8
C	> C
	[1] "a" "b" "c" "d" "e" "f" "g" "h"
D	> D
	[1] FALSE FALSE FALSE FALSE TRUE
	[6] TRUE TRUE TRUE

We start by creating four vectors called A, B, C, and D. A vector is simply a series of values of the same kind. The first vector uses the : (colon) to create a sequence of integers from 1 to 8. Notice the <- (less than sign followed by a dash) that we use to set A equal to the result of executing the command on the right. R will also understand a simple = (equals sign) here, but it is clearer to use <- since the equals sign can be used in several ways in R. Also note that we used capital letters for our variable names. Lowercase would also work, but the two are not interchangeable so that variables named y and Y are not the same. We can refer to A as a variable, but in R it is also an object. In R objects include data and functions (sequences of commands) are also objects. Functions in R pay attention to what kind of object they receive and adjust their behavior accordingly.

Then we use A to create three more vectors. B is just each value in A divided by 10 to create a numeric vector. Numeric vectors can have decimal values and they are stored differently than integer variables. C uses the built-in variable let-ters to create a vector consisting of the first eight lowercase letters in the alphabet. Since letters is a vector, we can refer to a position in the vector with a number, letters[1] is "a" and letters[8] is "h". Finally D is a logical vector, which is TRUE if A is greater than 4 and FALSE if it is not.

We can access part of the vector by putting the index values we want in square brackets so A[3:5] prints values 3, 4, and 5 and A[-(3:5)] prints all the values except 3, 4, and 5. The parentheses are needed so that R does not look for index values –3, –4, and –5, which do not exist. If the values we want are not sequential, we use the c() function to combine them into a vector so A[c(3, 5, 7)] prints values 3, 5, and 7.

Integer vectors are useful for recording count data such as the number of artifacts in an excavation unit or the number of flake scars on a tool. Numeric vectors are useful for measurements such as length, breath, weight, and area. Character vectors allow us to store character strings representing things like site names. Logical vectors can be used for storing presence/absence or other kinds of dichotomous data. In addition to integer, numeric, character, and logical vectors, there are vectors that contain date/time information and vectors that contain factors. A factor is a useful way of representing categorical data such as type designations (e.g. scraper, point, or burin). The main rule for vectors is that they must contain all of the same kind of data. You cannot mix numbers and characters together for example. If you try, R will convert all of the numbers to character strings.

Now we expand vectors to two dimensions by constructing a matrix:

Type this into the R Editor	Output in the R Console
E <- matrix(1:12, 3, 4)	> E <- matrix(1:12, 3, 4)
E	> E
	[,1] [,2] [,3] [,4]
	[1,] 1 4 7 10
	[2,] 2 5 8 11
	[3,] 3 6 9 12

```
F <- matrix(LETTERS[1:12],      > F <- matrix(LETTERS[1:12],
   4, 3)                             4, 3)
F                                 > F
                                       [,1] [,2] [,3]
                                  [1,] "A"  "E"  "I"
                                  [2,] "B"  "F"  "J"
                                  [3,] "C"  "G"  "K"
                                  [4,] "D"  "H"  "L"
```

Matrix E contains the integers from 1 to 12 arranged into three rows and four columns using the matrix() function. Matrix F contains the capital letters from A to L arranged into four rows and three columns. By default the matrix() function places the values by columns, but it is possible to force it to fill them by rows instead. Just as with vectors, all of the values in a matrix must be of the same type. We can expand beyond two dimensions to three or more using the array() function.

If you have studied a programming language, vectors and matrices will seem familiar. But R can also label the values in a vector or the rows and columns in a matrix:

Type this into the R Editor	Output in the R Console
str(A)	> str(A) int [1:8] 1 2 3 4 5 6 7 8
names(A) <- letters[1:8] A	> names(A) <- letters[1:8] > A a b c d e f g h 1 2 3 4 5 6 7 8

str(A)	> str(A)
	Named int [1:8] 1 2 3 4
	  5 6 7 8
	- attr(*, "names")= chr
	  [1:8] "a" "b" "c" "d" ...

names(A)	> names(A) [1] "a" "b" "c" "d" "e" "f" "g" "h"
A[3]	> A[3] c 3
A["c"]	> A["c"] c 3

When we look at the structure of A with the `str()` function, it shows that we have a vector of eight integer values. Using the `names()` function we can assign names to each of the values in the vector A. Now when we print A, we get the value names above each value and when we use the `str()` function, it indicates that now we have "Named" integers. R stores the names as an attribute called `names`. We can print out the names with the `names()` function. We can extract a value or values from a vector by specifying its index or name. Earlier we used the minus sign (−) to exclude index values, but that works only with numbers, not with names.

With matrices we can label the rows and columns:

Type this into the R Editor	Output in the R Console

`str(E)`	`> str(E)`
	`int [1:3, 1:4] 1 2 3 4 5 6 7 8 9`
	`10 ...`

`colnames(E)`
`  <- c("Type 1",`
`"Type 2", "Type 3",`
`"Type 4")`
	`> colnames(E) <- c("Type 1",`
	`  "Type 2", "Type 3", "Type 4")`

`rownames(E)`
`  <- c("Site 1", "Site`
`2", "Site 3")`
	`> rownames(E) <- c("Site 1",`
	`  "Site 2", "Site 3")`

`E`	`> E`
	`      Type 1 Type 2 Type 3 Type 4`
	`Site 1    1      4      7     10`
	`Site 2    2      5      8     11`
	`Site 3    3      6      9     12`

`str(E)`	`> str(E)`
	`int [1:3, 1:4] 1 2 3 4 5 6 7 8`
	`9 10 ...`
	`- attr(*, "dimnames")=List of 2`
	`..$ : chr [1:3] "Site 1" "Site`
	`  2" "Site 3"`
	`..$ : chr [1:4] "Type 1" "Type`
	`  2" "Type 3" "Type 4"`

`colnames(E)`	`> colnames(E)`
	`[1] "Type 1" "Type 2" "Type 3"`
	`"Type 4"`

`rownames(E)`	`> rownames(E)` `[1] "Site 1" "Site 2" "Site 3"`

cont.

Type this into the R Editor	Output in the R Console
dimnames(E)	> dimnames(E) [[1]] [1] "Site 1" "Site 2" "Site 3" [[2]] [1] "Type 1" "Type 2" "Type 3" "Type 4"
E[1,]	> E[1,] Type 1 Type 2 Type 3 Type 4 1 4 7 10
E["Site 1",]	> E["Site 1",] Type 1 Type 2 Type 3 Type 4 1 4 7 10
E[, 2]	> E[, 2] Site 1 Site 2 Site 3 4 5 6
E[, "Type 2"]	> E[, "Type 2"] Site 1 Site 2 Site 3 4 5 6

When we look at the structure of E with the str() function, it shows that we have an integer matrix with three rows and four columns. Using the colnames() and rownames() functions we can assign names to the rows and columns. Now when we print E, we get the row and column labels and when we use the str() function, it indicates that now we have a matrix with a dimnames attribute. We can print out the names with colnames() and rownames() or both with dimnames(). We can extract rows or columns using the row or column number or name. If we specify both the row and column, the value at the intersection is returned (without names).

Vectors, matrices, and arrays are considered to be "*atomic*" by R because they are the elements from which other data structures such as data frames and lists are constructed. This would be an arcane bit of trivia except for the fact that error messages produced by R often complain that something is or is not atomic. Knowing that atomic means vectors, matrices, and arrays will make it easier to figure out what the problem is.

If we want to combine vectors with different types of data, we use a data structure called a data.frame:

Type this into the R Editor	Output in the R Console
`G <- data.frame(A, B, C, D`	`> G <- data.frame(A, B, C, D`
	`+ )`
`G <- data.frame(A, B, C, D)`	`> G <- data.frame(A, B, C, D)`
`View(G)`	`> View(G)`
`str(G)`	`> str(G)`
	`'data.frame':  8 obs. of  4`
	`  variables:`
	`$ A: int  1 2 3 4 5 6 7 8`
	`$ B: num  0.1 0.2 0.3 0.4`
	`  0.5 0.6 0.7 0.8`
	`$ C: Factor w/ 8 levels`
	`  "a","b","c","d",..: 1 2 3`
	`  4 5 6 7 8`
	`$ D: logi  FALSE FALSE`
	`  FALSE FALSE TRUE TRUE ...`
`G[ , 2]`	`> G[ , 2]`
	`[1] 0.1 0.2 0.3 0.4 0.5 0.6`
	`  0.7 0.8`
`G[ , "B"]`	`> G[ , "B"]`
	`[1] 0.1 0.2 0.3 0.4 0.5 0.6`
	`  0.7 0.8`
`G$B`	`> G$B`
	`[1] 0.1 0.2 0.3 0.4 0.5 0.6`
	`  0.7 0.8`

The first line illustrates a common error in R. We forgot to add the closing parenthesis before pressing the Enter key. R responded with a "+" instead of a ">" discreetly telling us that we made a mistake. We can type the closing parenthesis on the same line and press Enter and R will execute the command. The command is repeated on the next line showing what we should have done in the first place. Whenever R changes the prompt from ">" to "+" it means that the command is not complete. Often you can just finish the command, but in other cases you need to press the **Escape** key to terminate the command. Then R will respond with a ">" prompt and you can retype the command. Forgetting a quotation mark is another common way to make this error.

We use the `data.frame()` function to combine vectors A, B, C, and D. Rather than printing out the new data frame we use `View()` to display it in a window. We also examine the data frame using the `str()` function. This tells us that G is a data frame with eight observations (rows) and four variables (columns). Furthermore, the type of each variable is noted and the first several values are printed. As you can see, the columns can be different data types, but they must each be the same length (one value for each row). Notice that one of the variables has changed type. Variable C has changed from a character string to a factor. The data.frame() function automatically converts character vectors unless you tell it not to do so. In a factor variable, the character strings become labels (called levels) and an integer index is saved for each row to indicate what level the variable has on that row. This is very compact when there are many rows but fewer categories, but in this case a character variable would be fine and later we will learn how to change it back to a character variable.

Whereas vectors and matrices can have names, data frames must have names. R used the name of each vector for the column names and it picked up the names that we added to A as the row names. Both colnames() and names() will extract the column names and both rownames() and row.names() will extract the row names.

Most of the time you will store your data in a data frame. Each row will represent an observation and each column a piece of information about that observation. The observations might be sites, pots, hand axes, excavation units, graves, or house pits. Data frames provide the flexibility of allowing you to store your information on an observation in many different ways and store it together. As with matrices, you can refer to rows and columns by their position number or their name, but there is a third option for columns because data frames are also considered to be lists. The "G$B" command above illustrates this new way of referring to a column using a dollar sign. This is the most common way you will extract a column from a data frame.

The last major data structure in R is a **list**. You can think of a list as a basket that contains any of the data structures we have discussed including lists. This makes lists more confusing than the other structures because there are essentially no rules. This also makes lists perfect for storing the results of a statistical analysis since the various parts of the analysis can all be stored together. Try these commands:

Type this into the R Editor	Output in the R Console

`H <- list(E=E, F=F, G=G)`
`str(H)`
	`> H <- list(E=E, F=F, G=G)`
	`> str(H)`
	`List of 3`
	`$ E: int [1:3, 1:4] 1 2 3 4 5 6 7`
	`  8 9 10 ...`

Type this into the R Editor	Output in the R Console
	`$ F: chr [1:4, 1:3] "A" "B" "C" "D" ...`
	`$ G:'data.frame':   8 obs. of  4 variables:`
	`..$ A: int [1:8] 1 2 3 4 5 6 7 8`
	`..$ B: num [1:8] 0.1 0.2 0.3 0.4 0.5 0.6 0.7 0.8`
	`..$ C: Factor w/ 8 levels "a","b","c","d",..: 1 2 3 4 5 6 7 8`
	`..$ D: logi [1:8] FALSE FALSE FALSE FALSE TRUE TRUE ...`
`H$E`	`> H$E`
	` `

```
        Type 1 Type 2 Type 3 Type 4
Site 1       1      4      7     10
Site 2       2      5      8     11
Site 3       3      6      9     12
```

We use the `list()` function to create a list from E, F, and G. Note that we have to label the parts using the equals sign. The `data.frame()` function did this for us automatically. We use `str()` to summarize the structure of the list in a compact form. Data frames require that the columns have the same number of rows. Here we have combined a matrix with three rows, another matrix with four rows, and a data frame with eight rows. Extracting parts of a list are complicated for two reasons. First, unlike matrices and data frames where we could use 2:5 to select rows or columns 2 through 5, we can select only a single element of a list at a time. Second, we can extract an element as a list with 1 element or just the element. Almost always you will want to extract just the element. For the example above, `H[[1]]`, `H[["E"]]`, or `H$E` will get you what you want. Using single brackets instead of double brackets creates a list with a single element, which is almost never what you want.

In these examples, we displayed the results using the `print()` function even though we never actually typed the command. By default, when you type an object name such as A, R executes the command `print(A)`. That is convenient, but even more convenient is that there are many different print commands depending on what kind of object we are printing. The print function will provide a summary of the most useful results, but often not all of the results. When a statistical function returns a list, the `print()` function usually returns only part of the list since they can be very long and complicated. Try the command `print(H)` to see all of the parts of the list we just created.

Before going any further, you should install the `archdata` package, which contains all of the data sets used in this book (Carlson and Roth, 2016). As before, type the commands in the R Editor and then select them and select Edit | Run line or selection (or just press Ctrl+R).

Type this into the R Editor	Output in the R Console

`install.`
`  packages("archdata")`
	`install.packages("archdata")`
	`trying URL`
	`  'https://cran.rstudio.com/`
	`  bin/windows/contrib/3.2/`
	`  archdata_1.1.zip'`
	`Content type 'application/zip'`
	`  length 143154 bytes (139 KB)`
	`downloaded 139 KB`
	
	`package 'archdata'`
	`  successfully unpacked and`
	`  MD5 sums checked`

`library(archdata)`	`> library(archdata)`
`data(package="archdata")`	`> data(package="archdata")`
`data(Acheulean)`	`> data(Acheulean)`

The `install.packages()` function goes to CRAN to get the package you have specified (you may first have to specify the mirror you want to use). The `archdata` package was created for this book to provide real archaeological data sets. Once a package has been installed on your computer, you use the `library()` function to load it. The `data(package="archdata")` command opens a new window that shows the data sets in the package. The `data(Acheulean)` command loads the `Acheulean` data set. The data sets are all stored as data frames similar to the one we created in the previous section. To see what is in `Acheulean`, add the following commands to the R Editor window and run them:

Type this into the R Editor	Output in the R Console
?Acheulean	> ?Acheulean starting httpd help server ... done
str(Acheulean)	> str(Acheulean) 'data.frame': 7 obs. of 14 variables: $ Lat : num -1.58 -7.9 -8.6 -19.92 -0.45 ... $ Long: num 36.5 35.6 31.2 29 36.3 ... $ HA : int 197 246 337 45 132 1 15 $ CL : int 96 208 264 13 56 8 19 . . . 8 lines deleted . . . $ SS : int 213 98 303 46 17 35 17 $ OST : int 218 64 48 22 25 18 70 - attr(*, "Variables")='data. frame': 14 obs. of 2 variables: ..$ Var : chr "Lat" "Long" "HA" "CL" ... ..$ Label: chr "Latitude" "Longitude" "Hand axes" "Cleavers" ...

The first command should open your web browser and display information about the Acheulean data set. You will see that the data comes from a paper by L. R. Binford (1972) and is based on analyses by M. R. Kleindienst (1961, 1962). The data consist of the approximate latitude and longitude for each site and the counts for 12 different stone tool types. Research questions regarding these data focus on how the site assemblages differ from one another. The original publication provides data on 32 different assemblages from the 7 sites. Here the assemblages are aggregated by site to keep things simpler.

We have used the str() command before to see what was inside an R object. Acheulean is a data frame with seven observations (rows) and 14 variables (columns). Each row represents a Lower Paleolithic site in Africa with Acheulean artifacts. It is an example of an assemblage composition data set as described in the Chapter 1. The first two columns (Lat and Long) contain the latitude and longitude (approximate) of the site and the remaining columns are abbreviations for the different tool types found at the site. A data frame can also contain attributes, additional information that is stored with the data frame. The print() function lists the data frame and the attributes() function shows us the attributes. To save space, we will only show the results of commands from here on, but you should continue to type the commands in the Editor window (and periodically save the file). If a command line wraps, R will start the continuation line with a "+". Do not type the "+", just continue the command on the following line in the R Editor window.

```
> Acheulean
              Lat    Long   HA   CL  KN  FS  D  CS   P  CH SP OLTSS  OST
Olorgesailie -1.58  36.45 197   96  58  17  5  11   3  32 52 6  213 218
Isimila      -7.90  35.61 246  208  30  28  6  30  16  62 17 15  98  64
Kalambo
  Falls      -8.60  31.24 337  264  59  96  8 124  18  69 6  17 303  48
Lochard     -19.92  29.02 45    13   3   2 12   1   0  32 3  8   46  22
Kariandusi   -0.45  36.26 132   56  47  23  3   5   7   6 5  8   17  25
Broken Hill -14.43  28.45 1      8   1   1  0   1   0   4 25 0   35  18
Nsongezi     -1.03  30.78 15    19   2   9  1  28   1  19 0  10  17  70

> attributes(Acheulean)
$names
 [1]  "Lat" "Long" "HA"  "CL"   "KN"  "FS"  "D"  "CS"  "P" "CH"
 [11] "SP"  "OLT"  "SS"  "OST"

$class
[1] "data.frame"

$row.names
[1] "Olorgesailie"  "Isimila"      "Kalambo Falls" "Lochard"
[5] "Kariandusi"    "Broken Hill"  "Nsongezi"

$Variables
     Var     Label
1    Lat     Latitude
2    Long    Longitude
3    HA      Hand axes
4    CL      Cleavers
5    KN      Knives
6    FS      Flake Scrapers
7    D       Discoids
8    CS      Core Scrapers
9    P       Picks
10   CH      Choppers
11   SP      Spheroids
12   OLT     Other large tools
13   SS      Small scrapers
14   OST     Other small tools
```

Typing just the name of the data frame lists it in the R Console and typing `View(Acheulean)` opens a new window displaying the same information so that you can keep it visible. All data frames will have the `names`, `class`, and `row.names` attributes. We have added a `Variables` attribute, a data frame listing the column names along with a more descriptive label. This makes it clear that the HA column refers to the number of hand axes at the site.

We can get some basic descriptive statistics for each column with the `summary()` function:

```
> summary(Acheulean[ , 1:4])
       Lat                Long              HA              CL
Min.    :-19.920   Min.    :28.45   Min.    :1.0     Min.    :8.00
1st Qu. :-11.515   1st Qu. :29.90   1st Qu. :30.0    1st Qu. :16.00
Median  :-7.900    Median  :31.24   Median  :132.0   Median  :56.00
Mean    :-7.701    Mean    :32.54   Mean    :139.0   Mean    :94.86
3rd Qu. :-1.305    3rd Qu. :35.94   3rd Qu. :221.5   3rd Qu. :152.00
Max.    :-0.450    Max.    :36.45   Max.    :337.0   Max.    :264.00
```

The output shows the minimum value, the maximum value, the mean (average), the median, and the first and third quartiles for the first four columns. All of these columns are numeric; character and factor variables will be described differently. Now try these two commands to summarize the sample sizes by rows and by columns:

```
> rowSums(Acheulean[ , 3:14])
Olorgesailie     Isimila   Kalambo Falls  Lochard      Kariandusi
         908         820           1349      187             334
   Broken Hill       Nsongezi
            94            191
> colSums(Acheulean[ , 3:14])
 HA   CL   KN    FS    D    CS    P    CH    SP   OLT   SS  OST
973  664  200   176   35   200   45   224   108    64  729  465
```

The `rowSums()` and `colSums()` functions sum a data frame by rows and columns respectively (and `rowMeans()` and `colMeans()` compute the means of each row or column). From the results we can see that Olorgesailie has the most artifacts and Broken Hill has the fewest. The largest tool class is hand axes (HA) followed by small scrapers (SS) and the smallest is discoids (D).

Whenever we use a new function you should type the command `help("function")` or `?function` to get more information about how the function works.

2.3 GETTING YOUR DATA INTO R

There are several ways to get your own data into R. If the data set is small you can create each column separately and then combine them into a data frame. For example, assume you have a set of six stone tools and you have recorded a catalog number, length, breadth, thickness, and material type for each one.

```
> catalog <- c("LN15", "LN17", "LN18", "LN21", "LN23", "LN24")
> length <- c(18, 14, 21, 14, 17, 16)
> breadth <- c(9, 7, 10, 7, 8, 8)
> thickness <- c(3, 2, 3, 3, 3, 2)
> material <- c("chert", "chert", "obsidian", "chert",
  "obsidian", "obsidian")
> Tools <- data.frame(catalog, length, breadth, thickness,
  material)
> str(Tools)
'data.frame':  6 obs. of  5 variables:
 $ catalog  : Factor w/ 6 levels "LN15","LN17",..: 1 2
   3 4 5 6
 $ length   : num  18 14 21 14 17 16
 $ breadth  : num  9 7 10 7 8 8
 $ thickness: num  3 2 3 3 3 2
 $ material : Factor w/ 2 levels "chert","obsidian": 1 1
   2 1 2 2
> Tools$catalog <- as.character(Tools$catalog)
> Tools
  catalog    length   breadth   thickness    material
1   LN15        18         9           3         chert
2   LN17        14         7           2         chert
3   LN18        21        10           3      obsidian
4   LN21        14         7           3         chert
5   LN23        17         8           3      obsidian
6   LN24        16         8           2      obsidian
> save(Tools, file="Tools.RData")
> write.csv(Tools, file="Tools.csv")
```

Type the commands into the R Editor window. We create each variable (column) by giving it a name and assigning six values to it. The c() function combines the individual values into a single vector. Then we combine the vectors into a data frame called Tools using data.frame(). When we look at the structure of the data frame with str(), we discover that the two character vectors have been converted to factors. That is fine for `Tools$material` since multiple speci-mens have the same material type, but each catalog number (`Tools$catalog`) is unique. It is not absolutely necessary, but we use `as.character()` to con-vert it back to character data. We print the data frame and then save it in the compact binary format that R uses using `save()` and as a comma separated file that can be imported into a spreadsheet using `write.csv()`. At this point, you could use `fix(Tools)` to add columns or rows to the data frame. Then save the modified file. If you make a mistake, just reload the file with `load("Tools.RData")`.

More likely, your data is already in an electronic form in a spreadsheet or data-base. The smoothest way to import that data into R is to use a comma separated file (.csv). All spreadsheet programs and many databases can produce such files. You can read the comma separated version of the `Tools` file that we just created into R as follows:

```
> Tools2 <- read.csv("Tools.csv")
```

The `read.csv()` function imports the comma separated file, `"Tools.csv"`, and creates a new object called `Tools2`. Box 1 provides more informa-tion on this very useful family of functions. If you use `str()`, you will see that `Tools2$catalog` is a factor variable again, but you can convert it back to char-acter as we did before.

Since we just created `"Tools.csv"` we knew that it was located in the current directory. If it is somewhere else, you can insert the path before the file name. Use "/" in defining the path even if you are using Windows since R will handle the change for you and the backslash "\" is a special character in R. For example, if there is a folder in your "LearnR" directory called "myfiles" that contains `"Tools.csv"`, use `read.csv("myfiles/Tools.csv")` or `read.csv("myfiles\\Tools.csv")` on Windows if you want to use the backslash.

If you want to search around for the file, the function `file.choose()` will let you navigate through the directory structure to find the file. We can locate the file and read it in a single step with

```
> Tools2 <- read.csv(file.choose())
```

R can also import files produced by SPSS®, SAS®, Minitab®, STATA®, and Systat® statistical packages using the `foreign` package which is automatically included when you install R.

2.4 STARTING AND STOPPING R

When you load R, you should make a habit of always running certain commands first:

```
> setwd("LearnR")
> library(archdata)
```

This will set your working directory so that any files you create and save will be where you can find them again. Loading the `archdata` package is optional, but we will use it in every chapter. Also run the following command at least once a week or use the R Console menu option "Packages | Update packages" to install the latest versions of any of the packages that you have installed:

```
> update.packages(ask=FALSE)
```

To exit R, use the command `q()` or `quit()` or select "File | Exit" from the R Console menu. R will ask if you want to "Save workspace image?" Just click "No" since saving the workspace image will save all of the objects you have created to a single file called `.RData`. When you return to R, it will load this file automatically. Especially when you are just beginning R, it is better to make a clean start each time. That way any options, graphics parameters, and objects that you have created will disappear when you exit. Of course, that means that you need to explicitly save any objects that you want to use again, but that is a good habit to develop.

Every 6–12 months you will probably need to upgrade R to the latest version. The simplest way to do that is to uninstall the current version and download and install the new one. You will have to re-install your packages, but just re-install the ones you are using. If you don't uninstall R, it will just add the new version to your system, so you will have more than one, which is fine if you want to be able to use previous versions, but unless you are actively developing R packages, you probably will not be doing that.

2.5 R FUNCTIONS

R is a language consisting of objects. Objects include variables and groups of variables organized into vectors, matrices, tables, arrays, data frames, lists, and other data types. Objects also include functions that perform certain actions. In the examples above, we have used several functions. Most functions accept some kind of data, operate on that data, and return results. You can capture the results by assigning them to a new object or just display them by letting R send the results to `print()`. Functions often have various options that affect how the data is processed and those options are specified when calling the function. So far, we have not made much use of these options which are called **arguments**.

You can get help on a particular function, including its arguments, by typing `?functionname` or `help("functionname")` in the R Console window to get the manual page for that function. Either command will load your default web browser and display the manual page. The manual pages all follow the same organization. The top left corner of the page lists the function name and the package containing that function. For example, the `mean()` function is found in the `base` package, one of the packages that is automatically included when you install R. Most manual pages include seven sections:

1. **Description** provides a brief description of what the function does. For `mean` it computes the arithmetic mean or, optionally, a trimmed mean. The term generic in the description indicates that the function behaves differently depending on what kind of data it receives so that it can handle dates or directional data.

2. **Usage** shows how the function is called (which may differ depending on what kind of data you are using). It indicates what arguments the function takes and their default values. For `mean()` this includes `x=`, `trim=`, and `na.rm=` arguments).

3. The **Arguments** section describes each argument and how it is used. In this case, `x` is the data, generally a single vector of numeric values. The `trim=` argument is used only if you want to compute a trimmed mean so that `trim=.1` would remove the lowest and highest 10 percent of the values before computing the mean. The `na.rm=` argument tells the function if it should remove missing values (represented as `NA` in R) before computing the mean. Note that in the **Usage** section the arguments are `trim=0` and `na.rm=FALSE`. These are the default values that will be used if these arguments are not specified. If you leave those arguments out, the function will use all of the values (no trimming) and will not remove missing values. If your data includes missing values, the mean function will fail with an error message. Adding `na.rm=TRUE` will remove the missing values before computing the mean. The `...` at the end indicates that additional arguments can be specified that will be used by functions called by `mean()`. If you specify the arguments in the same order as they appear in the **Usage** section, you do not need to name them. If you are specifying only a few, you need to include their names.

4. The **Value** section tells you what the mean function returns. For mean, this is just the value computed by the function. For other functions, multiple values may be returned. Functions for more complicated statistical tests usually return lists.

5. The **References** section provides bibliographic references describing the function and how it works.

6. The **See Also** section provides links to other related functions.

7. Finally, the **Examples** section provides examples of the function that you can run by typing the command `example(mean)`.

If a function is not working the way you expect or you are receiving error or warning messages, check the manual page to make sure you are using the function correctly. It is easy to forget the names of some argument, but it takes only seconds to bring up the manual page.

2.6 GETTING HELP

Just as with any software, you may run into problems along the way. Things won't work the way you expected or you will get a cryptic error message. You will probably want to learn more about something covered in this book or use functions that are not covered here. R has an extensive set of resources to get you started and help you find out about more advanced methods and techniques.

First there is extensive, free documentation about every aspect of R. Some of this documentation is copied to your computer when you install R. There are several ways to access this information. If you know the name of a function, you can access its manual page as described in the previous section. Each R package has a manual page documenting each function and each data set in the package. If you don't know the exact function name, but you know it is included in a package that you have installed on your computer, the command `??mean` will search for the word "mean" anywhere in any installed package. Your web browser will display a page with the results.

Some packages include short documents called **vignettes** in addition to the manual. Whereas the manual for a package consists of an alphabetical listing of the functions and data sets, a vignette describes how to use the package in a more holistic fashion. To see what vignettes are available for the packages you have installed on your computer, type the command `vignette()` and a list will appear in a pop up window. Using the function with the name of the vignette will bring up a window with the vignette.

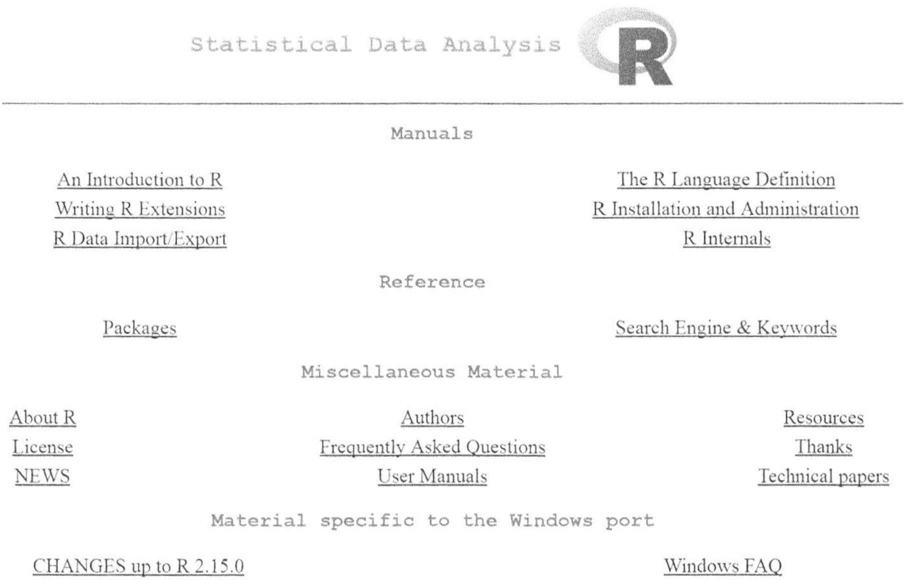

Statistical Data Analysis R

Manuals

An Introduction to R   The R Language Definition
Writing R Extensions   R Installation and Administration
R Data Import/Export   R Internals

Reference

Packages   Search Engine & Keywords

Miscellaneous Material

About R   Authors   Resources
License   Frequently Asked Questions   Thanks
NEWS   User Manuals   Technical papers

Material specific to the Windows port

CHANGES up to R 2.15.0   Windows FAQ

FIGURE 3 Main "HTML help" page.

The extensive help system is accessed from your web browser. From the R Console, select "Help | Html help" or type `help.start()` at the command line. Either will cause your default web browser to load with the main help page (Figure 3). That page contains links to various documents such as frequently asked questions (FAQ) and Packages, a page listing the manual for every package you have installed.

Online the main R Project web page (www.r-project.org) has manuals, lists of books, a journal, and links to free beginners guides in multiple languages (https://cran.r-project.org/other-docs.html). A Google® search including R as a term (e.g., cluster analysis R) will usually return useful results.

2.7 OTHER WAYS TO USE R

In this book, we are interacting with R using the R Console and using the R Editor to type our commands and send them to the R Console for execution. This approach will allow you to save commands and the results of those commands in separate files. As with virtually everything in R, you have choices. There are several other ways to interact with R and this section will mention three options: R Commander, R Studio, and Rattle. Each of these has advantages and disadvantages.

R Commander adds a GUI to R that can be useful if you want to avoid typing the commands yourself (Fox 2005). R Commander combines the R Editor (called R Script) window and the R Console (called Output) window by placing one over the other and amplifying the menu bar to include many additional commands. A row of buttons under the menu tabs includes options to select, edit, or view a data set.

No menu system can include every possible R command, but R Commander is strong for generating descriptive statistics, graphics, hypothesis testing, and regression models of various kinds. It also supports some basic multivariate methods and provides a number of ways of importing data, extracting subsets of the data, adding and removing variables, and transforming variables. It also prompts you to save your files when you exit.

R Commander includes a tabbed window (R Markdown) that builds a markdown file. Markdown files are simple text files that include any descriptive text that you want to include. When the file is processed, the commands are run and the results, including figures, are embedded into a single html file. This is a useful way to combine your description of what you did and why with the commands you used and the output they produced. If an error in the data is discovered and corrected, a revised version of the report is easy to generate. You can create markdown files without R Commander, but R Commander automates the process.

To install R Commander, use `install.packages("RCmdr")` within R. When you first run it, it will ask to install some additional packages and utilities. To start R Commander, open R and type `library(RCmdr)`. For more information see online documents by Fox and Bouchet-Valat (2014) and Karp (2014).

RStudio is an integrated development environment (IDE) for R that is particularly useful if you are accustomed to programming where IDEs are common (Racine, 2012). The goal is to arrange a number of windows so that you have everything at your disposal while you are working. In RStudio, the window is arranged into four panes that can be resized. The top left pane includes the R Editor window and tabs for viewing data and markdown files. The R Console window is in the bottom left pane (although you can change these positions). The upper right pane includes tabbed windows for the environment (all of the variables that are currently loaded or have been created) and the history (all of the commands you have executed). The bottom right pane includes tabbed windows showing the files in the current directory, plots, packages you have installed, help pages, and a viewer for local html content.

RStudio includes debugging tools for writing your own functions and extensive support of markdown files, which can be processed into html, Microsoft Word, or pdf files. If your research routinely involves quantitative methods, you will probably want to move to RStudio as you get more familiar with R and move toward larger and more complex projects.

RStudio is installed outside of R by installing the file for your operating system at www.rstudio.com. Support is provided at the RStudio website. To use the program, you run RStudio and it will load R for you.

The **Rattle** package is a GUI that is focused on data mining (Williams, 2011). It provides menu-based access to a wider variety of multivariate methods commonly used in data mining or statistical learning. You install the `rattle` package with the `install.packages()` function and start it with `library(rattle)`. The first time it will probably need to install additional packages. Support is available at the developer's webpage: http://rattle.togaware.com/.

For the examples in the book, we will stick with the simple interface that comes with R consisting of the R Console window, the R Script Window, your web browser (for help files), and windows for graphics and data display.

2.8 ARCHAEOLOGICAL DATA FOR LEARNING R

To make it simpler to learn R using archaeological data, I created a package of data files containing data sets used in this book. The package is called `archdata` (Carlson and Roth 2016) and we installed it at the beginning of the chapter to use the `Acheulean` data set. The data include examples of compositional data, assemblage data, artifact measurements, and spatial distribution data. The package includes additional data sets that are not used in the book. The latest version (1.1) includes 25 different data sets.

BOX 1 THE `read.csv()` FUNCTION IN THE `base` PACKAGE

```
read.csv(file, header = TRUE, sep = ",", quote = "\"",
dec = ".", fill = TRUE, comment.char = "", ...)
```

The main way of importing plain text, delimited data into R is to use the `read.table()` family of functions. There are a large number of optional arguments so each variant of `read.table()` uses different default values. For `read.csv()` the defaults are as follows:

- The text file has variable names in the first row (`header=TRUE`).
- The separator for different values on each row is a comma (`sep=","`).

- Character strings are separated by double quotation marks (`quote="\""`).
- Decimal numbers are indicated with a period (`dec="."`).
- If a line does not have enough values, pad it with missing values (fill=TRUE).
- There is no comment character (`comment.char=""`).

For countries in which decimal numbers are indicated with a comma, use `read.csv2()`. All spreadsheet programs are able to create comma separated delimited (csv) files. If you have many spreadsheets, it may be worth exploring some packages that can read the spreadsheet file directly such as `xlsx`. If the data are tab separated instead of comma separated, use `read.delim()` or `read.delim2()`.

The defaults for `read.table()` are that no header is present; the separator is any white space (space, tab, newline, carriage return); character strings are separated by single quotation marks; lines with fewer than expected values are not filled; and the "#" character is treated as a comment so the rest of the line is ignored.

There are several other options that may be useful in certain circumstances:

- Specify a string that should be interpreted as a missing value, `na.strings`.
- Skip lines at the beginning of the file, `skip`.
- Do not convert character strings to factors, `stringsAsFactors`.

For more information use `?read.table` (or `?read.csv`)

Table 1 *Functions introduced in Chapter 2*

Function	Package	Description
:	base	Generate an integer sequence from:to
?	utils	Get the manual page for a function or data set
??	utils	Search system for documentation
array	base	Create a multidimensional array
as.character	base	Convert values to character strings
attributes	base	Show the attributes in an object
c	base	Combine objects into a single object
colMeans	base	Return the mean of each column
colnames	base	Column names of a matrix or data.frame
colSums	base	Return the sum of each column

Table 1 (*cont.*)

Function	Package	Description
data	utils	Load or list data sets
data.frame	base	Create a data frame
dimnames	base	Retrieve or set dimension names of an object
dir.create	base	Create a folder/directory
example	utils	Run examples in a help topic
file.choose	base	Choose a file interactively
fix	utils	Make changes in a data frame
getwd	base	Get the current working directory
help	utils	Get help on a function or data set
help.search	utils	Search system for documentation
help.start	utils	Display help files in web browser
install.packages	utils	Download and install a package
library	base	Load an installed package
list	base	Create a list object
load	base	Load an R object or objects
matrix	base	Create a matrix object
print	base	Prints contents of an object
q or quit	base	Quit R
read.csv	utils	Read a comma separated file and create a data frame
read.table	utils	Read a delimited file and create a data frame
readLines	base	Read lines from a text file
row.names	base	Row names of a data frame
rowMeans	base	Return mean of each row
rownames	base	Row names of a matrix
rowSums	base	Return the sum of each row
save	base	Save an R object or objects to a file
setwd	base	Set the current working directory
str	utils	Display the structure of an object
summary	base	Summarize an object
update.packages	utils	Download and install updates for a package
View	utils	View a data frame
vignette	utils	Display or list vignettes
write.csv	utils	Write a data frame or matrix to a comma separated file

Note: Packages `base`, `datasets`, `graphics`, `grDevices`, `methods`, `stats`, and `utils` are automatically loaded when R starts.

Looking at Data – Numerical Summaries

Archaeological data come in all sizes, shapes, and quantities ranging from Egyptian pyramids (large in size, small in the number of specimens) to micro-debitage from a lithic workshop or molecular residues in a ceramic bowl. Because the questions we ask of the data are different, our representations of those data differ. One way of representing the data dominates however, because it is so flexible. That is a rectangular arrangement of data so that each row represents an observation and each column represents a measurement on that observation. Some of those measurements can be counts, and each count is a potential observation for another data table.

For example, we may have located a variety of archaeological sites in a river valley. One data table could consist of the grid units that were surveyed so that each row of the table is a grid square (e.g., 100 m on a side). The columns of the data set include the coordinates of the unit and the number of sites and isolated artifact finds discovered during the survey. There could be other columns identifying when the unit was surveyed and information about the location of the unit with respect to topographic features such as dominant soil type, major waterways, lakes, and so on. This data set would be relevant to exploring questions about site density. For example, are there more sites near water features and fewer in upland areas away from any water source?

Each of the counts in this data set is a potential row in another data set. That data set consists of a row for each site and columns for the location of the site, the area of the site, the physical characteristics around the site (e.g., slope, elevation, aspect, soil type), and the number of different kinds of artifacts and features found on the site. This data set would be relevant to questions regarding where sites are located and how the artifacts and features found on sites differ.

Each of the artifacts and features in the site data set is a potential row in another data set (or more likely multiple data sets). At this point it may make sense to create separate data sets for projectile points, flakes, cores, pottery sherds, shells, bones, and other categories of material. Each of the artifacts from the site is a row in the data set and the columns are measurements for each specimen including such categories as raw material, length, width, weight, decoration, temper, type, elemental composition, and so on. Generally, this is the end of the series of data sets, but we could go further by measuring line thicknesses on pottery or locations of use-wear on stone tools.

We get another series of data sets if we excavate one of the sites. The site is divided horizontally into a set of grid squares or trenches and vertically into a set of depositional units or arbitrary levels. Some items are recorded in terms of three-dimensional position within the site and others are recovered from screened sediment and bagged according to their excavation unit (square, trench, augur hole, etc.).

At each level in this hierarchical series of data sets, the organization is the same. By adding identification fields to the rows in each of them, we can link them up from bottom to top. The collection of tables with their linkages is called a relational database. Software such as Microsoft Access®, Filemaker®, Libre Office Base®, and the various flavors of SQL (structured query language) such as MySQL® and PostgreSQL® make it relatively easy to organize relational databases.

But we don't only proceed in one direction in creating data sets. Some of the measurements we take on a particular type of artifact are categorical and those categories provide a basis for aggregating (counting the number of) rows so that all of the artifacts in a row share certain characteristics. Notice that now the row is not the same kind of observation. It is not a unit of space or an object. Now the row is a collection of items that are similar to one another. We can produce this data set from the earlier ones, but we often create them directly for certain types of artifacts that are small and abundant. The flakes from an excavation unit could be described individually, but often they are grouped into categories (complete flakes, broken flakes, and shatter or rim sherds, basal sherds, and body sherds).

In R we refer to all of these data sets as data frames. A data frame consists of a set of columns and the columns can be numeric, character, factor, or logical, but each column can contain only one kind of data.

The second most common format for archaeological data is the cross-tabulation table. Here the rows and columns are the categories of two (or more) nominal variables that can be observed on each object. The counts in each cell represent the number of objects that fall into a particular combination of categories. R uses a special kind of matrix called a table object to store cross-tabulation data. In a table, all of the cell values defined by the intersections of the rows and columns are numeric and the rows and columns are labeled.

Some kinds of data are inherently difficult or impossible to represent as a data frame. Site or feature boundaries are a good example. Boundaries are represented by a series of points but the number of points is not the same for all sites or all features of a particular kind. The mapping packages in R use lists to store site boundaries as polygons.

Sometimes the value for a variable is not available for a particular observation. Missing data may result from broken specimens (e.g., a broken projectile point has a missing value for its length), recording errors, equipment errors, or values below the detection limits of the equipment. Regardless of their source, these missing data must be coded in some way so that they are clearly identifiable. R uses the designation NA to identify missing values. If you import a spreadsheet into R and some of the cells are empty, R will insert NA's. If some other value has been used to mark the missing values, such as 0 or 9.999, they must be changed to NA's for R to recognize them. Data sets that contain missing values will require decisions about how to handle those values at every step in the analysis. R provides several ways of handling missing data and we will discuss several approaches in Chapter 7.

The first step in analyzing new data is to look at it. R provides several ways of looking at data using numerical summaries (this chapter), tables (Chapter 4), and graphs and charts (Chapter 5). Looking at the data is an essential first step to identifying measurement or coding errors before you begin an analysis. We generally assume that the archaeological record is patterned in some way, but what does that mean? For a single variable, a pattern could be a distribution that is unusual. For two variables, a pattern could be an association between the variables. We will talk about associations between variables later (Chapter 9). But what is an unusual distribution? Before we answer that question, we should learn a little more about R and how it handles arithmetic operations.

3.1 ARITHMETIC WITH R

Start R and change your working directory to "LearnR". Then use the menu option "File | New script" to open a blank editor window for the commands in this chapter. R can handle all of the basic arithmetic operations – addition, subtraction, multiplication, and division work as you would expect:

```
> 2 + 5
[1] 7
```

```
> 7 - 3
[1] 4
> 5 * 6
[1] 30
> 8 / 2
[1] 4
```

In addition, R handles exponents, square roots, and logarithms:

```
> 2 ^ 5    # or 2 ** 5
[1] 32
> sqrt(2) # or 2 ^ .5
[1] 1.414214
> log(1000)
[1] 6.907755
> log10(1000)
[1] 3
> exp(2)
[1] 7.389056
```

The exponentiation operator is the caret "^" and sqrt() computes square roots. The # symbol is used to begin a comment. R ignores the rest of the line following # so you can add some information that only humans will see. The log() function computes natural logs using base e (exp(1) = 2.718282) and log10() computes common logs using base 10. The exponential function, exp(), raises its argument as a power of e. The previous examples used both binary operators (+, -, *, /, ^) and functions, but R actually interprets binary operators as functions:

```
> "+"(2, 5)
[1] 7
> "^"(2, 5)
[1] 32
> ?"+" # Brings up help for arithmetic operators
```

Usually this just means more typing, but there are circumstances where it can be handy to know this. The last command opens the manual page in your web browser for all of the operators. When you combine operators in a single command, you need to be aware of the precedence of operations that R uses. Exponentiation comes first, then multiplication/division, and then addition/subtraction. Within a group, operations proceed from left to right. It is generally best to specify how you want R to do things using parentheses:

```
> 2 + 5 / 3 ^ 2
[1] 2.555556
> 2 + (5 / (3 ^ 2))
[1] 2.555556
> 2 + (5 / 3) ^ 2
[1] 4.777778
> (2 + 5) / 3 ^ 2
[1] 0.7777778
> ((2 + 5) / 3) ^ 2
[1] 5.444444
```

The first command shows the answer using the default order of operation and the second command uses parenthesis to show that that order involves squaring 3 first, then dividing it into 5, and then adding 2. You can specify the order of operations using parentheses "()" or curly braces "{}", but not square brackets "[]," which are used only for identifying elements in matrices, data frames, and lists.

These operators work element-by-element on vectors and matrices as long as they have the same dimensions (number of rows and columns):

```
> x <- c(1, 2, 3)
> y <- c(1, 5, 2)
> x + y
[1] 2 7 5
> x - y
[1]  0 -3  1
> x * y
[1]  1 10  6
> x / y
[1] 1.0 0.4 1.5
> x ^ y
[1]  1 32  9
> x + 1
[1] 2 3 4
> c(x, x) + y
[1] 2 7 5 2 7 5
```

In R, this is called **vectorization** and it makes operations on vectors and matrices much easier. Many other programming languages would require a programming loop to get the same results. Look at the last two examples above. In next to last example, we add 1 to the vector x. R adds 1 to each value in x. This is called **recyc-ling** and it is very handy as long as you remember that R does it. In the last example we double the x vector and add y. Since the length of y is a multiple of the length of the doubled x, R automatically doubles the y vector before adding. If the vectors are not multiples of one another, R will issue a warning message after recycling as much of the shorter vector as it needs.

The number you see in the R Console is usually an approximation of the result; it is not a direct copy of the number as it is stored in your computer. This applies not just to R, but to any software that performs numerical opera-tions. Decimal numbers (also known as floating point numbers) cannot always be precisely represented in the binary number system that computers use. This is important for two reasons. First, you can control how precisely R displays the results. In many cases, R gives you more information than you need to compare values. Second, because numbers are stored as very good approximations, it is possible that two numbers that should be equal are not quite equal. For an exam-ple, see "Frequently Asked Questions on R # 7.31. Why doesn't R think these numbers are equal?"

There are two options in R that control how numbers are displayed, digits= and scipen=, and they are accessible using the options() function:

```
> options("digits", "scipen")
$digits
[1] 7

$scipen
[1] 0
```

The default number of significant digits is 7. Significant digits do not include the 0's that are place holders. For example, seven significant digits for 123456789 would be 123456800 and for .123456789 would be .1234568. In this case R prints the whole number for the first value, but rounds the second value. Significant digits are not the same as rounding. As we generate descriptive statistics in this chapter, we will use several approaches to reducing the number of digits displayed to make it easier to compare values. This affects only how the numbers are displayed, not how they are stored.

The second option, scipen=, is short for "scientific notation penalty" and it controls when R shifts to scientific notation to represent very large numbers and numbers very close to 0. The default is 0, but we can change it to larger values to force R to print numbers in standard notation. The default value shifts to scientific notation when there are four or more leading zeros so that .0000123456789 is represented as 1.234568e-05 and when there are more than 12 digits before the decimal so that 1234567890000 becomes 1.234568e+12. We can also use the round() and signif() functions to simplify the output.

3.2 FOUR COMMON DISTRIBUTIONS

Archaeological data can be described by many theoretical distributions. Here we will just consider four very common distributions: binomial, Poisson, normal, and lognormal. The first two are discrete distributions because they deal with observations that are recorded as whole numbers (e.g., the number of sites, hand axes, decorated pots, or utilized flakes). The second two are continuous distributions because they deal with observations that can take any real value (e.g., length, width, weight, area).

3.2.1 Binomial Distribution

Binomial distributions are used to represent observations that must fall into one of two categories (e.g., decorated/undecorated, present/absent, burned/unburned). One of the two categories is arbitrarily designated as a "success" and the probability of a "success" is designated as p and the probability of a "failure" is 1 – p. Given the number of trials or observations, we can generate the probability of any number of successes.

$$\Pr(X = k) = \binom{n}{k} p^k (1-p)^{n-k}$$

where $\binom{n}{k} = \dfrac{n!}{k!(n-k)!}$; $k = 0, 1, 2, \ldots, n$; n is the number of trials; and p is the probability of a success, and $n!$ means that we multiply the numbers from 1 to n (1 x 2 x 3 x 4 x … n). The right side of the equation gives the probability of k successes out of n trials. If we compute the probability for each value of k from 0 to n, the sum of those probabilities will be 1.

Binomial distributions are expected whenever there are only two outcomes possible. For example, a tossed coin can land heads or tails, a site can be within 100 meters of a water source or not, a house can contain decorated ceramics or not, a point is made of obsidian or it is not, and a site contains a palace complex or it does not. Even if there are more than two outcomes, we can focus on one of them and lump all of the others together.

We can produce a quick plot of the binomial distribution using R. To plot this and the following distributions, we will use the plotDistr() function in package RcmdrMisc (Fox 2016). This package includes functions that are used with R Commander (discussed in Chapter 2), but they are very useful even without using R Commander. To use a function in a package, we have to install the package with install.packages() and then load the package with library(). We only install the package once, but we have to load it whenever we want to use it during a new R session.

```
> install.packages("RcmdrMisc")
also installing the dependencies 'car', 'sandwich'
. . . various informational messages . . .
> library(RcmdrMisc)
Loading required package: car
Loading required package: sandwich
```

The install.packages("RcmdrMisc") function generates a number of messages. Some functions in RcmdrMisc use functions in other packages (dependencies) so the car and sandwich packages are also installed. Then we load the package with library(RcmdrMisc), which also loads the dependent packages. Now we can plot the binomial distribution. Let's assume that we have 30 trials (n) so k ranges from 0 to 30, and the probability of a success, p, equals .4. Using R commands, we create these variables and then pass them to the dbinom() function to compute the probability for each value of k, which we will call Pk using the above equation (Pk <- dbinom(k, n, p)). The dbinom() function is the **d**ensity function for the **binom**ial distribution.

```
> n <- 30
> k <- 0:n
> p <- .4
> Pk <- dbinom(k, n, p)
> Pk[1:5]
 [1] 2.210739e-07 4.421478e-06 4.274096e-05 2.659437e-04
 1.196747e-03
> round(Pk[1:5], 4)
 [1] 0.0000 0.0000 0.0000 0.0003 0.0012
```

```
> sum(Pk)
[1] 1
> plotDistr(x=k, p=Pk, discrete=TRUE)
```

The values for Pk are all less than 1. We list the first five values only, but you can list them all by leaving off [1:5]. By default, they are represented in scientific notation so the first value is 2.210739 x 10^{-7} or .0000002210729. This is the probability that 0 successes will occur with 30 trials. To make the values more readable, we use round() to show only four decimal places. The last command uses the plotDistr() function to plot the distribution. This opens a plot window containing the plot (Figure 4a). Looking at the plot, you can see that it has a single

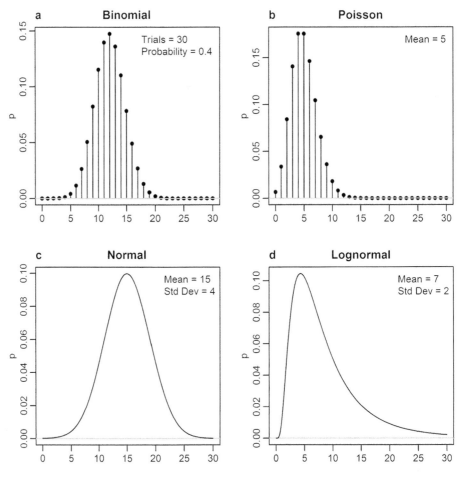

FIGURE 4 Four probability distributions: a. Binomial, b. Poisson, c. Normal, d. Lognormal.

peak and is not quite symmetrical. The height of the bar gives the probability that a sample of 30 would have x successes. The highest probability is at x=12 where the probability is .1474 (14.74 percent). This is the 13th value in the list of Pk values since we started at 0 (i.e., Pk[13]).

Use the "File | Save" option on the R Editor window to save your file as Chapter03.R, but keep it open since you will use it for the rest of the chapter.

To make the theoretical distribution more concrete, imagine that we have a cemetery consisting of 30 graves. Based on demographic data and excavations at other cemeteries, we believe that about 60 percent of the graves should be children and 40 percent should be adults. The binomial distribution we just computed tells us how many adult burials we should expect to have in the cemetery. By looking at the figure, you can see that a range of 7 to 17 adult burials would be likely (if you sum the range, sum(Pk[8:18]), it comes to about 96 percent). If the cemetery had 25 adult burials, we would suspect that this cemetery was different from our expectations.

Generate some more binomial distributions by changing the number of trials and the probability of success. As the probability of success gets farther away from .5, the distribution becomes less symmetrical.

3.2.2 Poisson Distribution

Poisson distributions are used to express the number of successes that will occur within a particular unit of time or space and the occurrence of each success is independent of the other occurrences. In archaeology, the Poisson distribution is routinely used as a null hypothesis in spatial analysis. The number of sites in a set of survey units or the number of pottery sherds in a set of excavation squares will follow a Poisson distribution if the observations are completely independent of one another. When we are dealing with by-products of human activity, the observations will not usually be independent and we can explore the degree to which they are uniformly distributed or clustered. The Poisson distribution is characterized by the parameter λ (lambda), which is the average number of specimens in each unit.

$$\Pr(X = k) = \frac{\lambda^k}{k!} e^{-\lambda}$$

where $k = 0, 1, 2, \ldots, k$; and λ is the mean number of observations in a unit, $k!$ means that we multiply the numbers from 1 to n (1 x 2 x 3 x 4 x ... k) and e is the base of the natural logarithm equal to approximately 2.71828. We can plot the Poisson distribution for lambda = 5 as follows (Figure 4b):

```
> max <- 30
> k <- 0:max
> lambda <- 5
> Pk <- dpois(k, lambda)
> round(Pk[1:5], 4)
 [1] 0.0067 0.0337 0.0842 0.1404 0.1755.
> sum(Pk)
[1] 1
> plotDistr(x=k, p=Pk, discrete=TRUE)
```

Notice that we created a variable called max rather than n. In the binomial distribution, we have to specify the number of trials (sample size). There is a different distribution for each sample size. The Poisson distribution is the same for all sample sizes that have the same lambda value. We use dpois() to get the density of the Poisson distribution. The x-axis represents the number of occurrences in a unit defined by space or time. For example, if we survey a 5 by 5 kilometer area divided up into square kilometer units and count the number of round barrows in each unit, we would have the number of barrows in each of 25 square kilometer units. Assuming the average number of barrows per square kilometer is 5 (that is 125 barrows were recorded in 25 square kilometers), we can compute the expected number barrows per unit as follows:

```
> round(Pk*25)
 [1] 0 1 2 4 4 4 4 3 2 1 0 0 0 0 0 0 0 0 0 0 0 0 0 0 0 0 0 0 0 0 0
```

We have rounded the numbers to integer values since we assign each barrow to the unit that contains its center even if part of the barrow extends over the boundary of the unit. If barrows were located independently, their distribution should follow a Poisson distribution and most of the survey units should contain four barrows (sum(Pk[4:7]) = 0.6375). If people tended to construct barrows near existing barrows or if they tended to construct barrows away from existing barrows, the distribution would not be Poisson. In the first case, more units will have 0 barrows and more units will have more than four barrows. In the second case, a higher proportion of the survey units would have five or six barrows. Generate some more Poisson distributions with larger and smaller values of lambda to see how the distribution changes.

3.2.3 Normal Distribution

The **normal** (also Gaussian or Bell) distribution is a continuous probability distribution that has a symmetrical shape and is defined by two parameters, μ and σ^2, the mean and the variance. For discrete distributions, only integer values are possible, but for a continuous distribution, any real number is possible. We plotted discrete distributions as vertical lines with the height of the line representing the probability of that outcome. Since it would take an infinite number of lines to represent a continuous distribution, we use a curve. Also since the probability of any specific value (e.g., 25.0000000···) is essentially 0, we can only refer to the probability of a range of outcomes (e.g., from 1.5 to 2.0) and that probability will be represented as the area under the curve over that range. Normal distributions are common enough that many statistical methods have been designed to work with them. The equation for the probability density of the normal distribution is as follows:

$$f\left(x\,|\,\mu,\sigma\right)=\frac{1}{\sigma\sqrt{2\pi}}e^{-\frac{(x-\mu)^2}{2\sigma^2}}$$

where μ is the mean of the distribution; σ is the standard deviation; and e is the base of the natural logarithm.

The following commands will plot a normal distribution with a mean of 15 and a standard deviation of 4 (Figure 4c):

```
> mean <- 15
> std <- 4
> x <- seq(0, 30, length.out=200)
> Dx <- dnorm(x, mean, std)
> plotDistr(x=x, p=Dx)
```

Since we are drawing a smooth curve we need many x values so we use `seq()` to generate 200 values between 0 and 30. Then we use `dnorm()` to get the **density** for the **norm**al distribution. To get probabilities, we need to use `pnorm()`:

```
> # Probability of 5 or less
> pnorm(5, mean, std)
[1] 0.006209665
> # Probability of 25 or more
> pnorm(25, mean, std, lower.tail=FALSE)
[1] 0.006209665
> # Probability between 14 and 16)
```

```
> pnorm(16, mean, std) - pnorm(14, mean, std)
[1] 0.1974127
```

As before # tells R to ignore the rest of the line so that we can add comments describing what we are doing. Strictly speaking, you do not need to include them in your Chapter03.R script file, but they will provide a useful reminder of what you are doing. Feel free to add additional comment lines. The first command computes the probability of an observation having a value of 5 or less and the second computes the probability of an observation having a value of 25 or more (the lower and upper tails of the distribution). The last command shows the probability of an observation having a value between 14 and 16. By default, the pnorm() function returns the area under the curve from negative infinity (−∞) to the value specified (the lower tail). To get the area under the curve from positive infinity (+∞) to the value (the upper tail), we use the lower.tail=FALSE argument. To get the area between two values we subtract the smaller area from the larger.

The normal distribution is very common in archaeological data. The central limit theorem holds that the sum of a large number of random variables (regardless of their distribution) will have an approximately normal distribution. As a result, any measurement that represents the sum of a number of different factors could be expected to have an approximately normal distribution. The assumption of a normal distribution underlies the statistical methods known as parametric statistics. Normal distributions play a large role in defining confidence limits and significance levels for parametric statistics (Chapter 8).

The dimensions of artifacts might be expected to follow a normal distribution under many circumstances, but distributions that differ from normal are potentially interesting. Multimodal distributions (distributions with more than a single peak) could indicate that two or more groups with different normal distributions are contained within the sample.

3.2.4 Log-Normal Distribution

The **log-normal** distribution is a continuous probability distribution of a random variable whose logarithm is normally distributed. A log-normal distribution is asymmetrical with a long tail extending to the right:

$$f\left(x\,|\,\mu,\sigma\right) = \frac{1}{x\sigma\sqrt{2\pi}}e^{-\frac{(\ln x - \mu)^2}{2\sigma^2}}$$

where μ is the mean of the distribution; σ is the standard deviation; and e is the base of the natural logarithm.

The following commands generate a log normal distribution for a mean of 7 and a standard deviation of 2. The function requires the natural logarithms of these values so we use the `log()` function in the following code to plot the lognormal distribution (Figure 4d):

```
mean <- 7
std <- 2
x <- seq(0, 30, length.out=200)
Dx <- dlnorm(x, log(mean), log(std))
plotDistr(x=x, p=Dx)
```

The log-normal distribution is also common in archaeological data. The central limit theorem leads to the log normal distribution when a variable is the product (as opposed to the sum) of a large number of random variables. As a result, any measurement that represents the product of a number of different factors (e.g., probabilities) could be expected to have an approximately log-normal distribution. Areas, volumes, and weights can be modeled as the product of a set of linear measures and will often be log-normally distributed.

3.3 DESCRIPTIVE STATISTICS – NUMERIC

Descriptive statistics include measures that try to describe a distribution in terms of a few numeric values. These include measures of central tendency, measures of dispersion or spread, and measures of shape. Generally, the data that we work with represent a sample from a larger population and we are more interested in the population than just the sample. Using the sample to estimate the population is the purpose of inferential statistics, which we will discuss in Chapter 8, but here we will identify measures that have slightly different definitions when we are interested in estimating the population, not just describing the sample.

Measures of central tendency indicate the middle of the data. The primary measures of central tendency are the arithmetic **mean**, the **median**, and the **mode**. The mean is the sum of the values divided by the number of values:

$$\bar{x} = \frac{\sum_{i=1}^{n} x_i}{n}$$

where $\bar{x}$ is the estimate of the mean using a sample; n is the number of values in the vector; and i is an index $i = 1, 2, 3, ..., n$.

The mean has the property that it provides an estimate that minimizes error. If we randomly select data values from any distribution and compare it to the mean, over the long run, the error (defined as the sum of the squares of the differences between the randomly selected values and the mean) will be smaller for the mean than for any other value. However, the mean is affected by extreme values so that it may not be the number that represents most of the values. One way to reduce the influence of extreme values is to use a **trimmed mean** by removing a percentage of the smallest and largest values before computing the mean. Another way is to use the **median**, which is the value at which half of the values are higher and half are lower. The **mode** is the most common value or the highest point on the density curve. Except for the mode, these are available in R as functions `mean()` for both the mean and the trimmed mean and `median()` for the median.

Measures of dispersion indicate the span of the data values. The primary measures of dispersion are the **variance, standard deviation, range, interquartile range, median absolute deviation**, and **coefficient of variation**. The variance is the sum of the squared deviations of each observation from the mean divided by the number of observations (or the number of observations minus 1 if we are estimating the population variance).

$$s^2 = \frac{\sum_{i=1}^{n}\left(x_i - \bar{x}\right)^2}{n-1}$$

where s^2 (and the square root, s, is the standard deviation); $\bar{x}$ is the mean; n is the number of values in the vector; and i is an index $i = 1, 2, 3, ..., n$.

The standard deviation is the square root of the variance. The variance and the standard deviation share the mean's sensitivity to extreme values so they are most applicable if the data follow a normal distribution. The **range** is simply the maximum value minus the minimum value so it is completely defined by the two most extreme values. The **interquartile range** is the difference between the third and first quartiles. The first quartile is the value that has 25 percent of the values falling below it and the third quartile has 75 percent of the values falling below it. The interquartile range therefore includes half of the data values.

The **median absolute deviation** is a robust measure of dispersion that is computed by taking the median of the absolute values of the difference between each value and the median. The **coefficient of variation** adjusts the standard deviation by dividing it by the mean to adjust for the fact that measurements with larger means also have larger standard deviations. The coefficient of variation is dimensionless so we can compare variables measured in different scales. The primary drawback of the coefficient of variation is that it becomes inflated as the mean approaches zero.

Functions for the variance, standard deviation, range, interquartile range, and median absolute deviation in R include `var()`, `sd()`, `IQR()`, and `mad()`. The coefficient of variation is just `sd()/mean()`. The R function `range()` computes the minimum and maximum so `diff(range())` computes the difference between them.

The principal **measures of shape** are **skewness** and **kurtosis**. **Skewness** helps identify distributions that are asymmetrical (skewed) in one direction or the other. Distributions that are skewed right have more extreme high values and those that are skewed left have more extreme low values. In Figure 4, the Poisson and log-normal distributions are skewed right. Recognizing skewness can help to determine if a transformation should be applied to the data and if so, which one (more details in Chapter 6). **Kurtosis** is a measure of how peaked or flat the distribution is and how thick or thin the tails are. Flatter distributions may be multimodal, suggesting that they represent a mixture of different types. In describing a sample, skewness and kurtosis are similar to the calculation of variance except that we take the third or fourth power of the differences between each observation and the mean. The population estimates are more complicated and there are three different versions all of which are available from the `skewness()` and `kurtosis()` functions in package `e1071` (Meyer et al., 2015).

Finally, we can also get information about dispersion and shape from looking at **quantiles**. Quantiles divide the data into groups so that the same number of values falls into each group. For example, quartiles divide the data into four groups, deciles divide them into 10 groups, and percentiles divide them into 100 groups. Quantiles are not uniquely defined since there are various ways to draw the boundaries between values. The `quantile()` function can use any of nine different definitions (Hyndman and Fan, 1996). Generally the differences will be minor unless the sample size is small.

3.4 DESCRIPTIVE STATISTICS USING R

To illustrate how to compute descriptive statistics using R, we need some data. The `archdata` package (Carlson and Roth, 2016) includes a range of archaeological data sets. Assuming you installed the package in Chapter 2, you now only need to load it with the `library()` command:

```
> library(archdata)
> data(DartPoints)
```

```
> ?DartPoints
> View(DartPoints)
> str(DartPoints)
'data.frame': 91 obs. of  17 variables:
 $ Name    : Factor w/ 5 levels "Darl","Ensor",..: 1 1 1 1 1
             1 1 1 1 ...
 $ Catalog : chr  "41-0322" "35-2946" "35-2921"
   "36-3487" ...
 $ TARL    : chr  "41CV0536" "41CV0235" "41CV0132"
             "41CV0594" ...
 $ Quad    : chr  "26/59" "21/63" "20/63" "10/54" ...
 $ Length  : num  42.8 40.5 37.5 40.3 30.6 41.8 40.3 48.5
   47.7 33.6 ...
 $ Width   : num  15.8 17.4 16.3 16.1 17.1 16.8 20.7 18.7
   17.5 15.8 ...
 . . . 9 lines deleted . . .
 $ Haft.Sh : Factor w/ 5 levels "A","E","I","R",..: 5 5 5 5
   5 3 3 5 5 5 ...
 $ Haft.Or : Factor w/ 5 levels "C","E","P","T",..: 2 2 2 2
   2 1 2 2 2 3 ...
```

The library(archdata) and data(DartPoints) commands load archdata and attach the DartPoints data frame so that we can use it. Load the manual page with ?DartPoints. View(DartPoints) provides a pop-up display of the data so that you can scroll through the rows and columns. Close the window when you are finished so that your desktop does not become too cluttered. The str(DartPoints) command summarizes the data set. Normally you should use some combination of these commands whenever you use a new R data set from archdata or any other R package.

DartPoints includes measurements on 91 complete dart points that were recovered during surface surveys at the Fort Hood military base in Texas (Figure 5). Only five types of points are included and the type is stored as a factor in the first column (Name). Other variables include the catalog number, site number (TARL), and survey quadrat, all stored as character variables. Then seven metric variables containing information about the dimensions of the points and six factors represented categorical variables coding shape information. These points were drawn from an analysis of a larger sample (Carlson et al., 1987) and the coding system for the shape variables was based on a system developed by Futato (1983). The points are classified on the basis of overall shape and manufacturing process so we can explore the

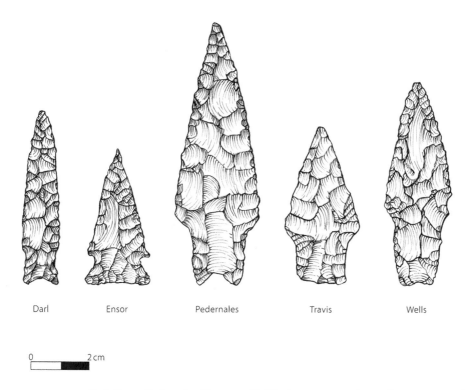

Darl   Ensor   Pedernales   Travis   Wells

0 _____ 2 cm

FIGURE 5 Darl, Ensor, Pedernales, Travis, and Wells dart points. Redrawn from Turner and Hester (1993).

degree to which the various measurements provide sufficient information to identify the types.

Whenever you begin working with a new data set, you should look at some basic descriptive statistics. Descriptive statistics help to characterize your data so that you have some idea of how well they fit one of the distributions we have just described. They also help you to catch obvious coding errors so you can correct them before proceeding and they will give you an indication of possible outliers, data that have substantially lower or higher values than the rest of the data.

Try the following commands:

```
> mean(Length)
Error in mean(Length) : object 'Length' not found
> mean(DartPoints$Length)
[1] 49.33077
> median(DartPoints[, 5])
```

```
[1] 47.1
> sd(DartPoints[, "Length"])
[1] 12.73619
> quantile(DartPoints$Length)
     0%    25%    50%    75%   100%
  30.60  40.85  47.10  55.80 109.50
```

The variables inside DartPoints are not visible to R functions. That is why the first command produced an error. The next three commands show three different ways to specify that we want the Length column, by column name, by column position, and by column name within brackets. The last version just looks like extra typing, but it can come in handy when you want to specify the names of several columns at once. Looking at the mean and the median, we can already tell that dart point length may be skewed right since the median is less than the mean. The quantiles confirm this suspicion. The difference between the minimum (0%) and the first quartile (25%) is about 10 (30.6 to 40.8) whereas the difference between the maximum (100%) and the third quartile (75%) is over 50 (55.8 to 109.5). Another sign that a distribution is skewed right is when the standard deviation is large relative to the mean, but that is not the case here since the standard deviation is about one-fourth the mean. Try these commands:

```
> attach(DartPoints)
> mean(Thickness)
[1] 7.271429
> mean(B.Width)
[1] NA
> mean(B.Width, na.rm=TRUE)
[1] 13.75072
> detach(DartPoints)
```

The first command attaches DartPoints to the search path so that R looks variable names there. That means you do not have to append DartPoints$ to the variable name, but it also means that you can get confused if you are working with multiple data sets at one time. If you use attach(), always be sure to detach() after you are finished working with the data set. Not using attach() is safer and we will not use it again. We compute the mean of thickness (Thickness) and then basal width (B.Width). Thickness is fine, but basal width produces NA as the result. If you use View(DartPoints) to look at the data and scroll right to see the B.Width column you will see several NAs in the column. NA stands for "Not Available" or missing. These values were not measured on the point for some reason.

All of the statistical functions described above have an na.rm= argument and the default value is FALSE. That means that if there are any missing values in the vector, the resulting value will be missing. Although it may seem annoying, it protects you from proceeding with your analysis under the mistaken assumption that there are no missing values in the data.

Generally you do not want to compute these statistics individually. Several functions provide summary statistics in tabular format and provide the ability to compute descriptive statistics on subsets of the data. We used one of them in Chapter 2:

```
> summary(DartPoints[, c(1, 5, 8, 12)])
          Name            Length            B.Width         Blade.Sh
 Darl       :28    Min.    :30.60    Min.    :7.10    E    :42
 Ensor      :10    1st Qu. :40.85    1st Qu. :11.70   I    :4
 Pedernales :32    Median  :47.10    Median  :13.60   R    :3
 Travis     :11    Mean    :49.33    Mean    :13.75   S    :40
 Wells      :10    3rd Qu. :55.80    3rd Qu. :15.50   NA's :2
                   Max.    :109.50   Max.    :21.20
                                     NA's    :22
```

To save space, we are only looking at four variables with summary() by specifying which columns to analyze. For factors (Type name and blade shape), summary() provides counts of up to five categories are shown along with the number of missing values (NA's). For numeric variables we get the quartiles and the mean along with the number of missing values. It is a quick way to get a basic description of the data, but it is not exactly elegant or easy to read.

We can get a more compact display of numeric variables with the numSummary() function in package RcmdrMisc (Box 2). But first we will use the options() function to set the number of significant digits:

```
> options(digits=3)
> numSummary(DartPoints[, 5:11])
             mean     sd    IQR     0%     25%    50%     75%    100%   n  NA
Length      49.33  12.74  14.95   30.6   40.85  47.1   55.80  109.5  91   0
Width       22.08   5.16   6.60   14.5   18.55  21.1   25.15   49.3  91   0
Thickness    7.27   1.53   2.00    4.0    6.25   7.2    8.25   10.7  91   0
B.Width     13.75   2.95   3.80    7.1   11.70  13.6   15.50   21.2  69  22
J.Width     15.40   2.73   3.95   10.6   13.12  15.6   17.08   21.2  90   1
H.Length    13.41   4.01   5.80    5.8   10.50  12.5   16.30   23.3  91   0
Weight       7.64   4.21   5.50    2.3    4.55   6.8   10.05   28.8  91   0
```

This is easier to read. Ehrenberg has suggested that we are better able to compare values in a table if only two significant digits are presented so you might want to try that (1977, 1981). The mean length is printed as 49.33, but internally it is stored as 49.330769230769228 (`print(mean(DartPoints$Length)`, `digits=22)`). When R prints values, it takes the value of `digits` as a guide not a law and it prints the same number of decimal places for each value in a column. Notice that mean length has four significant digits, while mean thickness has three, but they both have two decimal places.

By default `numSummary()` provides the mean, standard deviation, interquartile range, quartiles, number of observations, and the number of missing values. Optionally it can also provide the standard error of the mean, the coefficient of variation, skewness, and kurtosis. The specific quantiles can also be changed and you can break the statistics into groups based on a factor:

```
> numSummary(DartPoints[, 5], statistics=c("mean", "sd",
+ "skewness", "kurtosis", "cv", groups=DartPoints$Name)
              mean      sd     cv  skewness  kurtosis  data:n
Darl          39.8    6.18  0.155     0.480    -0.292      28
Ensor         42.7    5.79  0.135     0.998     1.546      10
Pedernales    57.9   14.13  0.244     1.708     4.789      32
Travis        51.4    9.90  0.193     0.488    -0.822      11
Wells         53.1    7.94  0.150     0.101    -0.970      10
```

From the output, it is clear that Pedernales points are the longest on average and Darl points are the shortest. Pedernales point lengths are also the most variable as measured by the coefficient of variability (cv).

The `numSummary()` function provides compact summaries of numeric data and it makes it very easy to compare values from different groups, but it does not summarize categorical data. The `Desc()` function in package `DescTools` provides descriptive statistics for numeric, categorical, and dichotomous data (Signorell et al., 2016). As a final example, we will install the package and generate some basic descriptive statistics for the `DartPoints` data set:

```
> install.packages("DescTools")
> library(DescTools)
> options(scipen=10)
> Desc(DartPoints[, c(1, 5, 12)])
```

```
---------------------------------------------------------------
'data.frame': 91 obs. of  3 variables:
 1 $ Name   : Factor w/ 5 levels "Darl","Ensor",..: 1 1 1 1 1
     1 1 1 1 1 ...
 2 $ Length : num  42.8 40.5 37.5 40.3 30.6 41.8 40.3 48.5
     47.7 33.6 ...
 3 $ Blade.Sh: Factor w/ 4 levels "E","I","R","S": 4 4 4 4 4
     4 2 1 1 1 ...
---------------------------------------------------------------
1 - Name (factor)

  length    n   NAs   levels   unique   dupes
      91   91     0        5        5       y
```

	level	freq	perc	cumfreq	cumperc
1	Pedernales	32	35.2%	32	35.2%
2	Darl	28	30.8%	60	65.9%
3	Travis	11	12.1%	71	78.0%
4	Ensor	10	11.0%	81	89.0%
5	Wells	10	11.0%	91	100.0%

```
---------------------------------------------------------------
2 - Length (numeric)

  length     n     NAs    unique     0s      mean   meanSE
      91    91       0        81      0     49.33     1.34


     .05    .10     .25    median    .75      .90      .95
   33.30  35.40   40.85     47.10  55.80    64.60    68.10


   range     sd   vcoef      mad     IQR     skew     kurt
   78.90  12.74    0.26    11.12   14.95     1.47     4.16

lowest : 30.6, 31.2, 32.0, 32.4, 33.1
highest: 69.0, 70.4, 78.3, 84.0, 109.5
---------------------------------------------------------------
3 - Blade.Sh (factor)

  length    n   NAs   levels   unique   dupes
      91   89     2        4        4       y
```

	level	freq	perc	cumfreq	cumperc
1	E	42	47.2%	42	47.2%
2	S	40	44.9%	82	92.1%
3	I	4	4.5%	86	96.6%
4	R	3	3.4%	89	100.0%

After loading the package, we set the `scipen=10` option to 10 to avoid scientific notation in the presentation of the results. To keep the output to a reasonable amount, we have only summarized the `Name`, `Length`, and `Blade.Sh` (blade shape). The `Desc()` function adapts to the kind of data so factor variables are handled differently from numeric ones (Box 3). As we will see in the Chapter 4, it can produce plots as well.

For `Name` (a factor variable), we get the number of each point type, the percentage, the cumulative frequency, and the cumulative percent. At the top, we get the length (number of values) and the number of non-missing values, missing values, levels, and unique values. The last two will agree unless some of the factor levels are empty. The "dups" column indicates if there are any duplicate values. The sample sizes for Pedernales and Darl points are substantially larger than for the Travis, Ensor, and Wells points. This is not necessarily a problem, but we should be aware of it.

For `Length` (a numeric variable), we get similar information and the number of zeros. This is helpful since a zero value should not occur as a measurement of length. Then we get the mean and the standard error of the mean. The second row gives quantiles proportions of .05, .10, .25, .50, .75, .90, and .95. On the third row, we get the range, standard deviation, coefficient of variation, mean absolute deviation, interquartile range, skewness, and kurtosis. The next row includes the five smallest and the five largest values. This is a good way to identify extreme values that may indicate coding errors. The longest point has a measurement of 109.5, which is much larger than the next longest. This measurement should be double-checked to be sure it is correct (it is). Also notice that the smallest length is 30.60 mm. That is a small value for a dart point so we should check the original data and a photograph to make sure this is not a fragmentary point (it is not).

The descriptive statistics for `Blade.Sh`, a factor, have the same format as the statistics for `Name`. Most of the points (92 percent) have either excurvate (E) or straight (S) blades. Also two points have missing values for blade shape.

If we analyze all of the variables for each of the five types we will generate a lot of output. Instead we will divert all of that output to a text file. The following commands will split the DartPoints data frame into a list of five data frames, one for each type. Then we will run Desc() on each of the data frames and send the output to a text file:

```
> DartPoints.split <- split(DartPoints[, 5:17],
  DartPoints$Name)
> sink("DartPointsDesc.txt")
> names(DartPoints.split)
> lapply(DartPoints.split, Desc)
> sink()
```

The first command uses the split() function to split the data frame DartPoints into a list of five data frames, one for each point type called DartPoints.split. We also leave out the first four columns of descriptive information. The second command uses sink() to divert the output of the following commands to a text file called DartPointsDesc.txt, which will be stored in the current working directory. The third command uses names() to list the names of the point types at the top of the file so we know which ones are being described. Unfortunately, this approach does not label each type group in the output, but you can add that later if you want. The fourth command runs the Desc() function on each of the five data frames stored in DartPoints.split using lapply(). The last command closes the output file. The file now contains 1219 lines with the descriptive statistics for each of the five types. You should be able to open it using the menu at the top of the R Console window, "File | Open script", but the file selection window that opens may be limiting the display to files with an R extension. If so, change it to show all the files. Then select DartPointsDesc.txt and scroll through the results. You can print the whole file (about 20 pages) or open it in a word processor or text editor and cut out the parts you need.

Some of the things to look for in the descriptive statistics include the categories of each factor variable. If any are empty or represented by a single specimen, they may be misspellings or categories that are present in a larger data set from which this one is a subset.

For the numeric variables, begin by examining the minimum and maximum values of each. Are there any values that seem too large or too small? Zeros probably indicate measurements that were not taken or could not be taken for some reason. If zero is not a valid value (for length, for example), it should be changed to NA (missing).

If you find errors in your data, you can correct them using the fix() function:

```
> fix(DartPoints)
> save(DartPoints, file="DartPoints.RData")
```

The fix() function displays the data frame. Make any modifications you want by clicking in a cell and typing new numbers. To change an entry to missing, double-click the cell and press the Delete key (or "Edit | Delete" on the top menu of the edit window). You have to save the data frame after editing it with save() to make a permanent copy in your folder. You can make any changes you want to DartPoints without affecting the original copy since that is stored in the archdata package in a different directory on your computer.

Correcting factor variables requires an extra step. If you correct a misspelled category and then run the levels() function on the factor column, you will see that the misspelled category is still there. You changed an entry, but you did not modify the list of factor levels. To do that, you have to regenerate the factor levels with the factor() function to eliminate the misspelled level from the list. In Chapter 5 we will discuss factors in greater detail.

If you want to include any of these tables in a paper, you can select, copy, and paste into the document, but you will need to select a monospaced font (e.g., Courier) for things to line up correctly. In Chapter 4 we will talk about other ways to export tables to a spreadsheet or word processing program.

Some values may seem much smaller or larger than the rest of the values. These outliers can affect descriptive statistics such as the mean and the standard deviation, so there is often a desire to identify them and remove them. That may be the best course of action if there is reason to believe that the outlier is a result of measurement or coding error and there is no way to re-measure the specimen or correct the coding error. With multivariate data, it is often the case that different specimens will seem to be outliers on different measurements. As a general rule, it is usually better to use robust statistics that are not as affected by outliers rather than to routinely remove them without some theoretical justification. If you look at the maximum values in the DartPoints data set, you will see indications of outliers. They will be easier to detect in the plots that we will create in Chapter 5.

Now save your command file using the R Editor menu option "File | Save". Then use the R Console menu option "File | Save to file" to save the output file as "Chapter03.txt." Then exit R. When R asks to save your workspace image, click "No."

There are a number of other packages that have functions to compute descriptive statistics, but these are some of the most useful. Using the search tools described in Chapter 2, you should be able to find more.

BOX 2   THE numSummary() FUNCTION IN THE RcmdrMisc PACKAGE

```
numSummary(data, statistics=c("mean", "sd", "se(mean)",
  "IQR", "quantiles","cv", "skewness", "kurtosis"),
  type=c("2", "1", "3"),
    quantiles=c(0, .25, .5, .75, 1), groups)
```

The function produces a neatly formatted table of various descriptive statistics, optionally broken down into groups on the basis of a variable. The defaults are as follows:

- Statistics including mean ("mean"), standard deviation ("sd"), quantiles ("quantiles"), and the interquartile range ("IQR")
- Quantiles including minimum (0%), first quartile (25%), median (50%), third quartile (75%), and maximum (100%).

Additionally, the following statistics can be included:
- By specifying the statistics= argument the default statistics can be removed and the standard error of the mean ("se(mean)"), coefficient of variability ("cv"), skewness ("skewness"), and kurtosis ("kurtosis") can be added.
- The quantiles to be computed can be changed with the quantiles= argument by specifying which proportions to use.
- The method for computing skewness and kurtosis can be changed (see the skewness and kurtosis functions in package e1071.

The groups= argument can be used to specify a variable that will be used to divide the data into groups and compute the statistics for each group.

The function returns an object of class numSummary, which is a list containing a matrix called table with one row for each variable and one column for each statistical value along with labels and information on the number of non-missing observations and the number of missing observations. When the groups= argument is used, the table is a three-dimensional array containing matrices for each group.

BOX 3 THE `Desc()` FUNCTION IN THE `DescTools` PACKAGE

```
Desc(x, ..., wrd = NULL)
```

This is a generic function that produces summaries of various types of variables. Normally, *x* would be a vector or a data frame and the function would generate statistics and optionally a plot for each variable. The summaries can include statistics, tables, and plots. Plots are selected with the argument `plotit=TRUE`. Summaries are produced for factors, ordered factors, integer, numeric, and date data types. Summaries for factor with factor, factor with numeric, and numeric with numeric can also be produced using a formula as the input.

Optionally the results of the function can be inserted directly into a Word® document if the user has Word® installed under the Windows operating system using the `wrd=` argument. For example, the following creates a Word® document, inserts descriptive statistics and plots, saves the file, and then closes it:

```
> setwd("LearnR")
> library(archdata)
> library(DescTools)
Loading required package: manipulate
> data(DartPoints)
> options(scipen=10, digits=3)
> wrd <- GetNewWrd()
Loading required namespace: RDCOMClient
> Desc(DartPoints[, c(1, 5:17)], plotit=TRUE, wrd=wrd)
> wrd$ActiveDocument()$SaveAs2(FileName="LearnR/DartPoints.
  docx")
NULL
> wrd$quit()
NULL
```

For numeric variables, a variety of statistics including the number of observations, number of 0 observations mean, standard error of the mean, quantiles (.05, .10, .25, .50, .75, .90, .95), range, standard deviation, coefficient of variation, mean absolute deviation, interquartile range, skewness, kurtosis, and the five largest and smallest values. The plot includes a histogram with a kernel density plot superimposed, a box and whiskers plot, and a cumulative plot (empirical distribution plot).

For factors and ordered factors, a frequency table of the factor levels including percentages and cumulative frequencies and percentages is produced. Bar plots can be drawn of frequency, percentage, and cumulative percent. For discrete data, a frequency table and descriptive statistics. Dot plots show the frequency of each value. For logical (dichotomous), a frequency table with upper and lower confidence intervals for the percentages and a stacked bar plot are made use of.

Table 2 *Functions introduced in Chapter 3*

Function	Package	Description
attach	base	Attach a database to the search path, see detach
dbinom	stats	Binomial density distribution
Desc	DescTools	Descriptive statistics
detach	base	Remove a database from the search path, see attach
diff	base	Compute differences between adjacent values
dlnorm	stats	Log-normal density function
dnorm	stats	Normal density function
dpois	stats	Poisson density distribution
exp	base	Exponential with base e
factor	base	Create a factor variable, or regenerate factor levels
IQR	stats	Compute interquartile range
kurtosis	e1071	Compute kurtosis
lapply	base	Apply a function to each element of a list or data frame
log	base	Natural logarithm (base e)
log10	base	Common, base 10 logarithm
mad	stats	Compute the median absolute deviation
mean	base	Compute mean or trimmed mean
median	stats	Compute median
names	base	Get or set names of an object
numSummary	RcmdrMisc	Summary statistics for numeric variables
options	base	Set or examine various options
plotDistr	RcmdrMisc	Plot a distribution
pnorm	stats	Normal distribution function
quantile	stats	Compute quantiles
range	base	Compute the minimum and maximum
round	base	Round a numeric value
sd	stats	Compute standard deviation

Table 2 (*cont.*)

Function	Package	Description
seq	base	Create a sequence of numbers
sink	base	Send output to a text file
skewness	e1071	Compute skewness
split	base	Split a vector or data frame into groups
sqrt	base	Compute the square root
sum	base	Sum the elements of a vector or matrix
var	stats	Compute variance

Note: Packages base, datasets, graphics, grDevices, methods, stats, and utils are automatically loaded when R starts.

4

4

Looking at Data – Tables

A table is simply a two-dimensional presentation of data or a summary of the data. We use tables to inspect the original data for errors or problems such as missing entries. We used tables to present condensed summaries of data values in Chapter 3 (e.g., numSummary()). Those summaries involved computing summary statistics by a categorical variable to see how the groups differed from one another. We can also use tables to see how categorical variables covary.

Nominal or categorical data play a large role in archaeological research. At the regional level, sites are the categories and we are interested in the number of different types of artifacts (also a category) found in each site. The same applies at the site level where the artifact categories are distributed across excavation units. Within sites, different kinds of features are present and features contain different types of artifacts. At the artifact level, some properties of artifacts are represented by categories. Because of this, the same data are often represented in different ways for different purposes. That is not a problem unless the statistical procedures we are using expect a format different from the one we are currently using. In Chapter 3, we created tables of descriptive statistics. In this chapter we are concerned with tables in which the cell entries consist of counts of objects.

R distinguishes between tables and data frames and some functions will work with one but not the other. Data frames have columns that represent different types of data (e.g., character strings, factors, numbers), but tables in R represent numeric data only. In fact, R tables are a kind of matrix. Before constructing tables, we will briefly describe how R encodes categorical data using factors.

4.1 FACTORS IN R

Factors are a way of storing categorical information in R. If you have coded a variable into a set of categories, you have the choice of storing the information as a character or factor vector. A factor stores each category as an integer and the category labels are stored as levels. If you import your data into a data frame, R will automatically convert character vectors into factors unless you use the argument `stringsAsFactors=FALSE`. Originally factors were just a compact way to store the data when computer memory was limited and in most cases R will use character vectors as smoothly as it uses factors. But factors have a number of advantages if you need to add categories, delete or combine them, or specify their order. Factors can also be used to specify graphical options such as symbol, color, or line type more easily than character strings. First, we can create a sample character vector and convert it into a factor:

```
> set.seed(42)
> size <- sample(c("Tiny", "Small", "Medium", "Large",
  "Huge"), 25, replace=TRUE)
> str(size)
 chr [1:25] "Huge" "Huge" "Small" "Huge" "Large" ...
> head(size)
[1] "Huge"  "Huge"  "Small"  "Huge"  "Large"  "Medium"
> sizef <- factor(size)
> str(sizef)
 Factor w/ 5 levels "Huge","Large",..: 1 1 4 1 2 3 2 5 2 2 ...
> head(sizef)
[1] Huge Huge Small  Huge Large  Medium
Levels: Huge Large Medium Small Tiny
> levels(sizef)
[1] "Huge"  "Large"  "Medium" "Small"  "Tiny"
```

The `set.seed(42)` function is used to set a random number seed before drawing random numbers. The random numbers will be drawn in the next command, which uses the `sample()` function. If you run this example, you should get exactly the same results as shown here. If you change the number, you will get a different sample. If you leave the command out, R will pick its own number to start generating random numbers. The `sample()` function randomly draws values from a vector, in this case the vector is `c("Tiny", "Small", "Medium", "Large", "Huge")`, but it could just as easily be numeric. By default, `sample()` draws values until the vector is exhausted, in this case, five values with each value occurring once. In this mode, `sample()` generates a random permutation, but we want 25 values so we set `replace=TRUE` so that the function can draw the values multiple times.

The result is a character vector called `size`. Then we turn `size` into a factor called `sizef` using the `factor()` function. Notice that the structure of the two vectors is different. In the factor the values are coded as numbers. The value `"Huge"` is coded as 1 and the value `"Large"` is coded as 2. But when we use `head()` to list the first six values, we do not get numbers, we get the labels, although they are not in quotation marks. We also get the complete list of factor levels, which is a reminder that this is a factor, not a character vector. We can list the factor levels with the `levels()` function.

We can convert a factor to its integer values with `as.integer()` or to its character labels with `as.character()`:

```
> as.character(sizef[15])
[1] "Medium"
> as.integer(sizef[15])
[1] 3
```

By default, factor levels are created by sorting the labels alphabetically. Often that is not really what you want. For example, we might prefer that the levels progress from smallest to largest:

```
> sizef <- factor(sizef, levels=c("Tiny", "Small", "Medium",
  "Large","Huge"))
> levels(sizef)
[1] "Tiny"  "Small"  "Medium" "Large"  "Huge"
```

We just rebuild the factor changing the order of the levels. Another handy feature of factors is that we can easily combine categories. For example, if the number of observations in the two largest and two smallest categories were small, we might decide to combine them:

```
> sizefc <- sizef
> levels(sizefc) <- c("Small", "Small", "Medium", "Large",
  "Large")
> head(sizefc)
[1] Large  Large  Small  Large  Large  Medium
Levels: Small Medium Large
```

Now there are only three categories, `"Small"`, `"Medium"`, `"Large"` with `"Tiny"` and `"Small"` combined into `"Small"` and `"Large"` and `"Huge"` combined into `"Large"`.

If you take a subset of a data frame containing a factor or a subset of the factor vector, R does not remove the empty factor levels. That can create problems in some cases, so you should rebuild the factor to get rid of the empty levels. For example, if we remove the two entries in the "Small" category (index numbers 3 and 14), R will not delete the category automatically:

```
> nosm <- sizef[-c(3, 14)]
> head(nosm)
[1] Huge  Huge  Huge  Large  Medium Large
Levels: Tiny Small Medium Large Huge
> nosm <- factor(nosm)
> head(nosm)
[1] Huge  Huge  Huge  Large  Medium Large
Levels: Tiny Medium Large Huge
```

After we rebuild the factor, the empty category disappears. If there are several factors in a data frame, you can drop all of the empty factor levels using droplevels().

In many cases, the categories of a factor will be inherently unordered such as color: red, green, blue; type: Darl, Ensor, Pedernales, Travis, Wells; or decoration: cord-marked, engraved, incised. In other cases, such as the example here, there is an ordering to the categories because the variable is ordinal rather than strictly nominal. An ordered factor preserves this ordering:

```
> sizeo <- ordered(size, levels=c("Tiny", "Small", "Medium",
  "Large","Huge"))
> head(sizeo)
[1] Huge  Huge  Small  Huge  Large  Medium
Levels: Tiny < Small < Medium < Large < Huge
> sizeo[1] > sizeo[3]
[1] TRUE
```

4.2 PRODUCING SIMPLE TABLES IN R

Load the archdata package, and the DartPoints data set by typing the following commands in the editor window and running them:

```
> library(archdata)
> data(DartPoints)
> options(digits=3)
```

The `DartPoints` data set contains a number of categorical variables or factors (`Name`, `Blade.Sh`, `Base.Sh`, etc.) and any of these can be the basis for creating a table. The functions for creating tables are `table()` and `xtabs()`. For the first function, we just list the variable names as arguments while the second one uses a formula to specify the table. To get a simple table of the number of points of each type, type the commands:

```
> (DartPoints.N <- table(DartPoints$Name))

     Darl   Ensor Pedernales    Travis    Wells
       28      10         32        11       10
> sum(DartPoints.N)
[1] 91
> prop.table(DartPoints.N)*100

    Darl     Ensor   Pedernales    Travis     Wells
    30.8      11.0         35.2      12.1      11.0
```

The first command creates a table object called `DartPoints.N` to store the table. Since we surrounded the command with parentheses, R also printed the results. This shows us that the categories are not equal in size. We have more Darl and Pedernales points than Ensor, Travis, or Wells points. The second command shows us how many observations we have in each type. We already know there are 91 points in the data frame, but `table()` ignores missing values so we now know that no points have a missing value for `Name`. The final command computes the percentages for each group using `prop.table()`, which computes proportions so we multiply them by 100 to get percentages. Two-thirds (30.8 + 35.2 = 66) of the points are Darl or Pedernales.

We can explore how categorical variables vary from one type to another by cross-tabulating point type with another categorical variable. While we can use the `table()` command for this, the `xtabs()` command lets us begin to learn about formulas, which will become important in later chapters (Box 4). The following commands will create a cross-tabulation of point type by blade shape using a formula:

```
> (DartPoints.NxBS <- xtabs(~Name+Blade.Sh, DartPoints))
            Blade.Sh
Name           E    I    R    S
   Darl       15    2    0   10
   Ensor       2    1    0    6
   Pedernales 15    1    3   13
   Travis      7    0    0    4
   Wells       3    0    0    7
```

```
> addmargins(DartPoints.NxBS)
              Blade.Sh
Name            E    I    R     S    Sum
   Darl        15    2    0    10     27
   Ensor        2    1    0     6      9
   Pedernales  15    1    3    13     32
   Travis       7    0    0     4     11
   Wells        3    0    0     7     10
   Sum         42    4    3    40     89
> addmargins(xtabs(~Name+addNA(Blade.Sh), DartPoints))
              addNA(Blade.Sh)
Name            E    I    R     S   <NA>   Sum
   Darl        15    2    0    10      1    28
   Ensor        2    1    0     6      1    10
   Pedernales  15    1    3    13      0    32
   Travis       7    0    0     4      0    11
   Wells        3    0    0     7      0    10
   Sum         42    4    3    40      2    91
```

We create a table called DartPoints.NxBS using xtabs() with the formula ~Name+Blade.Sh. Normally a formula will contain something on both sides of the tilde (~), but not in this case. Notice that we just list the variable names without identifying the data frame that they come from. The second argument of xtabs() is the name of the data frame so we do not have to type the name twice. The table has a row for each point type and columns for each blade shape (Excurvate, Incurvate, Recurvate, and Straight). Looking at the table, we see that 15 Darl points and 15 Pedernales points have excurvate blades and 10 and 13 straight blades respectively. Not many points have incurvate or recurved blades. Blade shape might be a basis for defining the point type, but it could also be a result of resharpening the point.

The second table uses addmargins() to add row and column totals to the table. The addmargins() function also has a margin= option so that we can specify summing only the rows (margin=1) or only the columns (margin=2). Notice that the row sums do not match the results we just computed for DartPoints.N. We are missing one Darl and one Ensor point. This means those points have missing values for blade shape. Points with missing values are excluded from the table. The third table shows how to add them using addNA() (there were no missing values for point type so we did not need to use it on the Name variable). Now we have another column, <NA>, that shows the points that have a missing value for blade shape. The counts are informative, but percentages would make it easier to compare the types:

```
> (DartPoints.NxBSP <- prop.table(DartPoints.NxBS,
  margin=1)*100)
            Blade.Sh
Name           E        I        R        S
  Darl       55.56     7.41     0.00     37.04
  Ensor      22.22    11.11     0.00     66.67
  Pedernales 46.88     3.12     9.38     40.62
  Travis     63.64     0.00     0.00     36.36
  Wells      30.00     0.00     0.00     70.00

> DartPoints.NxBSP[c(4, 1, 3, 5, 2), c(1, 4, 2, 3)]
            Blade.Sh
Name           E        S        I        R
  Travis     63.64    36.36     0.00     0.00
  Darl       55.56    37.04     7.41     0.00
  Pedernales 46.88    40.62     3.12     9.38
  Wells      30.00    70.00     0.00     0.00
  Ensor      22.22    66.67    11.11     0.00
```

The margin= argument to prop.table() lets us choose how to compute the proportions. If the argument is missing, the proportions are based on the total number of observations. If margin=1, we get row proportions and if margin=2, we get column proportions. Then we multiply the table by 100 to get percentages. This table shows that Travis points have the highest percentage of excurvate blades and Wells points have the highest percentage of straight blades. Incurvate and recurved blades are never more than 12 percent. These tables express the patterning between point type and blade shape pretty well. But Ehrenberg has pointed out that ordering the rows and columns according to magnitude makes it easier to read the values and see systematic changes (1977, 1981). It would be easier to see the pattern if we rearranged the order of the rows and columns so that the columns ranged from the most common to the least common blade shape (instead of alphabetical order which is the default) and the rows were organized by the percentage of excurvate specimens. Since a table is a matrix, we can just rearrange the index values of the rows and columns. For the columns we want E, S, I, R since there are 42, 40, 4, and 3 points in each of those blade shape categories so the new ordering of the columns would be 1, 4, 2, 3. For the rows we will put them in decreasing order of percentage excurvate so the rows would be 4, 1, 3, 5, 2.

Now the table shows clearly that Travis points have the highest percentage of excurvate edges and Ensor points have the lowest. Wells and Ensor have the highest percentages of straight edges.

4.3 MORE THAN TWO VARIABLES

The DartPoints data set illustrates data that is organized in rows and columns such that each row is a single observation, in this case a dart point. But when all of the variables are categorical, it can be more compact to organize the data so that each row represents a combination of the categorical variables and a column is added to show how many observations share that combination. The EndScrapers data set is organized this way. The data consist of 48 rows and six columns representing 3,000 Upper Paleolithic scrapers from two sites (Sackett, 1966, Figure 6). There are $2 \times 2 \times 3 \times 2 \times 2 = 48$ possible combinations of the five categorical variables so recording that there are 33 Narrow, Parallel, Round, Unretouched end scrapers from Castenet A on a single line is more compact than repeating that line 33 times. Let's generate some tables with these data:

```
> data(EndScrapers)
> str(EndScrapers)
'data.frame':  48 obs. of  6 variables:
 $ Width    : Factor w/ 2 levels "Narrow","Wide": 1 1 1 1 2 2
    2 2 1 1 ...
 $ Sides    : Factor w/ 2 levels "Convergent","Parallel": 2 2
    1 1 2 2 1 ...
 $ Curvature: Factor w/ 3 levels "Round","Medium",..: 1 1 1
    1 1 1 1 2 ...
 $ Retouched: Factor w/ 2 levels "Retouched","Unretouched":
    2 1 2 1 2 1 ...
 $ Site     : Factor w/ 2 levels "Castenet A","Ferrassie H":
    1 1 1 1 1 ...
 $ Freq     : int  33 170 2 84 15 81 1 2 96 191 ...
> xtabs(Freq~Site, EndScrapers)
Site
 Castenet A  Ferrassie H
      1198         1802
```

You should also use View(EndScrapers) to browse through the data and ?EndScrapers to look at the manual page, which describes the data in more detail. While the formula method of specifying tables in xtabs() may seem awkward, it has the advantage that it can handle this compact way of storing categorical data. On the left side of the tilde (~), we put the name of the variable that has the count and on the right side we put one or more categorical variables. The table() function cannot handle this data format.

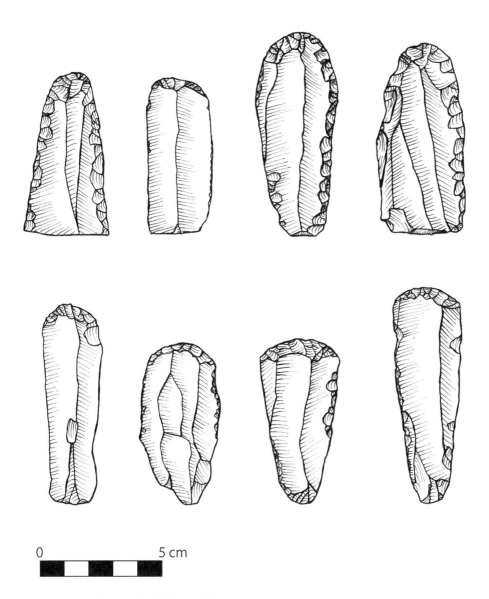

FIGURE 6 Upper Paleolithic end scrapers.
Redrawn from Sackett (1966).

A simple question to raise about the data is if there are differences in the kinds of end scrapers between the two sites. The following command compares the two sites according to the amount of lateral retouch found on the scrapers:

```
> (EndScrapers.SxR <- xtabs(Freq~Site+Retouched,
  EndScrapers))
```

```
                      Retouched
Site              Retouched    Unretouched
 Castenet A          868           330
 Ferrassie H         592          1210

> prop.table(EndScrapers.SxR,   1)*100
                      Retouched
Site              Retouched    Unretouched
 Castenet A          72.5          27.5
 Ferrassie H         32.9          67.1
```

Even without computing the row percentages, we can see that there are many more end scrapers with lateral retouch at Castenet A. The row percentages make it even clearer. Nearly three-quarters of the end scrapers at Castenet A have lateral retouch whereas only a third from Ferrassie H have lateral retouch. We can add another variable indicating parallel or convergent sides:

```
> (EndScrapers.SxRxSd <- xtabs(Freq~Site+Retouched+Sides,
  EndScrapers))
, , Sides = Convergent

                      Retouched
Site              Retouched    Unretouched
 Castenet A          138            25
 Ferrassie H          50            91

, , Sides = Parallel

                      Retouched
Site              Retouched    Unretouched
 Castenet A          730           305
 Ferrassie H         542          1119

> prop.table(EndScrapers.SxRxSd, 1)*100
, , Sides = Convergent

                      Retouched
Site              Retouched    Unretouched
 Castenet A         11.52          2.09
 Ferrassie H         2.77          5.05

, , Sides = Parallel
```

	Retouched	
Site	Retouched	Unretouched
Castenet A	60.93	25.46
Ferrassie H	30.08	62.10

Now we have two tables, one for convergent sides and one for parallel sides. Notice that the row percentages sum across both tables (11.5 + 2.1 + 60.9 + 25.5 = 100). Very quickly it becomes difficult to interpret the results and the multiple tables can be confusing. One solution is to use the ftable() function to flatten the three-dimensional table into two dimensions (Box 5):

```
> ftable(prop.table(EndScrapers.SxRxSd, 1)*100, row.vars=1,
  col.vars=2:3)
```

	Retouched		Unretouched	
Sides	Convergent	Parallel	Convergent	Parallel
Site				
Castenet A	11.52	60.93	2.09	25.46
Ferrassie H	2.77	30.08	5.05	62.10

The row.vars= and col.vars= arguments are used to specify which variables are collapsed on the rows and columns. The numbers relate to the order we used in building the table: Site × Retouched × Sides so Site will be the only row variable and Retouched and Sides will be combined to make the columns. Now we can more easily compare the sites. Most Castenet A end scrapers are retouched with parallel sides (61 percent) and most of the Ferrassie H end scrapers are unretouched with parallel sides (62 percent).

We do not have to stop at three dimensions since xtabs() will keep going. We could include all five variables:

```
> EndScrapers.tbl <- xtabs(Freq~Site+Width+Sides+Curvature
+    Retouched, EndScrapers)
> str(EndScrapers.tbl)
 int [1:2, 1:2, 1:2, 1:3, 1:2] 84 13 2 0 170 63 81 46 31 20 ...
 - attr(*, "dimnames")=List of 5
  ..$ Site     : chr [1:2] "Castenet A" "Ferrassie H"
  ..$ Width    : chr [1:2] "Narrow" "Wide"
  ..$ Sides    : chr [1:2] "Convergent" "Parallel"
  ..$ Curvature: chr [1:3] "Round" "Medium" "Shallow"
  ..$ Retouched: chr [1:2] "Retouched" "Unretouched"
```

```
 - attr(*, "class")= chr [1:2] "xtabs" "table"
 - attr(*, "call")= language xtabs(formula = Freq ~ Site +
 Width + Sides + Curvature + Retouched, data = EndScrapers)
```

EndScrapers.tbl is a five-dimensional array, [1:2, 1:2, 1:2, 1:3, 1:2], where the first dimension is Site (two categories), then Width (two categories), then Sides (two categories), then Curvature (three categories), and finally Retouched (two categories). If you print EndScrapers.tbl you will get 12 two-way tables of Site by Width for each combination of the other three variables. Fortunately, ftable() provides ways of flattening the table by nesting the variables:

```
> ftable(EndScrapers.tbl, row.vars=c("Curvature", "Width",
+    "Sides"), col.vars=c("Site", "Retouched"))
```

		Site	Castenet A		Ferrassie	H
		Retouched	Retouched	Unretouched	Retouched	Unretouched
Curvature	Width	Sides				
Round	Narrow	Convergent	84	2	13	8
		Parallel	170	33	63	96
	Wide	Convergent	2	1	0	0
		Parallel	81	15	46	50
Medium	Narrow	Convergent	31	13	20	38
		Parallel	191	96	123	274
	Wide	Convergent	2	0	1	2
		Parallel	112	59	103	208
Shallow	Narrow	Convergent	19	7	14	39
		Parallel	98	57	115	290
	Wide	Convergent	0	2	2	4
		Parallel	78	45	92	201

You can also specify the variables by number according to their order in the table (i.e., EndScrapers.tbl not the original data set) so ftable(EndScrapers.tbl, row.vars=c(4, 2, 3), col.vars=c(1, 5)) will produce the same table. If you leave out a variable or two, ftable() will sum over those dimensions for you.

Since the sample sizes are not equal, percentages would make it easier to compare the two sites in terms of the different combinations:

```
> round(ftable(prop.table(EndScrapers.tbl, 1)*100,
+    row.vars=c("Curvature", "Width", "Sides", "Retouched"),
+    col.vars="Site"), 1)
```

The resulting table is Table 3. It is easy to see the differences between the two sites when the table is arranged this way. We used prop.table() on EndScrapers.

`tbl` by specifying that the proportions should be computed according to the 1st variable (`Site`). While the command looks complicated, it is built up from functions we have already used. Just work from the inside out: `prop.table()` to get percentages goes to `ftable()` to be flattened goes to `round()` to round off to one decimal place for readability.

Sometimes you may want to collapse a table by summing over categories that are not important rather than folding it. You can always rebuild the table without the variables you do not need, but the function `margin.table()` will collapse a multidimensional table for you:

```
> margin.table(EndScrapers.tbl, c(1, 4))
              Curvature
Site          Round   Medium   Shallow
  Castenet A    388      504       306
  Ferrassie H   276      769       757
```

4.4 BINNING NUMERIC VARIABLES

So far we have dealt only with factor variables (nominal or categorical variables), but sometimes it is useful to group a numerical variable into a small number of categories (called binning or cutting). R provides the function `cut()` for this purpose, but the function `bin.var()` in package `RcmdrMisc` is more user-friendly. Returning to the `DartPoints` data set, we can cut the `Length` variable into five groups and then compare it to the point types:

```
> data(DartPoints)
> library(RcmdrMisc)
> Length.bin1 <- bin.var(DartPoints$Length, bins=5,
+ method="intervals", labels=NULL)
> addmargins(table(DartPoints$Name, Length.bin1))
  Length.bin1
```

	(30.5,46.4]	(46.4,62.2]	(62.2,77.9]	(77.9,93.7]	(93.7,110]	Sum
Darl	23	5	0	0	0	28
Ensor	8	2	0	0	0	10
Pedernales	5	18	6	2	1	32
Travis	5	4	2	0	0	11
Wells	3	5	2	0	0	10
Sum	44	34	10	2	1	91

```
> Length.bin2 <- bin.var(DartPoints$Length, bins=5,
+ method="proportions", labels=NULL)
> addmargins(table(DartPoints$Name, Length.bin2))
  Length.bin2
         [30.6,40] (40,43.7] (43.7,49.1] (49.1,58.9] (58.9,110] Sum
Darl            14         8           4           2          0  28
Ensor            3         5           1           1          0  10
Pedernales       1         2           8           7         14  32
Travis           1         2           3           3          2  11
Wells            0         1           3           4          2  10
Sum             19        18          19          17         18  91
```

The default labeling for binned variables is to use numbers: 1, 2, 3, 4, 5 to label the categories. When the option `labels=NULL` is specified, the categories are named using the range for each category, which is cluttered, but more informative. A square bracket means the group includes that value and a parenthesis means the group includes greater or less than that value but not the value. The category `(30.5,46.4]` includes values over 30.5 and less than or equal to 46.4. You can also specify your own labels (e.g., `labels = c("Tiny", "Small", "Medium", "Large", "Gigantic"))`.

The `bin.var()` function provides three methods for binning the variables. The default value is `method="intervals"`, which divides the **range** of the variable into equal intervals. Notice that with this method there is only one point in the largest group. The second example uses `method="proportions"`, which divides the data into **quantiles** so that there are approximately the same number of values in each group. Now there are 17–19 points in each group, but the ranges within groups are very different ranging from 3.7 in the second group to 51.1 in the fifth group. The third approach, `method="natural"`, uses k-means clustering to divide the variable into "**natural**" groups, but it is not illustrated here.

4.5 SAVING AND EXPORTING TABLES

To save a table for future use in R, you can use the `save()` command. The command `save(EndScrapers.tbl, file="EndScrapers.tbl.RData")` will save the five-dimensional array for the end scrapers. You can load the table with the command `load("EndScrapers.tbl.RData")`. To save the printed version of the table, use the `sink()` function:

```
> sink(file="EndScrapers.tbl.txt")
> ftable(EndScrapers.tbl, row.vars=c(4, 2, 3), col.
  vars=c(1, 5))
> sink()
```

This will create a text file called "EndScrapers.tbl.txt" containing the table. You can open the file in a word processor or a spreadsheet. In a word processing document, you will want to select the table and set the font to a monospaced font such as Courier, Consolas, Lucinda Console, or Monaco so that the columns line up properly. In a spreadsheet, you will be able to use a proportional font if you help the spreadsheet find the column boundaries. For EndScrapers.tbl.txt, Microsoft Excel® was able to find the boundaries once it knew that the columns were fixed. LibreOffice Calc® needed a little help with the column boundaries by clicking on a ruler. The advantage of importing into a spreadsheet is that you can then copy/paste the table into your word processor and format it the way you want without having to use a monospaced font. You may have to do some additional editing to get the column headings to line up correctly. You can also set the number of decimal places to be displayed. Figure 7 shows examples of the EndScrapers.tbl.txt file opened into Microsoft® and LibreOffice® programs.

Another way to move tables and data frames from R into documents and spreadsheets is to use the xtable package (Dahl 2016). The xtable() function formats the output from many R functions into LaTeX or HTML format. The former is not used in archaeological publications (or most word processing software), but many word processing programs and some spreadsheets can import HTML files. The table can then be edited for publication:

```
> install.packages("xtable")
> library(xtable)
> print(xtable(DartPoints[1:10 ,1:8]), type="html",
  file="DartPoints.html")
> print(xtable(numSummary(DartPoints[,c("Length", "Width",
+    "Thickness")])$table), type="html",
+    file="numSummary.html")
> print(xtable(xtabs(~Name+Blade.Sh, DartPoints), digits=0),
+    type="html", file="CrossTabs.html")
```

These commands will produce and save three HTML files containing the tables. The first table includes just the first 10 rows and columns 1 through 8. The second

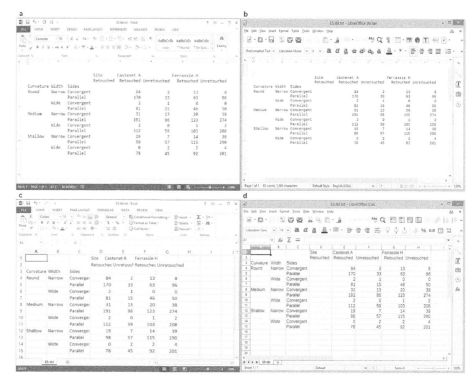

FIGURE 7 Imported tables in Microsoft® (a) Word and (c) Excel and LibreOffice®
(b) Writer and (d) Calc

table uses `numSummary()`, which produces a list containing the results as a table
so we have to access just the table part of the list. Also, the default number of decimal
places in `xtable()` is 2 so we change that to 0 for the third table. Unfortunately,
`xtable()` currently cannot handle more than two-way tables so it will not work
on tables produced using `ftable()`.

Figure 8 shows the html tables pasted to a single page in Microsoft Word®.
Selecting a table then makes it possible to use the Design tab in Word® to change the
formatting. The first table uses the "Plain Table 5" while the second table uses "Plain
Table 2." The bottom table shows an unmodified table. LibreOffice Writer® imports
html tables into a style similar to "Plain Table 2" except that the column headings
are in bold instead of the row labels. The tables also have extra space at the bottom of
each row, which can be eliminated by selecting the table and changing the "Format
| Paragraph" setting.

Tables provide ways of looking at data as long as there are not too many values.
They also provide a way to communicate summary statistics such as those we used

The screenshot shows a Microsoft Word window with several tables:

	Name	Catalog	TARL	Quad	Length	Width	Thickness	B.Width
1	Darl	41-0322	41CV0536	26/59	42.80	15.80	5.80	11.30
2	Darl	35-2946	41CV0235	21/63	40.50	17.40	5.80	
3	Darl	35-2921	41CV0132	20/63	37.50	16.30	6.10	12.10
4	Darl	36-3487	41CV0594	10/54	40.30	16.10	6.30	13.50
5	Darl	36-3321	41CV1023	12/58	30.60	17.10	4.00	12.60
6	Darl	35-2959	41CV0235	21/63	41.80	16.80	4.10	12.70
7	Darl	35-2866	41CV0855	25/65	40.30	20.70	5.90	11.70
8	Darl	41-0323	41CV0536	26/59	48.50	18.70	6.90	14.70
9	Darl	35-2325	41CV0795	20/48	47.70	17.50	7.20	14.30
10	Darl	40-0847	41CV1287	05/48	33.60	15.80	5.10	

	mean	sd	IQR	0%	25%	50%	75%	100%
Length	49.33	12.74	14.95	30.60	40.85	47.10	55.80	109.50
Width	22.08	5.16	6.60	14.50	18.55	21.10	25.15	49.30
Thickness	7.27	1.53	2.00	4.00	6.25	7.20	8.25	10.70

	E	I	R	S
Darl	15	2	0	10
Ensor	2	1	0	6
Pedernales	15	1	3	13
Travis	7	0	0	4
Wells	3	0	0	7

FIGURE 8 Tables produced by xtable and imported as html files in Microsoft Word illustrating different design styles.

in Chapter 3. Finally tables let us look for relationships between two or more categorical variables. In Chapter 5, we will look at how to summarize quantitative information graphically rather than with lists or tables of numeric values.

BOX 4 THE xtabs() FUNCTION IN THE stats PACKAGE

```
xtabs(formula, data, subset, sparse = FALSE, na.action,
    exclude = c(NA, NaN), drop.unused.levels = FALSE)
```

Create a contingency table by cross-classifying factors, usually from a data frame, using a formula interface. The specification of the formula differs depending the structure of the data frame. If each row in the data frame contains a single observation (i.e., there is no column of counts), then formula= is specified as ~Factor1 + Factor2 + Factor3+ … where Factor1, Factor2, Factor3 are factor or character variables.

If each row in the data frame represents a combination of categorical variables with a column indicating the number of observations with that combination (e.g., Frequency or Count), then `formula=` is specified as `Frequency~ Factor1 + Factor2 + Factor3+ . . .` where `Frequency` is a numeric variable containing the count and Factor1, Factor2, Factor3 are factor or character variables. The data frame containing the variables is identified with the `data=` argument. If a subset of the data frame is to be used, then a logical expression is used with the `subset=` argument. The `sparse=` argument identifies the table as a special type of sparse matrix. You will not need to use this.

The `na.action=` and `exclude=` arguments handle missing values and are only relevant if you want to include missing values in the table. But they only work if the variables are character, not if they are factors so it is better to use the `addNA()` function to include missing variables as a factor level, for example, `~ addNA(Factor1) + addNA(Factor2)` as this will work for factor and character variables.

The argument `drop.unused.levels=FALSE` keeps empty factor levels in the table. Changing it to TRUE will remove empty factor levels. The most common cause of empty factor levels is when a subset of a data frame is used and the subset does not include observations on some of the factor levels.

The function returns a table, a matrix with `dimnames()` that provide labels for the rows and columns of the table.

BOX 5 THE `ftable()` FUNCTION IN THE `stats` PACKAGE

```
ftable(..., exclude = c(NA, NaN), row.vars = NULL, col.
    vars = NULL)
```

Create a flat, two-dimensional version of a multidimensional table by nesting variables on rows and columns. The first argument is either a table object created with `table()` or `xtabs()`, multiple factors, or character strings, or a data frame containing factors or character strings.

The `exclude=` argument indicates what should be excluded from the table. Generally you will not use this argument.

The next two arguments, `row.vars=` and `col.vars=`, indicate what variables should be nested to create the rows and columns in the flattened table. They can be identified by number (their order in the table) or by name. If these are not specified, all of the variables except the last one will be on the rows and the last one will form the columns.

It is also possible to use a formula with `ftable()` in the same manner as `xtabs()` (Box 4).

There are also `read.ftable()` and `write.ftable()` functions that allow you to write an `ftable` in a plain text format and a `format()` function that allows simple changes to be made in how the table is formatted. The file produced by `write.ftable()` can be imported into word processing or spreadsheet software, but it does not have advantages over using `sink()` as described in Chapter 4. For retrieving the table in R, using `save()` and `load()` is preferable.

Table 3 *Percentage of end scraper varieties in each site*

Curvature	Width	Sides	Retouched	Site Castenet A	Ferrassie H
Round	Narrow	Convergent	Retouched	7.0	0.7
			Unretouched	0.2	0.4
		Parallel	Retouched	14.2	3.5
			Unretouched	2.8	5.3
	Wide	Convergent	Retouched	0.2	0.0
			Unretouched	0.1	0.0
		Parallel	Retouched	6.8	2.6
			Unretouched	1.3	2.8
Medium	Narrow	Convergent	Retouched	2.6	1.1
			Unretouched	1.1	2.1
		Parallel	Retouched	15.9	6.8
			Unretouched	8.0	15.2
	Wide	Convergent	Retouched	0.2	0.1
			Unretouched	0.0	0.1
		Parallel	Retouched	9.3	5.7
			Unretouched	4.9	11.5
Shallow	Narrow	Convergent	Retouched	1.6	0.8
			Unretouched	0.6	2.2
		Parallel	Retouched	8.2	6.4
			Unretouched	4.8	16.1
	Wide	Convergent	Retouched	0.0	0.1
			Unretouched	0.2	0.2
		Parallel	Retouched	6.5	5.1
			Unretouched	3.8	11.2

Table 4 *Functions introduced in Chapter 4*

Function	Package	Description
addmargins	stats	Add marginal totals to a table
addNA	base	Include missing values as a factor level
as.integer	base	Convert to integer
bin.var	RcmdrMisc	Bin a numeric variable
cut	base	Cut a numeric variable into groups
droplevels	base	Drop empty factor levels
ftable	stats	Flatten a multidimensional table
head	utils	Returns first values or rows of an object
levels	base	List the levels in a factor variable
margin.table	base	Collapse a contingency table summing over margins
ordered	base	Create an ordered factor
prop.table	base	Compute table proportions
sample	base	Takes a random sample with or without replacement
set.seed	base	Set the random number seed for reproducible results
table	base	Create a table by listing variables
xtable	xtable	Format table in latex or html
xtabs	stats	Create a table using a formula

Note: Packages `base`, `datasets`, `graphics`, `grDevices`, `methods`, `stats`, and `utils` are automatically loaded when R starts.

5

Looking at Data – Graphs

Tables of counts and statistical summaries are quick and compact ways to begin exploring a new data set, but they are limited. To really visualize data distributions and the relationships among variables, we need charts and graphs. R has extensive graphic capabilities including the standard pie charts, bar charts, histograms, box-and-whisker plots, and scatter plots. Newer methods such as dot plots, kernel density plots, violin plots, and ways of representing three or more variables simultaneously are also available.

R has several graphics systems. One is the base graphics system that is included in R. With this system, graphs and charts are created using functions that write directly to a graphics output device that can be a window on your computer screen or a file. Graphs can be built up using multiple functions that can be stored as R script files, allowing you to regenerate the graph whenever needed (Murrell, 2011). A second graphics system focuses on interactive graphs and 3D graphs using the `rgl` package. We will use `rgl` to create an interactive 3-D plot. A third system, `lattice`, sets up the graph as a `grid` object (just like data frames or tables are created as objects) and then that object is printed to a graphics device (Sarkar, 2008). Lattice rolls all of the steps you would use with base graphics into a single function call. It is more difficult to learn, but it provides a very easy way to make multiple graphs showing different samples or subgroups of the data set all at once. Finally, a relatively new system that tries to combine the best of base and lattice graphics with a consistent command structure is `ggplot2` (Wickham, 2009). We will not try to cover `lattice` or `ggplot2`. One of the advantages of R is the large community of people using R and adding new functions. Graphics is a perfect example of this productivity.

There are a number of sources available that describe how to produce graphs and charts that are clear, informative, and easy to interpret. They range from graphs that can be produced simply using a pencil and paper (Tukey, 1977) to graphs that communicate information clearly based on experiments on human perception to see what kinds of depictions are correctly interpreted (Cleveland, 1993, 1994) to graphs that retain an aesthetic quality while communicating effectively (Tufte, 1983, 1990). Using R will not prevent you from creating misleading, ugly graphs, but it does give you the tools to avoid doing that.

5.1 TRUE AND FALSE IN R

In Chapter 3 we looked at how R handles arithmetic operations. Another type of operation, logical expressions, have only two possible answers, TRUE or FALSE. These are special words in R and R will accept T and F as nicknames, but you should avoid using them to save typing because R will not let you redefine TRUE or FALSE (e.g., FALSE <- 42 will produce an error), but it will let you redefine F (F <- 42 will set the value of F to 42). That will almost certainly lead to misleading results if you then use F in a logical expression. Logical expressions can be useful for transforming values and for extracting rows from a data frame, as well as other uses. The logical operators for comparison are less than (<), greater then (>), less than or equal (<=), greater than or equal (>=), equal (==), and not equal (!=). Note that logical equal has two equals signs and that greater than or less than signs come before the equals sign. These operators work on single values and element-by-element on vectors and matrices (vectorization and recycling as described in Chapter 2):

```
> x <- c(1, 2, 3)
> y <- c(1, 5, 2)
> x < y
[1] FALSE  TRUE FALSE
> x > y
[1] FALSE FALSE  TRUE
> x <= y
[1]  TRUE  TRUE FALSE
> x >= y
[1]  TRUE FALSE  TRUE
> x == y
[1]  TRUE FALSE FALSE
> x != y
[1] FALSE  TRUE  TRUE
```

Look at each of the examples and make sure you understand how the operators work. There are also operators for combining the results of logical expressions, including not (!), and (& and &&), or (| and ||), and exclusive or (xor()):

```
> x < y
[1] FALSE   TRUE FALSE
> !(x < y)
[1]   TRUE FALSE   TRUE
> (x < y) & (x > y)
[1] FALSE FALSE FALSE
> (x < y) | (x > y)
[1] FALSE   TRUE   TRUE
> xor((x < y), (x > y))
[1] FALSE   TRUE   TRUE
```

The not operator (!) inverts the result. The and operator (&) is only true if both expressions are true (never in the example) and the or operator (|) is true if either expression is true. The exclusive or operator (xor()) is true if the expressions differ (one is true and one is false). If you need to compare more than two expressions use the functions any() and all(). The && and || operators return a single result and are used only in programming, particularly when using if statements.

Logical expressions are used in R to select elements from a vector or rows in a data frame and to convert values based on a logical expression:

```
> xy <- c(x, y)
> xy
[1] 1 2 3 1 5 2
> xy[ xy < 3 ]
[1] 1 2 1 2
> xy[ xy > 1 ]
[1] 2 3 5 2
> xy[ xy <= 3 & xy > 1 ]
[1] 2 3 2
> (a <- ifelse(xy > 2, "Big", "Little"))
[1] "Little" "Little" "Big"   "Little" "Big"   "Little"
> (b <- factor(ifelse(xy > 2, "Big", "Little")))
[1] Little Little Big   Little Big   Little
Levels: Big Little
```

After combining *x* and *y*, we extract the values that are less than 3, then the values more than 1, and finally the values greater than 1 and less than or equal to 3. The last two examples create a character vector and a factor using the ifelse() function. The function takes a logical expression followed by the value to return if the expression is true and the value to return if the expression is false.

5.2 PLOTTING ONE OR TWO CATEGORICAL VARIABLES

Simple graphs are easy to create, often with a single command. Load archdata and select the Fibulae data set, which includes measurements on 30 bronze fibulae:

```
> data(Fibulae)
> View(Fibulae)
> View(attr(Fibulae, "Variables"))
> ?Fibulae
```

The only new command here is attr(Fibulae, "Variables"). The attr() function lets you add or display attributes that are attached to the data frame. It is a good idea when looking at a new data set (even if it is your own) to look at the structure with str(), browse through it with View(), and pull up the manual page, if there is one, with ?Fibulae. Instead of browsing the data, you can just list the first six lines with head() or the last six lines with tail().

Fibulae are brooches or pins for fastening garments that were especially popular before the widespread use of buttons. They can be very elaborate and the ones in this data set are made of bronze and were recovered from an Iron Age cemetery in Switzerland except for two specimens (Hodson, 1968; Doran and Hodson, 1975). They look something like elaborate safety pins (Figure 9).

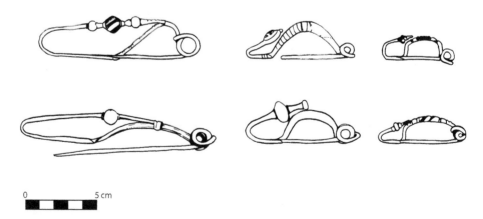

FIGURE 9 Bronze fibulae. Redrawn from Doran and Hodson (1975).

One of the simplest graphs to produce is a pie chart, which is often used to summarize categorical data. The main problem with pie charts is that people do not perceive differences in area as well as differences in length or height so bar charts are usually a better choice. For the `Fibulae` data set, there are no strictly categorical variables, but number of coils is a discrete value. To create a simple pie chart, we need to get the number of specimens in each category:

```
> (NCoils <- table(Fibulae$Coils))

  3   4   6  10  12  22
  1  12  13   1   2   1
> pie(NCoils)
```

Most of the fibulae have four or six coils. The default settings for `pie()` use a set of six pastel colors that will recycle if there are more than six groups. Labels and the first slice of the pie begin at 3 o'clock and run counterclockwise. We can add some labels and change the origin by specifying some of the arguments:

```
> pie(NCoils, main="La Tene Bronze Fibulae", xlab="Number of
+    Coils", clockwise=TRUE)
```

Now the pie chart begins at 12 o'clock and runs clockwise. A title and a label for the *x*-axis are also included. This may be enough, but if you are planning to include the plot in a publication, you may not be able to use color so we might want to change to shades of gray. Also the labels of the individual slices are straightforward, but in some cases you might want to include a legend:

```
> (gcol <- gray(c(1, .9, .8, .6, .4, 0)))
[1] "#FFFFFF" "#E6E6E6" "#CCCCCC" "#999999" "#666666"
 "#000000"
> pie(NCoils, main="La Tene Bronze Fibulae", xlab="Number of
  Coils",
+ clockwise=TRUE, col=gcol)
> legend("topright", legend=names(NCoils), title="Coils",
  fill=gcol)
```

The results are shown in Figure 10a. Now the pie chart is in shades of gray. The `gray()` function takes a value or values from 0 (black) to 1 (white) and returns the hexadecimal color value that `pie()` will use. Since `gray(1)` is white, "#FFFFFF" is the hexadecimal value for white and `gray(0)` is black, "#000000" is the value

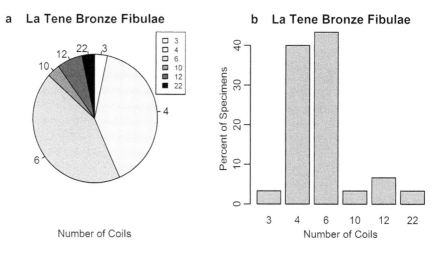

FIGURE 10 Pie chart (a) and bar chart (b) showing the number of coils on bronze fibulae.

for black. Colors can also be referred to by name so we could have called these colors
"white" and "black" instead (Box 6). Generally you do not need to worry
about the hexadecimal values, just let R create them for you. In this case we need
them in the col=gcol argument of pie(). We also add a title (main="") and a
label for the *x*-axis (xlab=""). The legend() function lets you place the legend
anywhere on the plot.

Load the help page by typing the command ?pie and be sure to look at the warning in the Note section: "Pie charts are a very bad way of displaying information. The
eye is good at judging linear measures and bad at judging relative areas. A bar chart
or dot chart is a preferable way of displaying this type of data."

Now switch to a bar chart with the barplot() function:

```
> barplot(NCoils, main="La Tene Bronze Fibulae",
  xlab="Number
+   of Coils", ylab="Number of Specimens")
```

We usually do not color the individual bars if we are representing a single variable
so we only need to use the main=, xlab=, and ylab= arguments. The bar chart
clearly shows that most of the specimens have four or six coils. By computing percentages, we can emphasize this point. Figure 10b shows that over 80 percent of the
fibulae have four or six coils.

```
> barplot(NCoils/sum(NCoils)*100, main="La Tene Bronze
+    Fibulae", xlab="Number of Coils",
+    ylab="Percent of Specimens")
```

Using the EndScrapers data, we can summarize two categorical variables using grouped or stacked bar charts. For example, we can compare the Castenet A and Ferrassie H sites in terms of the curvature of their end scrapers:

```
> data(EndScrapers)
> (EndScrapers.CxS <- xtabs(Freq~Curvature+Site,
  EndScrapers))
           Site
Curvature    Castenet A      Ferrassie H
  Round             88              276
  Medium           504              769
  Shallow          306              757
> barplot(EndScrapers.CxS, ylab="Number of End Scrapers",
+    main="End Scraper Curvature", legend.text=TRUE,
+    args.legend=list(x="topleft"))
```

Figure 11a shows the results. First, we load the EndScraper data set and make a table. The *x*-axis on the plot will be the columns of the table and each row is stacked on top of the preceding row. The barplot() function can call the legend() function, which saves us having to specify the labels and the shading. The legend.text=TRUE argument causes the legend to be constructed. The args. legend = list(x = "topleft") argument passes a list of arguments to the legend() function (see ?legend for the description of those arguments). The arguments must all be named when doing this (x="topleft", not just "topleft").

The main thing the graph shows is that there are more end scrapers at Ferrassie H so the chart is not very informative. It would be better if we used percentages by site instead. That is going to create problems with the legend since the two bars will be the same size:

```
> options(digits=3)
> (EndScrapers.CxSp <- prop.table(EndScrapers.CxS, 2) *100)
           Site
Curvature    Castenet A      Ferrassie H
  Round          32.4             15.3
  Medium         42.1             42.7
  Shallow        25.5             42.0
```

```
> barplot(EndScrapers.CxSp, ylab="Percentage of End Scrapers",
+    ylim=c(0, 110), main="End Scraper Curvature",
+    legend.text=TRUE, args.legend=list(x="top", ncol=3))
```

Figure 11b shows that the percentage of round end scrapers is substantially greater at Castenet A and there are more shallow end scrapers at Ferrassie H, but it is still hard to compare the medium end scrapers. To make room for the legend, we used xlim=c(0, 110) to increase the *y*-axis beyond the range of the data so that

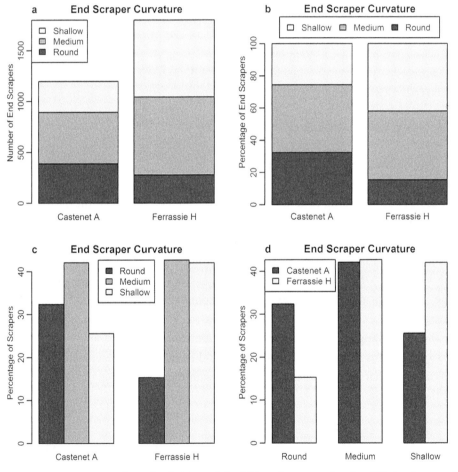

FIGURE 11 Bar charts for the Upper Paleolithic end scrapers showing differing degrees of curvature: (a) stacked bars of frequency by site, (b) stacked bars of percent by site, (c) side-by-side bars of percentage grouped by site, (d) side-by-side bars of percentage grouped by curvature.

there would be room for the legend. We also centered the legend at the top and put the labels horizontally (`ncol=3`).

To make it easier to compare the middle category, we could plot the bars side-by-side:

```
> barplot(EndScrapers.CxSp, ylab="Percentage of Scrapers",
+    main="End Scraper Curvature", legend.text=TRUE,
+    beside=TRUE, args.legend=list(x="top"))
```

Figure 11c shows that the medium end scrapers are comparable between the sites (a little over 40 percent) while the round scrapers are more common at Castenet A and the shallow scrapers are more common at Ferrassie H. If we are more interested in comparing the categories than comparing the overall differences between the sites, we could group the bars by `Curvature` rather than `Site`, but keep the percentages based on site (Figure 11d):

```
> barplot(t(EndScrapers.CxSp), ylab="Percentage of Scrapers",
+    main="End Scraper Curvature", legend.text=TRUE,
+    beside=TRUE, args.legend=list(x="topleft"))
```

Now we can compare the `Curvature` categories directly. Changing from grouping the bars by `Site` to grouping by `Curvature` just required flipping the table on its side or transposing it, which is what the `t()` function does. Figure 11 shows all the four bar charts.

A chart type that is often preferable to pie charts or bar charts is a dot plot using the `dotchart()` function. Dot plots represent magnitude using a dot placed on a horizontal line. They are a good example of Tufte's rule to maximize the information/ink ratio (1983):

```
> dev.new(width=10, height=5)
> oldp <- par(mfrow=c(1, 2), mar=c(4.1, 3.1, 2.1, 1.1))
> dotchart(t(EndScrapers.CxSp), xlim=c(0, 50),
+    xlab="Percentage of Scrapers", bg="gray")
> dotchart(t(EndScrapers.CxSp), xlim=c(0, 50),
+    gdata=rowMeans(EndScrapers.CxSp),
+    xlab="Percentage of Scrapers",
+    pch=21, gpch=3, bg="gray")
> par(oldp)
> dev.copy(tiff, "Dotplots.tif", width=1000, height=500,
  compression="lzw")
```

```
tiff
  3
> dev.off()
```

Figure 12 shows the plots. Since we are plotting side-by-side, we created a new window that is twice as wide as it is long using dev.new(). Then we used the `par()` function to divide the window in half and reduce the margins. The only difference between the two is that the second plot includes the mean percentages for each `Curvature` category computed using `rowMeans()`. This is more useful when there are more than two sites. We reach the same conclusions about the differences between the sites, but the dot chart is more compact so that we could easily compare more than two sites. Comparing more than about four groups gets difficult with side by side bar charts, but not with dot charts. The final commands reset the graphics parameters and copy the plot as a tiff image to a file named "Dotplots.tif". This is an easy way to save a plot that you have just produced, but it is usually better to plot directly to a graphics file, a topic we will discuss at the end of the chapter.

The `pch=` argument is used to specify plot symbols. There are 26 characters built into R numbered 0 through 25. Box 6 shows them all. Numbers 0 through 6 are basic unfilled geometric shapes along with the plus and the *x*. Numbers 7 through 14 overprint two of the first group to make more complex symbols. Numbers 15 through 20 are filled versions of the geometric shapes. Number 21 through 25 are filled geometric shapes where the fill can be specified separately. The `col=` argument sets the color for a symbol and the default is black. The `bg=` argument sets the fill color for symbols 21 through 25. These arguments are used in many different plot functions, not just the dot chart. In addition to the symbols, the `pch=` argument

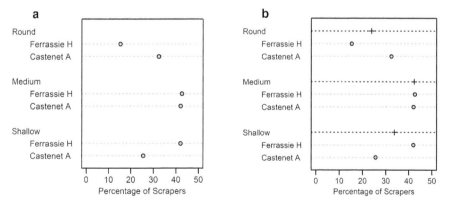

FIGURE 12 Dot charts showing percentage of end scrapers with different degrees of curvature: (a) grouped by curvature and (b) grouped by curvature with group means.

can take a single character so that any character on the keyboard can be used as a plotting symbol.

5.3 ONE NUMERICAL VARIABLE

For numeric variables, there are a number of ways to examine the distribution of values. One of the simplest, the stem-and-leaf plot, was designed by Tukey (1977) to allow researchers to create a quick histogram with a small batch of data. The key is a "small" batch of data since the stem-and-leaf plot becomes unwieldy when the sample size is too large. The main advantages of the plot are that it can be constructed by hand and, if the range of values is small, the original values are all preserved. Beyond that, it is primarily of historical interest:

```
> sort(Fibulae$Length)
 [1]  26  28  35  36  38  39  40  41  44  44  45  45  47  47  49  50  53
[18]  53  54  55  56  59  60  68  71  74  78 110 114 128
> stem(Fibulae$Length, scale=2)

  The decimal point is 1 digit(s) to the right of the |

   2 | 68
   3 | 5689
   4 | 014455779
   5 | 0334569
   6 | 08
   7 | 148
   8 |
   9 |
  10 |
  11 | 04
  12 | 8
```

The `sort()` function sorts the fibulae length values so we can see how the stem-and-leaf plot is constructed. The `stem()` function constructs the plot by separating the last digit of each number so 26 and 28 become 2 | 6 and 2 | 8 so they go on the first line. The 30's go on their line and so on. The stem can be stretched or squashed using the `scale=` argument. The default value of 1 squashed the stem so that 20's and 30's shared a line, 40's and 50's shared a line, and so on because the number of values is small. This display differs somewhat from the classic Tukey stem-and-leaf plot, but there are other versions in package `aplpack` called `stem.leaf()` and `stem.leaf.backback()`.

Another standard way of displaying the distribution of numerical values is the histogram. A histogram is similar to a bar chart in that we represent the values by binning them into categories and then plotting them much like a bar chart. In a bar chart, the bars represent categories that have no particular order. R emphasizes this fact by placing gaps between the bars (which you can remove if you want). Histograms are constructed with adjacent bars and the *x*-axis is numeric:

```
> hist(Fibulae$Length, main="", col="gray")
> (brk <- seq(20, 130, by=10))
 [1]   20   30   40   50   60   70   80   90  100  110  120  130
> hist(Fibulae$Length, main="", breaks=brk, col="gray")
> hist(Fibulae$Length, main="", breaks=brk, col="gray",
  freq=FALSE)
> library(RcmdrMisc)
> Hist(Fibulae$Length, main="", breaks=brk, scale="percent",
  col="gray")
```

These commands produce the four different histograms of the fibulae lengths shown in Figure 13a–d. The first is the basic plain vanilla histogram using the `hist()` function leaving all the decisions up to R. The main decision for a histogram is how many bins to use. The default is to use Sturges' formula. For 30 observations, the formula recommends six bins, which is what we get in the first histogram and you can see they are centered at 30, 50, … 130. We specify that the bars should be filled with gray since otherwise they will be empty. This is enough to make it clear that over half of the fibulae have lengths between 40 and 60 mm and that the distribution is skewed to the right.

The `hist()` function includes an argument to specify the breaks either by specifying a number of bins (which it sometimes ignores), or the boundaries (aka breakpoints) of the bins. We do that in the second example using `seq()` to create a vector of boundaries from 20 (below the minimum value of 26) to 130 (above the maximum value of 128) in increments of 10 mm. That gives us 11 bins that are centered on 25, 35, … 125. We use that vector in the second histogram and it emphasizes the conclusions we reached on the basis of the first histogram.

The third histogram specifies the argument `freq=FALSE`, which gives us a density histogram. On a density histogram, the areas of the bars (bar width * bar height) sums up to 1. The bars are all 10 mm wide and the tallest bar has a height of 0.03 so it contains 0.3 (30 percent) of the area of the histogram. This is often

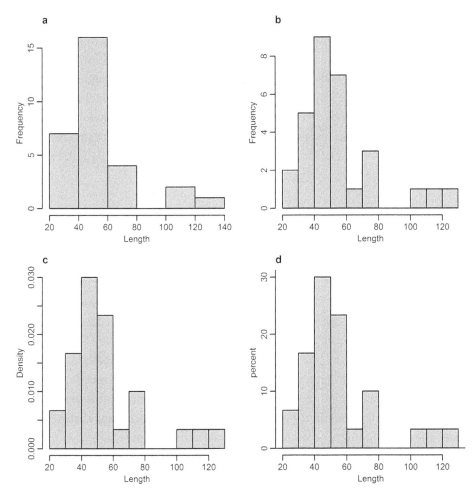

FIGURE 13 Histograms of fibulae lengths: (a) frequency using the default number of bars, (b) frequency setting 12 bars at 10 mm increments, (c) density setting 12 bars at 10 mm increments, (d) percentage setting 12 bars at 10 mm increments.

confusing to people who are not statisticians, but it is similar to the density plots we constructed in Chapter 3 and does not assume that all of the bars are the same width. The Hist() function in package RcmdrMisc has an option to create a histogram that scales the y-axis by percentage rather than frequency or density and the fourth example does this. The **heights** of the percentage histogram will sum to 100 while the **areas** of the density histogram sum to 1. The shapes of the frequency, density, and percentage histograms are all the same, and only the y-axis scale is different.

Histograms are a reasonable way to summarize a continuous numeric variable, but their shape is affected by the number of bins and the midpoints of those bins so the same set of numbers can produce histograms that look very different from one another. The histogram of fibulae lengths does show a single peak in the distribution, but the tails on either side of the peak are not symmetrical. Three fibulae have lengths over 100 whereas the other 27 fall between 20 and 80. The lengths are skewed right, a sign that fibulae lengths may not be well described by a normal distribution.

Histograms are easy to construct by hand, but by using a method called kernel density estimation, we can approximate the distribution of values as a smooth curve. The easiest way to illustrate the approach is by using the densityPlot() function in package car:

```
> library(car)
> densityPlot(Fibulae$Length)
```

The curve is called a density curve because, just as with the density histogram, the area under the curve sums to 1 (Figure 14a). The kernel density curve is constructed by looking at the values within a band on either side of each point along the x-axis. The size of that band is called the bandwith and the distribution used to estimate the density at each point is called the kernel. The default values are to use a Gaussian kernel (normal distribution) and a bandwith estimated using the SJ method (Sheather and Jones, 1991). This method should work well for many data sets, but you are free to experiment with other values using the bw= argument. The bandwidth used for Figure 14a was 6.85 (bw.SJ(Fibulae$Length)). Increasing that value will make the plot smoother and decreasing will make the plot more jagged. At the bottom of the plot is a rug, short vertical lines marking each fibula length.

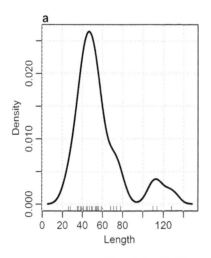 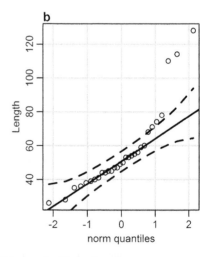

FIGURE 14 Kernel density (a) and QQ (b) plots for fibulae lengths.

The QQ plot lets us compare our data directly to a normal (or some other) distribution. It gives us a visual indicator of how the data deviate from the theoretical distribution:

```
> qqPlot(Fibulae$Length)
```

The `qqPlot()` function, also in package `car`, plots the original data against a normal distribution and places a confidence envelope around the expected line (Figure 14b). If the data points fall along the line and remain within the band marked by the dashed lines, the data are reasonably approximated by the distribution. In this case, the six largest values are all outside the envelope, indicating that the distribution is skewed to the right.

5.4 ONE NUMERICAL VARIABLE AND ONE CATEGORICAL VARIABLE

Box-and-whisker plots summarize numerical data in terms of five quantiles: 0, .25, .50, .75, 1 (minimum, first quartile, median, third quartile, maximum). These numbers are also known as Tukey's five-number summary and are available using the R functions `quantile()` or `fivenum()`. Box plots can be constructed for a single variable, but histograms, kernel density plots, and QQ plots provide more information. Because they are compact, box-and-whisker plots are often used to summarize a single numeric variable by a categorical variable. We will use the `DartPoints` data set to illustrate box-and-whiskers plots as well as some other approaches:

```
> with(DartPoints, numSummary(Length, statistics="quantiles",
   groups=Name))
               0%    25%    50%    75%   100%     n
Darl         30.6   34.3   40.1   42.4   54.2    28
Ensor        34.9   39.0   42.3   43.4   55.2    10
Pedernales   35.4   48.1   55.8   64.2  109.5    32
Travis       39.6   43.9   49.1   57.0   69.0    11
Wells        41.2   46.6   53.7   58.0   65.4    10
> Boxplot(Length~Name,  DartPoints)
[1]   "34"   "44"
> DartPoints[c("34", "44"), c(1, 5:7)]
           Name      Length     Width    Thickness
34        Ensor        55.2      22.5          7.0
44   Pedernales       109.5      49.3          7.5
```

The first command uses numSummary() to show the five-number summary for each point type. To avoid typing the name of the data frame (i.e., DartPoints$Length and DartPoints$Name), we use the with() function. It allows us to specify where to look for the variables used in the function and can save a great deal of extra typing. Also, when used with plot commands, the default axis labels will use only the variable names and not the data frame name.

Then we use the Boxplot() function in package car to draw a box-and-whiskers plot for the length of each point type (Figure 15). The main advantage of Boxplot() over the boxplot() function is that it identifies the outlier points automatically (or interactively if you want) and it provides x-axis and y-axis labels automatically. Notice that the plot is specified using the formula method that we used with xtabs() in the Chapter 4. The left side of the formula is the numeric variable (Length), then the tilde (~), and the right side is the categorical variable (Name). The formula is followed by the name of the data frame (DartPoints).

Each box shows the upper and lower hinges (25 and 75 percent quartiles) so for the Darl points the lower hinge is 34.3 and the upper hinge is 42.4. The dark horizontal line within the box shows the median (40.1 for the Darl points). The midspread (also called the interquartile range [IQR]) is the distance between the upper and lower hinges (42.4 − 34.3 = 8.1) for the Darl points. The whiskers extend above and below the box for 1.5 midspreads (8.1 × 1.5 = 12.2) unless the minimum or maximum are closer to the box in which case the whisker ends at the minimum or the maximum. Points identify values that lie above or below 1.5

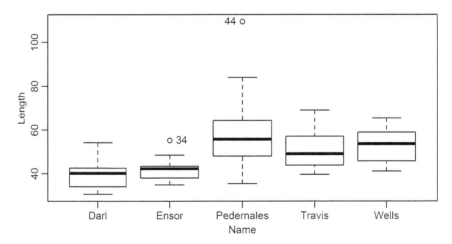

FIGURE 15 Box-and-whiskers plots for dart point lengths.

midspreads. There are no points above or below the whiskers for the Darl points so we know those whiskers end at the minimum (30.6) and maximum (54.2) values. There are points above the boxes for the Ensor and Pedernales points so these mark the maximum values for those types (55.2 and 109.5 respectively). The points are labeled with their row names so we can print out those rows in the data frame to examine their other values. To save space we printed only four columns.

Box-and-whiskers plots provide a summary of the distribution, let us compare groups to see if they are similar or different, and help to identify extreme values. But for small samples they may hide significant variability. When the sample size is small, a better way of displaying the data is a strip chart using the function `strip-chart()`. The values of the variable are simply placed along a line so this works well only if there are not so many observations that they overprint (approximately 30 or fewer). Strip charts show the actual values so it is possible to see if there are gaps in the distribution and where the concentrations of points lie, but they do not show the five-number summary.

Violin plots are a variant on box-and-whiskers plots that replace the box with a kernel density plot. The violin plot produces a symmetrical kernel density distribution truncated at the minimum and maximum values. Inside that distribution is a thick line showing the first and third quartiles and the median is identified with a dot. Bean plots combine kernel density plots with strip plots. The violin plot is available as function `PlotViolin()` in package `DescTools` (Andri Signorell et al., 2016) and the bean plot as function `beanplot()` in package `beanplot` (Kampstra, 2008).

The following code draws horizontal versions of all four (Figure 16). You will have to install package `beanplot` before running the following code:

```
> oldp <- par(las=1, mar=c(3.1, 5.6, 1.1, 1.1),
+    mfrow=c(2, 2), mgp=c(1.9, .75, 0))
> Boxplot(Length~Name, DartPoints, col="gray", xlab="Length",
+    ylab="", horizontal=TRUE)
[1] "34" "44"
> stripchart(Length~Name, DartPoints, pch=1)
> PlotViolin(Length~Name, DartPoints, xlab="Length",
+    horizontal=TRUE, col="gray")
> beanplot(Length~Name, DartPoints, xlab="Length", log="",
+    col="gray", overallline="median", horizontal=TRUE)
> par(oldp)
```

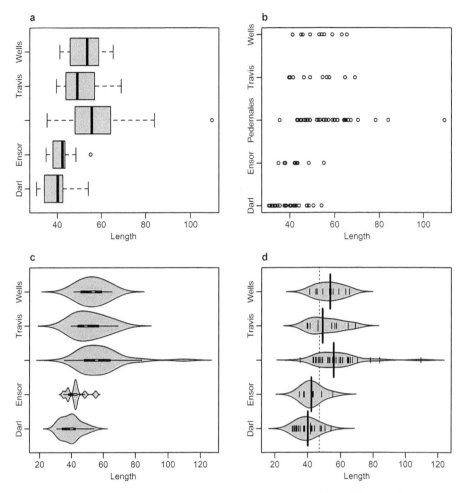

FIGURE 16 Box-and-whiskers (a), strip (b), violin (c), and bean (d) plots of the dart point lengths.

First, we set four graphics parameters with the par() function (see Box 6 for more information about graphics parameters). We want the y-axis labels to be printed horizontally (las=1) so we need more space on the left side of the plot. The parameter mar=c(4.1, 5.6, 1.1, 1.1) sets the outside margins of the plot window. The four values represent the number of lines on the bottom, left, top, and right. Also we want to plot all four graphs in a single windows two across and two down (mfrow=c(2, 2)). Finally, we reduce the space between the x-axis tick marks, the numeric labels, and the axis label since with small graphs the default spacing is a bit too much. Then we produce a boxplot using Boxplot(), a strip chart using `stripchart()`, a violin plot using `PlotViolin()`, and a bean plot using `beanplot()`. Finally we change the graphics parameters back to their original values.

5.5 TWO NUMERICAL VARIABLES

The previous plots make it easier to see differences in a numeric variable between groups defined by a categorical variable. To look at the relationship between two numeric variables, we use a scatter plot (or *x–y* plot) on the `Fibulae` data. The `plot()` function lets us do that:

```
> plot(BH~Length, Fibulae, ylab="Bow Height", main="Bronze
  Fibulae")
```

Figure 17a shows the basic scatter plot. Longer points tend to have greater bow heights, but the relationship is not very strong. Either the relationship is curved, rising from 35 to about 60 and then flattening out or there is a linear relationship for fibulae with lengths less than 80 and the longer fibulae form a different group. We can make these patterns easier to examine by adding a grid to the plot, by labeling the three longest fibulae, and by identifying the two fibulae that are not from Munsingen cemetery (labeled in the data set as "Thames" and "Halstatt"). This example illustrates several of the plotting functions described in Box 7.

```
> grid()
> Fibulae.big <- subset(Fibulae, subset=Fibulae$Length>85,
+    select=c(Length, BH))
> text(Fibulae.big, labels=rownames(Fibulae.big), pos=2)
> Fibulae.ex <- subset(Fibulae, Fibulae$Mno %in% c("Thames",
+    "Hallstatt"), select=c(Length, BH))
> points(Fibulae.ex, pch=16)
> legend("bottomright", legend=c("Munsingen",
+    "Thames/Hallstatt"), pch=c(1, 16), bg="white")
```

The new graph is shown in Figure 17b. The `grid()` function adds a grid to an existing plot, which makes it easier to estimate the values of the variables for individual points. Then we labeled the plot by identifying two groups of observations using the `subset()` function. First, we identify the three largest specimens by creating a subset of the original data called `Fibulae.big` that includes fibulae

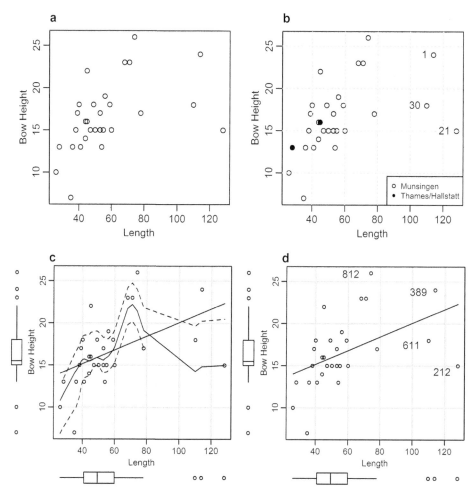

FIGURE 17 Scatter plots of length by bow height for the bronze fibulae: (a) original *x, y* plot, (b) identifying particular specimens, (c) function scatterplot(), and (d) function scatterplot() showing outliers.

that are longer than 85 mm and only includes the two variables we are plotting (Length and BH). We use the text() function to plot the row names and specify pos=2 to get the labels printed to the left of each point (1=below, 2=left, 3=above, 4=right with a default of printing the text centered on the point). Second, we create a subset of the two specimens that are not from the Munsingen cemetery by identifying the ones with Mno (Museum Numbers) of "Thames" or "Hallstatt" and call that Fibulae.ex. The %in% binary operator provides an easy way to do this. We use the points() function with the argument pch=16 to plot solid circles on top of the open circles for these two specimens. Now we can see that the non-Munsingen fibulae are not the large specimens. They fit well with the group on the left. Finally we add a legend in the lower right corner using `legend()` and include `bg="white"` to put a white background inside the legend box to cover up the grid lines.

This example illustrates the way we can start with a basic plot and then add information to it with various functions. By saving the commands required to create the plot, it is easy to regenerate if the data changes, you find an error in the original data, or you need to produce the figure in another format for a publication (e.g., tiff or postscript).

Package `car` has a `scatterplot()` function that provides a great deal of information in a single command:

```
> library(car)
> scatterplot(BH~Length, Fibulae, ylab="Bow Height",
  main="Bronze Fibulae")
```

This produces the rather busy graph in Figure 17c. Outside the x and y axes on the plot are box-and-whiskers plots showing the distributions for each variable. We already knew that the fibulae lengths were skewed to the right and now we can see that the bow heights also do not appear to be normally distributed (you could use `qqPlot()` to check). The `scatterplot()` function adds other features to the plot including a grid, a solid straight line, and a curving line with dashed bounds. The straight line is the least squares line that minimizes the squared vertical distances of the points to the line (Chapter 9). The second line tries to fit the points more closely using locally weighted scatterplot smoothing (LOESS or LOWESS, Cleveland, 1994). It may indicate that a straight line does not fit the data very well, but it really requires more points to do this effectively. The `scatterplot()` function also has options to identify groups in the data with different symbols and colors and by drawing ellipses around each group. It can also identify specific points on the plot that might be outliers, automatically or interactively. It can generate a legend for the plot when there are several groups present. For now, we can simplify the plot by removing the curved lines and label some outliers interactively:

```
> scatterplot(BH~Length, Fibulae, ylab="Bow Height",
+    main="Bronze Fibulae", smoother=FALSE,
+    id.method="identify", labels=Fibulae$Mno)
[1] "389" "812" "212" "611"
```

When you run the command, the cursor will change to a plus sign. You can click on the graph and the closest point will be labeled with its museum number

(Fibulae$Mno). Click on as many points as you want and then click the Stop label at the top left corner of the plot window. Depending on where you click, the label will be added to that side of the point so if you click just above the point the label will go above the point. That way you can add the labels so that they do not overlap or get cut off at the edge of the plot window. When you stop, the labels of the points you selected will be printed out in the R Console. Figure 17d shows the results with labels for four points.

Earlier, we compared dart points lengths using box-and-whiskers, strip, violin, and bean plots. The scatterplot function lets us plot the five types by length and width to see how different types may be characterized by differences in size and in the relationship between length and width.

```
> scatterplot(Width~Length | Name, DartPoints,
+    main="Texas Dart Points", smoother=FALSE,
+    legend.coords="topleft")
```

Notice the formula is different. In addition to the tilde (~) we also have a vertical bar (|) to indicate that we are separating the data into groups defined by point name (Figure 18a). The points are plotted using five different plotting symbols and colors (not shown in the figure) and each group gets its own regression line. The colors are taken from the default palette (type palette() to see them and see Box 6 for more details). The five groups overlap in length as we saw earlier, but the Darl points are generally shorter and the Pedernales points are generally longer. They also vary in width with the Darl points being narrower and the Pedernales points being wider. Notice that four of the five regression lines are roughly parallel and the lines for Ensor, Pedernales, and Wells points are very close together. The line for the Darl points is parallel, but it starts lower down so that a Darl point that is the same length as one of the other three is narrower. For the Travis points, the line is nearly horizontal, in other words, Travis points tend to have the same width regardless of their length. It is difficult to see the differences because most of the points fall in the lower left quarter of the plot. We can spread things out more by plotting on log scales for both variables:

```
> scatterplot(Width~Length | Name, DartPoints,
+    main="Texas Dart Points", smoother=FALSE,
+    legend.coords="topleft", log="xy")
```

If you look at the axes, you will see that the ticks are not evenly spaced (Figure 18b). The log scale compresses larger values and expands smaller values. In the process the points are more evenly spread across the plot window.

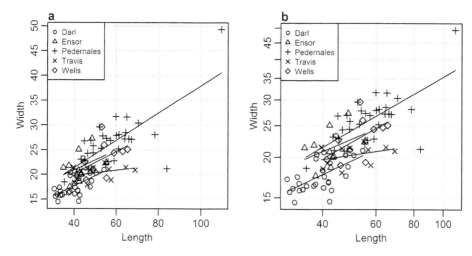

FIGURE 18 Texas dart point scatter plots with regression lines by point type: (a) linear scale and (b) log scales.

If you are plotting discrete variables, you will probably run into a problem with over-plotting With count data, 0, 1, 2, or values measured with limited precision, this will be very common, but it may not be obvious from the scatter plot since the symbols lie on top of one another. This is a problem in the fibulae data where some variables have only a few distinct values. For example, bow front angle (BFA) and bow rear angle (BRA) are measured to the nearest 10 degrees so there are only seven and six distinct values respectively. If you plot these two variables, there will only be 16 points visible on the plot despite the fact that there are 30 fibulae. A simple solution is to use the `jitter()` function to add a small value to each point so that they do not overlay one another:

```
> set.seed(42)
> plot(jitter(BRA)~jitter(BFA), Fibulae, xlab="Bow Front Angle",
+    ylab="Bow Rear Angle", main="Jitter Plot")
> points(BRA~BFA, Fibulae, pch=20)
```

In Figure 19a the open circles are the jittered points and the solid circles are the overprinted points. If we were looking at the solid circles, we would greatly under-estimate the number of fibulae with values of 1 and 1 since there are seven fibulae represented by this one solid dot. You don't need to use `set.seed(42)`, but if you do, your plot will look exactly like Figure 19a. Another approach, the sunflower plot, adds rays to each point to indicate how many fall on that location (Figure 19b):

```
> sunflowerplot(BRA~BFA, Fibulae, xlab="Bow Front Angle",
+    ylab="Bow Rear Angle", main="Sunflower Plot")
```

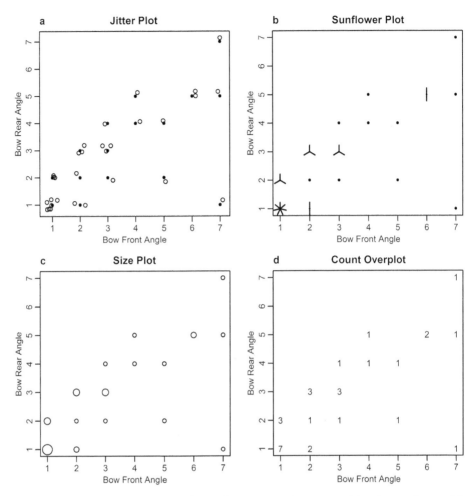

FIGURE 19 Ways to deal with overplotting points by jittering (a), using sunflowers (b), using size of plotting symbol (c), and using counts (d).

The next three approaches to overplotting are found in package `plotrix` so you will have to install that package and load it. The `sizeplot()` function increases the plot symbol size when there are multiple points (Figure 19c):

```
> library(plotrix)
> sizeplot(Fibulae$BFA, Fibulae$BRA, xlab="Bow Front Angle",
+   ylab="Bow Rear Angle", main="Size Plot")
```

The exact number of overplotted points is not clear, but visually the plot shows the concentration at 1/1. Since `sizeplot()` does not accept the formula method of specifying the data, we have to list the variables in *x, y* order. Neither does `count.overplot()`, which plots the number of overplotted points (Figure 19d):

```
> count.overplot(Fibulae$BFA, Fibulae$BRA, xlab="Bow Front Angle",
+    ylab="Bow Rear Angle", main="Count Overplot")
```

The last option works only for cases of nine or fewer overplotted points. The points are arranged in a 3×3 grid around the center point. First, we use `cluster.overplot()` to identify the overplotted points and give them coordinates to position them around the center point and then the `plot()` function can be used to plot them:

```
> pts <- cluster.overplot(Fibulae$BFA, Fibulae$BRA)
> plot(pts, xlab="Bow Front Angle", ylab="Bow Rear Angle",
+    main="Bronze Fibulae")
```

5.6 MORE THAN TWO NUMERICAL VARIABLES

More than two numerical variables can be difficult to display on a two-dimensional screen or page, but R has a number of ways of dealing with three or more variables. One is a matrix of scatterplots showing the relationships of pairs of variables. The basic R function is `pairs()`, but we will use a fancier version, `scatterplotMatrix()` from the RcmdrMisc package. Using the DartPoints data set, we can see how the length, width, and thickness variables are related to one another:

```
> scatterplotMatrix(~Length+Width+Thickness, DartPoints,
  smoother=FALSE)
```

Scatter plots are produced for each pair of variables (actually two for each pair) and the diagonal includes a density plot and a rug (Figure 20). This approach allows you to see the relationships between pairs of variables, but not three at a time. It readily expands to more than three variables, but the plots get smaller as each variable is added. The regression lines make it clear that all three variables are related. Longer points are also wider and thicker and shorter ones are narrower and thinner. The density plots and the rug show us that length and width are skewed right while thickness is relatively symmetrical. But how do these measurements vary by type? The next command helps to answer that question:

```
> scatterplotMatrix(~Length+Width+Thickness | Name, DartPoints,
+    smoother=FALSE, diagonal="boxplot", cex.labels=1.25,
+    cex=.8, legend.pos="topleft")
```

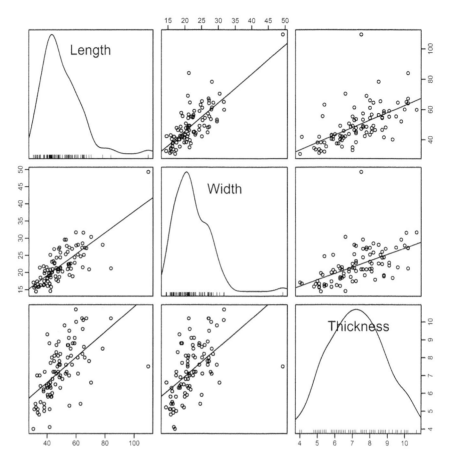

FIGURE 20 Scatterplot matrix for three Dart point measurements.

The boxplots show how each point type differs like the boxplots we constructed earlier (Figure 21). Differing symbols and colors identify each group. Here the regression line is for all of the points. We could get separate lines by adding the argument by.group=TRUE or remove it entirely with reg.line=FALSE. As with scatterplot(), we can add a LOESS line or ellipses around each group. In this example, the cex.labels=1.25 and cex=.8 arguments scale down the size of the variable name and the size of the legend text so they do not overlap.

To view all three dimensions simultaneously, we need to project the three dimensions onto two dimensions. We can do that interactively with the plot3d() function in package rgl, but the scatter3d() function in package car is easier to use.

```
> library(rgl)
> open3d(windowRect=c(50, 50, 650, 650))
> scatter3d(Thickness~Length+Width, DartPoints, surface=FALSE)
```

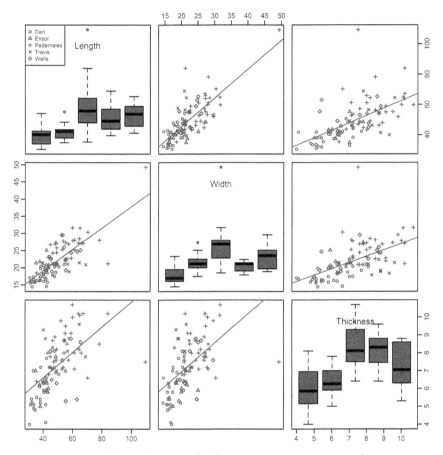

FIGURE 21 Scatterplot matrix for three Dart point measurements by type.

These commands open a window and draw a 3-D plot showing the points. The default window will be small. Just grab a corner of the window and drag to make it bigger. If you want to start out with a bigger window, use `open3d(windowRect=c(50, 50, 650, 650))` to get something larger, 600×600 pixels on the screen starting 50 pixels from the top and 50 pixels from of the left side of the monitor. Dragging with the left mouse button rotates the view and dragging with the right button (or using the wheel) zooms in and out. It is very clear that all three variables are correlated. When you get to a good viewing angle you can save the window as a png image file:

```
> snapshot3d("DartPts3d.png")
```

The `scatter3d()` function is a nice way to interactively explore three variables at once and you can capture the results. You can also color the points by group just as we did for the scatterplot matrix, but for printed plots you will probably want `scatterplot3d()` in the `scatterplot3d` package (Ligges and Mächler, 2003). Install the package and then run the following commands:

```
> library(scatterplot3d)
> pchars <- 21:25
> list3d <- with(DartPoints, scatterplot3d(Length, Width,
+    Thickness, color="darkgray", type="h", lty.hplot=3,
+    bg="black", pch=pchars[Name], angle=60, scale.y=.5))
> legend(list3d$xyz.convert(20, 50, 11),
+    levels(DartPoints$Name), pch=pchars, pt.bg="black",
+    yjust=0, ncol=3, xpd=TRUE)
```

Each type is plotted using a different symbol (Figure 22). By adding arguments to the basic function, you can rotate the plot and control the plotting symbol and whether lines are dropped to the floor of the plot. The arguments can be confusing, but there is a vignette (`vignette("s3d")`) that illustrates how to use the function. After loading the `scatterplot3d` package, we define a vector of five plotting characters from 21 to 25. These are the characters that are filled in with a background color. The next command is complicated. We use `with()` so that we do not have to type `DartPoints$` before each variable name. Within that function, we use `scatterplot3d()` to draw the plot. First, we list the three variables. Then we set the color to dark gray (so the vertical lines are not so prominent). The `type="h"` argument indicates that we want symbols and vertical lines dropped to the bottom of the plot, which makes it a bit easier to see depth. We set the line type for the vertical lines to short dashes and the background color for the symbols to black. We could also use different colors to further distinguish the point types. The plotting characters argument, `pch=pchars[Name]`, requires some explanation. The `Name` variable is a factor so the point type names are represented as the numbers 1 to 5. As a result, Darl points will be plotted with the first `pchar` value (21) and so on (see Box 6 for information about plotting characters).

You cannot rotate the figure interactively, but two arguments control the rotation (`angle=`) and the degree of compression of the y-axis as if you were moving toward or away from the graph (`scale.y=`). The default values are 45 and 1 respectively. Adding the optional legend is more complicated because we need to convert the coordinates. The `scatterplot3d()` function returns a list that includes a function called `xyz.convert()` to convert coordinates from three dimensions to the two dimensions used on the plot window. To place the legend, we identify the where

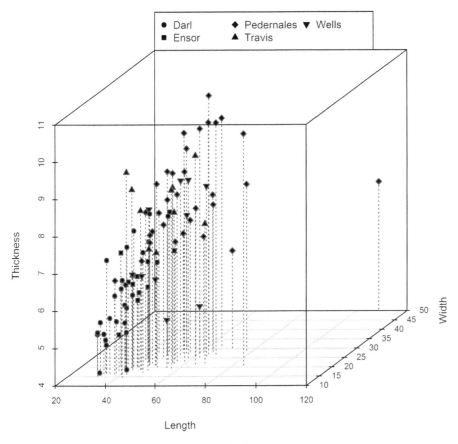

FIGURE 22 Using scatterplot3d() on the dart points data.

we want it to appear and use the function to convert that to a location on the figure. We want to place the legend on top of the plot so the top, left corner is Length=20, Width=50, and Thickness=11. The levels() function returns the factor levels (the type names). We want the same plotting characters and the same color(s) for those characters. We specify three columns for the plot (ncol=3) and tell R to plot into the top margin of the plot window (xpd=TRUE). Spend some time changing the angle= and the scale.y= arguments to see how the plot changes.

We have talked about the fact that lists in R contain different types of data. This example illustrates that a list can also contain a function (in fact 4 functions) that can be used to add to the 3-D plot. There is often some trial and error involved in getting the legend in the right place. Saving the commands in a script file or a markdown file makes it easy to regenerate the plot whenever needed.

Another way to examine three variables is to use a conditioning plot. The conditioning plot divides one of the variables into a series of overlapping groups (called shingles) so that you can see how the relationship between two variables changes with changes in a third variable (the conditioning variable):

```
> coplot(Width ~ Length | Thickness, data=DartPoints, pch=16)
```

Six plots of length by width are created and each uses a different range of thickness values (Figure 23). The plots go from left to right, from bottom to top. For each plot, the range of thickness values is shown at the top so the first plot represents thickness values range from just under 4 to a little over 6 in the first panel (bottom left) while the last panel (upper right) contains thickness values from just over 8 to

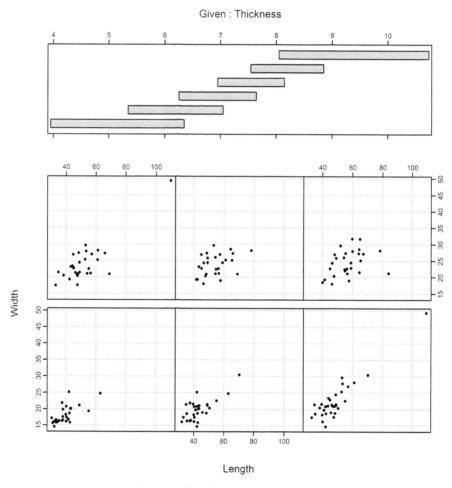

FIGURE 23 A conditioning plot of the dart point length and width by thickness.

almost 11. Just like the shingles on a roof, the thickness shingles overlap. Looking at the plots, it is clear that the linear relationship between length and width is stronger for thickness values below about 7.5 while for larger thickness values, the relationship is much weaker. This pattern was not immediately apparent from the 3-D plots and it illustrates the value of conditioning plots in examining multivariate data.

Finally, we can easily plot three variables in two dimensions if the three variables sum to a constant in each row. For assemblage data, we often transform the raw counts into proportions or percentages so this condition will be met. The data set `Olorgesailie.maj` contains the number of artifacts in each of 6 broad categories for 19 different Lower Paleolithic assemblages in Kenya (Isaac, 1977). We will spend more time with these data later, but for now, we want to illustrate how to plot a ternary (or triangle or triax) plot using three variables that sum to 100:

```
> data(Olorgesailie.maj)
> colSums(Olorgesailie.maj)
Large.cutting.tools       Heavy.duty.tools        Large.scrapers
                1035                    115                    94
  Other.large.tools           Small.tools             Spheroids
                 129                    829                    39
> rowSums(Olorgesailie.maj)
 LS1  LS2  LS3  LS4  LS5 MS1a MS1b MS2a MS2b  MS3  MS4  MS5
  61   68   54    1  219  198   50  103  581   77   78  211
 MS6  MS7  MS8  MS9  US1  US2  US3
  30  112  147   22  147   63   19
```

After loading the data, we look at the counts for each of the six tool categories and the number of tools in each assemblage. Small samples usually create problems since they may not have enough artifacts to be representative of the assemblage. There are several ways to decide how big a sample needs to be, but here we will use only assemblages with 50 or more artifacts. That means we will eliminate four rows (assemblages LS4, MS6, MS9, and US3). Also we need to combine tool categories since we can only plot three variables. The two big categories are large cutting tools and small tools so we will keep those two categories and combine the other four into a single category called other tools. Then we can plot the ternary (aka triax, triangle) plot using function `triax.plot()` in the `plotrix` package:

```
> Olorgesailie.maj$Other.tools <- rowSums(Olorgesailie.maj[,
  c(2:4, 6)])
> Olorgesailie.tri <- subset(Olorgesailie.maj,
+   subset=rowSums(Olorgesailie.maj)>=50,
```

```
+    select=c(Large.cutting.tools, Small.tools, Other.tools))
> Olorgesailie.tri <- Olorgesailie.tri/rowSums(Olorgesailie.
  tri)
> library(plotrix)
> triax.plot(Olorgesailie.tri, pch=16, label.points=TRUE,
+    show.grid=TRUE, main="Olorgesailie",
+    axis.labels=c("Large cutting tools",
+    "Small tools", "Other tools")
```

The first command creates a new variable, `Olorgesailie.maj$Other.
tools`, that contains the sum of columns 2, 3, 4, and 6 (heavy duty tools, large
scrapers, other large tools, and spheroids). The second command uses `subset()`
to keep the rows with 50 or more tools and select three columns (large cutting tools,
small tools, and other tools) and calls the new data set `Olorgesailie.tri`. The
third command replaces the counts in each row with proportions and the last one
produces the plot.

The ternary plot uses three axes to form an equilateral triangle (Figure 24). Each
axis represents an artifact type and ranges from 0 to 1. The axis for other tools is on
the left with the top of the triangle representing an assemblage consisting only of
other tools. In fact, other tools never exceeds 0.26 so none of the points lie above
the 0.3 horizontal grid line. Small tools are on the right side with the scale ranging
from 0 at the top of the triangle to 1 at the lower right corner. Small tools range from
0.04 (MS7) to 0.97 (LS1). Large cutting tools are shown at the bottom ranging from
0 (right corner) to 1 (left corner). They range from a low of 0.02 (LS1) to a high of
0.79 (MS7). It appears that there are two clusters of assemblages distinguished by
the importance of large cutting tools (the group on the left) versus small tools (on
the right), a pattern that has been noted by Isaac and others working with Acheulian
assemblages.

5.7 PRINTING GRAPHS

Eventually you will want to save your graphs for reports and publications. You can
do this quickly from the menu on the graphics window, but the results will not be
publication quality. Instead it is best to print directly to a graphics file. Graphics are
stored as files on your computer in two different ways: raster and vector.

The raster or bitmap format creates a grid across the page and stores a value for the
color of each point on that grid. If you want a resolution of 300 dpi (dots per inch)

Olorgesailie

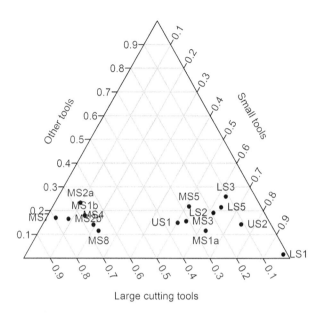

FIGURE 24 Triangle graph of Olorgesailie assemblages.

for an 8 × 10 inch graph, the grid will be 2400 × 3000 (for a total of 7,200,000) points. This is the resolution of many desktop printers, but high-quality printers range from 600 to 1200 dpi and higher. In contrast, the plots produced on your computer screen (about 96 dpi) will be about 672 × 672 (for a total of 451,584) points. Usually the information will be compressed to make the file size smaller. There are two broad kinds of compression. One compresses the information by reducing redundancy so that the image can be reconstructed without any loss of information (lossless). The other method creates even smaller file sizes by discarding some of the information so that the image loses detail (lossy). For publication, you should use only lossless compression. The two main file types are tiff (Tagged Image File Format) with LZW (Lempel-Ziv-Welch) or zip compression and png (Portable Network Graphics). R can produce files in both of these formats. There are a number of programs that can display and edit files in these formats (e.g., Adobe Photoshop®, Gimp®, IrfanView®). The main thing to remember about raster graphs is that you should plot to the size and resolution that you will use for printing. Expanding a small graph will generally produce jagged lines, especially for curves and text.

The vector graphics uses a series of descriptions regarding how to construct the graph. Lines are specified in terms of their beginning and ending points along with the color, line type, and line width. The resulting file is usually plain text, but it may be compressed so that you cannot read it directly. The main vector formats are eps (Encapsulated Postscript®) and the related pdf (Portable Document Format®) by Adobe® and the open source svg (Scalable Vector Graphics). For a simple graph, these files will be small, but for more complex graphs, they can be very large. The biggest advantage of the vector format is that it scales readily to any size and it is easier to edit the graph to change the color of a line or the font or size of text. R can produce files of all three types. There are several programs that can display and edit files in these formats (e.g., Adobe Illustrator® (all 3), Inkscape® (all 3), LibreOffice® (pdf and svg)).

To create a pdf file with the ternary plot, we just created (Figure 24) use the pdf() device:

```
> pdf("Olor.pdf", paper="letter")
> triax.plot(Olor.tri, pch=16, label.points=TRUE,
+    show.grid=TRUE, main="Olorgesailie",
+    axis.labels=c("Large cutting tools", "Small tools",
+    "Other tools"))
> dev.off()
```

This will save a file called Olor.pdf in your current working directory. In this example, we set the page size, but there are also width and height arguments. The pdf() function opens a device to create the plot. You need to close that device with dev.off() to have the plot actually written to a file on your computer. To create an encapsulated postscript file (preferred by some publishers) the commands are very similar:

```
> postscript("Olor.eps", width=7, height=7)
> triax.plot(Olor.tri, pch=16, label.points=TRUE,
+    show.grid=TRUE, main="Olorgesailie",
+    axis.labels=c("Large cutting tools",
+    "Small tools", "Other tools"))
> dev.off()
```

Finally to create a tiff image file, we use the tiff() device:

```
> tiff("Olor.tif", width=2100, height=2100,
+    compression="lzw", res=300, pointsize=10)
> triax.plot(Olor.tri, pch=16, label.points=TRUE,
+    show.grid=TRUE, main="Olorgesailie",
```

```
+    axis.labels=c("Large cutting tools", "Small tools",
+    "Other tools"))
> dev.off()
```

Notice that for the tiff file, we specify the width and height in pixel (dots) as 2100 and the resolution as 300 so the image size is 7×7 inches, just as the previous example. We also set the point size to 10. You may have to adjust these settings to get exactly what you want, but this will get you started. The compressed file is about 88 kilobytes whereas the uncompressed version is almost 13 megabytes.

This chapter introduces some of the basic graph types available in R. As we use them in subsequent chapters, we will introduce additional details about how to alter their basic format for specific circumstances. Boxes 6 and 7 provide additional information.

BOX 6 GRAPHICS PARAMETERS, THE par() FUNCTION

```
par(..., no.readonly = FALSE)
```

The par() function is used to set or query graphical parameters. For example, par("cex") returns the current value of cex while par(cex=1.5) sets the value to 1.5. Most parameters can be included in graphics functions (Box 7), but those that involve setting up the graphics window can only be set using par() before using a graphics function. The term "figure" refers to the graphics window and "plot" refers to the area within the axes.

1. Symbol arguments
    • pch= sets the symbol used for plotting points. Either an integer between 0 and 25 or a single letter or symbol in quotation marks (e.g., "x"). The col= argument sets the color of the symbol and the bg= argument sets the color of the fill in 21–25:

        0 1 2 3 4 5 6 7 8 9 10 11 12 13 14 15 16 17 18 19 20 21 22 23 24 25
        □ ○ △ + × ◇ ▽ ⊠ ✳ ⊕ ⊕ ⊠ ⊞ ⊗ ⊠ ■ ● ▲ ◆ ● • ○ □ ◇ △ ▽

2. Line arguments
    • lty= sets the line type: 0 or "blank"; 1 or "solid"; 2 or "dashed"; 3 or "dotted"; 4 or "dotdash"; 5 or "longdash"; 6 or "twodash". It is also possible to

construct additional patterns using different dash and gap lengths (see the documentation for `par`).

0   1 ——— 2 ----- 3 ·········· 4 ········· 5 ---- 6 ·—·—·

- `lwd=` the line weight. The default is 1 with larger numbers increasing the width of the line (note 0 is the same as 1):

0 ——— 1 ——— 2 ━━ 3 ━━ 4 ━━ 5 ━━ 6 ━━

- Arguments `lend`, `ljoin`, and `lmitre` control ends and corners of lines

3. Text arguments
   - `cex=` and its variants (`cex.axis`, `cex.lab`, `cex.main`, `cex.sub`) control the character expansion of symbols, text where the default size is 1 except for the title (main) where it is 2.
   - `family=` sets the font family. The default is set by the graphics device. Standard values are "serif" (comparable to Times), "sans" (comparable to Helvetica), and "mono" (comparable to Courier). There are packages that provide access to a wider variety of font families if needed.
   - `font=` and its variants (`font.axis`, `font.lab`, `font.main`, `font.sub`) control the specific font type: 1 corresponds to plain text (the default); 2 to bold face; 3 to italic; and 4 to bold italic. Also, font 5 is expected to be the symbol font, in Adobe® symbol encoding.
   - `adj=` controls text justification where 0 is left-justified, .5 is centered (the default), and 1 is right-justified.
   - `srt=` sets string rotation in degrees. Used only in `text()`.
   - Several arguments return the size of a default character in different units, but you cannot set them including `cin`, `cra`, `crt`, `csi`, `cxy`.
   - Other miscellaneous arguments include `lheight` (text line height), `mex` (margin text character expansion), `ps` (point size), and `ylbias` (positioning text in the margins).

4. Color arguments can be specified using numbers 1:8 to access the current color palette, a vector of colors ("black", "red", "green3", "blue", "cyan", "magenta", "yellow", "gray"). The palette can be changed to user selected colors or by using a function to generate colors such as `rainbow()`. The arguments also accept color names (e.g., "red", "blue", "black") and the function `colors()` returns a vector of 657 color names that R understands. The

hexadecimal representation of the color can also be specified (e.g. "#FF0000", "#0000FF", "#000000" for red, blue, and black).

- `bg=` and `fg=` control the color of the background and foreground.
- `col=` and its variants (`col.axis`, `col.lab`, `col.main`, `col.sub`) control the color of symbols, text, lines, and other parts of the plot.

5. Axes arguments
- `las=` controls how axis (tick) labels are printed, (0, the default, parallel to the axis; 1, horizontal, 2; perpendicular; 3, vertical).
- `mgp=` controls the placement of the axis title, axis labels, and axis line. The default is c(3, 1, 0). For example c(2, .75, 0) will move the labels closer to the axis line and the title closer to the labels.
- `lab=` suggests the number of tick marks on each axis, but `xaxp=`, `yaxp=` are preferable.
- `xaxp=`, `yaxp=` let you specify the tick marks on the x and y axes in the form (minimum, maximum, number of intervals). The specification is different for log axes.
- `xaxs=`, `yaxs=` provide two ways to specify "pretty" labels for the axes. The options are `"r"`, regular (the default) and `"i"`, internal. The first extends the axes slightly beyond the data and the second does not.
- `xaxt=`, `yaxt=` allow suppressing the *x*- or *y*-axis by setting the value to `"n"`. Useful if you are using the `axis()` function to specify a custom axis.
- `xlog=`, `ylog=` indicate whether or a not logarithmic scale is in use (returns TRUE). Does not set a logarithmic scale, use the `log=` argument in the plot command.
- `tck=` and `tcl=` set the length of the tick marks with positive values putting the marks inside the plot window and negative values (the default) putting them outside the plot window.

6. Plot window. Most of these arguments must be specified using par().
- `ann=` suppresses printing titles (`FALSE`).
- `ask=` when set to TRUE requires user input before a new plot is drawn with the message "Waiting to confirm page change...".
- `bty=` indicates what type of box to draw around the plot: `"o"` (the default), `"l"`, `"7"`, `"c"`, `"u"`, or `"]"`. This can be used in a `plot()` function.
- `din=` returns the size of the graphics device in inches.
- `fig=` sets the NDC coordinates of a figure region.
- `fin=` sets the figure region dimensions in inches.

- `mai=`, `mar=` set the 4 margins (bottom, left, top, right) in inches or lines.
- `mfcol=`, `mfrow=` divide the graphics window into multiple plots by specifying the number of rows and columns. Subsequent graphs are plotted by columns or rows.
- `mfg=` used with `mfcol` or `mfrow` specifies which row, column should be plotted next.
- `new=` when set to TRUE does not clear the current plot before drawing.
- `oma=`, `omd=`, `omi=` specify the outer margin using lines, normalized device coordinates, or inches.
- `page=` indicates if the next plot command will start a new page.
- `pin=` shows the current plot dimensions in inches.
- `plt=` shows the coordinates of the plot region as fractions of the figure region.
- `pty=` sets the type of plot region to be used (`"m"` (default) for maximal and `"s"` for square) and opens a plot window.
- `usr=` returns the coordinates of the plot region `c(x1, x2, y1, y2)`.
- `xpd=` sets the clipping region. If FALSE (default), all plotting is clipped to the plot region; if TRUE, all plotting is clipped to the figure region, and if NA, all plotting is clipped to the device region.

BOX 7 FUNCTIONS FOR PLOTTING

```
plot(x, y, ...)
```

The basic plotting function in R is the generic function `plot()`. Many statistical functions in R return an object that is associated with a specific version of the `plot()` function. When you first load R, typing the command `methods(plot)` will show the currently available methods, usually over 25 depending on what packages are currently loaded. Depending on what type of object the x= argument is, R will select the appropriate method for plotting. For example, if the first argument is a formula such as y~x, R will automatically use the `plot.formula` method. In addition to the manual page that comes up with `?plot`, the page for `?plot.default` has more information for the common situation where x= and y= are vectors. There are a number of arguments that work with many versions of plot:

- x=, the values to be plotted on the horizontal axis.
- y=, the values to be plotted on the vertical axis.

- `type=`, a character indicating what kind of plot to produce: "p" for points, "l" for lines, "b" for both points and lines, "c" for empty points joined by lines, "o" for overplotted points and lines, "s" and "S" for stair steps and "h" for histogram-like vertical lines, and "n" for no plotting (used to set up an empty plot window for plotting with other plotting functions).
- `main=`, a title for the plot (printed at the top in bold with characters twice the standard size).
- `sub=`, a subtitle for the plot (printed at the bottom in characters the standard size).
- `xlab=`, `ylab=`, labels for the horizontal and vertical axes.
- `xlim=`, `ylim=`, a vector with two values to set the plotting limits: c(min, max).
- `asp=`, the y/x aspect ratio for the plot, used to force the scales on x and y to match (`asp=1`) or to exaggerate one or the other. The default is to scale the axes independently to fill the plot window.
- `log=`, a string to indicate which axes should use a log scale: `"x"`, `"y"`, `"xy"`.

Many graphical parameters (Box 6) will also be accepted within the `plot()` function including `col=, bg=, pch=, cex=, lty=, lwd=)`.

Plotting in R often includes adding elements to the plot after the initial `plot()` command. The following functions are particularly useful:

- `abline()` adds horizontal and/or vertical lines that span the plot window. It can also plot any line given the intercept and slope or the results of a linear regression using `lm()`.
- `arrows()` adds arrows to a plot.
- `axis()` allows you full control over the construction of the axes of the plot.
- `grid()` adds grid lines to a plot.
- `legend()` adds a legend to a plot.
- `lines()` adds lines to a plot.
- `matlines()` adds multiple lines to a plot.
- `points()` adds points to a plot.
- `polygon()` adds polygons to a plot.
- `rect()` adds rectangle to a plot.
- `segments()` adds line segments to a plot.
- `text()` adds text to a plot.

Table 5 *Functions introduced in Chapter 5*

Function	Package	Description
%in%	base	Find matches in two sets
all	base	Given a set of logical vectors, are all of the values true?
any	base	Given a set of logical vectors, is at least one of the values true?
arrows	graphics	Add arrows to a plot
attr	base	Get or set specific attributes
axis	graphics	Add axis to a plot
barplot	graphics	Draw a bar chart
beanplot	beanplot	Draw a bean plot
boxplot	graphics	Draw a box-and-whiskers plot
Boxplot	car	Boxplots with point identification
bw.SJ	stats	Estimate bandwidth using Sheather and Jones, 1991
cluster.overplot	plotrix	Show overplotted points on a 3×3 grid
coplot	graphics	Plot two variables by ranges of a third variable
count.overplot	plotrix	Plot showing the number of overplotted points
densityPlot	car	Plot a kernel density estimate
dev.copy	grDevices	Copy current plot to a file
dev.new	grDevices	Open a new graphics device
dev.off	grDevices	Close a graphics device (and write the file)
dotchart	graphics	Draw a dot chart
fivenum	stats	Tukey's five-number summary
gray	grDevices	Specify a gray level from 0 (black) to 1 (white)
grid	graphics	Add a grid to a plot
hist	graphics	Draw a histogram
Hist	RcmdrMisc	Draw a histogram
ifelse	base	Creates a new object based on a logical expression
jitter	base	Add a small amount of noise to a numeric vector
legend	graphics	Add a legend to a plot
lines	graphics	Add lines to a plot
matlines	graphics	Plot multiple lines
open3d	rgl	Open a 3-D window and set options
pairs	graphics	Scatterplot matrix
par	graphics	Get and set graphics parameters
pdf	grDevices	Create a pdf file of a graph
pie	graphics	Draw a pie chart
plot`	graphics	Draw a bivariate plot

Table 5 (*cont.*)

Function	Package	Description
plot3d	rgl	Plot three dimensions, interactively zoom and rotate
PlotViolin	DescTools	Create a violin plot
points	graphics	Add a point to a plot
polygon	graphics	Add polygon to a plot
postscript	grDevices	Create an encapsulated postscript file of a graph
qqPlot	car	Draw a quantile comparison plot
rect	graphics	Add a rectangle to a plot
scatter3d	car	Plot three dimensions with options
scatterplot	car	Scatterplot with extras
scatterplot3d	scatterplot3d	Plot a 3-D graph
scatterplotMatrix	RcmdrMisc	Scatterplot matrix with options
segments	graphics	Draw line segments between pairs of points
sizeplot	plotrix	Plot overplotted points with a larger symbol
snapshot3d	rgl	Save a 3-D window as a png file
sort	base	Sort a vector
stem	graphics	Draw a stem and leaf plot
stem.leaf	aplpack	Draw Tukey stem and leaf plot
stem.leaf.backback	aplpack	Draw back-to-back stem and leaf plot
stripchart	graphics	Draw a strip chart
subset	base	Subset matrix or data frame
sunflowerplot	graphics	Create a sunflower plot using petals to show overplotted points
svg	grDevices	Create an svg file of a graph
t	base	Transpose a table or matrix
tail	utils	Returns last lines of an object
tapply	base	Apply a function after grouping by a factor
text	graphics	Add text to a plot
tiff	grDevices	Create a tiff file of a graph
triax.plot	plotrix	Draw a ternary (triax, triangle) plot
with	base	Evaluate a function using a data frame
xor	base	Exclusive or
xyz.convert	scatterplot3d	Coordinate conversion function returned by scatterplot3d

Note: Packages `base`, `datasets`, `graphics`, `grDevices`, `methods`, `stats`, and `utils` are automatically loaded when R starts.

6

Transformations

Raw data comes in many sizes and shapes and occasionally they are the wrong sizes and shapes for what we want to do with them. In those situations, it can be useful to transform them before analysis. Transforming data is often useful to balance a non-symmetric distribution or to pull in outlying observations to reduce their influence in the analysis. Transformations can be applied down columns (e.g., standard scores to weight each variable equally) or across rows (e.g., percentages to weight each assemblage equally). In general, there are four data problems that can sometimes be resolved with transformations.

First, transformations can help to produce a distribution that is closer to a normal distribution, making it possible to use parametric statistical methods (such as t-tests). In this case, we are looking at the raw data distribution and using an order-preserving transformation that makes the data more symmetrical. The alternative to transforming the data is to use nonparametric tests that do not require a normal distribution or robust statistical methods that are not as influenced by extremely large or small values.

Second, transformations can make it possible to use simple linear regression to fit nonlinear relationships between two variables. Transforming one or both variables makes the relationship between them linear. The drawback with this approach is that the errors are transformed as well so that additive errors become multiplicative errors when using a log transform. The alternative to transformation is to use nonlinear regression.

Third, transformations can be used to weight variables equally so that differences in measurement scales or variance do not give some variables more influence than others in the analysis. This is particularly important when we are using the concept of "distance" between observations (Chapter 14).

Fourth, transformations can be used to control for size differences between assemblages or specimens that we want to exclude from the analysis in order to focus on shape or relationships between variables that are independent of differences in size. In this case the transformation is applied to the rows of the data. First, we will consider a collection of R functions that are useful for a number of purposes, including transformation.

6.1 THE APPLY FAMILY OF FUNCTIONS IN R

R has several functions that allow us to write simple statements that execute a function repeatedly. In most programming languages, you would write a loop and R has similar programming commands, but using one of the apply functions often involves less typing.

The first apply function, `apply()`, operates on matrices, arrays, and data frames. There are three required arguments, the name of the matrix, array or data frame, the margin (rows=1, columns=2), and the name of a function. While R has built-in functions to compute the sums and means of rows and columns (`rowSums()`, `rowMeans()`, `colSums()`, `colMeans()`), there are many other functions that we might want to use on rows and columns. For example, the median, range, quantiles, coefficient of variation, and so on. Load the `Fibulae` data set and try the following commands:

```
> data(Fibulae)
> options(digits=3)
> apply(Fibulae[, 3:16], 2, median)
     FL      BH     BFA      FA      CD   BRA     ED   FEL       C
  21.50   15.50    2.00    8.00    7.00  2.00   8.00    NA   15.00
     BW      BT     FEW   Coils Length
   5.65    3.85      NA    6.00   49.50
```

We need to remove the first two columns since they do not contain numeric data. The `apply()` function converts `Fibulae[, 3:16]` to a matrix and returns a vector or a matrix. Since the margin is 2, we get medians for each column, but note that FEL and FEW have missing values, so the median is listed as missing. The `median()` function has an argument for removing missing values, and we just have to specify it after the function name.

```
> apply(Fibulae[, 3:16], 2, median, na.rm=TRUE)
     FL      BH     BFA      FA      CD    BRA     ED    FEL      C
  21.50   15.50    2.00    8.00    7.00   2.00   8.00   7.00  15.00
```

```
    BW      BT     FEW   Coils  Length
   5.65    3.85    2.50   6.00   49.50
```

Now we have all of the medians. If the function returns two or more values, we get a matrix:

```
> apply(Fibulae[, 3:16], 2, range, na.rm=TRUE)
      FL BH BFA  FA CD BRA ED FEL   C   BW   BT FEW Coils Length
[1,]  9  7   1   6  4   1  2   0   8  2.0  1.4 0.0    3     26
[2,] 94 26   7  10 16   7 14  50  50 17.6  7.7 8.6   22    128
```

The range function does not label the minimum and maximum for us, but it is clear that the first row contains the minimums and the second row contains the maximums. Other functions return labeled values:

```
> apply(Fibulae[, 3:16], 2, quantile, na.rm=TRUE)
        FL   BH BFA FA CD  BRA    ED FEL    C    BW   BT FEW Coils Length
0%     9.0  7.0   1  6  4 1.00  2.00   0  8.0  2.00 1.40 0.0    3   26.0
25%   19.2 15.0   1  8  6 1.00  5.00   4 11.2  4.00 3.05 1.9    4   41.8
50%   21.5 15.5   2  8  7 2.00  8.00   7 15.0  5.65 3.85 2.5    6   49.5
75%   28.8 18.0   4  9  9 3.75  9.75  11 18.0  8.17 4.77 3.9    6   59.8
100% 94.0 26.0   7 10 16 7.00 14.00  50 50.0 17.60 7.70 8.6   22  128.0
```

If we change the margin from 2 to 1, we can apply the function to the rows instead of the columns. That does not make much sense in this case since the columns are different measurements on a single specimen, but if the data are assemblages where the columns were counts of different artifact types, it might.

This works well if a single R function does exactly what we want with a vector of data, but sometimes we want to combine two or more functions. The apply() function lets us create an unnamed function on the fly:

```
> apply(Fibulae[, 3:16], 2, function(x) sd(x, na.rm=TRUE)/
  mean(x, na.rm=TRUE))
    FL     BH    BFA     FA     CD   BRA    ED    FEL     C    BW    BT
 0.744  0.247  0.699  0.135  0.312 0.619 0.467  1.135 0.559 0.532 0.392
   FEW  Coils Length
 0.742  0.602  0.432
```

The standard deviation divided by the mean is the coefficient of variation (some variants multiply this value by 100 to express it as a percent of the mean). Since we need to use two functions to compute the coefficient of variation, we have to tell `apply()` how do it. The `apply()` function passes each column (or row) as a vector to the function created in the third argument. We create a function that calls the vector x (you can pick another name if you wish) and then passes it to `sd()` and `mean()` so that we can divide them to get the coefficient of variation.

If the coefficient of variation is greater than 1, it indicates that the data are highly variable and probably skewed to the right. All of these values are relatively large and suggest that the collection is highly variable. Since these represent specimens recovered from graves that span about 2 centuries, that is not too surprising.

If the data consist of a list object (including a data frame), we can process each part of the list using the `lapply()`/`sapply()` functions. Since `Fibulae` is a data frame, we could use them instead as long as we are working with the columns (margin=2):

```
> sapply(Fibulae[, 3:16], range, na.rm=TRUE)
      FL BH BFA  FA  CD BRA  ED FEL   C   BW  BT  FEW Coils Length
[1,]   9  7   1   6   4   1   2   0   8  2.0 1.4  0.0     3     26
[2,]  94 26   7  10  16   7  14  50  50 17.6 7.7  8.6    22    128
```

Notice that we did not have to specify the margin (1 for rows, 2 for columns) because `sapply()` operates on lists and the columns are the list elements. If you give `sapply()` a matrix, it will process each cell separately, which is rarely what you want. The difference between `lapply()` and `sapply()` is that `sapply()` tries to return a vector or matrix, but `lapply()` always returns a list. Try running the previous command with `lapply()`. Whereas `apply()` always passes a vector to the function, `sapply()`/`lapply()` pass whatever the list element is.

There are a number of other functions. The `tapply()` function uses a factor to split a vector into groups and applies a function to each group and `by()` expands that to work with data frames. The `mapply()` function applies multiple arguments to a function. The `replicate()` function executes an expression a given number of times. There are others, but these are the ones most commonly used. We will use several of them in later chapters.

6.2 TRANSFORMING VARIABLES (COLUMNS)

When the data are skewed right, the standard transformations involve taking roots or logarithms. Square roots and cube roots are the most commonly used, but higher roots can be taken as well. Root transforms handle zero values without difficulty, but they can fix only moderate asymmetry in the distribution. Log transforms are better at fixing strong asymmetry, but the logarithm of zero is undefined so we must add a small value to zero entries before converting.

Figure 25a–d compares four data distributions. The first is a normal distribution. The second is slightly skewed, but is normal with a square root transformation. The third is more skewed, but is normal with a cube root transformation and the fourth is extremely skewed, but is normal with a logarithmic transformation.

Left-skewed distributions are not common in archaeological data, but the same approach applies. Taking the square (x^2), cube (x^3), exponential $(e^x$ or $10^x)$, or negative reciprocal $(-1/x)$ of the value will pull in the left tail. Figure 26a–d shows four

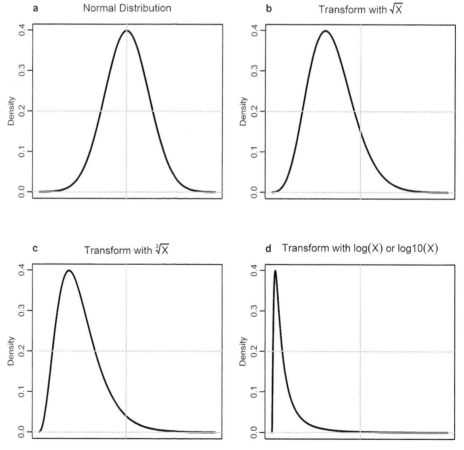

FIGURE 25 Transformations for right-skewed data: (a) normal, (b) transform with square root, (c) transform with cube root, and (d) transform with logarithm.

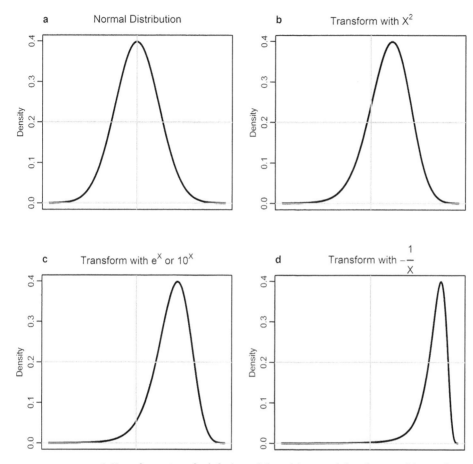

FIGURE 26 Transformations for left-skewed data: (a) normal distribution, (b) transform with square, (c) transform with exponential, and (d) transform with negative reciprocal.

data distributions. The first is a normal distribution. The second is slightly skewed, but is normal with a square transformation. The third is more skewed, but is normal with an exponential transformation and the fourth is extremely skewed, but is normal with a negative reciprocal transformation. The negative reciprocal and the negative square root reciprocal can also improve right-tailed distributions. As with the log transform, you must add a small value 0's.

Real data will generally not be as straightforward as Figures 25 and 26. The qqPlot() function in package car lets us plot our data against a normal distribution along with a confidence envelope. The symbox() function in the same package lets us produce boxplots of different transformations. For data, we will use the bronze fibulae data from Munsingen, Germany. We also need to load the `car` package to use `qqPlot()` (Chapter 5).

```
> library(car)
> data(Fibulae)
> qqPlot(Fibulae$Length)
> qqPlot(log10(Fibulae$Length))
> qqPlot(-1/Fibulae$Length)
> qqPlot(-1/sqrt(Fibulae$Length))
```

Figure 27a–d shows the QQ plots for the original values, the log-10 transformed values, the negative reciprocal transformed values, and the negative reciprocal square root transformed values. While none of the transformations put all of the observations between the dashed lines, any of the transformations, makes the data closer to a normal distribution. It would be reasonable to use the log 10 transform on fibulae length although the QQ plots suggest that the negative reciprocal transformed values match the normal distribution more closely. All three of the transformations would be undefined if any of the values were 0, but that is not the case here. To add a new variable to the `Fibulae` data set, in this case the log 10 transformed values of length takes a single command:

```
> Fibulae$logLength <- log10(Fibulae$Length)
```

You might want to save the data set to your computer using the `save()` function if you will be using it later. We could have used the `log()` function instead of `log10()`, which would use natural logs (base e = 2.718282). The effect on the distribution would be the same, but base 10 logarithms are easier to interpret since `log10(10)=1`, `log10(100)=2`, `log10(1000)=3`, and so on. If you have 0 values for some of the observations, you will have to add a constant to all of the values to make them positive (e.g., add 1 so 0 becomes 1). If you have a small number of 0's, you can just add a small value to the 0's (e.g., 0.5 or 0.05).

Closely related to the transformations, we have already described is a family of transformations known as the Box–Cox transformations (Fox and Weisberg, 2011: 131–132). These are defined in terms of an exponent, λ, as follows:

$$T_{BC}(x,\lambda)=\begin{cases}\dfrac{x^{\lambda}-1}{\lambda}; \text{ when } \lambda\neq0 \\ \log_e x; \text{ when } \lambda=0\end{cases}$$

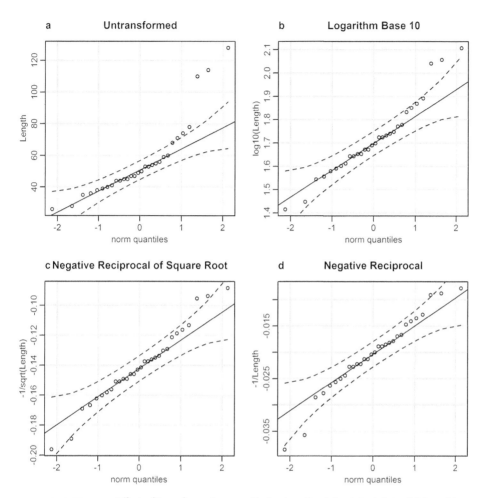

FIGURE 27 Effect of transformations on fibulae lengths: (a) original data, (b) logarithm base 10, (c) negative reciprocal square root, and (d) negative reciprocal.

where $T_{BC}(x, \lambda)$ are the transformed values; x are the raw values; λ is the exponent; and when λ is zero, we use the natural log transform. The transformation is defined only for positive values.

The symbox() function in package car provides boxplots of a number of Box–Cox transformations on a single plot:

```
> symbox(Fibulae$Length, powers=c(-2, -1, -.5, 0, .5, 1, 2))
```

The boxplots are shown in Figure 28. The λ value for each transformation is shown on the x-axis. By default we get powers –1, –0.5, 0, and 1, but here we expand the range to include –2 and 2. When λ (power) is 1, the "transformed" values are just

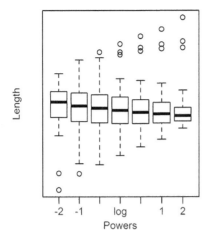

FIGURE 28 Boxplots for various transformations on fibulae length.

1 minus the original value. We are looking for a box with the median in the middle of the box and either no outliers or the same number of outliers above and below the box. The best choices seem to be for power (λ) –0.5 or –1. We could create a transformed variable for length using bcPower(Fibulae$Length, -.5) or bcPower(Fibulae$Length, -1).

If you are planning to transform many variables, it will be simpler if you can use the same transformation on all of them. Let's assume that we have looked at all of the numeric variables in the Fibulae data set and concluded that a log-10 transformation would work reasonably well for all of them. To make things simpler, we will eliminate the two variables that have missing values and zero entries, FEL (Foot Extension Length) and FEW (Foot Extension Width). We also want to eliminate the first two columns that contain provenience information (Grave and Mno). We need to extract all of the columns except these:

```
> (colnum <- which(!colnames(Fibulae) %in% c("Grave", "Mno",
  "FEL", "FEW")))
 [1]  3  4  5  6  7  8  9 11 12 13 15 16
> (colnam <- setdiff(colnames(Fibulae), c("Grave", "Mno",
  "FEL", "FEW")))
 [1] "FL"    "BH"    "BFA"   "FA"    "CD"    "BRA"   "ED"
     "C"     "BW"
[10] "BT"    "Coils"  "Length"
> Fibulae.log <- log10(Fibulae[ , colnum]) #  or
  log10(Fibulae[ , colnam])
> View(Fibulae.log)
```

The first command used compares the column names to a list of the four we want to exclude. If the column name is one of the four, the logical expression evaluates to TRUE otherwise it is FALSE. But we want to eliminate those four, so the exclamation point switches TRUE to FALSE and FALSE to TRUE. The which() function tells us which index numbers in the vector are TRUE so we get the column numbers of the columns we want to include. The second approach compares the two vectors of column names and returns the entries in the first that are not found in the second using the setdiff() function. Either approach lets us extract the columns we want from Fibulae so we can use log10() to create Fibulae.log. If you plot individual columns from Fibulae.log, you will see that we were only partly successful at getting normal distributions. We probably need to transform each variable separately. However, we did greatly reduce the size differences between the columns. Before transformation, FL and Length had much larger standard deviations than any of the other variables (21.2 and 24.3 respectively) and FA and BT had the smallest (1.1 and 1.6 respectively). After transformation, FL is still larger (0.25), but not by as much (0.06 and 0.19).

Taking the logarithm of the variables can reduce differences in magnitude and variance and it is commonly used in compositional analysis. If your data are approximately normal, but they are measured on completely different scales you may just want to eliminate the scale without changing the shape. Converting to standard scores (z-scores) will remove all differences in magnitude and standard deviation since each variable will have a mean of 0 and a standard deviation of 1.

The scale() function computes z-scores for a numeric variable. To convert all of the numeric variables to z-scores in the Fibulae data set, we first remove the first two columns and then create a new data set with the z-scores:

```
> Fibulae.z <- scale(Fibulae[ , -(1:2)])
> str(Fibulae.z)
 num [1:30, 1:14] 3.034 -0.356 0.209 -0.262 -0.403 ...
 - attr(*, "dimnames")=List of 2
  ..$ : NULL
  ..$ : chr [1:14] "FL" "BH" "BFA" "FA" ...
 - attr(*, "scaled:center")= Named num [1:14] 28.57 16.5 2.93
   8.4 7.9 ...
  ..- attr(*, "names")= chr [1:14] "FL" "BH" "BFA" "FA" ...
 - attr(*, "scaled:scale")= Named num [1:14] 21.24 4.08 2.05
   1.13 2.47 ...
  ..- attr(*, "names")= chr [1:14] "FL" "BH" "BFA" "FA" ...
```

The `scale()` function creates *z*-scores for each column in `Fibulae` by center-ing, subtracting the mean from each observation and scaling, dividing the centered value by the standard deviation. The result is returned as a matrix with attributes that record the mean and standard deviation of each column (`Fibulae.z`). If you want to convert the matrix to a data frame, use `Fibulae.zdf <- data.frame(Fibulae.z)`, but you will lose the attributes containing the means and standard deviations of the original values.

6.3 TRANSFORMING OBSERVATIONS (ROWS)

If we are looking for differences between observations such as shape differences between artifacts or features or differences in assemblages, we often want to control for size first. Differences in the shapes of projectile points, hand axes, or houses, dif-ferences in shape can be obscured by size differences. Differences in assemblage size can obscure relationships between artifact types.

These size effects can be reduced by transforming the rows of the data set. A stand-ard method of controlling for object size is to divide the measurements by the geomet-ric mean of the measurements (Mosimann, 1970; Jungers et al., 1995). The geometric mean is the *N*th root of the product of the values where *N* is the number of values.

$$gm = \left(\prod x_i \right)^{1/N}$$

where x_i are the values for length, width, thickness, and any other measurements on the artifact and *N* is the number of measurements.

Base R does not come with a function for the geometric mean, but a number of packages do. Package `DescTools` (Andri Signorell et al., 2016) has `Gmean()`; package `psych` (Revelle, 2016) has `geometric.mean()`; and package `compositions` (van den Boogaart, et al., 2014) has `geometricmean()`. Then divide each of the values by the geometric mean to produce transformed values. The meas-urements must all be at the same scale so you cannot mix linear measures with area or mass measures or measurements in meters with measurements in millimeters.

To see what difference removing size can make, run the following commands on the `Fibulae` data:

```
> library(DescTools)
> Geomean <- apply(Fibulae[, c(3:4, 7:9, 11:13, 16)], 1,
  Gmean, na.rm=TRUE)
> Fibulae.gm <- Fibulae[, c(3:4, 7:9, 11:13, 16)]/Geomean
```

We need to use measurements that are on the same scale, so we eliminate the angle measurements (BFA, FA, and BRA) and the measurements that have missing values or zeros (FEL, FEW) and the count measurement (Coils). That leaves us with nine metric variables. The geometric mean of these variables is used to create a new data set, Fibulae.gm where the variables on each row have been divided by their geometric mean. Now plot Length and Bow Height (BH) for the original and transformed measurements:

```
> scatterplot(BH~Length, Fibulae, main="Raw Data",
+    smoother=FALSE, cex=2, pch=20)
> scatterplot(BH~Length, Fibulae.gm, main="Size Adjusted",
+    smoother=FALSE,    cex=2, pch=20)
```

In the original data, there is a clear linear relationship between length and bow height shown by the straight line sloping from the lower left to the upper right. This reflects the fact that larger fibulae are both longer and wider. After using the geometric mean to remove size from the variables, the line is now horizontal (Figure 29a,b). Fibulae lying above the line have greater bow heights for their length and fibulae lying below the line have smaller bow heights for their length. Notice that size adjustment has also made each variable more symmetric.

Another way to create shape variables is to use ratios. For example, we can create a length to width ratio by dividing length by width or a width to thickness ratio by dividing width by thickness to measure aspects of point shape. Interpretation can be

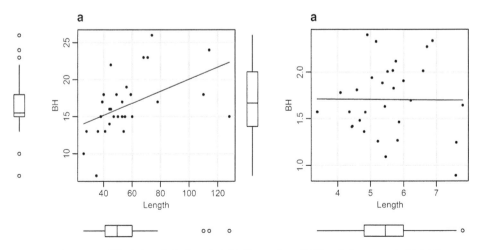

FIGURE 29 Fibula length by bow height. Raw values (left) and size corrected (right).

complicated by the fact that "size" is not controlled the same way for all of the ratios unless they use a common divisor.

Another kind of size effect is sample size. Some layers, houses, sites, or floors have more artifacts and the differences may reflect the intensity of the investigation, depositional rates, sampling strategies, or excavation areas. We do not want our analysis of the assemblages to be affected by the fact that different assemblages have different numbers of artifacts. In this case, we want to control for the assemblage size. A common way of handling counts of different artifact types in an assemblage is to compute proportions or percentages. The practice is common although geologists have noted the potential problems with the practice (Aitchison, 1986; Chayes, 1971).

An example of assemblage data is `Olorgesailie.maj`, the data we used in Chapter 5 to make the ternary plot (Isaac, 1977). This data set has one row for each site locality (19 rows) and a column for each major artifact class (six classes):

```
> data(Olorgesailie.maj)
> View(Olorgesailie.maj)
> Totals <- rowSums(Olorgesailie.maj)
> sort(Totals)
  LS4   US3   MS9   MS6  MS1b   LS3   LS1   US2   LS2   MS3   MS4  MS2a   MS7   MS8
    1    19    22    30    50    54    61    63    68    77    78   103   112   147
  US1  MS1a   MS5   LS5  MS2b
  147   198   211   219   581
> dotchart(sort(Totals), main="Olorgesailie - Assemblage Size", pch=16)
```

The `sort()` function shows the assemblage sizes sorted from smallest to largest and the second command produces a dot plot showing assemblage size again sorted from smallest to largest (Figure 30). One assemblage contains only a single artifact (L4), two more less than 25 and one more has less than 50. The largest contains 581 artifacts (M2b), more than twice the next largest assemblage. Depending on the next stage of the analysis, we will have to make some decisions about the minimum assemblage size to include. For example, we might exclude the three assemblages with fewer than 25 artifacts. Now we can create a separate data set with the percentages and remove the small assemblages:

```
> Olorgesailie.pct <- subset(Olorgesailie.maj/Totals*100,
+    subset=Totals >= 25)
```

Computing proportions or percentages is often done when analyzing assemblages since the sample size of each assemblage is usually not controlled directly by the

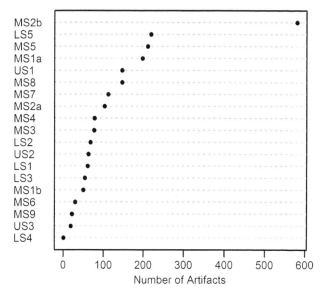

FIGURE 30 Assemblage sizes at Olorgesailie.

investigator. The area excavated or the time devoted to excavation is controlled, but not how many artifacts are recovered. As a result, the number of artifacts in a collection of assemblages can vary widely.

The problem with computing percentages or proportions is that it closes the assemblage. The values in each assemblage sum to the same number (1 for proportions or 100 for percentages). If we know the values for all but one artifact type, we can compute the value for the last one. This closure can introduce spurious negative correlations into the analysis. When the data are closed, increasing the proportion for one type must lead to decreases in the proportions of one or more of other types. Closure is the reason that triangle graphs allow us to plot three variables in a two-dimensional plane. Since only two values are free to vary, the third one is fixed. The same principle applies to compositional analysis where the constituents are expressed as parts per million or parts per billion.

Another problem with proportions or percentages is that they are bound between 0 and 1 (or 100 for percentages) so their distributions will often be asymmetric. Two transformations are used to handle this asymmetry. The arcsine square root transformation, `asin(sqrt(p))`, stretches the range of the data to 0 to `asin(1)`, 1.5708, and pushes points near the ends of the range toward the center. It is commonly used in ecology and biological anthropology. The other choice is the logit transformation, `log(p/(1-p))`, which stretches the range from negative to positive infinity. It is commonly used in regression analysis, particularly logistic regression (Chapter 10).

The closure problem is clear if we plot the original counts and the percentages for the Olorgesailie data:

```
> plot(Small.tools~Large.cutting.tools, Olorgesailie.maj,
+    pch=16, main="Oloregesailie - Raw Counts",
+    subset=Totals >= 25)
> plot(Small.tools~Large.cutting.tools, Olorgesailie.pct,
+    pch=16, main="Olorgesailie - Percentages")
```

In the original counts, there does not seem to be any relationship between small tools and large cutting tools (Figure 31a), but when we compute percentages, there is a strong negative relationship (Figure 31b). This is because these are the two largest

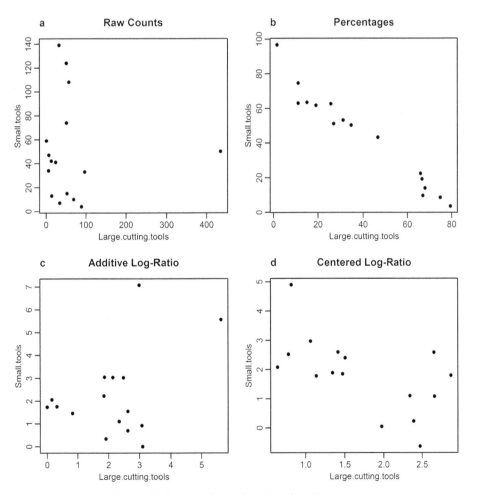

FIGURE 31 Olorgesailie large cutting tools and small tools.

classes, if the percentage of one increases, the other must decrease because the total is fixed.

A strategy for overcoming this is to transform the data using log-ratios relative to the last component (Aitchison 1986) although it has not been widely applied in archaeology and its use in compositional analysis has produced mixed results (Baxter and Freestone 2006). Its use in assemblage composition has probably been limited because the transformations cannot be applied to zero values unless types or elements containing zeros are modified by adding a small value to the zero. The use of log-ratios has also been limited because correspondence analysis provides an alternative way to work with assemblage data without transforming the raw counts first (Chapter 13).

However, the field has grown dramatically in the last 25 years and the `compositions` package has been designed specifically for compositional analysis. The primary approach is to convert the data using the **additive log-ratio**, which is simply the log of the ratios of each variable to the last (or some other) variable. The process reduces the number of variables by one. It can often be useful to try several different variables as the denominator since the results will vary. The **centered log-ratio** is the log of the ratios of each variable to the geometric mean for that row of data. Documentation that accompanies package `compositions` provides a clear introduction to the approach (van den Boogaart, 2008; and van den Boogaart and Tolosana-Delgado, 2008).

We can briefly illustrate the additive log-ratio and the centered log-ratio for the Olorgesailie data using package `compositions`. First, we create a copy of the original data, add a small amount to the zero values, and remove the assemblages with fewer than 25 specimens:

```
> library(compositions)
> Olor.adj <- Olorgesailie.maj[rowSums(Olorgesailie.maj) >= 25, ]
> Olor.adj[Olor.adj < .0001] <- .05
> Olor.alr <- alr(Olor.adj, ivar=4)
> View(Olor.alr)
> plot(Small.tools~Large.cutting.tools, Olor.alr, pch=16,
+     main="Oloregesailie - Additive Log-Ratio")
> Olor.clr <- clr(Olor.adj)
> plot(Small.tools~Large.cutting.tools, Olor.clr, pch=16,
+     main="Oloregesailie - Centered Log-Ratio")
```

The second command just copies the data to a new object called `Olor.adj`. after removing the rows with fewer than 25 tools and the third identifies 0 values and replaces them with .05. Note that the logical expression uses $<$ .0001 instead of ==0 because R could be storing the number as a very tiny positive or negative number. That is not the case here because the counts are being stored as integer values rather than numeric values (floating, decimal numbers), but it never hurts to be careful.

Next we compute and plot the additive log-ratio using the alr() function and specifying Other.large.tools (column 4) as the divisor. I chose this variable because it was not the smallest or largest of the artifact classes. The last artifact class, Spheroids, is relatively small and a third of the entries are zeros. So we are reducing the data to five artifact classes. Now the values are the logarithm of the ratio between each artifact class and other large tools. Figure 31c shows that there is a slight positive correlation between the two variables but the contrast with the percentage values is striking. A value of zero in this data set indicates that for that assemblage, an artifact class had a count equal to the count for other large tools.

Next we compute and plot the centered log-ratio using the clr() function. Figure 31d shows the plot. There is still a distinct negative correlation between the two variables, but it is much smaller (–0.98 for the percentage data and –0.59 for the centered log-ratio). The additive log ratio has a small positive correlation (.38).

The issues of closure using percentages are greater when the number of variables and the number of observations is small. This may be one reason that the problem does not seem to be as great for artifact compositional data where there are 20–40 variables and they often represent a small percentage of the total artifact composition.

The package compositions provides many ways of analyzing compositional data. There is no simple answer to which method is the best. The centered log ratio has several advantages. It does not depend on the selection of one of the variables as the base for the ratios. It preserves all of the original variables. Finally, it is easier to interpret the results since the relationship between two variables is not mediated by a third variable.

Transformations are used to shift data distributions to make them approximately normal, to straighten nonlinear relationships between variables, and to standardize the magnitude of multiple variables. Transformations on rows (objects or assemblages) help to remove size effects and to focus our analysis on relative changes among the variables that are independent of size.

Table 6 *Functions introduced in Chapter 6*

Function	Package	Description
alr	compositions	Additive log ratio transform
apply	base	Apply a function across rows or columns
asin	base	arc-sine function
bcPower	car	Transform a vector using the Box–Cox transformation
by	base	Apply a function to several groups
clr	compositions	Centered log ratio transform
geometric.mean	psych	Compute geometric mean
geometricmean	compositions	Compute geometric mean
Gmean	DescTools	Compute geometric mean
scale	base	Center and scale columns of a matrix
setdiff	base	Find differences between sets (asymmetric)
symbox	car	Box plots of Box–Cox transformations
which	base	Give indices of an object for a logical condition

Note: Packages `base`, `datasets`, `graphics`, `grDevices`, `methods`, `stats`, and `utils` are automatically loaded when R starts.

7

Missing Values

Given the fragmentary nature of the archaeological record, it should be no surprise that missing data are often an important consideration. Data are missing because specimens are fragmentary, because measurements were incorrectly recorded or not recorded at all, or because data from several different projects, each with a somewhat different recording system, are being combined. Data can also be missing because of our inability to measure values below a certain threshold. These and other factors mean that our data sets have holes, but fortunately R provides several ways of dealing with holes.

Missing data are said to be "missing completely at random" (MCAR) if the probability that a value is missing is unrelated to its value on that variable or to the values on any other variables in the analysis (Allison, 2001; McKnight et al., 2007). Essentially this means that you cannot predict when a value will be missing on a variable. You can create an MCAR data set by randomly selecting values and changing them to missing. You would not normally want to do this, but it makes the point that the data do not contain any information that would allow you to predict that a value would be missing. It is often easier to describe clearly what MCAR is not. For example, in compositional analysis, elemental data can be missing when the concentration is below the detection limits of the equipment. In this case, only small values are missing. This kind of missing data is called left censored because it is the small values that are missing. If larger projectile points are more likely to break, length measurements might be more likely to be missing for larger points. In both cases, the pattern of missing values is not random. The assumption that the data are MCAR is a strong one and will usually be difficult or impossible to confirm for archaeological data.

Missing data are said to be "missing at random" (MAR) if the probability that a value is missing is unrelated to its value on that variable after controlling for the other variables in the analysis. For example, the probability that a point is broken could be based on thickness and we have measurements of thickness. In this case, length is MAR. If values are MAR, and we can assume that the variables that govern the missing data process are observed and unrelated to the variables we are estimating, we can consider the missing data process to be ignorable. That means that we can estimate the missing values without modeling the process that led to values being missing.

If the missing data are not MAR, then we must model the missing data process in order to get good estimates and that generally requires detailed information that we do not have. When the missing data process is non-ignorable, we usually must fall back on ways of eliminating (rather than estimating) the missing values from the analysis and even then there may be unknown biases in our analysis.

7.1 MISSING VALUES AND OTHER SPECIAL VALUES IN R

R has four special values that are labeled using reserved words (names that cannot be assigned other values): NA, NaN, Inf, NULL. Of these, you are most likely to come across the first one, which is used to represent missing values, NA ("Not Available").

When a value is missing in a vector (or matrix, array, data frame, list), the missing value will be represented as NA. These values occur as a result of mistakes in recording or coding the data before we import it into R and they can be produced by operations (usually errors) in R. When you are importing data from a spreadsheet, you need to be careful when it comes to identifying missing values. A blank in a numeric column will be correctly read as a missing value and assigned a value of NA, but a blank in a character column will be assigned a blank string (""), which is not automatically considered a missing value. Either replace blank cells with NA before exporting the spreadsheet, or tell R to treat empty text cells as missing by using the argument na.string=="" in read.csv().

Missing values are special in the sense that any operation that involves a missing value produces a missing value as a result:

```
> NA + 1
[1] NA
> NA/NA
[1] NA
> NA > 1
[1] NA
> NA == NA
[1] NA
```

Notice the last example. You cannot test for missingness using a simple logical expression. Fortunately, there is a special function for determining if a value is missing:

```
> is.na(NA)
[1] TRUE
> (a <- 1:5)
[1] 1 2 3 4 5
> a[4] <- NA
> is.na(a[2]) <- TRUE
> a
[1]  1 NA  3 NA  5
> is.na(a)
[1] FALSE  TRUE FALSE  TRUE FALSE
```

The is.na() function returns TRUE if the value is missing. The function will also indicate which elements of a vector are missing and which are not. We can set a value to missing by specifying its index number and set it to NA using the <- operator. Alternatively, we can specify the index and set the value of is.na() to TRUE which also changes the value to missing. Most of the time, the first way will be simpler.

The values Inf and -Inf refer to positive and negative infinity and are most likely to occur when you try to divide by 0:

```
> 1/0
[1] Inf
> -1/0
[1] -Inf
```

The value NaN (Not a Number) is most likely to occur when you accidentally try to take the square root or logarithm of a negative number since these operations are not defined for real numbers:

```
> log(-1)
[1] NaN
Warning message:
In log(-1) : NaNs produced
> sqrt(-1)
[1] NaN
Warning message:
In sqrt(-1) : NaNs produced
```

Although they are defined for complex numbers:

```
> log(as.complex(-1))
[1] 0+3.141593i
> sqrt(as.complex(-1))
[1] 0+1i
```

Finally, NULL usually arises when a function does not return anything. For example, the plot() function draws a plot, but does not return any value. Also arguments to a function can have NULL default values.

7.2 ELIMINATING CASES OR VARIABLES WITH MISSING VALUES

The simplest way to eliminate missing values from the data is to drop any row that contains missing data (listwise deletion). In some R functions, this is the default behavior. The advantage of this approach is that it is simple and if the missing values are MCAR, the parameters estimated will be unbiased. Listwise deletion also produces unbiased estimates if the data are MAR and the probability of missing values among the dependent (explanatory) variables does not depend on the value of the independent (response) variable.

The cost of listwise deletion is that the standard errors of our estimates will be larger since they are based on fewer observations. If the number of observations with missing data is small, the increase will be small (about a 5% increase if 10% of the data are missing and 12% if 20% of the data are missing). This reduces the power of any statistical test, making it more difficult to reject the null hypothesis (Chapter 8).

When the data consist of several groups (e.g., artifact types, regions, strata), listwise deletion can reduce small groups to the point that their variability is not well represented and it can become impossible to use certain multivariate approaches because the sample size for the group is too small. In these circumstances, it may be necessary to consider alternatives.

One alternative is to delete columns (variables) with many missing values before listwise deletion. Preserving as many variables and observations as possible can be a balancing act between eliminating columns and rows. The danger in eliminating columns is that they may be important in helping to understand the patterns in the data. By now you should be getting the idea that there are no simple solutions and you will have to use your professional judgment in making decisions about missing values. In reporting your analysis, you should describe clearly what data (observations or variables) were eliminated and why.

We can easily determine how many rows and columns of the data are affected by missing values. The DartPoints data set has a number of missing values. The following commands will give us the necessary information:

```
> data(DartPoints)
> library(archdata)
> data(DartPoints)
> options(digits=3)
> sum(is.na(DartPoints$Name))
[1] 0
> nrow(DartPoints)
[1] 91
> sum(complete.cases(DartPoints[, 5:17]))
[1] 68
```

After loading the data, we check to see if point type name is missing for any observations. We do that with is.na(), which returns a logical vector identifying any missing values in dart point name. When we pass this to the sum() function, it gets converted to an integer vector where FALSE becomes 0 and TRUE becomes 1 so we get the number of missing values. Point type (Name) is not missing for any of the observations. Now we can focus on the numeric and categorical variables. The nrow() function tells us how many rows a data frame (or matrix) has so we know that there are 91 dart points. Then we use complete.cases() on columns 5 through 17 of DartPoints, which contain the measurements. The complete.cases() function scans each row for missing values and returns FALSE if there are any and TRUE if not. So now the sum tells us how many points we have with no missing values, 68, which means that 23 points have some missing data (91 − 68 = 23). The next command tells us how many missing values we have on each column sorted from the column with the most missing values to the least:

```
> sort(colSums(is.na(DartPoints[, 5:17])), decreasing=TRUE)
 B.Width   Blade.Sh   Base.Sh   Should.Sh   Should.Or   Haft.Sh   Haft.Or
      22          2         2           2           2         2         2
 J.Width     Length      Width   Thickness    H.Length    Weight
       1          0          0           0           0         0
```

Blade width is missing from 22 of the 23 points that have missing values. The other missing values are all coming from the categorical variables. How many cases do we have if we eliminate the B.Width variable (column 8)?

```
> nomiss <- complete.cases(DartPoints[, c(5:7, 9:17)])
> sum(nomiss)
[1] 88
```

The result is 88 so by excluding B.Width (column 8) and three cases with missing values on other variables, we could create a data set of 88 points with no missing values:

```
> DartPoints.new <- na.omit(DartPoints[, -8])
> DartPoints[!nomiss, 1:4]
            Name     Catalog       TARL     Quad
28          Darl     35-2928   41CV0132    20/63
38         Ensor     41-0210   41CV0481    16/59
68    Pedernales    44-1315M   41CV0449    20/55
```

The na.omit() function removes cases that have missing values. We remove column 8 (B.Width) first so that we get 88 complete cases. We could have just as easily used nomiss to extract the rows using DartPoints.new <- DartPoints[nomiss, -8]. The second command lists the first four columns of the three rows that we have eliminated from the full data set. Now we have a data set with no missing values by removing only 3.3 percent of the data called DartPoints.new.

There are a number of statistical analyses that do not use the original data once a distance (Chapter 14) or covariance matrix (Chapter 9) has been computed. An alternative to listwise deletion is pairwise deletion. In pairwise deletion, the correlation/covariance value for a pair of variables uses all of the rows that have no missing values for that pair of variables. That means that the number of cases used for each entry in the correlation or covariance matrix can be different. Pairwise deletion uses more of the data so that the standard errors are generally smaller than with listwise deletion. For covariance/correlation matrices, it can lead to a matrix that is not positive definite, which can create problems for principal components, factor analysis, and multiple regression analysis.

A distance matrix involves a computation on pairs of rows in the data set. Pairwise deletion means that the distance is measured using all of the variables that have non missing values for each pair. This generally requires scaling the distance up to adjust for the variables being left out.

If you are just using the correlation matrix to look at the correlations between variables as an initial step of your analysis, you can easily implement pairwise deletion:

```
> cor(DartPoints[, 5:11], use="pairwise.complete.obs")
          Length  Width Thickness  B.Width J.Width H.Length Weight
Length     1.000  0.769     0.589  -0.2839  0.4541    0.509  0.880
Width      0.769  1.000     0.546  -0.2407  0.6456    0.496  0.826
Thickness  0.589  0.546     1.000  -0.2062  0.5091    0.467  0.600
B.Width   -0.284 -0.241    -0.206   1.0000 -0.0425   -0.506 -0.264
J.Width    0.454  0.646     0.509  -0.0425  1.0000    0.435  0.503
H.Length   0.509  0.496     0.467  -0.5060  0.4352    1.000  0.486
Weight     0.880  0.826     0.600  -0.2641  0.5026    0.486  1.000
```

We will talk about correlation and distance matrices in later chapters, but the `dist()` function uses pairwise deletion when computing the distance between a pair of observations. The distance is then scaled up proportionally to the number of columns used.

7.3 IMPUTING MISSING VALUES

Since listwise deletion can reduce sample sizes severely and pairwise deletion will work only in limited circumstances, various ways of imputing missing data have been developed to overcome these limitations.

A traditional approach is to replace each missing value with the mean or the median for that variable. The main drawback is that it affects the variance of that variable and its covariance with other variables. We could replace the missing values for B.Width in DartPoints with the mean, 13.75 (or the median, 13.6):

```
> BW <- DartPoints$B.Width
> HL <- DartPoints$H.Length
> BW.orig <- c(sd=sd(BW, na.rm=TRUE), cor=cor(BW, HL,
  use="complete.obs"))
> BWmean <- BW
> BWmean[is.na(BW)] <- mean(BW, na.rm=TRUE)
> BWImp.mn <- c(sd(BWmean), cor(BWmean, HL))
> (results <- rbind(BW.orig, BWImp.mn))
           sd     cor
BW.orig  2.95 -0.506
BWImp.mn 2.56 -0.467
```

We start out by creating copies of the two variables we are using to reduce the amount of typing and to avoid changing our original data. Then we compute the standard deviation for BW and its correlation with HL so we can compare the original values using listwise deletion to those obtained after imputing missing values. We create a copy of the BW, which has missing values and impute the mean to all of the missing values in BWmean. You should print out BW and BWmean to see what is happening. BWmean has the value 13.8 inserted whenever there is a missing value in BW. For the original values, the standard deviation is 2.95 using the 69 non-missing values and the correlation with HL is –0.506. After we replace the 22 missing values with 13.75, the standard deviation drops to 2.56, and the correlation with HL decreases to –0.47. To compare the results of different imputation methods, we start building a table called `results`. The decrease in the standard deviation means that we will underestimate the variability in base width when we use inferential statistics (Chapter 8).

A similar procedure is often used in compositional analysis to replace zeros that represent elements that are below the detection limits of the equipment. Options include using a value of 0.5 or one-half the detection limit for that element or one-half the minimum value observed for that element if the actual detection limit is not known.

The package `Hmisc` contains a function `impute()` that imputes values based on a function or a random sample from the data. The function returns the data with imputed values and keeps track of which values were imputed (Harrell, et al., 2016). You specify a function to use in imputing the values (`median` is the default) or `random` to draw random values from the vector. Other options are also possible by using the `transcan()` function for more complex imputed values.

```
> install.packages("Hmisc")
> library(Hmisc)
> BWmed <- impute(BW)
> head(BWmed, 10)
    1      2     3     4     5     6     7     8     9    10
 11.3  13.6* 12.1  13.5  12.6  12.7  11.7  14.7  14.3  13.6*
> BWImp.md <- c(sd(BWmed), cor(BWmed ,HL))
> (results <- rbind(results, BWImp.md))
            sd    cor
BW.orig   2.95 -0.506
BWImp.mn  2.56 -0.467
BWImp.md  2.56 -0.466
```

The default for impute () is to use the median. The results are very similar since the two values are very close (13.75, 13.6). The advantage of using impute () is that it labels the missing values so that you do not lose track of them. Printing out the first 10 values shows that imputed values are flagged with an asterisk. Now we try randomly selecting one of the 69 non-missing values for each of the 22 missing values:

```
> set.seed(42)
> BWrand <- impute(BW, fun="random")
> head(BWrand, 10)
    1      2      3      4      5      6      7      8      9     10
 11.3   7.1*   12.1   13.5   12.6   12.7   11.7   14.7   14.3   10.3*
> BWImp.rnd <- c(sd=sd(BWrand), cor=cor(BWrand, HL))
> (results <- rbind(results, BWImp.rnd))
              sd      cor
BW.orig     2.95   -0.506
BWImp.mn    2.56   -0.467
BWImp.md    2.56   -0.466
BWImp.rnd   2.84   -0.421
```

The set.seed(42) function sets the random seed so that your results will match these. Now the imputed values are not all the same, but they are restricted to being a value that appears in the non-missing data. Notice that the standard deviation is much closer to the original value, but the correlation coefficient is even smaller than the value using the mean or median.

These approaches to missing data do not take much information about the data into account. In particular, there are relationships among the variables in the data set that should allow us to make better estimates of the missing values. Two other approaches to imputing missing values use the existing data (or at least some of it) in order to make better estimates. The hot deck procedure sorts the data set according to one or more variables and then uses an adjacent value to impute the missing value. The package VIM has an implementation of the hot deck procedure that is easy to use (Templ et al., 2016). We can divide the data into groups and select a value randomly from within that group. For example, assuming that B.Width varies by point type (Name), we can impute missing values by randomly selecting from the other specimens that are of the same type.

Alternatively we can sort the data by one or more variables and replace missing values with the value of the row just preceding it. This works better for the points if we use a categorical variable and a metric variable that is correlated with the variable containing the missing values. For this example, we will use Name as the categorical variable and Width as the metric variable:

```
> set.seed(42)
> BWHD1 <- hotdeck(DartPoints, variable="B.Width", domain_
  var="Name")
> View(BWHD1)
> BWImp.hd1 <- with(BWHD1, c(sd(B.Width), cor(B.Width,
  H.Length)))
> BWHD2 <- hotdeck(DartPoints, variable="B.Width", ord_
  var=c("Name", "Width"))
> BWImp.hd2 <- with(BWHD2, c(sd(B.Width), cor(B.Width,
  H.Length)))
> (results <- rbind(results, BWImp.hd1, BWImp.hd2))
            sd    cor
BW.orig    2.95 -0.506
BWImp.mn   2.56 -0.467
BWImp.md   2.56 -0.466
BWImp.rnd  2.84 -0.421
BWImp.hd1  2.92 -0.511
BWImp.hd2  3.12 -0.490
```

The hotdeck() function takes the entire data set and imputes all of the variables with missing values, or just the ones specified and returns a new data set with all of the same variables, but with imputed values. The first time we use random selection within point type and the second time we sort by Width within point type and use the B.Width of the point with the value just below the one with missing data. If you look at BWHD1 and BWHD2, you will find a new column at the end called B.Width_imp that indicates which values of B.Width have been imputed. The two hot deck procedures do very well at reproducing the standard deviation and the correlation of the original data.

While the hot deck method requires us to choose variables to order or group the data, the k-nearest neighbor approach combines multiple variables into a distance measure to find cases that are similar to the one containing missing values. The k-nearest neighbors are used to impute the missing values. The kNN() function in package VIM can use information from ratio, ordinal, and nominal variables to find the closest points to the ones with missing values. Then it uses the median of the k-nearest neighbors to impute the missing value. The following example uses point type and all of the numeric and categorical variables to find the three nearest neighbors:

```
> BWkNN <- kNN(DartPoints, variable="B.Width", k=3,
+   dist_var=colnames(DartPoints)[c(1, 5:17)])
Time difference of 0 secs
> BWImp.knn <- with(BWkNN, c(sd(B.Width), cor(B.Width,
  H.Length)))
> (results <- rbind(results, BWImp.knn))
              sd      cor
BW.orig     2.95  -0.506
BWImp.mn    2.56  -0.467
BWImp.md    2.56  -0.466
BWImp.rnd   2.84  -0.421
BWImp.hd1   2.92  -0.511
BWImp.hd2   3.12  -0.490
BWImp.knn   2.82  -0.499
```

In the *k*-nearest neighbor imputation, the standard deviation and correlation are about as similar to the original values as the hot deck imputations. These methods are not substantially more difficult to implement, but they give much better results than simply using the mean, median, or a random value. Methods based on random numbers (BWImp.rnd, BWImp.hd1) will change if you re-run the commands with a different random seed or with no seed. You should re-run these code blocks to see how much the results can change. In contrast, BWImp.mn, BWImp.md, BWImp.hd2, and BWImp.knn are not based on random selections so they should not vary.

All single imputation methods have the advantage of giving you a single data set to work with and the disadvantage of potentially underestimating the standard errors. A solution is to incorporate more variability in the imputation process by working with multiple sets of imputed data (multiple imputation).

There are several packages for multiple imputation available in R, particularly Amelia (Honaker et al., 2011), Hmisc (function aregImpute()), mi (Su et. al., 2011), mice (van Buuren and Groothuis-Oudshoorn, 2011), and packages cat, mix, norm, and pan (Schafer, 1997a, 1997b). Multiple imputation creates several (often five) data sets that are analyzed separately and then the statistics are combined into a single estimate (Allison, 2001; McKnight et al., 2007, Schafer, 1997a, 1999). They are routinely used in social science research when fitting multiple regression models, but there is less support for the kind of programs that archaeologists typically use such as principle components, discriminant analysis, and cluster analysis. However, you can still generate multiple data sets and run your analyses on all of them to make sure your conclusions are not based on a particular set of imputed data.

Function `mice()` in package `mice` uses a multiple imputation method called "multivariate imputation by chained equations." The function constructs an equation for each variable that has missing values. The equation is used to predict the values for that variable. For each observation with a missing value on that variable, the predictions are used to find five (or some other number) observations without missing data on that variable whose predicted values are close to the predicted value for the missing observation. Then one of the five values is randomly selected and used for the missing value. The process is repeated five (or some other number) times to create five data sets with imputed values. The approach is called predictive mean matching and it has the advantage that the imputed values will have the same range as the non-missing data and it does not make any assumptions about the underlying distribution like multiple imputation methods that assume a multivariate normal distribution.

As a simple example install package `mice` and run the following commands to create multiple imputations based on point type and the numeric variables:

```
install.packages("mice")
library(mice)
> set.seed(42)
> BWmice <- mice(DartPoints[, c(1, 5:11)], print=FALSE)
> sds <- sapply(1:5, function(x) sd(complete(BWmice, x)$B.
  Width))
> names(sds) <- paste0("BWImp.mi", 1:5)
> cors <- sapply(1:5, function(x) with(complete(BWmice, x),
+    cor(B.Width, H.Length)))
> (results <- rbind(results, cbind(sds, cors)))
            sd     cor
BW.orig    2.95  -0.506
BWImp.mn   2.56  -0.467
BWImp.md   2.56  -0.466
BWImp.rnd  2.84  -0.421
BWImp.hd1  2.92  -0.511
BWImp.hd2  3.12  -0.490
BWImp.knn  2.82  -0.499
BWImp.mi1  2.83  -0.484
BWImp.mi2  2.89  -0.526
BWImp.mi3  3.04  -0.504
BWImp.mi4  2.88  -0.500
BWImp.mi5  3.02  -0.474
```

We impute five data sets (all stored in BWmice) containing the point type and the metric variables by imputing the missing values in B.Width (and the single missing value in J.Width). Then we extract the five data sets using the complete() function. To get the standard deviations and the correlations for each set, we use the sapply() function to extract B.Width from each of the five data sets and compute the standard deviation and the correlation with H.Length. We add names to the standard deviations (sds) as labels using paste0() and use cbind() to combine the five imputations. Now results contains the results of all of the missing value imputations. Notice that the original standard deviation and correlation are generally close to the imputed values, but again these values are based to some degree on the random seed so you should re-run them to see how the results can change.

With a few commands, we can summarize the various imputation methods in a plot:

```
> lbls <- c("Orig", "mn", "md", "rnd", "hd1", "hd2",
+    "knn", "mi1", "mi2", "mi3", "mi4", "mi5")
> plot(results, xlim=c(2.5, 3.2), main="Imputation Methods",
  typ="n", las=1)
> text(results, lbls)
> abline(h=results[1, 2], v=results[1, 1], lty=3)
```

Figure 32 shows the results. The first command just creates short labels that will be printed on the plot. The plot() command sets up the plot, but does not plot anything and the text() command plots the labels on the plot. Finally abline()

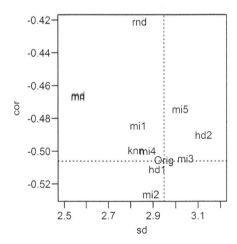

FIGURE 32 Comparison of imputation methods.

adds dashed lines centered on the values for the original data with listwise deletion. Points to the left of `Orig` have smaller standard deviations and points above `Orig` have smaller correlation coefficients. For this example, the hot deck method sorting by point type only (`hd1`) is very close to the original values. Hot deck using point type and width, k-nearest neighbor, and the multiple imputation values surround the original results. Simple methods of imputation such as using the mean, median, or choosing a random value did poorly (`mn`, `md`, and `rnd`).

Random selection within point type (`hd1`) is closest to the original values, but if you re-run the code with a different seed, it rarely gets this close. The hot deck method using `Name` and `Width` (`hd2`) worked well and is not based on a random process, but it is heavily dependent on picking the right variable. Using one of the other variables generally produces worse results. Overall, the best choice for estimating a single set of missing values seems to be k-nearest neighbor, but that may not be the case with different data. Multiple imputation works well and by looking at five sets of results, you get a better understanding of how much your results are affected by the missing values. All of the imputed data sets preserve the sample size of 91 so the standard error will be 14 percent smaller than using listwise deletion.

There is an extensive literature on imputation and multiple imputation. R makes it possible to use the most recently developed techniques, but you should read some of the references included in this chapter before doing more than simple imputation based on the hot deck or k-nearest neighbors.

Table 7 *Functions introduced in Chapter 7*

Function	Package	Description
abline	graphics	Add a regression, vertical, or horizontal line to a plot
aregImpute	Hmisc	Multiple imputation using additive regression, etc.
cbind	base	Combine vectors, matrices, or data frames by column
complete	mice	Extract an imputed data set after using mice
complete.cases	base	Test to see if a case (row) contains any missing values
cor	stats	Compute a correlation matrix
hotdeck	VIM	Impute missing values using hot deck method
impute	Hmisc	Impute missing values
is.na	base	Test a value to see if it is NA (missing)
kNN	VIM	k-nearest neighbor imputation using Gower distance
mice	mice	Multiple imputation by chained equations
na.omit	base	Remove rows with missing values

Table 7 (*cont.*)

Function	Package	Description
nrow	base	Number of rows in a matrix or data frame
paste0	base	Concatenate character strings with no separator
predict	stats	Compute fitted values from a model
rbind	base	Combine vectors, matrices, or data frames by row
sapply	base	Apply a function to each element of a list or data frame
transcan	Hmisc	Nonlinear additive transformation and imputation

Note: Packages `base`, `datasets`, `graphics`, `grDevices`, `methods`, `stats`, and `utils` are automatically loaded when R starts.

8

Confidence Intervals and Hypothesis Testing

When we plotted the dart point lengths, some types seemed similar to one another and some seemed different. Under most circumstances, we assume that the data we are analyzing is a sample of a larger population to which we do not have access. When we computed the mean and the standard deviation of length for different point types, we were computing sample **statistics**, values that characterized the distribution of values in the sample. If we increase the sample by adding more points, the statistics would change somewhat. If we could collect all of the points of a particular type and compute the mean and the standard deviation, those values would now be **parameters**. They would represent the entire population of a point type.

Of course, we cannot hope to find all of the points of a particular type, or all of the pots of a particular type. We never have more than a sample to work with, but we would like to estimate the population parameters on the basis of a sample. Since two samples contain only estimates of the population, it also makes sense to wonder if the two samples are part of the same population or if they come from two different populations. It is only when we are looking at a part of the whole that we have to consider if the statistics computed from the sample are representative of the population as a whole. One of the goals of inferential statistics is to formalize the concepts of similar and dissimilar in terms of probability and this leads to the concepts of **confidence intervals** and **hypothesis testing**.

Confidence intervals provide a probability distribution around a statistic such that if we had many samples, we can say that a certain percentage of the confidence intervals of those samples would include the population value. **Hypothesis testing** allows us to assign a probability to the possibility that two samples were drawn from the same population (or from populations with the same parameters).

Classical inferential statistics often depends upon the normal or Gaussian distribution to determine those probabilities. These methods are generally referred to as parametric statistics. Inferential statistics that do not assume a normal distribution are referred to as

nonparametric statistics. This chapter covers both approaches and will introduce a relatively new and powerful approach to nonparametric statistics, the bootstrap.

8.1 PROGRAMMING R – WRITING FUNCTIONS

We are not limited to using the functions that come with R or the many packages
that we can install. We can also create our own functions. Defining a function consists of giving the function a name, specifying its arguments and any default values
for those arguments, writing the commands that will be executed, and identifying
the results that should be returned. There are entire books written on how to write
functions in R, but we can cover the basics here since knowing how to write simple
functions is useful when working with the apply family of R functions and when you
want to run the same basic analysis with different sets of data without retyping the
commands over and over again.

To illustrate the process, we can write a function that takes two numbers and
returns their sum, difference, product, and quotient.

```
> four <- function(x, y) {
+    return(c(x + y, x - y, x * y, x / y))
+ }
> four(3, 6)
[1]  9.0 -3.0 18.0  0.5
```

The function four() takes two numbers and returns a vector. It is a pretty simple function since it consists of a single command. It actually does not need the
return() function since a function automatically returns the result of the last
operation and in this case there is only one operation. There is no error checking in
this function, but R will return reasonable error messages:

```
> four()
Error in four() : argument "x" is missing, with no default
> four(3)
Error in four(3) : argument "y" is missing, with no default
> four("a", "b")
Error in x + y : non-numeric argument to binary operator
```

Calling four() without the correct number of arguments causes the function
to fail and calling it with the wrong kind of values (characters instead of numeric)
causes it to fail. A useful function will generally have a number of arguments with

some of them taking default values. We can make a slightly more complex function that will take a vector of numbers and compute the coefficient of variation, which is the standard deviation divided by the mean and, optionally, multiplied by 100 to express it as a percentage.

```
> CV <- function(x, pct=FALSE, na.rm=TRUE) {
+        cv <- sd(x, na.rm=na.rm) / mean(x, na.rm=na.rm)
+        if (pct) cv <- cv*100
+        return(cv)
+ }
> set.seed(42)
> a <- runif(25)*100
> CV(a)
[1] 0.5001117
> CV(a, pct=TRUE)
[1] 50.01117
```

The CV() function has three arguments: a data vector, a logical argument to determine if the CV is multiplied by 100, and a logical argument to determine if missing values should be removed from the data. The default values are to not multiply by 100 and to remove the missing values. We create the function and then a set of 25 uniform random numbers using runif() between 0 and 100 to test the function.

Most programming languages have ways of controlling the flow of the program. In R these are referred to as control-flow constructs (?Control to get the manual page; you have to put the individual commands in quotation marks, for example, ?"for" and ?"function"). In the this example, we use if to multiply the value of cv by 100 if pct is set to TRUE. Other control-flow words create loops that repeat a certain number of times (for loops) or until a condition has been reached (while loops). Loops are less commonly used in R because many functions can operate on whole vectors rather than single values and the apply family of functions has various ways of generating loops. If you write a function that works on one variable or for one sample, you can use apply functions to run it multiple times. But there are times when a loop is helpful, especially when you want to repeat something without storing the results.

As an example of a programming loop in a function, we can write a function to take samples of four different sizes from a specified uniform distribution and plot them on a single page:

```
> Plot4 <- function(from=0, to=1, sizes=c(15, 50, 100, 200)) {
+        oldp <- par(mfrow=c(2, 2))
```

```
+       for (i in sizes) {
+           hist(runif(i, from, to), freq=FALSE, xlab="",
+               main=paste0("Sample Size: ", i))
+       }
+       par(oldp)
+ }
> Plot4()
> Plot4(0, 100, sizes=c(25, 100, 200, 500))
```

Create the function first and make sure you do not have any error messages. The `for` loop will set `i` equal to each of the values in `sizes` and create a histogram. The first example, `Plot4()`, will create a page with four histograms using the default values. The second will change the range and the sample sizes. You can see the code of your R function just by typing its name without parentheses:

```
> CV
function(x, pct=FALSE, na.rm=TRUE) {
    cv <- sd(x, na.rm=na.rm) / mean(x, na.rm=na.rm)
    if (pct) cv <- cv*100
    return(cv)
}
```

This will also work with many, but not all R functions. We will need to create some simple functions to explore confidence intervals and hypothesis testing in the remainder of the chapter.

8.2 CONFIDENCE INTERVALS

In Chapter 3 we computed a number of descriptive statistics. We could construct confidence intervals around any of these, but typically we are interested in confidence intervals around the mean. To see how this works, pretend that we know the mean and standard deviation of the length of all of the La Tène bronze fibulae. We can never really know this, but if we assume that fibulae lengths follow a normal distribution, we can explore the results of different sample sizes from this unknown population. R has functions to generate pseudo-random numbers from many different distributions. We can use the `rnorm()` function to generate random samples from a normal distribution with a particular mean and standard deviation and then we can look at the distribution of those samples. We need to distinguish between the **sample distribution**, which is the distribution of the observations in the sample, from the **sampling distribution**, which is the distribution of the means (or some other statistic) of many samples.

```
> data(Fibulae)
> options(digits=3)
> (Fm <- mean(Fibulae$Length))
[1] 56.2
> (Fs <- sd(Fibulae$Length))
[1] 24.3
> set.seed(42)
> estimates <- replicate(1000, mean(rnorm(10, mean=Fm,
  sd=Fs)))
> quantile(estimates, prob=c(.025, .975))
 2.5% 97.5%
 40.6  70.5
```

The first four commands load the `Fibulae` data set and compute the mean and standard deviation for `Length`. Then we use `set.seed(42)` to set the random number generator. The next command is complicated by the fact that several functions are nested. The outermost function is `replicate()`, which is part of the `apply` family (Chapter 6). The first argument tells the function how many times to run the command (which is the second argument). So we know that we are going to run the command 1,000 times and return the results to the object called `estimates`. The second argument is the function `mean()`. So we are going to compute 1,000 means. Inside the `mean()` function is another function, `rnorm(10, mean=Fm, sd=Fs)`. The `rnorm()` function generates pseudo-random numbers according to a normal distribution. We are asking for 10 random numbers from a normal distribution with the same mean and standard deviation as the 30 fibulae lengths in `Fibulae`. The last command prints the 2.5 and 97.5 percent quantiles. Of the 1,000 sample means, 95 percent range from 40.6 to 70.5. Recall that the population mean is 56.2 so there is quite a bit of variation around that value. Now we can plot the results:

```
> library(car)
> densityPlot(estimates, xlim=range(Fibulae$Length),
+    ylim=c(0, 16), xlab="Fibulae$Length",
+    rug=FALSE, lwd=2)
> lines(density(Fibulae$Length, bw="SJ"), lty=3, lwd=2)
> abline(v=Fm, lty=2, lwd=2)
> legend("topright", c("Sample Means (n = 10)",
+    "Population Mean", "Münsingen Fibulae Length"),
+    lty=1:3, lwd=2, bg="white")
```

First, we plot the kernel density distribution for the sample means (the 1,000 values in estimates), which is the **sampling distribution**. We set the *x*-axis range large enough so that we can add the distribution of the actual fibulae lengths to the plot (the **sample distribution**) and the *y*-axis so that we will have the same scale as the next plot. We use density() to plot the kernel density for the original fibulae lengths and use lines() to add it to the plot. Then abline() adds a vertical line representing the mean fibula length that we used to generate the random samples and legend() identifies the elements in the plot (Figure 33a).

What happens if the sample size is 100?

```
> set.seed(42)
> estimates <- replicate(1000, mean(rnorm(100, mean=Fm,
  sd=Fs)))
> print(quantile(estimates, prob=c(.025, .975)), digits=3)
 2.5% 97.5%
 51.3  60.9
> densityPlot(estimates, xlim=range(Fibulae$Length),
  ylim=c(0, .16),
+        xlab="Fibulae Lengths", rug=FALSE, lwd=2)
> lines(density(Fibulae$Length, bw="SJ"), lty=3, lwd=2)
> abline(v=Fm, lty=2, lwd=2)
> legend("topright", c("Sample Means (n = 1000)",
+    "Population Mean", "Münsingen Fibulae Lengths"),
+    lty=1:3)
```

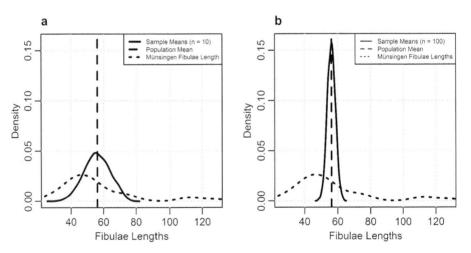

FIGURE 33 Distribution of sample means from a normal distribution: (a) sample size 10 and (b) sample size 100.

Now 95 percent of the sample means range from 51.3 to 60.9, much closer to 56.2. We would expect that samples of 100 would give us a better estimate of the population mean than samples of 10 and Figure 33b shows how much better they do. This is the basic idea behind confidence intervals, but in the real world, we do not know what the population mean (a parameter) is so we construct a confidence interval around the sample mean (a statistic). A 95 percent confidence interval means that 95 percent of such samples will include the population mean in that interval. To construct a confidence interval, we need the sample mean, the sample standard deviation, and the sample size. From these, we can construct confidence intervals using the t distribution. The basic formula for the confidence interval for the mean is the following:

$$\bar{Y} \pm t_{1-\frac{\alpha}{2}, N-1} \frac{s}{\sqrt{N}}$$

where $\bar{Y}$ is the sample mean; s is the sample standard deviation; and N is the sample size; $t_{1-\frac{\alpha}{2}, N-1}$ is the value of the t distribution at $1 - \frac{\alpha}{2}$ with $N - 1$ degrees of freedom and the confidence interval is $1 - \alpha$.

The t-distribution is very similar to the normal distribution and when the sample size is large they are effectively equal. At small sample sizes, the t distribution has fatter tails so the confidence interval is wider. It adjusts for the fact that we do not really know the population parameters (mean and standard deviation) and are using the sample statistics to estimate them. The t-distribution has one parameter, the degrees of freedom, which is just the sample size minus 1. In the formula, α represents the probability that the sample does not contain the population mean, so for a 95 percent confidence interval α = 1 - .95 = .05. This 5 percent is divided with half on the left side and half on the right side of the symmetrical t distribution. So 1 – α/ 2 = 0.975 is the tail on the right side and 2.5 percent is the tail on the left side. That is why we used those quantiles in the previous example.

To construct a parametric confidence interval, we compute the standard error, which is the standard deviation divided by the square root of the number of cases. We multiply the standard error by the quantile in the t distribution that represents the probability interval we have chosen (often 95 percent). We can illustrate the steps by constructing a confidence interval for fibula mean length. We can compare that to the results of using the function `MeanCI()` in package `DescTools`, which will be simpler for general use:

```
> Ybar <- mean(Fibulae$Length)
> s <- sd(Fibulae$Length)
```

```
> N <- length(Fibulae$Length)
> alpha <- 1-.95
> t <- qt(1-alpha/2, N-1)
> Ybar + c(-t, t)*s/sqrt(N)
[1] 47.2 65.3
> library(DescTools)
> MeanCI(Fibulae$Length)
  mean lwr.ci upr.ci
  56.2   47.2   65.3
```

So our 95 percent confidence interval for fibulae mean length is 47.2 to 65.3, which is in between the two estimates we created before since our sample size is 30. We use the qt() function to get the quantiles of the t-distribution that would include 95 percent of the area under the curve. Figure 34a shows the t-distribution and the confidence interval.

If the data are not normally distributed, or if we want confidence intervals for a robust measure of location such as the median, the best solution is to use bootstrapping. Bootstrapping uses multiple random samples from the original data to construct confidence intervals. The samples are the same size as the original data set, but they are drawn randomly with replacement so that some observations do not appear in a particular sample and others appear more than once. To construct confidence intervals for mean length, we could take a large number of samples of size 30 (the same sample size as our data) and compute the mean for each sample. The 2.5 and 97.5 percent quantiles of those samples would be our confidence

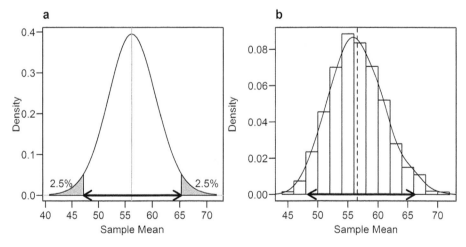

FIGURE 34 Ninety-five percent confidence interval for fibulae length based on (a) a t-distribution and (b) a 1,000-sample bootstrap.

interval. The following is is not always the most efficient estimate, but it is easy to illustrate:

```
> set.seed(42)
> means <- replicate(2000, mean(sample(Fibulae$Length,
  replace=TRUE)))
> mean(means)
[1] 56.5
> quantile(means, prob=c(.025, .975))
 2.5% 97.5%
 48.2  65.9
```

After setting the random number seed, we draw a sample of size 30 from the Length values with replacement and compute the mean for the sample using `rep-licate()` to do this 2,000 times and store the 2,000 means as the vector `means`. Then we display the mean of the 2,000 means, which is 56.5 (compared to mean length for the 30 fibulae in `Fibulae` of 56.2) and the 2.5 and 97.5 percent quantiles. The bootstrapped confidence interval is similar to the one we calculated using the t-distribution, but slightly narrower (65.8 – 48.2 = 17.6 instead of 65.3 – 47.2 = 18.1) and shifted to the right by about 0.5 mm. Also the t-distribution confidence interval is symmetric, the distance from the mean to the lower bound is the same as from the mean to the upper bound. But with the bootstrapping estimate, the lower bound is 8.3 mm smaller than the mean, while the upper bound is 10.37 mm larger than the mean. This reflects the fact that the distribution of fibulae lengths is asymmetrical (Figures 13 and 14). Figure 34b shows a histogram of the 2,000 bootstrapped sample means with a kernel density plot superimposed.

This method gives you a quick way to generate bootstrapped confidence intervals based on quantiles, but under some circumstances, it can underestimate the true confidence interval. The `boot` package in R makes it relatively simple to bootstrap confidence intervals that perform well under a wider variety of circumstances (Canty and Ripley, 2016). Minimally the `boot()` function needs the data, the function that computes the statistic for which we want confidence intervals, and the number of samples to draw. We can use `boot()` to bootstrap standard R functions but we need to create a simple function so that `boot()` can generate the necessary samples.

```
> install.packages("boot")
> library(boot)
> wmean <- function(x, d) { return(c(mean(x[d]), var(x[d])/
  length(d))) }
> set.seed(42)
```

```
> means.boot <- boot(Fibulae$Length, wmean, R=2000)
> plot(means.boot)
> boot.ci(means.boot, type="stud")
BOOTSTRAP CONFIDENCE INTERVAL CALCULATIONS
Based on 2000 bootstrap replicates

CALL :
boot.ci(boot.out = means.boot, type = "stud")

Intervals :
Level    Studentized
95%   (48.5, 68.1 )
Calculations and Intervals on Original Scale
```

After installing and loading the boot package, we create a function called wmean(). The function has two arguments, x (the variable to be used in creating the bootstrapped confidence intervals) and d, an index that boot() will use to draw the samples. The function has a single command between the curly braces. It returns the mean of x[d] and the variance (the sample variance divided by the number of observations). Next we pass wmean() to boot() along with the data we plan to use and the number of samples to generate. We save the results as means.boot.

The plot() command shows the histogram of the sample means on the left and compares the sample means to a normal distribution on the right (Figure 35). Then we extract the Studentized confidence intervals from boot.out using boot. ci().The Studentized estimate uses the variances in each bootstrap sample to

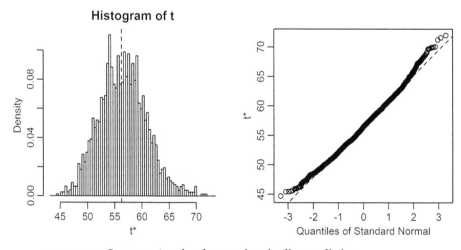

FIGURE 35 Bootstrapping plots for mean length of bronze fibulae.

adjust the interval. It performs well in many circumstances and Venables and Ripley recommend using it (2002: 137). Since bootstrapping is based on drawing random samples, the results will change slightly each time you run the function (assuming you do not set the random seed to the same number for each run). In particular the upper bound varies more than the lower bound.

For an introduction to bootstrapping, see *Bootstrapping: A Nonparametric Approach to Statistical Inference* by Mooney and Duval (1993) and *Bootstrap Methods and Their Applications* by Davison and Hinkley (1997). There are several other packages that provide bootstrapping. In particular, `simpleboot` is easier to use for simple bootstrapping problems such as getting confidence intervals for simple statistics or regression coefficients. It provides the percentile estimate of the confidence interval, but not the Studentized interval. The `bootstrap` package is a companion to *An Introduction to the Bootstrap* (Efron and Tibshirani, 1993).

8.3 HYPOTHESIS TESTING

One of the reasons for computing confidence intervals is to compare one sample to another sample. For example, we might want to know if two types of projectile points have the same average length or if graves containing males are as likely to contain spindle whorls as those containing females.

For each of these tests, the basic procedure is the same. We establish a null hypothesis that the two groups have the same distribution (i.e. there is no difference between them). The test involves computing the probability that we would get the observed results if there was no difference between the two groups. If that probability is small enough, we reject the null hypothesis and conclude that there is a statistically significant difference between the groups. Rejecting the null hypothesis provides support for the conclusion that there is a difference between the groups and we might then proceed to look for ways of explaining that difference. If we do not reject the null hypothesis, we cannot accept the alternate hypothesis (there is no difference between the groups), but we usually accept that failure to reject the null hypothesis provides support for the conclusion that there is no difference between the two samples. It is an oversimplification, but failing to reject the null hypothesis often suggests that there is nothing to explain, while rejecting the null hypothesis implies that something is going on that we do not understand.

How small does the probability have to be before we reject it? Often in the social sciences, the significance level (the probability that will trigger rejection of the null hypothesis) is set to .05. In other words, the observed data would be obtained only one time in 20 if the null hypothesis is true. Statisticians usually discuss this decision in terms of type I (α) and type II (β) errors. A type I error is the probability that you will reject the null hypothesis of no difference when the null hypothesis is actually true so the type I error rate is the same as the significance level. If rejecting the null hypothesis leads to more investigation to see what is going on and accepting the null hypothesis (or failing to reject it) leads to no further investigation, then in a practical sense, the type I error is the probability of heading down a "blind alley" – looking for something that is not there.

We could make the significance level smaller (e.g., .01 or even .001) so we have a smaller chance of making a type I error. But then we face an increase in the type II error rate. The type II error is the chance of accepting (or failing to reject) the null hypothesis when it is actually false. If accepting the null hypothesis means that we conclude that there is no difference and therefore nothing further to investigate, then the type II error is a "missed opportunity." If we decrease the type I error rate, we increase the type II error rate, but how much it increases depends on the power of the statistical test.

In some fields, the types I and II error rates have life and death consequences that must be weighed. For example, a type I error could mean recommending that an expensive and painful treatment provided real benefits to patients when it does not and a type II error could mean telling patients they do not have a serious disease, when they do. As a result, there is a substantial literature on error rates and how to weigh them in the literature. Since archaeologists deal with people who are already dead, the consequences of these errors generally amount to wasted time or failing to recognize an interesting pattern in the archaeological record. That does not mean that you should ignore the difference between type I and type II errors. You should always consider the degree to which a "statistically significant" result actually provides an important understanding of the archaeological record and that the failure to find something statistically significant may simply be a problem of sample size or measurement techniques.

Table 8 summarizes the details of these error types. The rows represent the decision to accept or reject the null hypothesis and the columns show whether the decision is wrong or correct. You should realize that although we can estimate the error rates, in a particular case, we do not know whether we have made an error or not. We always know what row we are on in Table 8, but we can never be sure which column.

The probability of obtaining the observed results if the null hypothesis is correct gives us an objective way to make a decision about the null hypothesis, but it does not give us information about how important the difference is. As sample sizes increase, you can reject the null hypothesis with smaller and smaller differences between the two samples. Those differences, although statistically significant, may be trivial as far as our understanding of the archaeological record is concerned.

Table 8 *Types of errors in statistical inference*

		Null Hypothesis (H_0) is	
		True	False
Decision	Reject H_0	**Error** **Type I, α**	Correct Decision
	Accept H_0 (fail to reject)	Correct Decision	**Error** **Type II, β**

8.4 COMPARING TWO SAMPLES

There are a number of ways of testing the null hypothesis of no difference between two samples. They include the proportions test, the difference of means test (aka, Welch two-sample *t*-test or Student's *t*-test), and the Wilcoxon rank sum test (Mann–Whitney *U* test). The first is based on the binomial distribution, the second on the normal distribution, and the third on the average difference in ranks between two groups.

As an example of the proportions test, we will look at the Snodgrass site. The Snograss site is a Mississippian site in Missouri, United States, that was occupied by maize agriculturalists about CE 1325–1420 (Figure 36). The site includes 91 pit houses located within a fortification wall. Some of the 91 houses at the site fall inside an area marked by an interior wall, which the excavators thought might reflect rank differences within the site. We would like to know if the proportion of houses containing arrow points is the same for houses inside and outside that wall. The variable `Inside` identifies houses inside versus outside the wall and the variable `Points` indicates how many arrow points were found in each house. For the proportions test, we just need the presence or absence of points so we need to create a new variable:

```
> data(Snodgrass)
> Points.pa <- ifelse(Snodgrass$Points>0, "Present", "Absent")
> Points.pa <- factor(Points.pa, levels=c("Present", "Absent"))
> Snodgrass.pts <- xtabs(~Inside+Points.pa, Snodgrass)
> addmargins(Snodgrass.pts)
         Points.pa
Inside    Present    Absent    Sum
  Inside       34         4     38
  Outside      24        29     53
  Sum          58        33     91
> prop.test(Snodgrass.pts, correct=FALSE)
```

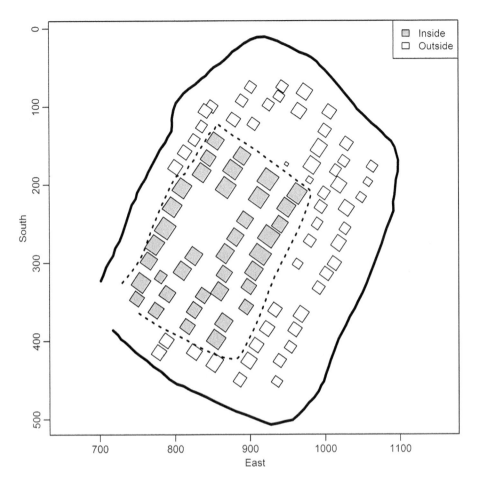

FIGURE 36 The Snodgrass site.

```
     2-sample test for equality of proportions without
continuity correction

data:  Snodgrass.pts
X-squared = 20, df = 1, p-value = 2e-05
alternative hypothesis: two.sided
95 percent confidence interval:
 0.276 0.608
sample estimates:
prop 1 prop 2
 0.895  0.453
```

First, we create character variable called Points.pa with values Absent or Present depending on whether arrow points were recovered from the house. Then we convert Points.pa to a factor with Present as the first level and Absent as the second level. This second step is not necessary, but it makes it easier to understand the results. The default would be to make `Absent` the first level since it starts with "A," but then we would be testing whether points are as likely to be absent in each group. The difference of proportions test is based on the binomial distribution (Chapter 3). One outcome is considered a "success" and one a "failure." It does not matter which is which but it is easier to talk about the presence of a point as a "success."

Then we create a table making sure that the variable that defines the samples is the row variable (`Inside`). This part is very important. We sampled houses to find which ones contained points. We did not sample points since we do not know where they were until we excavate them. If you look at the table, you can see that almost 90 percent of the houses inside the wall have arrow points (34/38 = .895) while for those outside the wall only 45 percent (24/53 = .453) have points. We want to know if this difference is simply due to random sampling. Could the probability that a house contains an arrow point be the same for both groups? The overall proportion of houses with points is 58/91 = .64. If the probability was .64 for both groups, how likely is it that we would get these results? Our null hypothesis is that the probability is the same for both groups and we use the `prop.test()` function to evaluate it.

The probability that the null hypothesis is correct is based on the Chi-squared distribution and for this example, the value is 18.7 with one degree of freedom, and a p-value of .00002 (R expresses this in scientific notation as 2e-5, which is the same as 2×10^{-5}). This is the probability that we would get the observed results if the null hypothesis is correct (the type I (α)). Only two times in 100,000 tries would we get samples that differed this much if the null hypothesis was correct. That is a very small number, but it is not 0. It is much smaller than .05 so at that significance level, we reject the null hypothesis and conclude that points are more likely to be found in structures inside the wall (conversely, they are less likely to be present in structures outside the wall). The difference between the proportions is .895 - .453 = .442. The 95 percent confidence interval for the difference in proportions is .276 to .608. That interval does not include zero (the null hypothesis), which confirms that the difference is significant at the .05 level.

The null hypothesis is that there is no difference between the proportions or that their difference is 0. The alternate hypothesis is that the proportions are different. The test is two-sided since we did not predict in advance which group of houses would be more likely to have arrow points.

We have computed the test without the continuity correction which would be advisable for small samples. With the continuity correction the p-value increases to .00004, which is still much smaller than .05. In the previous section, we set the number of significant digits to three. If you want to display more decimal places for the Chi-squared value, increase the number of digits with `options(digits=7)` and rerun the test.

The **degrees of freedom** determines which version of the Chi-square distribution we need to use. Given the sample size (91), the number of houses with points (58), and the number of houses inside the inner wall (38), there is only one more value that we can freely choose. For example, the number of houses inside the wall containing arrow points could have any value from 0 to 38, but once that value is chosen, the rest of the values in the table are determined by the row and column totals (the marginals). Most of the other tests we use will have a value for degrees of freedom that indicates how much flexibility we have in choosing values.

To compare a numeric variable between two groups, the difference of means or *t*-test is the main parametric test and the Wilcoxon test (also known as the Mann Whitney test) is the main nonparametric test. The *t*-test compares the means of two distributions and there are two versions. One assumes the variances of the two samples are the same and one that they are different. The default for the `t.test()` function is to assume the variances are not equal (the more conservative approach). To use `t.test()` we must have two groups with a numeric variable. For the Snodgrass site, we can use the `Area` variable, which contains the area of each house in square feet. As before, our grouping variable will be `Inside` and our null hypothesis is that houses inside and outside the walled area are the same size. The formula for the *t*-test depends on whether or not the variances of the two samples are equal. If they are equal, we combine the variances to create a single estimate of the variance:

$$t = \frac{\bar{X}_1 - \bar{X}_2}{\sqrt{\frac{(n_1 - 1)s_1^2 + (n_2 - 1)s_2^2}{n_1 + n_2 - 2}} \sqrt{\frac{1}{n_1} + \frac{1}{n_2}}}$$

where t is value of the statistic; $\bar{X}_1$ and $\bar{X}_2$ are the sample means; n_1 and n_2 are the sample sizes; and s_1^2 and s_2^2 are the squared standard deviations of the each sample.

The numerator is just the difference between the means of the two samples and the denominator is the pooled standard error. The result has $n_1 + n_2 - 2$ degrees of freedom. The test involves three assumptions. First, that the two samples are independent of one another. In this case, it means areas of houses inside the wall are unrelated to the mean areas of houses outside the wall. Second, that the samples are drawn from normal populations. Finally, that the sample variances in the samples are equal. If the variances are different, we need to use an alternate version of the test, called Welch's *t*-test:

$$t = \frac{\bar{X}_1 - \bar{X}_2}{\sqrt{\frac{s_1^2}{n_1} + \frac{s_2^2}{n_2}}}$$

where t is value of the statistic; $\overline{X}_1$ and $\overline{X}_2$ are the sample means; n_1 and n_2 are the sample sizes; and s_1^2 and s_2^2 are the squared standard deviations (i.e. variances) of the each sample.

In this case, the degrees of freedom is a more complicated function of the variances and sample sizes that will be smaller than the degrees of freedom for the pooled estimate. From a practical standpoint, this makes the test less powerful (more likely to make a type II error).

Since the t-test is a parametric test, we should consider the degree to which Snodgrass house areas within each group diverge from a normal distribution. The t-test is relatively robust against deviations from normality, but we should know where we stand so we can consider transforming the data or switching to a nonparametric test. The null hypothesis is that the values fit a normal distribution. We can easily check this using the `tapply()` function (part of the `apply` family, Chapter 6), which takes a vector (in this case the area of each house, `Area`), divides it into groups based on a factor (`Inside`), and passes each group to a function, `shapiro.test()`:

```
> options(digits=6)
> with(Snodgrass, tapply(Area, Inside, shapiro.test))
$Inside

        Shapiro-Wilk normality test

data:  X[[i]]
W = 0.9816, p-value = 0.775


$Outside

        Shapiro-Wilk normality test

data:  X[[i]]
W = 0.9821, p-value = 0.607
```

The Shapiro–Wilk test prints the results at fewer significant digits than the current value so we increase the value to 6. The result is the same for the `Inside` and `Outside` houses, the p-values are much larger than .05 so we fail to reject the null hypothesis that the distribution is a normal one. This suggests that the use of a parametric test such as the t-test is appropriate. With large sample sizes, smaller and smaller deviations from normality will be statistically significant so you should not necessarily abandon the use of parametric statistical methods since many can handle small departures from normality. Use tests of normality as a guide in making informed decisions, not as law.

Second, we would like to know if the variances for the areas of houses inside and outside the wall are the same.

```
> with(Snodgrass, tapply(Area, Inside, var))
 Inside Outside
5789.38 3112.03
> var.test(Area~Inside, Snodgrass)


        F test to compare two variances

data:  Area by Inside
F = 1.86, num df = 37, denom df = 52, p-value = 0.0388
alternative hypothesis: true ratio of variances is not
  equal to 1
95 percent confidence interval:
 1.03255 3.45742
sample estimates:
ratio of variances
        1.86032
```

The first command computes the variances for each group. They are quite different with the inside variance nearly twice as large as the outside variance. The second command uses var.test() to compare the two variances. Notice that we use a formula to specify the test with Area on the left and Inside on the right. The test uses the ratio of the two variances and the F-value is 1.86. The p-value is .039, which is less than .05, so we reject the null hypothesis that the variances are equal. We will use the separate variances option in the t-test.

Notice that there are two values for the degrees of freedom, one for the numerator (houses inside) and one for the denominator (houses outside). For each, the degrees of freedom is one less than the number of houses.

Third, we are ready to compare the mean areas of the two groups.

```
> t.test(Area~Inside, Snodgrass)


        Welch Two Sample t-test

data:  Area by Inside
t = 9.52, df = 64.23, p-value = 6.81e-14
alternative hypothesis: true difference in means is not
  equal to 0
95 percent confidence interval:
```

```
109.293 167.336
sample estimates:
 mean in group Inside mean in group Outside
             317.371                  179.057
```

By default t.test() does a two-sided test assuming the variances are not equal (Box 8). We are doing a two-sided test since we did not predict which group has the larger houses before seeing the data. The alternate hypothesis for a two-sided test is that the difference between the means is not 0. In a one-sided test, the alternate hypothesis would be that difference in mean areas of the houses is greater or less than 0. That would require some basis for expecting one group of houses to be larger before we actually looked at the data.

The t-statistic is 9.52 and the p-value is essentially 0 so we reject the null hypothesis that the difference in areas between Inside and Outside houses is 0. The difference is not actually printed out, but it is 138.3. The confidence interval for the difference between the two groups ranges from 109.3 to 167.3. The test is symmetrical so the p-value is the same if we subtract Outside from Inside or the Inside from Outside (except that the t-value would be –9.5204 and the confidence interval would be –167 to –109). The group means show how different they are, Inside=317 and Outside=179. If we had specified var.equal=TRUE in the t.test() function, the label would have been "Two Sample t-test" instead of "Welch Two Sample t-test."

We conclude that arrow points are more likely to be found in houses inside the walled area and those houses are larger. That raises a question that will can explore later: Are points more likely inside the wall because the houses are larger inside the wall? In other words, the probability of finding a point is not fixed for all houses; larger houses have a higher probability of having a point.

If the level of measurement is ordinal (rank) or the distribution is not normal, a nonparametric test called the Wilcoxon rank sum (or Mann–Whitney U) test can compare whether the rank values of one sample tend to be larger than the rank values in the other sample. This is roughly, but not exactly, equivalent to comparing the medians of the two samples:

```
> wilcox.test(Area~Inside, Snodgrass)

        Wilcoxon rank sum test with continuity correction

data:  Area by Inside
W = 1879, p-value = 2.31e-12
alternative hypothesis: true location shift is not equal to 0
```

Notice that the *p*-value is very small so we reject the null hypothesis that the sums of the rank values in the groups are the same. The *W* value is the sum of the ranks in the first group adjusted by the sample size for that group:

$$W = \Sigma R_1 - \frac{n_1 (n_1 + 1)}{2}$$

where *W* is the statistic; ΣR_1 is the sum of the ranks in the first group; and n_1 is the number of observations in the first group. The following code illustrates how to compute the Wilcoxon test using the formula:

```
> Area.rank <- rank(Snodgrass$Area)
> tapply(Area.rank, Snodgrass$Inside, sum)
 Inside Outside
   2620    1566
> table(Snodgrass$Inside)
 Inside Outside
     38      53
> 2620 - 38*39/2
[1] 1879
```

So *W* equals 1879, which matches the output from the `wilcox.test()` function. The first command ranks the house areas from smallest (1, where the area is 20) to the largest (91, where the area is 472.5). Ties are averaged so that if two houses with the same area are tied for ranks 9 and 10, they both receive a rank of 9.5. For reasonable sample sizes, the distribution of *W* can be approximated by a normal distribution to get the *p*-value.

8.5 COMPARING MORE THAN TWO SAMPLES

If there are more than two groups, we could construct all possible *t*-tests, but it is much better to use tests designed for more than two groups such as analysis of variance (ANOVA) and the Kruskal–Wallis test to compare all of the groups simultaneously. In ANOVA we are basically comparing the sum of the squared deviations of the values from their group means (the within group sum of squares [SSW]) to the sum of the squared deviations of the group means from the grand mean weighted by the number in each group (the between group sum of squares [SSB]). The sum of these is the sum of squared deviations of each observation from the grand mean (the total sum of squares [TSS]). If the groups overlap, their means will not be very different from the grand mean. If they are very separate, the group means will be farther away from the grand mean:

$$\text{TSS} = \Sigma \left(y_{ij} - \bar{y}_{..} \right)^2$$

$$\text{SSW} = \Sigma \left(y_{ij} - \bar{y}_{i.} \right)^2$$

$$\text{SSB} = \Sigma n_i \left(\bar{y}_{i.} - \bar{y}_{..} \right)^2$$

TSS=SSW+SSB

where y_{ij} is the jth observation in the ith group; $\bar{y}_{..}$ is the grand mean over all of the groups; $\bar{y}_{i.}$ is the mean of the ith group; and n_i is the number of observations in the ith group.

The sums of squares are divided by their respective degrees of freedom to form mean squares. The degrees of freedom for SSB is $k-1$ where k is the number of groups and the degrees of freedom for SSW is $n - k$ where n is the total number of observations. The ratio of the between and within mean squares is the F statistic. An example should make this clearer.

The houses at Snodgrass were originally placed into three groups. Those inside the wall belong to Segment 1. Segment 2 houses are to the north and west of the inner wall and Segment 3 houses are to the east and south. We can use analysis of variance to see if the house areas are different across the three segments:

```
> Snodgrass.aov <- aov(Area~Segment, Snodgrass)
> Snodgrass.aov
Call:
    aov(formula = Area ~ Segment, data = Snodgrass)

Terms:
                    Segment    Residuals
Sum of Squares       432327       367107
Deg. of Freedom           2           88

Residual standard error: 64.5885
Estimated effects may be unbalanced
> summary(Snodgrass.aov)
             Df    Sum Sq    Mean Sq    F value     Pr(>F)
Segment       2    432327     216164       51.8    1.3e-15    ***
Residuals    88    367107       4172
```

```
---
Signif. codes:  0 '***' 0.001 '**' 0.01 '*' 0.05 '.' 0.1 ' ' 1
> with(Snodgrass, tapply(Area, Segment, mean))
      1       2       3
317.371 166.795 192.790
```

The results of the analysis are stored in Snodgrass.aov as a list with 13 parts (Box 9). The warning message "Estimated effects may be unbalanced" indicates that the number of houses in each group is not the same. For a one-way analysis of variance, that will not be a problem. The default printout for the results is not very informative. You will usually want to store the output as an object and use summary(), which gives us a traditional analysis of variance table. In the table, the row labeled Segment has the between sum of squares and mean square (the sum of squares divided by the degrees of freedom) and the row labeled Residuals has the within sum of squares and mean square. Dividing the mean squares gives an F-value of 51.8 with a p-value of nearly 0 so we can reject the null hypothesis of no difference between the group means for the three groups. This implies that at least one mean is different from the others. The output also includes significance codes. The three asterisks indicate a p-value of less than .001.

Although we have rejected the null hypothesis of no difference between the groups, we do not know which groups are different without additional analysis. We could to t-tests between all of the combinations of groups (1 with 2, 1 with 3, 2 with 3), but there is a problem. Our significance level of .05 means that we will make a type I error one time in 20, but if we do three tests, the probability will increase. This is the multiple comparisons problem. It is easier to calculate the probability of not making an error at the .05 level (1 - .05 = .95) and asking what the chances of not making an error on three comparisons would be. If the probability of not making a mistake on one test is .95, then the probability of not making any mistakes on three tests is .95 × .95 × .95 ($.95^3$ = .857). So now the probability of making at least one type I error in three tests is 1 − .857 = .143! In three tests, we have a 14 percent chance of making at least one type I error when the significance level for each test is .05. The number of comparisons grows rapidly with the number of groups ($k(k - 1)/2$ where k is the number of groups). With three groups, there are three comparisons, but with four groups, there are six comparisons and with five groups there are 10 comparisons. This problem is not unique to ANOVA. It occurs whenever we test multiple null hypotheses. If we want to control the type I error rate of the whole group of comparisons to .05, we have to reduce the error rate of each comparison. Generally we can let R figure this out for us since there

CONFIDENCE INTERVALS AND HYPOTHESIS TESTING 181

are several ways of adjusting the per comparison *p*-values, but the basic formulas are simple:

```
> # Type I error rate for m comparisons
> m <- 3
> 1 - (1 - .05)^m
[1] 0.142625
> # p-value needed to keep overall error rate at .05
> 1 - (1-.05)^(1/m)
[1] 0.0169524
```

So for three comparisons at .05, our overall error rate is .14 as just mentioned. To keep the overall error rate at .05, we need to set the significance level to .017 for each test. While we could use *t*-tests at this significance level, there is an easier way to figure out which groups are different using Tukey's honest significant differences:

```
> TukeyHSD(Snodgrass.aov, ordered=TRUE)
  Tukey multiple comparisons of means
    95% family-wise confidence level
    factor levels have been ordered

Fit: aov(formula = Area ~ Segment, data = Snodgrass)

$Segment
          diff        lwr        upr       p adj
3-2    25.9954   -16.3740    68.3647    0.313807
1-2   150.5764   112.2265   188.9263    0.000000
1-3   124.5811    84.9284   164.2337    0.000000
> plot(TukeyHSD(Snodgrass.aov, ordered=TRUE), las=1)
```

The table shows the difference between the means for each comparison and the 95 percent confidence intervals for that difference. By specifying ordered=TRUE, the segments are sorted from smallest mean area to largest mean area so that all of the differences would be positive. This does not change the results; it just makes them easier to interpret. The adjusted *p*-values take multiple comparisons into account so that you can treat .05 as a significant difference. The plot (Figure 37a) shows these confidence limits graphically. If the horizontal line crosses the dashed vertical line marking 0, the difference is not significant. We conclude that segment 1 (Inner) houses are larger than segments 2 and 3 (Outer), but that segments 2 and 3 are not significantly different in area.

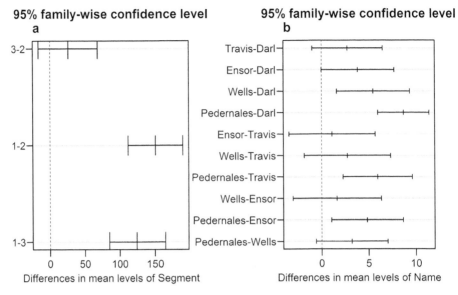

FIGURE 37 Multiple comparison analyses of (a) Snodgrass house areas and (b) dart point widths using Tukey honest significant difference.

The Kruskal–Wallis test is a nonparametric test that compares rank sums between groups in the same way that the ANOVA compares means. Function DunnTest() in package DescTools (Signorell et al., 2016) runs a nonparametric multiple comparisons test.

```
> kruskal.test(Area~Segment, Snodgrass)

        Kruskal-Wallis rank sum test

data:  Area by Segment
Kruskal-Wallis chi-squared = 50.44, df = 2, p-value = 1.11e-11

> library(DescTools)
> DunnTest(Area~Segment, Snodgrass)

 Dunn's test of multiple comparisons using rank sums : holm

    mean.rank.diff      pval
2-1          -43.1 1.7e-10 ***
3-1          -35.2 4.4e-07 ***
3-2            7.9  0.2771
---
Signif. codes:  0 '***' 0.001 '**' 0.01 '*' 0.05 '.' 0.1 ' ' 1
```

As expected, we reject the null hypothesis of no difference between the groups. Dunn's multiple comparison test compares the observed differences between each pair to a critical difference and identifies significant differences. In this case, the results agree completely with the Tukey test.

The multiple comparison analysis of the Snodgrass house areas is relatively easy to interpret. The houses within the walled area are larger than the houses outside. The houses outside the wall are similar in area. Things are not always so simple. Earlier we looked at the length and width of the Fort Hood dart points and noted that the lengths of the points overlapped substantially, but there were differences between the types in width. We can run the same analysis on those data for a more complex example:

```
> data(DartPoints)
> options(digits=3)
> sort(with(DartPoints, tapply(Width, Name, mean)))
      Darl     Travis      Ensor      Wells Pedernales
      17.7       20.4       21.5       23.1       26.4
> DartPoints.aov <- aov(Width~Name, DartPoints)
> summary(DartPoints.aov)
            Df  Sum Sq  Mean Sq  F  value    Pr(>F)
Name         4    1173    293.2     20.7   5.8e-12  ***
Residuals   86    1220     14.2
---
Signif. codes:  0 '***' 0.001 '**' 0.01 '*' 0.05 '.' 0.1 ' ' 1
> TukeyHSD(DartPoints.aov, ordered=TRUE)
  Tukey multiple comparisons of means
    95% family-wise confidence level
    factor levels have been ordered

Fit: aov(formula = Width ~ Name, data = DartPoints)

$Name
                   diff      lwr     upr    p adj
Travis-Darl        2.74  -0.9970    6.47    0.255
Ensor-Darl         3.84  -0.0279    7.71    0.053
Wells-Darl         5.47   1.6021    9.34    0.002
Pedernales-Darl    8.68   5.9626   11.39    0.000
Ensor-Travis       1.10  -3.4849    5.69    0.963
Wells-Travis       2.73  -1.8549    7.32    0.464
Pedernales-Travis  5.94   2.2726    9.61    0.000
Wells-Ensor        1.63  -3.0637    6.32    0.869
Pedernales-Ensor   4.84   1.0377    8.64    0.006
Pedernales-Wells   3.21  -0.5923    7.01    0.139
```

```
> oldp <- par(mar=c(5.1, 8.1, 4.1, 2.1))
> plot(TukeyHSD(DartPoints.aov), las=1)
> par(oldp)
```

After loading the data and setting the number of significant digits, we print out the mean dart point widths from smallest to largest. Darl points are the narrowest and Pedernales points are the widest. Travis, Ensor, and Wells are relatively close together. The summary of the ANOVA model shows a *p*-value very close to zero so we can reject the null hypothesis of no difference in width between the point types. Tukey honest significant differences test comes next. The Snodgrass example had only three comparisons, but the dart point example has 10. Of the 10 comparisons four are significant at the .05 level (Pedernales-Darl, Wells-Darl, Pedernales-Ensor, and Travis-Pedernales). Whereas the three Snodgrass house locations fell into two non-overlapping groups, the five dart point types fall into three overlapping groups: (Darl, Ensor, Travis), (Ensor, Travis, Wells), (Wells, Pedernales). Within each group, there are no significant differences in width. The plot shows this as well (Figure 37b). Notice that we had to increase the size of the left margin on the plot to make room for the labels and rotate them 90 degrees using the `mar=` and `las=` arguments. The last command resets the margin to the default values.

It can be difficult to identify the groups when they are overlapping as they are here. One way of showing the results is called the "compact letter display," but to get it, we need to run the Tukey HSD test with the `glht()` function in package `multcomp`. Install the package and then generate the compact letter display with `cld()`.

```
> library(multcomp)
> DartPoints.mc <- glht(DartPoints.aov, linfct=mcp(Name="Tukey"))
> summary(DartPoints.mc)
```

```
         Simultaneous Tests for General Linear Hypotheses

Multiple Comparisons of Means: Tukey Contrasts


Fit: aov(formula = Width ~ Name, data = DartPoints)

Linear Hypotheses:
                    Estimate Std. Error t value  Pr(>|t|)
Ensor - Darl == 0      3.839      1.388    2.77   0.0504 .
Pedernales - Darl == 0 8.679      0.975    8.90   <0.001 ***
Travis - Darl == 0     2.738      1.340    2.04   0.2473
```

```
Wells - Darl == 0              5.469   1.388    3.94     0.0014**
Pedernales - Ensor == 0        4.840   1.365    3.55     0.0054**
Travis - Ensor == 0           -1.101   1.646   -0.67     0.9610
Wells - Ensor == 0             1.630   1.684    0.97     0.8644
Travis - Pedernales == 0      -5.941   1.316   -4.51     <0.001***
Wells - Pedernales == 0       -3.210   1.365   -2.35     0.1336
Wells - Travis == 0            2.731   1.646    1.66     0.4548
---
Signif. codes:  0 '***' 0.001 '**' 0.01 '*' 0.05 '.' 0.1 ' ' 1
(Adjusted p values reported -- single-step method)
> cld(DartPoints.mc)
   Darl    Ensor Pedernales    Travis    Wells
    "a"     "ab"        "c"      "ab"     "bc"
```

There is also a `plot()` method that works with the object that `glht()` returns that is a bit nicer if you are planning to include the plot in a publication. The comparisons are flagged, making it easier to see which ones are significant. The Ensor–Darl comparison is significant at the $p < .1$ significance level, but we are using the .05 level so we did not include it as a significant difference. The compact letter display gives a letter designation to each group and since we have three groups, they are identified by letters "a", "b," and "c." All of the points that have an "a" underneath them form the "a" group and so on. The same groups are identified as above, but the `cld()` function does it for us. This also makes it easy to see that Darl and Pedernales points are in a single group while Ensor, Travis, and Wells points are in two groups each.

There are other methods for post hoc multiple comparisons and there is a substantial literature comparing different approaches. Most of the methods have been developed to deal with controlled experiments which occur rarely in archaeology except in experimental archaeology. Tukey HSD is one of the few that can handle groups of different sizes and different variances.

As mentioned before, the need to adjust our significance levels for multiple comparisons is not limited to analysis of variance or the Kruskal–Wallis test. Whenever we test multiple statistical hypotheses, we should adjust the p-values for multiple comparisons. It is useful to distinguish between two error rates: comparisonwise and familywise. The first is the significance level for a single hypothesis test and the second is the significance level for a group of tests. For example, if the comparisonwise error rate (significance level) is .05, then the familywise error rate on three tests is .14. The familywise error rate is the probability of making at least one type I error in the group of comparisons. The Tukey HSD test adjusted the comparisons of the groups so that the familywise error rate was .05.

If we are doing a large number of t-tests (e.g., comparing two point types on the basis of length, width, thickness, and weight), one way to deal with the multiple comparisons problem is to select a smaller probability of making a type I error for each test. With a comparisonwise significance level of .01, five tests have a family-wise error rate of .05. At a comparisonwise significance level of .001, 50 tests will have a familywise error rate just below .05. Of course, there is a cost to this approach and that cost is an increase in the type II error rate, the probability of accepting the null hypothesis when it is false (Table 8). Ultimately you will have to weigh the two error rates and make a decision about how to proceed.

The p.adjust() function adjusts p-values for multiple tests. If you have just conducted a series of hypothesis tests such as difference of proportions tests on all of the tool types in two assemblages, you just place all of the p-values in a vector and use p.adjust(). For example, assume you have conducted six t-tests with p-values of .001, .008, .015, .04, .075, and .10. At the .05 comparisonwise signifi-cance level, four of these values are significant. Correcting for multiple comparisons changes that conclusion:

```
> pvals <- c(.001, .008, .015, .04, .075, .10)
> p.adjust(pvals)
[1] 0.006 0.040 0.060 0.120 0.150 0.150
```

This scales up the p-values to adjust for the fact that you have six tests. Now only two are significant at the .05 familywise significance level. The default adjustment uses the Holm (1979) method for adjusting p-values. There are five other meth-ods including the better known Bonferroni correction. The Bonferroni correction is simple to compute by hand, but it is conservative. The Holm method is valid under the same assumptions so it is generally preferable.

BOX 8 ONE-SAMPLE, TWO-SAMPLE, AND PAIRED *T*-TESTS USING FUNCTION `t.test()`

```
t.test(x, y = NULL,
    alternative = c("two.sided", "less", "greater"),
    mu = 0, paired = FALSE, var.equal = FALSE,
    conf.level = 0.95, ...)

t.test(formula, data, subset, na.action, ...)
```

This test performs difference of means or *t*-tests depending on the data received. The common two-sample *t*-test can be specified by providing numeric vectors x and y representing the values for each sample or by using the formula method (numeric vector~factor) where the numeric vector will be divided into two groups using the values of the factor. If the factor has more than two levels, the test will halt and return an error message. By default the function will assume that the variances of the two samples are different (the more conservative approach). To use the equal variances test, set `var.equal=TRUE`.

The one sample *t*-test involves comparing the mean of a numeric vector to a population parameter. For this test, only x is provided.

The paired *t*-test involves comparing the paired differences between two vectors (e.g., a before and after experimental setting). Numeric vectors *x* and *y* must be of the same length and the `paired=TRUE` argument must be set.

The default null hypothesis for all three is that the difference between the means is 0 or the population parameter is 0 (for the one sample test), but you can specify a different null hypothesis by setting the `mu=` argument. The default test is `"two.sided"` assuming that the direction of the difference was not specified, but one sided tests can be specified by setting the `alternative=` argument to `"less"` or `"greater"`. Confidence intervals are provided at the .95 level unless the value is changed using the `conf.level=` argument.

BOX 9 ANALYSIS OF VARIANCE USING aov() AND MULTIPLE COMPARISONS USING TukeyHSD() AND glht()

```
aov(formula, data = NULL, projections = FALSE, qr = TRUE,
    contrasts = NULL, ...)

TukeyHSD(x, which, ordered = FALSE, conf.level = 0.95, ...)

Package multcomp:
glht(model, linfct, ...)
cld(object, level = 0.05, decreasing = FALSE, ...)
```

The `aov()` function fits a traditional analysis of variance model using the linear model function (`lm()`) in order to present the results using the traditional language of the analysis of variance. The function `anova()` is used to compare two nested models and should not be confused with `aov()`.

The analysis of variance is expressed as a formula in the form Response variable ~ Explanatory variable where the Response variable is numeric and the Explanatory variable is a categorical variable (factor). For a simple one-way analysis of variance, you will generally need only the formula and the name of the data frame containing the data. It is also possible to add a `subset=` argument, which will be passed to `lm()` to extract part of the data frame for the analysis.

The function returns a list containing 13 elements, including a section called `model` that includes the data used in the analysis. For a simple one-way analysis of variance, you will not generally use the elements of the list except to produce the summary table with `summary()`.

The null hypothesis for a one-way analysis of variance is that all of the group means are equal. If the null hypothesis is rejected, at least one group mean is different from the others. To identify which groups are significantly different from one another, multiple comparisons analysis tests all of the possible paired comparisons and controls for the familywise error rate. Function `TukeyHSD()` handles this comparison using the Tukey honest significant difference method and creates a summary table which can be passed to plot() for plotting. Setting `ordered=TRUE` sorts the groups by increasing mean value so that all of the differences are positive.

The Tukey's honest significant difference method can also be computed using function `glht()` in package `multcomp`. The `glht()` function provides hypothesis tests and multiple comparisons for various regression models. For one-way analysis of variance, the Tukey test is specified using `linfct=mcp(GroupVar="Tukey")` where the `model` argument is the object returned by `aov()`. The object produced by `glht()` can be used to produce a plot using `plot()` or a compact letter display using `cld()`.

Table 9 *Functions introduced in Chapter 8*

Function	Package	Description
aov	stats	Analysis of variance
boot	boot	Bootstrap replicates of a statistic
boot.ci	boot	Bootsrapped confidence limits
cld	multcomp	Compact letter display
density	stats	Compute kernel density estimate
dt	stats	Density of the *t* distribution
DunnTest	DescTools	Dunn's test of multiple comparisons using rank sums
function	base	Define a new function
glht	multcomp	General linear hypotheses (inc. multiple comparisons)
kruskal.test	stats	Kruskal–Wallis rank sum test
length	base	Get the length of a vector or list
MeanCI	DescTools	Confidence interval for mean
p.adjust	stats	Adjust p-values for multiple comparisons
prop.test	stats	Proportions test
qt	stats	Quantiles of the *t* distribution
rank	base	Rank the values in a vector
replicate	base	Repeat an expression multiple times
return	base	Return a result from a function
rnorm	stats	Generate random numbers from a normal distribution
runif	stats	Generate random numbers from a uniform distribution
shapiro.test	stats	Shapiro–Wilk test of normality
t.test	stats	One- and two-sample *t* test
TukeyHSD	stats	Tukey honest significant difference
var.test	stats	*F* test to compare variances of two samples
wilcox.test	stats	One- and two-sample Wilcoxon test (Mann–Whitney)

Note: Packages `base`, `datasets`, `graphics`, `grDevices`, `methods`, `stats`, and `utils` are automatically loaded when R starts.

9

Relating Variables

In Chapter 8, we used one categorical variable to define groups and examined differences in a numeric variable between the groups. The grouping variable was treated as an explanatory or independent variable while the numeric variable was the response or dependent variable. This relationship was indicated by the fact that the explanatory variable was on the right-hand side of the formula and the response variable was on the left side of the formula (for the Snodgrass example, Area~Segment). This terminology suggests some kind of causal relationship between the variables.

Statistical tests do not tell us which one is which or even if the relationship is causal, but they can draw our attention to the fact that when one variable changes, another one changes as well. Another way of looking at this is to say that one variable allows us to make predictions (or projections or forecasts) about another variable. This chapter focuses on methods we can use to identify variables that vary with one another. In some cases, it is clear which variable is the explanatory variable and which is the response. In other cases, the distinction is irrelevant because the statistic is symmetrical. In looking for relations between variables, we usually have one of two goals. Either we are looking for a measure of association that tells us how strongly two variables co-vary (e.g., correlation) or we are looking for a way to use one variable to make predictions about another variable (e.g., regression).

9.1 CATEGORICAL DATA

When the two variables are categorical, we generally use the Chi-square test to determine if the two variables are independent or associated. If they are independent, knowing the value of one variable does not improve our ability to guess the value of the second variable. Coin tosses are independent. If I toss a coin and the result is heads, it does not improve my ability to predict a second toss of the coin.

This concept of independence underlies the Chi-square test and represents the null hypothesis.

Computing Chi-square involves creating a table of expected values with the same marginal frequencies as the data (row and column sums). If we have a table showing the cross-tabulation of two categorical variables, we want to know if knowing which row an observation is in helps us to predict what column it is in. For example, in the following table, if I know that an observation falls in the first row, can I predict which column it falls in or vice versa? If I can, then the row and column variables are related (associated) in some way. If not, they are independent. To test the null hypothesis that the two variables are independent, we need to construct a table of the frequencies that would be expected if the variables were independent. The following table illustrates the computation for a 3×3 table:

Row Variable	Column Variable			
	Column $j=1$	Column $j=2$	Column $j=3$	
Row $i=1$	y_{11}	y_{12}	y_{13}	$\Sigma y_{1.}$
Row $i=2$	y_{21}	y_{22}	y_{23}	$\Sigma y_{2.}$
Row $i=3$	y_{31}	y_{32}	y_{33}	$\Sigma y_{3.}$
	$\Sigma y_{.1}$	$\Sigma y_{.2}$	$\Sigma y_{.3}$	$\Sigma y_{..}$

$$E\left(y_{ij}\right) = \frac{\Sigma y_{i.} \Sigma y_{.j}}{\Sigma y_{..}}$$

where $E\left(y_{ij}\right)$ is the expected frequency; y_{ij} is the observed frequency in row i, column j; $\Sigma y_{i.}$ is the sum of the frequencies in row i; $\Sigma y_{.j}$ is the sum of the frequencies in column j; and $\Sigma y_{..}$ is the total sum.

Once we have the table of expected values, we compare them to the observed values. If the deviations are too great, we reject the null hypothesis of independence and conclude that the two variables are associated to some degree. The Chi-square statistic is just the sum of the squared deviations between the observed values and the expected values divided by the expected value. We compute the deviation for each cell and sum the results:

$$X^2 = \Sigma \frac{\left(y_{ij} - E\left(y_{ij}\right)\right)^2}{E\left(y_{ij}\right)}$$

where X^2 is the Chi-square statistic; y_{ij} are the observed values; and $E\left(y_{ij}\right)$ are the expected values.

The *p*-value is based on the Chi-square distribution where the degrees of freedom is the number of rows minus 1 times the number of columns minus 1. For a 2×2 table the degrees of freedom is 1 and for a 3×3 table, it is 4.

The Chi-square test assumes that the data being tabulated represent discrete counts and that each observation is independent of the other observations. This can create problems for archaeologists. Many archaeological specimens are fragments of a larger object. Fragments from the same object are not independent of one another. Also, as with most statistical tests, as the sample size increases, smaller deviations from independence become statistically significant. There is no simple way out of this quandary except to be cautious about attaching too much importance to a significant Chi-square test if the data consist of thousands of stone flakes or pottery sherds. For pottery sherds and animal bones, it may be possible to estimate the true sample size with the minimum number of individuals or pots, but this is more difficult for stone flaking debris.

The data set `PitHouses` in package `archdata` contains six categorical variables for each of 45 Late Stone Age pithouses from Arctic Norway (Engelstad, 1988). To start with, we will look for a possible association between pithouse size and depth. We would like to know if larger pithouses are more likely to have deep pits or if depth is independent of house size:

```
> data(PitHouses)
> PitHouses.SxD <- xtabs(~Size+Depth, PitHouses)
> addmargins(PitHouses.SxD)
      Depth
Size       Deep    Shallow       Sum
  Small      18          3        21
  Medium      8         13        21
  Large       1          2         3
  Sum        27         18        45
> (PitHouses.SxD.chi <- chisq.test(PitHouses.SxD))


        Pearson's Chi-squared test

data:  PitHouses.SxD
X-squared = 10.873, df = 2, p-value = 0.004355

Warning message:
In chisq.test(PitHouses.SxD) : Chi-squared approximation may
be incorrect
```

Note that we saved the table as `PitHouses.SxD` and the results of the function `chisq.test()` as `PitHouses.SxD.chi`. After creating the table, we print it using `addmargins()` to get row and column totals. There seems to be a tendency for small pithouses to be deep and medium/large pithouses to be shallow. The *p*-value indicates that we should reject the null hypothesis of independence if we are using a significance level of .05. Notice that there are only three large pithouses. In the row of `Large` pithouses, the cell values are 1 and 2. This can create problems in estimating the Chi-square statistic since the squared deviations are divided by the expected value for the cell. We will check on this shortly by looking at the expected values directly. If some of the expected values are small, it could inflate the value of Chi-square and lead us to reject the null hypothesis when we should accept it (a type I error).

The `chisq.test()` function returns a warning message "Chi-squared approximation may be incorrect." First, note that this was a *warning* not an *error*. A warning means that the function was able to compute a result, but there may be a problem with the results. An error message means that the problem was severe enough that the function could not produce a result. In this case, the warning means that some of the expected cell values are small enough that the Chi-square value could be inflated. An inflated Chi-square produces a smaller *p*-value. That means that our type I error rate (rejecting the null hypothesis when it is correct) is actually larger than it appears to be. Fortunately, `chisq.test()` has some solutions. By default, a continuity correction is added to 2×2 tables that can reduce the degree to which the value is inflated. But our table is 3×2 so that does not help here.

More useful is an option to randomly generate multiple tables with the same marginal values (row and column sums) as ours and computing Chi-square for those randomly generated tables. By default 2,000 tables are generated and the *p*-value is based on this simulation. Also we will look at the expected values directly:

```
> set.seed(42)
> chisq.test(PitHouses.SxD, simulate.p.value=TRUE)

	Pearson's Chi-squared test with simulated p-value
	(based on 2000 replicates)

data:  PitHouses.SxD
X-squared = 10.873, df = NA, p-value = 0.003998
```

```
> PitHouses.SxD.chi$expected
          Depth
Size       Deep    Shallow
  Small    12.6        8.4
  Medium   12.6        8.4
  Large     1.8        1.2
```

In this case the *p*-value increases slightly so the small expected values have not inflated the Chi-square value by very much. We would still reject the null hypothesis that the pithouse size and depth are independent. Looking at the expected values, we see that two are less than 2 (both in the Large row). In general, we want the expected values to be greater than 5 (some authors say 3 but R is more conservative). If you compare the expected and observed tables, you will see that the expected table predicts 12.6 small deep pithouses, but there are 18 and it predicts 8.4 medium shallow pithouses, but there are 13.

The chisq.test() function returns a list that contains a great deal of information, which is why we saved the results. Those results include the original data, the expected values, the residuals (the difference between the observed and expected value divided by the square root of the expected value), and standardized residuals (Box 10). If we square the residuals and sum them over the table, we get the Chi-square value:

```
> PitHouses.SxD.chi$residuals
          Depth
Size              Deep      Shallow
  Small       1.5212777   -1.8631770
  Medium     -1.2959032    1.5871508
  Large      -0.5962848    0.7302967
> sum(PitHouses.SxD.chi$residuals^2)
[1] 10.87302
```

The residuals are a gauge of which cell values diverge the most from the expected values. The largest residual (−1.86) is for small shallow pithouses.

Another test for independence is Fisher's exact test. It is usually recommended for 2×2 tables with small sample sizes where Chi-square values might be inflated. The R version runs on larger tables and larger sample sizes so it is an alternative test in many situations.

```
> fisher.test(PitHouses.SxD)

        Fisher's Exact Test for Count Data
```

```
data:  PitHouses.SxD
p-value = 0.003027
alternative hypothesis: two.sided
```

Both tests agree that we should reject the null hypothesis. It appears that smaller pithouses are more likely to be deep and medium and large pithouses are more likely to be shallow. While the Chi-square and Fisher's exact tests let us evaluate a null hypothesis of independence, they do not tell us how strong the relationship is. There are many measures of association: some applicable to categorical variables, some to ordinal (rank) variables, and some applicable to interval or ratio variables. Ordinal and interval measures can be used with dichotomous data so we can use the Assocs() function in package DescTools to give us an extensive list of choices.

```
> library(DescTools)
> options(scipen=10)
> Assocs(PitHouses.SxD)
                           estimate     lwr.ci       upr.ci
Phi Coeff.                   0.4916        -            -
Contingency Coeff.           0.4411        -            -
Cramer V                     0.4916      0.1600       0.7656
Goodman Kruskal Gamma        0.7546      0.4767       1.0000
Kendall Tau-b                0.4686      0.2262       0.7111
Stuart Tau-c                 0.4859      0.2324       0.7394
Somers D C|R                 0.4339      0.2044       0.6634
Somers D R|C                 0.5062      0.2036       0.8088
Pearson Correlation          0.4603      0.1928       0.6641
Spearman Correlation         0.4813      0.2186       0.6789
Lambda C|R                   0.3333      0.0000       0.7689
Lambda R|C                   0.4167      0.1672       0.6662
Lambda sym                   0.3810      0.0752       0.6867
Uncertainty Coeff. C|R       0.1918     -0.0086       0.3921
Uncertainty Coeff. R|C       0.1447     -0.0090       0.2985
Uncertainty Coeff. sym       0.1650     -0.0085       0.3384
Mutual Information           0.1862        -            -
```

After loading the package, we use the options() function to set scipen=10. Without this, R will display all of the results using scientific notation so that the phi coefficient would be printed as 4.9160e-01. By changing the default value of 0 to 10, non-zero values will have to be more than 10 decimal places before R switches to scientific notation. The `Assocs()` function wraps together several association measures for simplicity, but normally you should just pick the ones you want to use and use the specific functions (e.g., `Phi()` for the Phi coefficient).

For categorical variables the Phi coefficient, the contingency coefficient, and Cramer's V (along with Yule's Q) are the traditional measures. They vary from 0 to 1, with 1 being the strongest relationship and 0 being complete independence, but values in between have no clear interpretation so they are useful only for comparing one table of the same size to another. The Phi coefficient is the square root of Chi-square divided by the number of observations $\phi = \sqrt{X^2/n}$ where $n = \Sigma y_{..}$ as defined above.

The Phi coefficient does not reach the maximum value of 1 if the table does not have the same number of rows and columns or if the row and column sums are not equal. Cramer's V adjusts the Phi coefficient by the square root of one less than the smaller of the number of rows or columns ($V = \phi / \sqrt{\min(cols-1, rows-1)}$). The contingency coefficient adjusts the Chi-square value differently, but also does not reach 1 under a number of situations ($C = \sqrt{X^2/(n+X^2)}$). You can see that the values for the first three rows are about the same, halfway between 0 and 1 which suggests an association between the two variables.

The next block of measures, Goodman and Kruskal's Gamma, Kendall Tau-b, Stuart Tau-c, and the Somers Delta, are designed for ordinal data. These measures compare pairs of observations (e.g., (x_1, y_1) and (x_2, y_2)). If $x_1 > x_2$ and $y_1 > y_2$, then the pair is considered concordant since the first observation is larger for both variables. The same is true if $x_1 < x_2$ and $y_1 < y_2$ since the first observation is smaller for both variables. If $x_1 < x_2$ and $y_1 > y_2$ or if $x_1 > x_2$ and $y_1 < y_2$, then the pair is considered discordant. If $x_1 = x_2$ or $y_1 = y_2$, the pair includes a tie. If most of the pairs are concordant, then as one observation is greater on one measurement, it is also greater on the second measurement so there is a positive association between the variables. If n is the number of observations, then $\frac{1}{2}n(n-1)$ is the number of comparisons. If n is 45, there are 990 comparisons and if n is 100, there are 4,950 comparisons. If most of the pairs are discordant, then as one observation is greater on one measurement, it is smaller on the second measurement or vice versa and there is a negative association between the variables. If the number of concordant and discordant pairs is about the same, there is no association between the two variables. The various measures differ in how they combine concordant and discordant counts into a measure, how they adjust the measure for tied observations, and whether they treat rows and columns symmetrically. Since pithouse size and depth are ordinal, these measures are appropriate and indicate that there is a significant positive association between pithouse size and depth. That may seem backward, but the order of the depth categories is Deep, Shallow, so larger pithouses are more shallow. If we reversed the categories, the association would be negative. For tabular data like these, Stuart's tau-c is probably the best choice.

Next are the Pearson and Spearman correlation measures for ordinal, interval, or ratio data. We will describe them in the next section.

The Lambda coefficients measure the proportional reduction in the error of using the row variable to predict the column variable or vice versa. The value of .33 means that knowing the row (`Size`) allows us to make 33 percent fewer errors predicting the column (`Depth`). The measure is asymmetric so, in this case, we make 42 percent fewer errors predicting `Size` from `Depth`. Lambda can be computed on tables of any size and the sampling distribution is known so that we can place confidence limits around our estimate.

To compute Lambda, imagine that we need to predict if a house is deep or shallow using what we know about our sample of 45 pithouses. We need a table with marginal totals to see how the measure is computed:

```
> addmargins(PitHouses.SxD)
          Depth
Size      Deep    Shallow    Sum
  Small     18          3     21
  Medium     8         13     21
  Large      1          2      3
  Sum       27         18     45
```

Without knowing about the size of the pithouse, we look at the column totals. Since 27 are deep and only 18 are shallow, we always predict the pithouse is deep and make 18 errors (45 – 27). But knowing pithouse size leads to fewer errors. If we know that the pithouse is small, we predict deep and make three errors (21 – 18). If we know the pithouse is medium, we predict it is shallow and make eight errors (21 – 13). If it is large, we also predict shallow and make one error (3 – 2). So knowing the pithouse size leads to 12 errors, which is fewer than 18 by 33 percent ((18 – 12)/18 = .333). If we predict pithouse size without knowing depth, we predict they are small or medium and make 24 errors (45 – 21). If the pithouse is deep, we predict small and make 9 errors (27 – 18) and if it is shallow, we predict medium and make 5 errors (18 – 13). So knowing pithouse depth leads to 14 errors, which is fewer than 24 by 42 percent ((24-14)/24 = .417).

The uncertainty and mutual information coefficients use the concepts of information and entropy so the values produced have meaning in terms of those concepts. Most archaeologists will probably find the Lambda coefficients easier to interpret. While Chi-square tells us if two variables are independent, measures of association tell us how strongly related they are. With large sample sizes, we can often reject the null hypothesis of independence, but our measure of association suggests they have very little substantive influence on one another.

9.2 NUMERIC DATA – ASSOCIATION

If the data are ordinal or interval, measures of association are more meaningful. The three most commonly used measures are the Pearson product–moment correlation coefficient for interval and ratio variables and Spearman's and Kendall's correlation coefficients for rank or ordinal data. These correlation coefficients range from –1.0 to +1.0, indicating how well one variable can predict the other variable. Positive correlations imply that as one variable increases, the other variable increases. Negative correlations imply that as one variable increases, the other variable decreases. These three measures are symmetric so the correlation of x with y is the same as y with x.

The Pearson product–moment correlation (also known as Pearson's r) measures linear correlation between two variables. If we plot the two variables on a scatterplot and the points lie exactly along a straight line, Pearson's r is +1 if the line increases from left to right and –1 if it decreases from left to right. If the points are scattered along to the line but not directly on it, Pearson's r measures how close they are to the line. The square of the Pearson correlation coefficient is the proportion of the variance in one variable that can be explained by variation in the other variable. The formula for Pearson's r sums the deviations of x and y pairs from their respective means and divides that sum by the product of their individual standard deviations:

$$r_{xy} = \frac{\Sigma(x_i - \bar{x})(y_i - \bar{y})}{\sqrt{\Sigma(x_i - \bar{x})^2}\sqrt{\Sigma(y_i - \bar{y})^2}}$$

where x_i, y_i are values of the two variables for a particular observation and $\bar{x}$, $\bar{y}$ are the means for each variable. Note that in the numerator the mean deviations are not squared so that if x and y are both greater or less than their respective means, the value is positive and if one is greater than its mean and one is less, the value is negative.

Load the DartPoints data set to compute the Pearson correlation coefficient between Length and Width:

```
> data(DartPoints)
> options(digits=3)
> with(DartPoints, cor(Length, Width))
[1] 0.769
> with(DartPoints, cor.test(Length, Width))
```

```
        Pearson's product-moment correlation

data:  Length and Width
t = 10, df = 90, p-value <2e-16
alternative hypothesis: true correlation is not equal to 0
95 percent confidence interval:
 0.669 0.842
sample estimates:
  cor
0.769
```

The correlation between dart point length and width is +.769, which means that as a point gets longer, it also gets wider. The square of the correlation coefficient is .591 so about 59 percent of the variability in width is "explained" by length or vice versa. But it also means that 41 percent of dart point width is not explained by length. The `cor()` function provides the correlation between two variables or a correlation matrix showing the correlation between all pairs of variables when given a matrix rather than two vectors. The `cor.test()` function tests the null hypothesis that the correlation coefficient is 0. In this case, the p-value is essentially 0 and we get a 95 percent confidence interval for the correlation that ranges from .67 to .84. Both functions can also compute the Kendall and Spearman rank correlations, which are appropriate for ordinal or rank data.

Computing the Kendall rank correlation (also known as Kendall's tau) involves counting concordant and discordant pairs as described in the previous section. The formula for Kendall's tau subtracts the number of discordant pairs from the number of concordant pairs and divides by the total number of pairs:

$$\tau_A = \frac{n_C - n_D}{\frac{1}{2}n(n-1)}$$

where n_C is the number of concordant pairs; n_D is the number of discordant pairs; and n is the number of observations.

This version of the formula assumes that there are no tied values within x or y. When there are tied values, the denominator is adjusted for the number of ties and often referred to as Kendall's tau-b (τ_B). The functions `cor()` and `cor.test()` in package `stats` automatically use tau-b if there are ties in the data (as there are in this example) and `KendallTauB()` in `DescTools` provides confidence intervals:

```
> with(DartPoints, cor.test(Length, Width, method="kendall"))

        Kendall's rank correlation tau
```

```
data:   Length and Width
z = 8, p-value = 9e-15
alternative hypothesis: true tau is not equal to 0
sample estimates:
  tau
0.555


> with(DartPoints, KendallTauB(Length, Width, conf.
  level=.95))
 tau_b lwr.ci ups.ci
 0.555  0.466  0.644
```

If the data come from a table where there are only a few categories and the number of rows and columns are different, there is a third version of the measure sometimes called Kendall's tau-c, but more properly called Stuart's tau-c. It is available in the function `StuartTauC()` in package `DescTools`.

Kendall's tau is somewhat complicated to compute, but has the straightforward interpretation that it is a measure of the predominance of concordant or discordant pairs so it is a measure of how well we can use the order of the values in length to predict the order of values in width (or vice versa). Spearman's rho is easier to compute, but does not have a straightforward interpretation:

$$\rho = \frac{6\sum\left(xr_i - yr_i\right)^2}{n\left(n^2 - 1\right)}$$

where xr_i are the x values that have been converted to ranks; yr_i are the y values that have been converted to ranks; and n is the number of values.

Actually it turns out that Spearman's rho is exactly the same as converting x and y to ranks and then computing the Pearson's r, except that the interpretation of square of the Pearson's r no longer relates to the percentage of variance explained since variance is not defined for rank variables. The functions `cor()` and `cor.test()` compute Spearman's rho and the second one provides a test of the null hypothesis, but `SpearmanRho()` in package `DescTools` provides confidence intervals:

```
> with(DartPoints, cor.test(Length, Width,
  method="spearman"))

        Spearman's rank correlation rho
```

```
data:  Length and Width
S = 30000, p-value <2e-16
alternative hypothesis: true rho is not equal to 0
sample estimates:
  rho
0.747


Warning message:
In cor.test.default(Length, Width, method = "spearman") :
  Cannot compute exact p-value with ties
> with(DartPoints, SpearmanRho(Length, Width, conf.
  level=.95))
   rho lwr.ci ups.ci
 0.747  0.640  0.826
```

We get a warning that there are ties in the data so that the *p*-value cannot be computed exactly, but it is so close to 0 that the association is clearly significantly different from 0. Since we are printing the results with three significant digits, the value for *S* is rounded (it is actually 31754). Normally you will not need this value, but if you do, just reset the digits value to the default of 7.

Comparing all three, the Pearson correlation is the highest (+0.769) while Spearman's rank correlation is slightly lower (+0.747), and Kendall's rank correlation is substantially lower (+0.555). This is not unusual. If you do get Spearman or Kendall correlations that are higher than Pearson, it often means that the relationship between the two variables is nonlinear.

If we want to look at patterns of correlations between several variables, `cor()` will produce a correlation matrix:

```
> vars <-  c("Length", "Width", "Thickness", "H.Length",
  "B.Width")
> cor(DartPoints[, vars], use="complete.obs")
            Length    Width  Thickness  H.Length   B.Width
Length       1.000    0.783      0.591     0.542    -0.284
Width        0.783    1.000      0.513     0.533    -0.241
Thickness    0.591    0.513      1.000     0.551    -0.206
H.Length     0.542    0.533      0.551     1.000    -0.506
B.Width     -0.284   -0.241     -0.206    -0.506     1.000
```

This gives us the correlations between five different variables in a matrix. The matrix is symmetrical since the correlation of B.Width with Length is the same as the correlation of `Length` with `B.Width`. The argument `use= "complete. obs"` is necessary since there are 22 missing values for `B.Width`. Without this argument all of the correlations involving `B.Width` are missing values (NA). The alternative is `use="pairwise.complete.obs"`, which excludes an observation only if it has a missing value on the variables being correlated. That means that the number of observations is different for different values in the correlation matrix.

The first four variables show modest positive correlations with one another. For measurements that reflect the size of an artifact, this is typical. As the length of a dart point increases, so does the width, thickness, and haft length. But basal width does not follow this pattern. In fact, it shows a small negative correlation with the other measurements, suggesting that basal width tends to get smaller with increases in the other measures, especially haft length.

This discrepancy from our expectations is interesting. First, we should check to see if the correlation is significant before trying to explain it. Second, we need to remember that the `DartPoints` data set includes five different point types and the correlations are an amalgam of those types. We should check the correlation matrices of each type separately to see if this relationship holds for all of the types. In Chapter 3, we used the `split()` and `lapply()` functions to produce descriptive statistics for each point type. The same approach would give us correlation matrices for each type, but even simpler is to use the `by()` function:

```
> by(DartPoints[, vars], DartPoints$Name, cor, use="complete.
  obs")
  . . . output not shown . . .
```

This will generate five correlation matrices, one for each point type. They are quite different across the point types. To determine the statistical significance of the correlations, we can use the `rcorr.adjust()` function in package `RcmdrMisc`:

```
> library(RcmdrMisc)
> rcorr.adjust(DartPoints[, vars], use="pairwise.complete.
  obs")
```

```
Pearson correlations:
          Length   Width   Thickness   H.Length   B.Width
Length    1.000    0.769     0.589       0.509     -0.284
Width     0.769    1.000     0.546       0.496     -0.241
Thickness 0.589    0.546     1.000       0.467     -0.206
```

H.Length	0.509	0.496	0.467	1.000	-0.506
B.Width	-0.284	-0.241	-0.206	-0.506	1.000

Number of observations:

	Length	Width	Thickness	H.Length	B.Width
Length	91	91	91	91	69
Width	91	91	91	91	69
Thickness	91	91	91	91	69
H.Length	91	91	91	91	69
B.Width	69	69	69	69	69

Pairwise two-sided p-values:

	Length	Width	Thickness	H.Length	B.Width
Length		<.0001	<.0001	<.0001	0.0181
Width	<.0001		<.0001	<.0001	0.0463
Thickness	<.0001	<.0001		<.0001	0.0892
H.Length	<.0001	<.0001	<.0001		<.0001
B.Width	0.0181	0.0463	0.0892	<.0001	

Adjusted p-values (Holm's method)

	Length	Width	Thickness	H.Length	B.Width
Length		<.0001	<.0001	<.0001	0.0542
Width	<.0001		<.0001	<.0001	0.0926
Thickness	<.0001	<.0001		<.0001	0.0926
H.Length	<.0001	<.0001	<.0001		<.0001
B.Width	0.0542	0.0926	0.0926	<.0001	

This time we used `use="pairwise.complete.obs"` to show the difference. The correlations involving B.Width will be the same as before, but the other correlations will be slightly different. We also get four matrices instead of one. The first is the correlation matrix. The second is the number of observations that were used for each correlation. If we had used `use="complete.obs"`, this would be a single line telling how many cases were used. The third matrix gives the p-values for each correlation. The only one that is not significantly different from 0 at the .05 level is B.Width with Thickness. But the table lists values for 10 different correlation values (and therefore 10 tests of the null hypothesis) so we have a multiple comparisons problem. The fourth matrix addresses this concern by showing adjusted p-values. This adjustment affects the correlations between B.Width and Length and B.Width and Width, which are now not significant.

We have been working with the entire sample of `DartPoints`. If we want to look at the correlations within types, we can use `by(DartPoints[, vars], DartPoints$Name, rcorr.adjust, use="pairwise.complete. obs")`, but the sample sizes within each type are so small that fewer of the correlations will be significant.

9.3 NUMERIC DATA – REGRESSION

Linear regression is a statistical technique that allows us to use one variable to predict another. In computing correlation coefficients, we do not need to distinguish between explanatory (independent) and response (dependent) variables because the coefficient is symmetric. When we use one variable to predict another, the analysis is no longer symmetric. In classical least squares regression, using length to estimate width is not the same as using width to estimate length because of the way we measure the errors. When we estimate width from length, we assume that length is measured without error so that we look at errors in width as deviations from the estimate of width that we get using length. In this example, there is no clear answer to the question of which should be the explanatory (independent) variable because both length and width are affected by a third variable, size, that we can only measure indirectly. In other cases, one variable is logically prior to the other variable. For example, the presence of decorated ceramics in a house at the Snodgrass site could be caused by the location or size of the house since the house must be constructed in a particular place before it can have any contents. It would not make sense to think of decorated ceramics as causing the location of the house.

Linear regression describes the relationship between two variables in the form of an equation that predicts the one variable (*Y*, response) by multiplying a second variable (*X*, explanatory) by a constant value and then adding another constant value (Predicted *Y* = a + b*X). To describe the line, we need to pick values for the two constants, a and b. The first constant, a, is called the *y*-intercept because it is the value of Predicted *Y* when the *X*=0. The second constant, b, is called the slope because is describes how much Predicted *Y* increases (or decreases if the value is negative) for every one unit increase in *X*. We are looking for the line that minimizes the sum of the squared differences between *Y*Predicted and *Y* (i.e., the sum of (*Y* – Predicted *Y*)²). The line also passes through the point marked by the mean value of *X* and the mean value of *Y*:

$$b = \frac{\sum (x_i - \bar{x})(y_i - \bar{y})}{\sum (x_i - \bar{x})^2}$$

$$a = \bar{y} - b\bar{x}$$

$$y_i = a + bx_i + \epsilon_i$$

where x_i, y_i are values of the two variables for a particular observation; $\bar{x}$, $\bar{y}$ are the means for each variable; ϵ_i is the error associated with the estimate of y_i.

Note that in the numerator the mean deviations are not squared so that if x and y are both greater or less than their respective means, the value is positive and if one is greater than its mean and one is less, the value is negative. We can estimate (predict) a value of y_i using the equation $a + bx_i$ but this estimate will be exact only if the correlation coefficient is +1 or –1. Otherwise we will miss the value of y_i by the amount ϵ_i. Our least squares formula guarantees that $\sum\epsilon_i^2$ will be as small as possible.

To illustrate the basics of linear regression, we will use the Darl points from the `DartPoints` data set. We will compute the correlation between `Length` and `Width` and compare their distributions to a normal distribution before computing the least squares regression:

```
> Darl <- subset(DartPoints, subset=Name=="Darl",
  select=c("Length", "Width"))
> with(Darl, cor.test(Length, Width))

        Pearson's product-moment correlation

data:  Length and Width
t = 3.5818, df = 26, p-value = 0.001377
alternative hypothesis: true correlation is not equal to 0
95 percent confidence interval:
 0.2568034 0.7805078
sample estimates:
      cor
0.5748093


> scatterplot(Width~Length, Darl, smooth=FALSE)
```

After extracting the Darl points and variables `Length` and `Width` from `DartPoints`, we use `cor.test()` to look at the Pearson product–moment correlation between length and width. The value of .57 is significantly different from 0 with a p-value of .0014. Then we use `scatterplot()` to look at the scatter of points and the distributions of each variable (Figure 38a). The scatterplot also shows us the regression line for the data and we can see that there is a fair amount of scatter

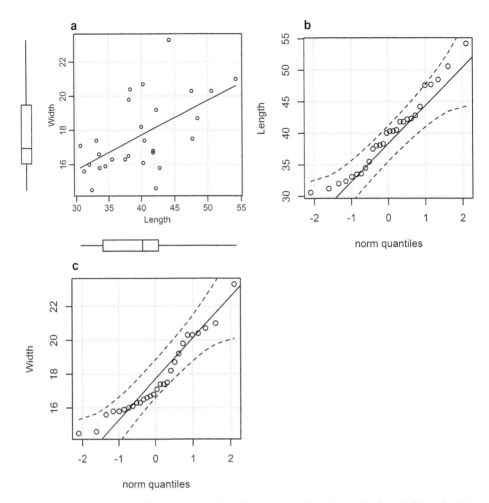

FIGURE 38 Plot of length and width of Darl points (a). QQ plots for length (b) and width (c) of Darl points.

around the line. In particular, the middle of the data range is more variable than either end. The box plots suggest that the distributions are slightly asymmetric so we use qqPlot() and shapiro.test() to see if we need to consider transforming the variables (Chapter 6):

```
> with(Darl, qqPlot(Length))
> with(Darl, qqPlot(Width))
> with(Darl, shapiro.test(Length))

        Shapiro-Wilk normality test
```

```
data:  Length
W = 0.95877, p-value = 0.3258

> with(Darl, shapiro.test(Width))

      Shapiro-Wilk normality test

data:  Width
W = 0.92265, p-value = 0.04035
```

The QQ plots (Figure 38b,c) indicate that the two variables are reasonably normal although the Shapiro–Wilk normality test produces a p-value of .04 for `Width` probably because although the points stay within the dashed lines, very few of them are close to the solid line. Next we use `lm()` to fit the linear model and then `summary()` and `plot()` to examine the results (Box 11).

```
> Darl.lm <- lm(Width~Length, Darl)
> summary(Darl.lm)

Call:
lm(formula = Width ~ Length, data = Darl)

Residuals:
     Min       1Q    Median       3Q       Max
   -3.569   -1.007   -0.377    1.016     4.724

Coefficients:
             Estimate  Std. Error  t value  Pr(>|t|)
(Intercept)   9.58124     2.28481    4.193  0.000282   ***
Length        0.20351     0.05682    3.582  0.001377   **
---
Signif. codes:  0 `***' 0.001 `**' 0.01 `*' 0.05 `.' 0.1 ` ' 1

Residual standard error: 1.823 on 26 degrees of freedom
Multiple R-squared:  0.3304,   Adjusted R-squared:  0.3047
F-statistic: 12.83 on 1 and 26 DF,  p-value: 0.001377
> oldp <- par(mar=c(3.1, 3.5, 2.1, 1.5), las=1, mgp=c(1.8,
  .6, 0),
+    mfrow=c(2, 2))
> plot(Darl.lm, ask=FALSE)
> par(oldp)
```

The (Intercept) estimate is 9.58 (the *y*-intercept or a in the equation above) and the *t*-test indicates that the value is significantly different from 0. This is not a test of the overall regression, just the intercept, and we might wonder how a dart point that has a length of 0 can be 9.58 mm wide. This may indicate that the relationship is not linear, but within the range of our data values for length (30–55 mm) it is essentially linear. The test of the significance for the slope value for Length does evaluate the significance of the linear relationship and the value of .204 is significantly different from 0 with a *p*-value of .0014. The slope (*b* in the equation above) indicates that we predict an increase in width of .2 mm for every increase in length of 1 mm. The *R*-squared value of .3304 is just the square of the correlation coefficient and the F-statistic produces the same p-value as the t-statistic for Length.

The plot() function produces four diagnostic plots for the regression analysis and you usually have to press Enter on the keyboard to cycle through them. However, we used par() to shrink the outside margins; plot the *y*-axis labels horizontally; close up the space between the axis titles, labels, and tick marks; and put all four plots on a single page (Figure 39a–d). The plot of "Residuals vs Fitted" shows that while the variability in the residuals (the difference between the observed width and the fitted or estimated width) is relatively small at either end of the distribution of the fitted values (the predictions of Width based on Length), but large in the middle. You could use the command Darl[c("12", "24", "27"),] to see the values for these specimens.

The "Normal Q-Q" plot compares the residuals to a normal distribution and the same points are noted as deviating from the expected normal distribution for residuals. The "Scale-Location" plot shows even more clearly that the variability in the residuals is greater in the middle of the distribution. The line across the plot would be horizontal if the variability was constant across the fitted values. This is a condition known as heteroscedasticity. It might be possible to correct the problem using a transformation of the Length and Width variables. Finally, the "Residuals vs Leverage" plot tells us if some of the observations are having excessive influence on the estimation of the regression coefficients. For more details on regression diagnostics and what they mean, see Fox and Weisberg (2011: 285–328) and Faraway (2002).

We can also look at the confidence and prediction bands around the regression line. The **confidence band** incorporates the confidence intervals of the intercept and the slope to define an area on the plot that contains the population regression line *x* percent of the time where *x* percent is the confidence limit (e.g., 95 percent). The **prediction band** involves the prediction of a single observation (e.g., what is the expected width of a Darl point that is 45 mm long). Both of these intervals will be

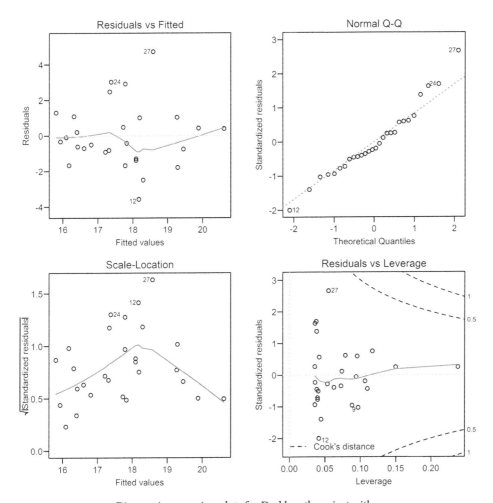

FIGURE 39 Diagnostic regression plots for Darl length against with.

larger when the *R*-square value is small (as in this case) and smaller when it is large. To predict a single value, we use the `predict()` function:

```
> predict(Darl.lm, data.frame(Length=45), level=.95,
  interval="prediction")
    fit  lwr  upr
1 18.7 14.9 22.6
```

The result indicates that a Darl point that is 45 mm long should be 18.7 mm wide with a 95 percent prediction band between 14.9 and 22.6 mm. We can plot the confidence and prediction bands for the regression line as follows (Figure 40):

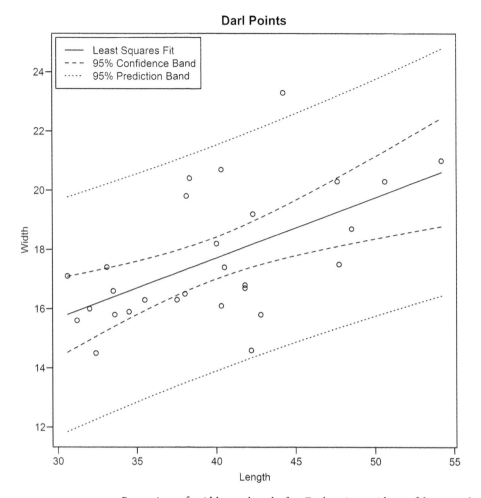

FIGURE 40 Regression of width on length for Darl points with confidence and prediction bands.

```
> xvals <- seq(min(Darl$Length), max(Darl$Length), length.
  out=100)
> FitCL <- predict(Darl.lm, data.frame(Length=xvals),
+    level=.95, interval="confidence")
> FitPL <- predict(Darl.lm, data.frame(Length=xvals),
+    level=.95, interval="prediction")
> plot(Width~Length, Darl, ylim=range(FitPL), main="Darl
  Points")
> matlines(xvals, FitCL, lty=c(1, 2, 2), col=c("black",
  "blue", "blue"))
```

```
> matlines(xvals, FitPL[,2:3], lty=c(3, 3), col=c("red",
  "red"))
> legend("topleft", c("Least Squares Fit",
+    "95% Confidence Band", "95% Prediction Band"),
+    inset=.01, lty=c(1, 2, 3), col=c("black", "blue",
  "red"))
```

The first command creates a vector of 100 numbers that span the range of the Length values. Since the confidence bands are curves, we need about 100 values to plot a smooth curve. The second and third commands compute the Width values for the regression line and the upper and lower confidence and prediction bands. Then we create a plot of Length against Width but we increase the y-axis (Width) limits to fit the prediction bands (we get the maximum and minimum values for the prediction bands with range(FitPL)). Next we add the regression line and the confidence limits using matlines() and set line types and colors for them. Then we add the prediction bands and a legend. The population regression line should fall within the dashed lines while a prediction for any single point is subject to the larger dotted lines, which very nearly cover the entire range of observed widths. The regression may be significant, but it will not help us predict width very precisely.

If there are extreme values in the data, it may be useful to use a robust linear regression model instead of classical least squares regression. There are a number of approaches to robust regression in R. The rlm() function in package MASS computes a linear model by robust regression using an M estimator (Venables and Ripley, 2002: 156–163). Tukey (1977) proposed a simple approach described variously as a "Tukey line," "Tukey's resistant line," or the "median-median line" (Hartwig and Dearing, 1979; Walters et al., 2006). It is available in R using the line() function (not to be confused with the lines() function that draws lines on a plot). If you try either of these, you will see that the result is not very different since the outliers are in the middle of the distribution and they offset one another.

Linear regression by least squares is the best way to construct an equation for predicting values of Y given values of X if the relationship between the variables is a straight line. It also provides a test of the significance of the slope value that provides a test of the null hypothesis that there is no relationship between the two variables. But regression by least squares is not symmetrical. The regression line predicting Y from X is not the inverse of the line predicting X from Y and it can underestimate the slope value between two variables, especially when the correlation between the two variables is low. If we are interested in allometric relationships (how variables change as overall size changes), two other methods of line-fitting, major axis (MA) and standardized major axis (SMA) are worth considering (Warton, et al., 2006). Also called type 2 regression, these methods are symmetrical and measure error on both variables (not just on *Y*). In R these line-fitting methods are provided by package smatr.

Other expansions of linear regression include adding additional explanatory variables (multiple regression), using categorical explanatory variables, and predicting dichotomous or Poisson variables (generalized linear models). We will consider several of these expansions in the Chapter 10. Nonlinear regression will be illustrated briefly in Chapter 18.

BOX 10 CHI-SQUARE TESTS, THE chisq.test() FUNCTION

```
chisq.test(x, y = NULL, correct = TRUE,
        p = rep(1/length(x), length(x)), rescale.p = FALSE,
        simulate.p.value = FALSE, B = 2000)
```

Performs the Chi-squared contingency table tests and goodness-of-fit tests. If x is a matrix or a table with at least two rows and two columns (for example produced using table() or xtabs()), the function computes the standard Chi-square contingency table test. The values in the matrix must be non-negative integers. If x and y are vectors of the same length, they are converted to factors to construct a contingency table and then compute the standard Chi-square contingency table test.

Finally, if x is a vector of non-negative integers, then a goodness-of-fit test is conducted using p to compute the expected values for each category. If *p* is not provided, the default is to assume equal counts in each category. If *p* is provided, it must be the same length as *x*. The values must be positive and should sum to 1 (although setting rescale.p=TRUE will cause the function to compute proportions from the vector by dividing each value by the sum).

If the table has two rows and two columns, the function uses a continuity correction of subtracting .5 from the absolute value of the difference between the observed and expected cell values. This lowers the Chi-square estimate (i.e., makes it more conservative). Set correct=FALSE to get the actual Chi-square value.

If there are small observed values (e.g., less than 3), the function will print a warning that the *p*-value may be an overestimate. In that situation, it is preferable to use Monte Carlo simulation of random tables with the same marginal values to estimate the *p*-value. Setting `simulate.p.value=TRUE` performs this test using 2,000 simulated tables. The number of tables can be changed using the `B=` argument.

The function returns a list of class "htest" with nine components. The first five summarize the results: `statistic` (the Chi-squared test statistic), `parameter` (degrees of freedom), `p.value` (the *p*-value for the test), `method` (Pearson's Chi-squared test and whether the *p*-value was simulated), and `data.name` (the name of the data set used). The last four components are tables: `observed` (the original counts), `expected` (the expected counts under the null hypothesis of no association), `residuals` (the Pearson residuals (observed − expected)/sqrt(expected)), and `stdres` (standardized residuals.

BOX 11   LINEAR LEAST SQUARES REGRESSION, THE `lm()` FUNCTION

```
lm(formula, data, subset, weights, na.action,
   method = "qr", model = TRUE, x = FALSE, y = FALSE,
   qr = TRUE,
   singular.ok = TRUE, contrasts = NULL, offset, ...)
```

The function is used to is used to fit linear models using least squares. The first three arguments specify the formula and data used to fit the linear model. The `formula=` argument will generally be of the form `Y~X1+X2+X3+`... where `Y` is the dependent or response variable and `X#` are the independent or explanatory variables, `data=` is the name of the data frame containing the variables, and `subset=` allows restricting the model to part of the data. The `weights=` argument allows differential weighting of the observations (weighted least squares).

The default behavior is to drop cases with missing values on any of the variables (i.e., `na.action=na.omit`) and you should not generally alter this argument. The remaining arguments relate to what results should be returned by the function and some technical settings.

The function returns a list of at least 12 components depending on the settings of some of the arguments. Some of these provide details of the model and formula and others provide details of the mathematical process used to estimate the model (QR decomposition). Generally the ones of most use will be `coefficients` (the intercept and slope coefficients), `residuals` (the difference between the observed value of the response/dependent variable and its fitted/

predicted value), `fitted.values` (the fitted or predicted values), and `df.residual` (the degrees of freedom). The `print()` function returns only the model coefficients.

Missing from these returned values are the statistics we would normally look at to evaluate the significance of the model and the coefficients. These are computed by passing the `lm()` results to `summary()`. The summary function for linear models (`?summary.lm`) computes the regression results table showing the overall significance of the model and the slope and intercept values and the multiple R-squared value.

There are a number of other functions that use the object returned by `lm()` including `coef()` to get the coefficients, `deviance()` to get the sum of the squared deviations from the model, `fitted()` to get the fitted/predicted values, `confint()` to get the confidence intervals of the intercept and slope parameters, `predict()` to use the linear regression model to predict values based on new data, and `residuals()` to get the residuals.

Table 10 *Functions introduced in Chapter 9*

Function	Package	Description
Assocs	DescTools	Compute various measures of association
chisq.test	stats	Compute the Chi-square statistic
coef	stats	Return regression coefficients
confint	stats	Confidence intervals for coefficients of a model
cor.test	stats	Confidence interval and significance of a correlation
deviance	stats	Compute sum of squared deviations from model
fisher.test	stats	Compute Fisher's exact test
fitted	stats	Compute predicted values from a model
KendallTauB	DescTools	Compute Kendall's tau-b
line	stats	Tukey line
lm	stats	Linear regression with least squares
max	base	Maximum value
min	base	Minimum value
rcorr.adjust	RcmdrMisc	Adjust *p*-values for multiple comparisons

Table 10 (*cont.*)

Function	Package	Description
residuals	stats	Return the residuals from a model (e.g., regression)
rlm	MASS	Robust linear regression
SpearmanRho	DescTools	Compute Spearman's rho
StuartTauC	DescTools	Compute Stuart's tau-c for tabular data

Note: Packages `base`, `datasets`, `graphics`, `grDevices`, `methods`, `stats`, and `utils` are automatically loaded when R starts.

Multivariate Methods

Multiple Regression and Generalized Linear Models

Multiple regression is a straightforward expansion of bivariate regression by increasing the number of explanatory variables. Jointly those variables may provide better estimates of the response variable. Traditional linear regression has been expanded over the last few years by the development of generalized linear models that allow the use of a wider range of measurement scales and response variables that are dichotomous (logistic regression) or discrete (log-linear models and Poisson regression). We can also specify models that include explanatory variables that are dichotomous and categorical.

10.1 MULTIPLE REGRESSION

The basic model for multiple regression can be written very simply in matrix form as follows:

$$y = X\beta + \varepsilon$$

where y is a vector $\{y_1, y_2, y_3, \ldots, y_n\}$ of n values on the response (or dependent) variable; β is a vector $\{\beta_1, \beta_2, \beta_3, \ldots, \beta_p\}$ of p slopes, one for each explanatory (or independent) variable; X is an n row by p column matrix containing n values for each of p explanatory variables; and ϵ is a vector $\{\varepsilon_1, \varepsilon_2, \varepsilon_3, \ldots \varepsilon_n\}$ of n error values.

Multiple linear regression involves making five assumptions about the data and their relationships.

First, we assume that the explanatory variables are measured without error. In Chapter 9 we measured the error as the discrepancy between y and the estimate of y that we obtained from the regression equation. If we have two explanatory variables, they will define a plane in three-dimensional space that give the predicted value for y for any combination of the explanatory variables. Beyond two explanatory variables, we will be defining a hyperplane that gives the predicted value of y for any combination of the explanatory variables. Regardless how many explanatory variables we are using, we estimate the model by minimizing the differences between the fitted (predicted) values and the observed values.

Second, we assume the relationship between the response variable and the explanatory variables is a linear one. We will multiply each explanatory variable by a slope value (β), add them together along with an intercept value to predict y. Sometimes we can incorporate nonlinear relationships by transforming variables (e.g., taking their logarithm) or by adding polynomials (e.g., x^2 and x^3).

Third, we assume that the errors have constant variance (**homoscedasticity**). No matter where we are on the hyperplane, the errors will have approximately the same variance. The main consequence of heteroscedasticity is that we will not estimate the parameters correctly (the slopes and the intercept) and we may get misleading estimates of the standard errors of those slopes.

Fourth, the errors in the response variable values are uncorrelated. When this assumption is violated it is usually because the observations are correlated as a result of their temporal or spatial position (autocorrelation and spatial autocorrelation).

Finally, the explanatory variables should be uncorrelated with one another. When this assumption is violated, the standard errors of the slope estimates may be inflated and the slope values do not provide accurate information on the relative importance

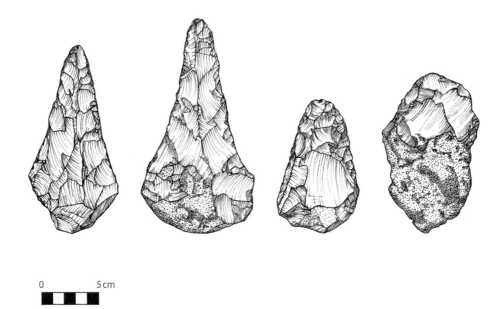

0   5 cm

FIGURE 41 Sample hand axes from Furze Platt.
Redrawn from Roe (1981).

of the various explanatory variables. Strong correlations between the explanatory variables is called **multicollinearity**.

There is an enormous literature on regression analysis and substantial resources on using R to overcome these problems (e.g., Berry and Feldman, 1985; Fox, 2008; Fox and Weisberg, 2011; Tabachnik and Fidell, 2007). This chapter will focus primarily on how to use multiple regression on archaeological data using R and how to diagnose potential problems.

Simple multiple regression is not widely used in archaeological research, but it is the basis for regression with dummy variables, logistic regression, and Poisson regression. Load the `Handaxes` data set, which consists of measurements on 600 hand axes from the Furze Platt site stored at the Royal Ontario Museum that were measured by William Fox (Figure 41). We will use these data to illustrate model-construction with multiple regression by attempting to predict hand-axe length from other variables. We might do this if we wanted to estimate the lengths for hand axes with broken tips:

```
> data(Handaxes)
> library(car)
> scatterplot(L ~ B, Handaxes, lwd=2, smoother.
  args=list(lty=2))
> Handaxes.lm1 <- lm(L ~ B, Handaxes)
> summary(Handaxes.lm1)

Call:
lm(formula = L ~ B, data = Handaxes)

Residuals:
    Min      1Q   Median      3Q     Max
-47.352 -11.560  -0.971  10.494  75.733

Coefficients:
            Estimate Std. Error t value Pr(>|t|)
(Intercept) 20.96764    3.47383   6.036 2.77e-09 ***
B            1.42450    0.04809  29.624  < 2e-16 ***
---
Signif. codes:  0 '***' 0.001 '**' 0.01 '*' 0.05 '.' 0.1 ' ' 1

Residual standard error: 16.53 on 598 degrees of freedom
Multiple R-squared:  0.5947,    Adjusted R-squared:  0.5941
F-statistic: 877.6 on 1 and 598 DF,  p-value: < 2.2e-16
```

We can use the regression of length (L) on breadth (B) to see how length changes for each increase in breadth (or any other dependent variable). After loading the data set and the car package, we use scatterplot() to look at the data (Figure 42). The extra arguments make the regression line thicker and the smooth line dashed. The boxplots suggest that breadth is slightly skewed right, but length is skewed more. The straight line is the regression line. The points clearly cluster along the line suggesting a strong correlation between length and breadth (.771 using cor()). The darker, curved line is the loess line and it suggests that the relationship may be slightly nonlinear.

Then, we use the lm() function to estimate the linear regression coefficients and save the results to an object (Handaxes.lm1). The lm() function uses the formula notation that we have used before. The variable being predicted goes to the left of the tilde (~) and the variable(s) being used to predict go on the right separated by plus signs (+).

The summary() function summarizes the results. After describing the model being estimated, we get the quartiles for the residuals. Ideally, the median should be 0, the first and third quartiles should be approximately the same, but of different sign, and the minimum and maximum should be approximately the same, but of different sign. Here the median is about –1 and the first and third quartiles are close to one another, but not identical. The maximum is much larger than the minimum. This is the point near the top of the scatterplot on Figure 42. The coefficients table gives us the estimates of the (Intercept), the estimated length of a hand axe with a breath of 0 is 20.97 mm. We also get the slope value for breadth. For every increase of 1 mm in breadth, hand axe length increases by 1.4 mm. This means that we can estimate the length of a hand axe with the following equation:

$$\hat{L} = 20.97 + 1.42B$$

where $\hat{L}$ is the fitted value of length (also called the predicted or estimated value) and B is the maximum breadth of the hand axe.

The other columns in the coefficients table show the standard error (how much variation there is in the intercept and slope estimates), the t-value (to test the null hypothesis that the estimate is 0), and the p-value of that test. Both the slope and the intercept are highly significant, but it is only the slope p-value that tests the null hypothesis of no relationship between the variables. The residual standard error 16.5 mm suggests that approximately 95 percent of the points should fall within 33 mm above and 33 mm below the line. The multiple R-squared value of .59 indicates that 59 percent of the variation in hand axe length is explained by breadth, but that also means that 41 percent is still unexplained. The adjusted R-square is used

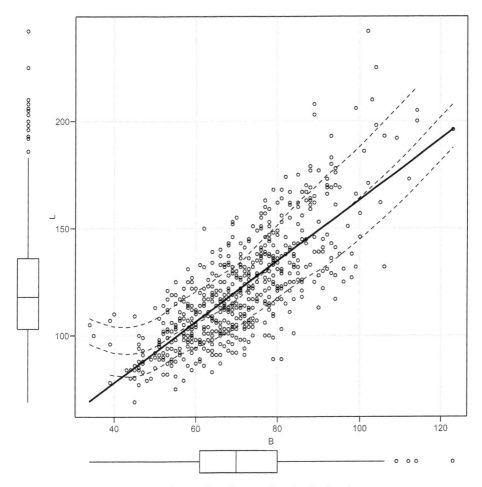

FIGURE 42 Scatterplot showing length versus breadth for hand axes.

to adjust R-square downward for multiple explanatory variables to make the value more realistic. We only have one explanatory variable so they are effectively the same. Finally the F-statistic is a test of the significance of the model. This test combines all of the explanatory variables for an overall test of significance. Since there is only one explanatory variable, the p-value is the same as the p-value for the slope of breadth.

We can easily get four diagnostic plots summarizing the results that will help us evaluate the degree to which the assumptions of linear regression have been met. We use the same approach as in the Chapter 9 to divide the plot window into four smaller windows:

```
> oldp <- par(mar=c(3.1, 3.5, 2.1, 1.5), las=1,
+     mgp=c(1.8,.6, 0), mfrow=c(2, 2))
```

```
> plot(Handaxes.lm1, ask=FALSE)
> par(oldp)
```

The results are shown in Figure 43a–d. First line sets the graphics parameter to divide the plot window into four windows (two rows and two columns) and the last line resets the parameter so further plots will use the whole window.

The "Residuals vs Fitted" plot shows the residuals by the fitted values (predicted lengths). The residuals should be evenly distributed around 0 and the spread should not increase or decrease along the x axis (the fitted values). Ideally, the residuals should be balanced above and below the horizontal dashed line at 0, but

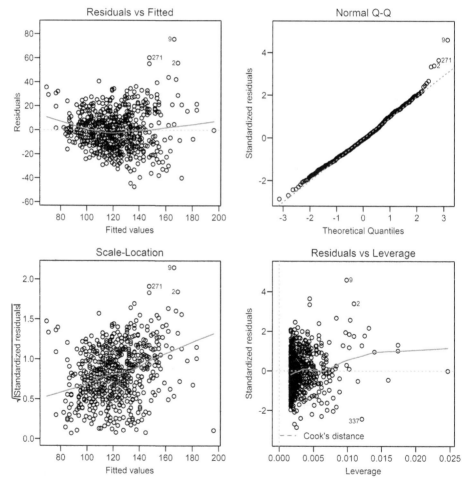

FIGURE 43 Regression diagnostic plots for hand axe length using breadth as the explanatory variable.

the curved line shows that they are positive at low and high values of length. This suggests that the relationship is not linear, something that Figure 42 also indicated. The plot also identifies hand axes 2, 9, and 271 as potential outliers with very large residuals.

The "Normal Q-Q" plot of the standardized residuals suggests the same thing. The residuals follow the dashed line closely in the middle, but curve above the line at both ends.

The "Scale-Location" plot compares the fitted values to the square root of the absolute value of the residuals. This effectively takes the first plot and folds it along the horizontal dashed line to see if there is any change in the variance along the line. The upward sloping line indicates that the variance in the residuals increases with increasing estimated length, a clear sign of heteroscedasticity.

Finally, the "Residuals vs Leverage" plot shows the standardized residuals by leverage with contour lines showing Cook's distance. Leverage is a measure of how far the values for the explanatory variable deviate from the mean (i.e., very broad or narrow). Those points can potentially have a large effect on the estimate of the regression slope coefficients. Cook's distance is a measure of how much influence a single observation has on the coefficient estimates. Points 2, 9, and 337 are potentially problematic.

Using breadth we can make a reasonable estimate of length, but the relationship does not seem to be linear and we have a problem with the error variance increasing with the estimated length (a violation of homoscedasticity). First, we can explore the degree to which other variables would help to improve the estimate of length. Normally we should only add variables that we have some reasonable expectation of having a relationship with the response variable. Here all of the variables are likely to be correlated to some degree with size, so any of them could contribute to estimating length:

```
> Handaxes.lm2 <- lm(L ~ L1 + B + B1 + B2 + T + T1, Handaxes)
> summary(Handaxes.lm2)

Call:
lm(formula = L ~ L1 + B + B1 + B2 + T + T1, data = Handaxes)

Residuals:
    Min      1Q   Median      3Q      Max
-36.826  -8.684   -0.917   8.061   52.285
```

```
Coefficients:
               Estimate Std.     Error  t value     Pr(>|t|)
(Intercept)     5.38496   2.90864    1.851       0.0646 .
L1              0.89025   0.06020   14.788     < 2e-16  ***
B               0.85936   0.10100    8.509     < 2e-16  ***
B1             -0.95354   0.07716  -12.358     < 2e-16  ***
B2              0.62872   0.08394    7.490    2.50e-13  ***
T               0.66960   0.08061    8.307    6.69e-16  ***
T1             -0.35634   0.16564   -2.151       0.0319 *
---
Signif. codes:   0 '***' 0.001 '**' 0.01 '*' 0.05 '.'
   0.1 ' ' 1

Residual standard error: 12.77 on 593 degrees of freedom
Multiple R-squared:   0.7603,    Adjusted R-squared:   0.7579
F-statistic: 313.5 on 6 and 593 DF,   p-value: < 2.2e-16
```

The residuals are more balanced in this model although the maximum value is still much larger in magnitude than the minimum value. The coefficients table shows the intercept value is now 5.4 and the p-value of .06 indicates that it is not significantly different from 0. This is what we would expect; a hand axe with 0 values on all of the explanatory variables should have a length of 0 mm. Now we have six slope values to look at. The slope values in a multiple regression will not be the same as the slope values for six bivariate regressions. Remember that the slope estimate for breadth was 1.42, but now it is 0.86. The multiple regression coefficients take the correlations between the explanatory variables into account and if they are highly inter-correlated (multicollinearity), the standard errors of the slopes will be larger. That makes it more likely that a slope value will not be significant although in this example, they are all significant at the .05 level. This also explains why some of the slope coefficients are negative although none of the explanatory variables has a negative correlation with length. Based on these slope values, we can compute the length of a hand axe with the following equation:

$$L = 5.38 + .89L1 + .86B - .95B1 + .63B2 + .67T - .36T1$$

where L is the fitted value of length; $L1$ is the distance from the butt of the hand axe to the point of maximum breadth; B is the maximum breadth; $B1$ is the breadth 1/5 of the length from the tip; $B2$ is the breadth 1/5 of the length from the butt; T is the maximum thickness; and $T1$ is the thickness 1/5 of the length from the tip.

The negative slope values for $B1$ and $T1$ indicate that hand axes with blunt (chisel-shaped) tips are generally shorter than pointed hand axes. The residual standard error with six explanatory variables is 12.77 (compared to 16.58 with only breadth) and the adjusted R-squared value is .76 so we are now explaining 76 percent of the variability in length instead of 59 percent. If some of the explanatory variables were not significant, we could refit the model excluding them. Generally that should be done one variable at a time since the slopes of all of the variables will change whenever we remove one. We can check to see if adding additional variables corrected the nonlinearity or increasing variance problems that we were having with the previous model:

```
> oldp <- par(mar=c(3.1, 3.5, 2.1, 1.5), las=1,
+    mgp=c(1.8, .6, 0), mfrow=c(2, 2))
> plot(Handaxes.lm2, ask=FALSE)
> par(oldp)
```

Figure 44a–d shows the results. Adding more variables did not correct any of the problems of the original bivariate regression. We may be able to correct the increasing variance of the residuals by transforming the length variable. In Chapter 6 on transformations we discussed the Box–Cox transformation (Box and Cox, 1964) in terms of transforming single variables, but we can also use it to transform the response variable taking the regression model into account as follows:

```
> library(MASS)
> Handaxes.bc <- boxcox(Handaxes.lm2)
> Handaxes.bc$x[which(Handaxes.bc$y==max(Handaxes.bc$y))]
[1] -0.02020202
```

After loading the MASS package, we use function boxcox() with the regression model to estimate the best Box–Cox transformation. The second line computes the log likelihood values for lambdas from –2 to 2 in .1 increments and plots the values (Figure 45). The third line finds the value of lambda with the maximum log likelihood value which is about –0.02. The optimal lambda value is very close to 0. Since the estimate of lambda is not much different from 0, we will use log10(L) as our transformation:

```
> Handaxes$L.log <- log10(Handaxes$L)
> Handaxes.lm3 <- lm(L.log ~ L1 + B + B1 + B2 + T + T1,
  Handaxes)
> summary(Handaxes.lm3)
```

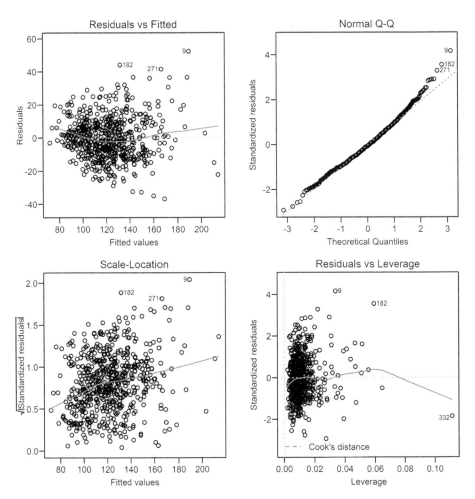

FIGURE 44 Regression diagnostic plots for hand axe length using six explanatory variables.

```
Call:
lm(formula = L.log ~ L1 + B + B1 + B2 + T + T1,
  data = Handaxes)

Residuals:
      Min        1Q     Median        3Q       Max
-0.117631 -0.029340 -0.002209  0.030216  0.135123

Coefficients:
            Estimate Std. Error t value Pr(>|t|)
(Intercept) 1.6792123  0.0099471 168.814  < 2e-16 ***
L1          0.0030683  0.0002059  14.904  < 2e-16 ***
```

```
B              0.0027595   0.0003454    7.989  7.09e-15 ***
B1            -0.0031372   0.0002639  -11.889   < 2e-16 ***
B2             0.0023079   0.0002870    8.040  4.88e-15 ***
T              0.0020482   0.0002757    7.430  3.81e-13 ***
T1            -0.0009084   0.0005665   -1.604     0.109
---
Signif. codes:  0 '***' 0.001 '**' 0.01 '*' 0.05 '.'
   0.1 ' ' 1

Residual standard error: 0.04366 on 593 degrees of freedom
Multiple R-squared:  0.7592,    Adjusted R-squared:  0.7567
F-statistic: 311.5 on 6 and 593 DF,  p-value: < 2.2e-16

> oldp <- par(mar=c(3.1, 3.5, 2.1, 1.5), las=1,
+   mgp=c(2.2, .6, 0), mfrow=c(2, 2))
> plot(Handaxes.lm3, ask=FALSE)
> par(oldp)
```

We create a new variable, L.log, and use it in the regression. Notice that the residuals are more balanced. The slope values are much smaller because the log values of length are much smaller. The thickness 1/5 of the length from the tip (T1) is no longer significant. For the final model, we could remove that variable, but it does not change the results much. Now the equation for predicting hand axe length is

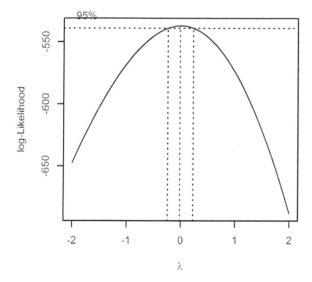

FIGURE 45 Box–Cox plot for hand axe regression model.

$$\hat{L} = 10^{1.6792 + .0031L1 + .0028B - .0031B1 + .0023B2 + .0020T - .0009T1}$$

where the variables are defined as before.

The diagnostic plots are shown in Figure 46a–d. Notice that the Residuals vs Fitted plot shows a nearly horizontal line, the Normal Q-Q plot shows very little deviation from a normal distributions for the standardized residuals, and the Scale–Location plot shows substantial improvement although there is still a slight upturn at the right side of the graph. The Residuals vs Leverage plot shows hand axes 290, 182, and 332 as outliers. We have several options at this point. We could try using a robust linear model to reduce the influence of the extreme values using $rlm()$ in package MASS. Alternatively, we could eliminate hand axes identified as outliers on any of the four plots from the analysis and recompute the multiple regression:

```
> Handaxes.lm4 <- lm(L.log ~ L1 + B + B1 + B2 + T, Handaxes)
> library(MASS)
> Handaxes.lm5 <- rlm(L.log ~ L1 + B + B1 + B2 + T, Handaxes)
> Handaxes.out <- Handaxes[-c(182, 290, 332, 337), ]
> Handaxes.lm6 <- lm(L.log ~ L1 + B + B1 + B2 + T, Handaxes.
  out)
```

You should run these commands and use $summary()$ and $plot()$ to look at the results. HA.lm4 is the same as Handaxes.lm3 except that variable T1 is excluded. Handaxes.lm5 is a robust regression using the $rlm()$ function in the MASS package, and Handaxes.lm6 is the same as Handaxes.lm4, but with hand axes 182, 290, 332, and 337 excluded. Neither the robust regression, Handaxes.lm5, nor the linear regression with outliers removed, Handaxes.lm6, is substantially different from Handaxes.lm4 so it should probably be our final model. Given that model, we predict the length of the first hand axe in the data as follows:

```
> Handaxes[1, ]
  Catalog  L L1  B B1 B2  T T1   L.log
1 896.4.1 134 69 79 65 57 41 22 2.127105
> predict(Handaxes.lm4, Handaxes[1, ])
       1
2.101479
> 10^predict(Handaxes.lm4, Handaxes[1, ],
  interval="prediction")
      fit       lwr       upr
1 126.322 103.5606 154.0861
> plot(Handaxes$L, 10^predict(Handaxes.lm4, Handaxes))
> abline(a=0, b=1, lty=2)
```

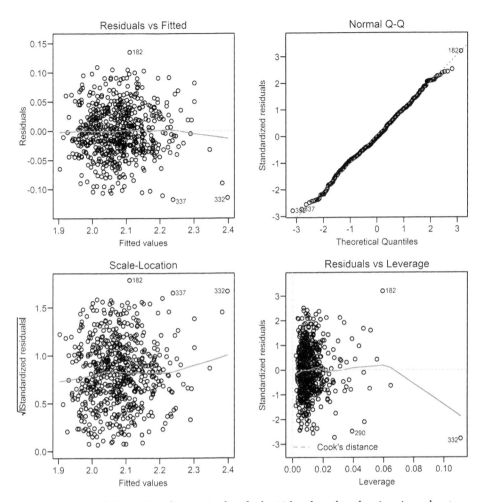

FIGURE 46 Regression diagnostic plots for log10 hand axe length using six explanatory variables.

Listing the first line of Handaxes shows us that the length of the hand axe is 134 and the base 10 log of 134 is 2.127. The predict() function is predicting L.log as 2.101. Normally we would want to transform back to the original measurements using the fitted value as a power of 10. When we do that and request prediction intervals, we get an estimated length of 126.3, an underestimate of about 8 mm, but well within the 95 percent prediction interval. Notice that because we used the log transform, the prediction interval is not symmetric. The fitted value is 22.8 mm larger than the lower bound, but the upper bound is 50.5 mm larger than the fitted value. The two commands produce a plot of the original hand axe lengths to their fitted estimates.

10.2 REGRESSION WITH DUMMY VARIABLES

In Chapter 8 we looked at the areas of the houses at the Snodgrass site to see if the houses in segment 1 are larger using an analysis of variance (and we discovered that they are). We can conduct a similar analysis using linear regression by specifying `Area` as the response variable and `Segment` as the explanatory variable:

```
> data(Snodgrass)
> Snodgrass.lm1 <- lm(Area~Segment, Snodgrass)
> summary(Snodgrass.lm1)

Call:
lm(formula = Area ~ Segment, data = Snodgrass)

Residuals:
    Min          1Q      Median         3Q         Max
-162.121     -36.831     -2.371     43.542     155.129

Coefficients:
              Estimate Std. Error t value Pr(>|t|)
(Intercept)    317.37      10.48   30.290  < 2e-16 ***
Segment2      -150.58      16.09   -9.361 7.43e-15 ***
Segment3      -124.58      16.63   -7.490 5.03e-11 ***
---
Signif. codes:  0 '***' 0.001 '**' 0.01 '*' 0.05 '.'
   0.1 ' ' 1

Residual standard error: 64.59 on 88 degrees of freedom
Multiple R-squared:  0.5408,     Adjusted R-squared:  0.5304
F-statistic: 51.82 on 2 and 88 DF,  p-value: 1.344e-15
```

The output will be a little confusing at first. Segment is listed twice, as `Segment2` and `Segment3`. When you use a factor as an explanatory variable, R automatically converts that variable into a set of $k - 1$ dichotomous variables where k is the number of categories. In this case, we have three categories so we get two variables. There are several ways to create the variables and the default method that R uses is called dummy coding. For the Snodgrass example, Segment2 has a value of 1 if the house is located within segment 2 and 0 otherwise. Segment3 is 1 if the house is in segment 3. Houses in segment 1 are identified by having 0 for both variables.

With this coding system, the (Intercept) is the mean area for houses located in Segment 1 (within the white wall). The `Segment2` estimate is the value that we add

to (Intercept) to get the average area of houses in segment 2 and the Segment3 estimate is the value that we add to (Intercept) to get the segment 3 area. The *t*-test for the
(Intercept) is not very useful since we don't expect that the area of any houses will be
zero, but the other two tests provide a test of the hypothesis that the houses in that segment are significantly different from the houses in segment 1. Both values are significant and we conclude that the houses in segments 2 and 3 are significantly smaller than
the houses in segment 1. We do not get a direct test of the hypothesis that houses in segments 2 and 3 are significantly different from one another, but they overlap one another
at 1 standard error so they are probably not significantly different (which is what we
learned from the Tukey HSD test in Chapter 8). The adjusted *R*-square indicates that
we can explain 53 percent of the variability in house area from segment, but this is a
little misleading since all of the houses in a segment are predicted to have the same area.

By using dummy variables in this way, multiple regression can accommodate a
mixture of numeric and categorical variables in a single model. For example, Types
is the number of different kinds of artifacts (projectile points, decorated ceramics,
effigies, etc.) found in the house so it is a measure of the diversity:

```
> Snodgrass.lm2 <- lm(Area~Segment+Types, Snodgrass)
> summary(Snodgrass.lm2)

Call:
lm(formula = Area ~ Segment + Types, data = Snodgrass)

Residuals:
     Min         1Q     Median         3Q        Max
-128.170    -38.199     -6.821     36.343    130.900

Coefficients:
            Estimate Std. Error t value Pr(>|t|)
(Intercept)  238.797     16.579  14.404  < 2e-16 ***
Segment2     -90.627     17.442  -5.196 1.33e-06 ***
Segment3     -63.186     17.971  -3.516 0.000699 ***
Types         10.225      1.811   5.647 2.02e-07 ***
---
Signif. codes:  0 '***' 0.001 '**' 0.01 '*' 0.05 '.'
  0.1 ' ' 1

Residual standard error: 55.57 on 87 degrees of freedom
Multiple R-squared:  0.664,      Adjusted R-squared:  0.6524
F-statistic:  57.3 on 3 and 87 DF,  p-value: < 2.2e-16
```

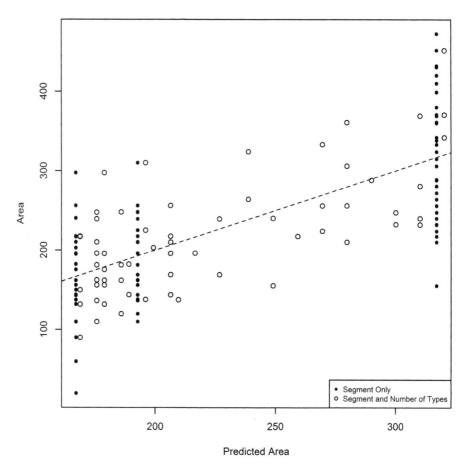

FIGURE 47 Comparison of actual and fitted areas of Snodgrass houses using segment and using segment and types.

Now the (Intercept) does not give us the mean area of houses in segment 1 because the influence of the number of types is incorporated into the model so that 238.8 is the estimated area of a house in segment 1 with 0 types. Starting with an area of 238.8 ft² we multiply the number of artifact types by 10.2 and add that to the area. That is our estimate for houses inside the wall (segment 1). For segment 2 houses we subtract 90.6 and for segment 3 houses we subtract 63.2 to get our estimate. The adjusted R-squared value increases to .65 and the slope value for Types is statistically significant. The slope indicates that area increases by 10.2 ft² per artifact type. We can compare the first and second models by plotting the fitted values against the observed house areas (Figure 47):

```
> plot(predict(Snodgrass.lm1), Snodgrass$Area, pch=20)
> points(predict(Snodgrass.lm2), Snodgrass$Area)
```

```
> abline(a=0, b=1, lty=2)
> legend("bottomright", c("Segment Only",
+    "Segment and Number of Types"),
+    pch=c(20, 1), cex=.75)
```

The first model simply predicts the mean area given the value of Segment. Adding information about the number of artifact types provides a wider range of estimates that more closely matches the observed areas. The current model assumes that the slope of artifact types is the same in each segment. We could test that by evaluating a model incorporating an interaction between segment and artifact types with the model:

```
> Snodgrass.lm3 <- lm(Area~Segment*Types, Snodgrass)
```

If you use summary(Snodgrass.lm3), you will see that the table indicates that Segment2:Types and Segment3:Types are both negative suggesting that area increases less with increasing types than in Segment 1, but they are not significantly different from 0. In other words, the estimate of 10.2 ft² per artifact type applies regardless of house location. Also, the adjusted R-squared value is slightly smaller than the previous model.

10.3 GENERALIZED LINEAR MODELS – LOGISTIC REGRESSION

Generalized linear models are an expansion of linear regression to include response variables that are not normally distributed. This includes variables that are dichotomies, proportions, or counts. These models have a wide range of uses within archaeology. Binary and proportional responses can be predicted using logistic regression. Count responses can be predicted using Poisson and negative binomial regression. Poisson regression can also be used in the place of log-linear models although R can compute log-linear models as well (loglin() in package MASS).

Logistic regression is used to specify a binary outcome (present/absent, male/female, large/small, etc.). Within archaeology, logistic regression has primarily been used to develop predictive models of archaeological site locations to estimate the probability that a site will be present within a particular area. As an illustration, we will see if we can predict if a house at Snodgrass is inside or outside the walled area using the area of the house and the number of types of artifacts found in the house. In the previous section, we predicted house area from location and number of artifact types. Now we are predicting location from house area and number of artifact types. We need to use function glm(), but otherwise the specification is very similar to the previous examples (Box 12):

```
> data(Snodgrass)
> Snodgrass$Inside <- factor(Snodgrass$Inside,
  levels=c("Outside", "Inside"))
> Snodgrass.lm4 <- glm(Inside~Area+Types,
  family=binomial(logit), Snodgrass)
> summary(Snodgrass.lm4)

Call:
glm(formula = Inside ~ Area + Types, family = binomial(logit),
    data = Snodgrass)

Deviance Residuals:
     Min           1Q       Median           3Q          Max
-1.76644     -0.42164     -0.13581      0.08721      2.77883

Coefficients:
              Estimate Std. Error z value Pr(>|z|)
(Intercept)  -8.908070   2.067910  -4.308 1.65e-05 ***
Area          0.029556   0.008283   3.568 0.000359 ***
Types         0.479797   0.177769   2.699 0.006955 **
---
Signif. codes:  0 '***' 0.001 '**' 0.01 '*' 0.05 '.' 0.1 ' ' 1

(Dispersion parameter for binomial family taken to be 1)

    Null deviance: 123.669  on 90  degrees of freedom
Residual deviance:  47.587  on 88  degrees of freedom
AIC: 53.587

Number of Fisher Scoring iterations: 7
```

After loading the data set, we change the order of the coding for Inside. Since we coded Inside as Inside and Outside, our factor levels are 1 for Inside and 2 for Outside which R would convert to a dichotomous variable with 0=Inside and 1=Outside. That means that the regression is predicting the probability that a house is outside the wall. By changing the order of the factor levels, we will be predicting the probability that a house is inside the wall. It is not really necessary since the results would be the same although the signs of the coefficients will be reversed.

The model specification is the same except for the introduction of a new argument, `family=binomial(logit)`. This tells R to compute a logistic regression by estimating the logarithm of the odds ratio of being inside the white wall. An odds ratio is a ratio of two probabilities. For example, if the probability of an event occurring is .25, then the probability that it will not occur is 1 - .25 = .75. The odds ratio of occurrence is .25/.75 = .33. If you are accustomed to probabilities, this may seem overly complicated, but probabilities are bound in the range of 0 to 1. Odds ratios range from 0 to infinity and the log of odds ratios ranges from negative infinity to positive infinity, which makes them easier to work with in a regression model.

The output is similar to that for linear regression, but there are differences. The estimates look familiar, but the confidence intervals are based on a normal distribution instead of the t distribution. The intercept and the slopes for both `Area` and `Types` are significantly different from 0. Instead of the residual standard error and the multiple R values that were part of the results of a linear regression, generalized linear models give us two kinds of deviance: the Akaike information criterion (AIC) and the number of iterations.

Generalized linear regression is not based on least squares, but on an iterative process that stops when the estimates no longer change. The two types of deviance represent a model with only the intercept (null deviance) and the fitted model (residual deviance). The deviances and their degrees of freedom are stored in the object returned by `glm()`. We can answer two different questions with the deviance estimates.

First, does the model represent an improvement on the null hypothesis? This question involves the difference between the null deviance and the residual deviance. We subtract the residual deviance from the null deviance and use the difference between the null degrees of freedom and the residual degrees of freedom. The null hypothesis is that the decrease in deviance is not significantly different from zero. We use the Chi-square distribution for the test:

```
> with(Snodgrass.lm4, 1 - pchisq(null.deviance - deviance,
+       df.null - df.residual))
[1] 0
```

The p-value is 0 so we reject the null hypothesis and conclude that the logistic model provides a significant improvement over the null model.

Second, does the residual deviance indicate that the model fits data poorly so we should look for a different model? This test involves only the residual deviance and the residual degrees of freedom. The null hypothesis is that the observed values differ significantly from fitted values:

```
> with(Snodgrass.lm4, 1 - pchisq(deviance, df.residual))
[1] 0.9998674
```

The second Chi-square is nearly 1 so we do not reject the null hypothesis that the observed values are significantly different from the fitted values. We conclude that the model is acceptable.

AIC stands for Akaike information criterion and it is used to compare several alternate models. If we construct several overlapping models, we generally select the one with the smallest AIC value. For example, we could compute models with `Inside ~ Area`; with `Inside ~ Area + Types`; with `Inside ~ Area + Types + Points`; and with `Inside ~ Area + Types + Points + Ceramics`. All of the models would be adequate as measured by the residual deviance, but the AIC values would be 61.7, 53.6, 55.5, 56.4. The model with `Area` and `Types` has the smallest AIC value. Additionally the estimates for `Points` and `Ceramics` are not significant, a further reason to choose the model with `Area` and `Types`.

The equation predicts the log odds ratio of a house being located outside the wall. The odds ratio is simply OR = $p/(1 - p)$, where p is the probability of a success. Given the odds ratio, we can convert it back to the probability with $p = $ OR/(1 + OR). The equation for estimating the odds ratio from the regression model is

$$\text{OR}(y) = e^{8.908 - .0296\,\text{Area} - .480\,\text{Types}}$$

$$\text{Pr}(y) = \frac{\text{OR}(y)}{(1 + \text{OR}(y))}$$

where OR(Y) is the estimated odds ratio for y and Pr(y) is the probability of success (being outside the wall) for y.

Since the coefficients are log odds ratios, we have to convert them to a simple odds ratio before computing the probability. The intercept for the model including `Area` and `Types` is –8.91, which is the value of the equation when the area of the house is 0 and the number of types is 0. The exponential of the intercept is `exp(-8.91) = .00014` and the probability is `.00014/(1+.00014) or .00014`, which is essentially 0. So houses with 0 area and 0 artifact types are very likely to be located outside the wall. Since `Area` and `Types` have positive coefficients, they increase the odds ratio and the probability of being inside. This would be a great deal of trouble to calculate by hand, but fortunately the `predict()` function will do it for us. Consider the first four rows in Snodgrass:

```
> head(Snodgrass[, c(6:7, 15)], 4)
   Inside   Area Types
```

```
1 Outside 144.0    1
2 Outside 256.0    1
3  Inside 306.0    4
4  Inside 451.5    8
> round(predict(Snodgrass.lm4, head(Snodgrass, 4),
  type="response"), 3)
     1     2     3     4
0.015 0.297 0.886 1.000
```

The first two cases are small houses with only one type that are located outside the wall. The second two houses are larger with multiple types that are located inside the wall. We use `type="response"` in the `predict()` function to get the results in probabilities rather than log odds. The first two houses have probabilities of .015 and .297 of being inside the wall. The second two have probabilities of .886 and 1 of being inside the wall. The regression model does not tell us what to predict, but a reasonable rule of thumb is to predict outside if the probability is greater than .5 and inside if it is smaller. We can compare the predictions to the actual locations with a cross-tabulation table.

```
> Predict <- ifelse(predict(Snodgrass.lm4,
+   type="response")<.5, "Outside", "Inside")
> Predict <- factor(Predict, levels=c("Outside", "Inside"))
> addmargins(xtabs(~Snodgrass$Inside+Predict))
                 Predict
Snodgrass$Inside Outside Inside Sum
        Outside       49      4  53
         Inside        6     32  38
            Sum       55     36  91
```

This is sometimes referred to as a confusion table. Of the 53 houses outside the wall, 49 were correctly predicted and four were wrongly predicted. Of the 38 houses inside the wall, 32 were correctly predicted and six were wrongly predicted. The overall rate is $(32 + 49)/91 = 0.89$ or 89 percent correctly predicted.

If you change the boundary from 0.5 to 0.6, you will see that one more inside house is wrongly predicted, but one less outside house is wrongly predicted so the overall rate is the same. Changing the boundary to 0.4 makes no difference in the results. Unless there is a reason for considering one kind of wrong prediction worse than the other kind of wrong prediction, just stay with 0.5.

The 89 percent success rate is misleading because we used the same data to build the model and to test it, which means our model is biased toward these particular data (also called overfitting). With new data, the success rate would be lower. We will

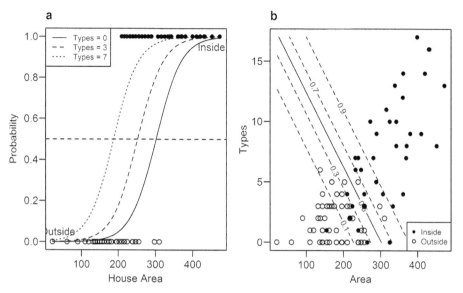

FIGURE 48 Logistic regression for Snodgrass houses: (a) regression lines, (b) regression plane.

revisit this issue in the Chapter 11 using discriminant analysis to illustrate the use of cross-validation to control for this source of bias.

Since the response variable has only two values, it can be challenging to create an informative plot. One solution is to create a strip chart and overlay curves representing the probability that a house is inside the wall (Figure 48a):

```
> sym <- ifelse(Snodgrass$Inside=="Inside", 16, 1)
> plot(Snodgrass$Area, as.numeric(Snodgrass$Inside)-1,
+    type="p", ylab="Probability", xlab="House Area",
+    pch=sym, las=1)
> x <- seq(min(Snodgrass$Area), max(Snodgrass$Area), length.
  out=100)
> lines(x, predict(Snodgrass.lm4, data.frame(Area=x,
+    Types=0), type="response"), lty=1)
> lines(x, predict(Snodgrass.lm4, data.frame(Area=x,
+    Types=3), type="response"), lty=2)
> lines(x, predict(Snodgrass.lm4, data.frame(Area=x,
+    Types=7), type="response"), lty=3)
> abline(h=.5, lty=2)
> legend("topleft", c("Types = 0", "Types = 3", "Types = 7"),
+    lty=1:3, bg="white")
> text(c(450, 35), c(.95, .05), c("Inside", "Outside"))
```

Run these lines one at a time to see how the plot is built up step by step. The first line creates a vector called `sym` to set the plotting symbol to 16 when the house is inside the wall (a solid circle) and 1 when it is outside (an open circle). Then we plot the house areas. They form two rows of points at 1 and 0 on the y-axis. Next we create a numeric vector of 100 areas that range from the smallest house to the largest. We will compute the value of the regression equation for each of those areas in order to plot smooth curves. If we were predicting house location only from area, we could plot a single curve, but since we are also using the number of artifact types, we have to show how the curve changes as the number of types changes. The three `lines()` functions do that for 0, 3, and 7 artifact types. The horizontal reference line at 0.5 indicates where we change our prediction from outside to inside. When there are 0 types, a house must be about 300 ft^2 before, we predict that it is inside the wall. If it has three types, a house of 250 ft^2 is predicted to be inside the wall and if it has seven types, a house of 185 ft^2 is predicted to be inside the wall. The last two lines add the legend and text labels to indicate which houses are inside and which are outside. Positioning the text labels involves a bit of trial and error to get them located properly.

An alternate way to display the results is to use the `contour()` function (Figure 48b):

```
> x <- with(Snodgrass, seq(min(Area), max(Area), length.
  out=50))
> y <- with(Snodgrass, seq(min(Types), max(Types), length.
  out=50))
> z <- outer(x, y, function(x, y) predict(SG.lm4, data.
    frame(Area=x, Types=y), type="response"))
> contour(x, y, z, levels=c(.1, .3, .5, .7, .9), lty=c(2, 2, 1,
    2, 2), xlab="Area", ylab="Types", labcex=.75, las=1)
> with(Snodgrass, points(Area, Types, pch=sym))
> legend("bottomright", c("Inside", "Outside"), pch=c(16, 1))
```

The contour map is laid over a scatterplot between `Area` and `Types`. Houses inside are shown as filled circles and those outside are shown as open circles. The contour lines show how the probability that a house is located outside the wall changes as area and the number of types increase. For houses in the lower left corner of the plot, the probability is greater than .9 that the house is outside the walled area and for houses in the upper right corner, the probability is less than .1 that they are outside the walled area (i.e., .9 that they are inside the walled area). The plot is constructed by creating two vectors, each with 50 values for `Area` and `Types` that range from the minimum to the maximum of each variable. The `outer()` function takes two vectors and creates a matrix (in this case a 50 × 50 matrix) showing the probability for every combination of Area and Types. The contour() function takes the same two vectors (x and y) along with the matrix (z) and draws the contour lines.

Using x, y, and z, you can also create a 3-D version of the probability surface. It is eye-catching, but not really as informative as the other two graphs:

```
> persp(x, y, z, xlab="Area", ylab="Types",
+    zlab="Probability", theta=20, phi=15,
+    ticktype="detailed")
```

BOX 12 THE GENERALIZED LINEAR MODEL FUNCTION, `glm()`

```
glm(formula, family = gaussian, data, weights, subset,
      na.action, start = NULL, etastart, mustart, offset,
      control = list(...), model = TRUE, method = "glm.fit",
      x = FALSE, y = TRUE, contrasts = NULL, ...)
```

The glm() function is used to fit generalized linear models. These are models in which the response or dependent variable is not necessarily normally distributed or continuous. It allows fitting models where the response variable is binomial (presence/absence) or Poisson (counts). The family= argument indicates what kind of response variable.

Logistic regression is specified using family=binomial("logit"), where the response variable is a dichotomous factor or coded numerically as 0, 1. The fitted value returned by the function is the log-odds which can easily be converted to a probability. The probability is then used to make a prediction for a particular combination of explanatory variables.

Poisson regression is specified using family=poisson("log") where the response variable is a count. The fitted value returned by the function is the natural log of the expected count.

As with lm() (Box 11), the formula specifies a response variable on the left of the tilde (~) and the explanatory variables on the right. Interactions between the explanatory variables are indicated with * or :. The data frame containing the variables (data=), weights (weights=), any subsetting of the data frame (subset=), and how to handle missing values (na.action=) are the same as lm(). The remaining arguments are not generally used unless you need to fine tune details of the analysis or include additional information in the output of the function.

The `glm()` function returns an object very similar to `lm()`. In addition, the same functions are available to summarize the results and extract parts of the object including `summary()`, `coef()`, `deviance()`, `fitted()`, `predict()`, `residuals()`, and `confint()` in package MASS.

Table 11 *Functions introduced in Chapter 10*

Function	Package	Description
boxcox	MASS	Compute and plot Box–Cox power transformation
confint	MASS	Confidence intervals for glm and nls models
contour	graphics	Produce a contour plot
glm	stats	Generalized linear models
loglin	stats	Fit log-linear models to contingency tables
pchisq	stats	Chi-square distribution function
persp	graphics	Draw perspective plot of surface

Note: Packages `base`, `datasets`, `graphics`, `grDevices`, `methods`, `stats`, and `utils` are automatically loaded when R starts.

11

MANOVA and Discriminant Analysis

In Chapter 10, we expanded on linear regression by using more than one explanatory variable on the right-hand side of the formula. In this chapter, we will expand on t-tests and analysis of variance from Chapter 8 by adding more than one response variable on the left-hand side of the formula. Hotelling's T test is a multivariate expansion of the t-test and multivariate analysis of variance (MANOVA) is a multivariate expansion of analysis of variance. In many cases, we have multiple measures of artifact shape or composition and running t-tests separately on each variable creates multiple comparisons problems. Also the tests are not really independent if the variables are correlated with one another as they often are. Hotelling's T and MANOVA provide an overall test of the difference between the groups based on all of the numeric variables. The tests of significance are on these linear combinations rather than the original separate variables.

Discriminant analysis involves a similar process in that we are looking for linear combinations of variables that allow us to predict a categorical variable. The most common archaeological application is in compositional analysis where we are trying to characterize different sources (geological sources or manufacturing sources) on the basis of molecular or elemental composition. Discriminant analysis includes two separate but related analyses. One is the description of differences between groups (descriptive discriminant analysis) and the second involves predicting to what group an observation belongs (predictive discriminant analysis, Huberty and Olejink 2006).

Descriptive discriminant analysis is based on multivariate analysis of variance. Instead of a single numeric dependent (response) variable, we have several variables. To test for differences between groups, we compute linear combinations of the original variables and then test for significant differences between the linear combinations. A linear combination is like a multiple regression equation in the sense that each variable is multiplied by a value and summed to produce a new value that summarizes variability in the original variables. Descriptive discriminant analysis is also described as canonical discriminant analysis and the linear components are referred to as canonical variates. The method is used to visualize the similarities and differences between groups in two or three dimensions.

Predictive discriminant analysis is a form of supervised classification. That just means that we can identify the group membership for at least some observations. We use the known group memberships to construct a predictive equation (or several equations) that allows us to assign new objects to one of the known groups. The converse, unsupervised classification involves the discovery of groups without prior knowledge of what groups exist within the data and will be described in Chapter 15.

Discriminant analysis can make substantial demands on sample size. The bare minimum is at least five more observations in each group than the number of variables, but recommendations run as high as two or three times as many observations as variables. Some of the discrepancy in recommendations relates to the difference between linear discriminant analysis and quadratic discriminant analysis. The first assumes that the groups share the same covariance matrix whereas the second uses separate covariance matrices for each group. For the second approach, there must be more observations than variables in each group. It is also true that with small sample sizes, there is a danger that discriminant analysis will over fit the data, which simply means that the prediction equations are tuned too closely to the specific data used in the analysis and may give less accurate results when applied to new observations.

The dependent or response variable in discriminant analysis is a categorical variable that identifies group membership. The explanatory variables are used to construct the linear equations that separate the group means. The first equation provides the maximum separation between the group means. Subsequent equations separate the means in additional dimensions under the constraint that they must be orthogonal (uncorrelated) to all of the preceding equations. There will be one fewer of these equations than the number of groups (e.g., one equation for two groups, two equations for three groups). If there are fewer independent variables than groups, there will be no more equations than the number of independent variables.

11.1 HOTELLING'S T AND MANOVA

Hotelling's T test is a multivariate expansion of the t-test. It is useful to perform a comparison of two groups on the basis of multiple variables simultaneously. The test is available in the `DescTools` package. As an example, we will use the Romano British glass data for major and minor elements (`RBGlass1`). The glass comes from two different sites, Leicester and Mancetter, and we want to know if the chemical composition of the glass at the two sites is different. Since there are 11 elements, we are testing the null hypothesis that differences between the means for all 11 elements are 0:

```
> library(DescTools)
> data(RBGlass1)
> dim(RBGlass1)
[1] 105  12
> colnames(RBGlass1)
 [1] "Site" "Al"  "Fe"  "Mg"  "Ca"  "Na"  "K"   "Ti"  "P"
     "Mn"  "Sb"  "Pb"
> HotellingsT2Test(as.matrix(RBGlass1[, -1])~Site, RBGlass1)


        Hotelling's two sample T2-test

data:   as.matrix(RBGlass1[, -1]) by Site
T.2 = 15.768, df1 = 11, df2 = 93, p-value < 2.2e-16
alternative hypothesis: true location difference is not equal
  to c(0,0,0,0,0,0,0,0,0,0,0)
```

After loading the DescTools package and the RBGlass1 data, we check the dimensions of the data with dim() and see that there are 105 rows and 12 columns. From colnames(), we see that the first column is Site and the remaining 11 are the major elements. The HotellingsT2Test() function uses the formula method. The response variables go on the left side of the tilde ($\sim$) and the grouping variable (with only two groups) goes on the right. We could have typed all 11 elements separated by "+", but it is easier to use the data frame after removing the first column and converting it to a matrix because the formula will not accept a data frame.

The p-value of the T.2 statistic is compared to an F distribution with $k - 1$ and $n - k$ degrees of freedom where k is the number of variables and n is the number of observations. The p-value is effectively 0 so we can reject the null hypothesis that the percentages of all of the major elements are identical. If we look at the means and standard deviations for the groups, we can see that the differences are small, generally within 1 standard deviation:

```
> Mn <- aggregate(RBGlass1[, -1], list(RBGlass1$Site), mean)
> Sd <- aggregate(RBGlass1[, -1], list(RBGlass1$Site), sd)
> print(rbind(Mn=Mn, Sd=Sd), digits=1)
```

```
       GROUP.1   AL   FE   MG   CA NA    K    TI    P    MN   SB   PB
MN.1 LEICESTER  2.4  0.7 0.55  6.6 18 0.71 0.10 0.12 0.27 0.26 0.03
MN.2 MANCETTER  2.5  0.5 0.53  7.2 17 0.72 0.08 0.14 0.41 0.09 0.03
SD.1 LEICESTER  0.1  0.2 0.03  0.8  1 0.09 0.01 0.01 0.08 0.12 0.01
SD.2 MANCETTER  0.1  0.1 0.05  0.6  1 0.18 0.01 0.02 0.17 0.10 0.02
```

The `aggregate()` function allows us to split a data frame by a categorical variable and compute a statistic by group. Here we use it to get a compact display of the means and standard deviations by `Site` for each element. The first argument is the data frame or matrix, the second is a list of the categorical variable or variables, and the third argument is the function to be used. The last line combines the two data frames so they will line up when we print them. The first two lines show the means for each element and the last two show the standard deviations. Notice that the elements do not differ by much and that when they do the differences overlap at 1 standard deviation.

Multivariate analysis of variance is an expansion of ANOVA (Chapter 8). Instead of one numeric variable, we use several. In ANOVA, we compared the sum of the squared deviations from the mean of the response variable within groups (**within groups** or **error sum of squares**) to the sum of the squared deviations of the group means from the grand mean (**between groups** or **hypothesis sum of squares**). Now instead of one value for each sum of squares, we have a symmetric matrix with one row and column for each variable.

The `RBPottery` data set contains the results of chemical analyses to measure the percentages of nine different oxides in 48 specimens of Romano-British pottery from five kilns in three regions (Tubb et al., 1980). We will examine the data to see if there are significant differences in composition between the three regions (Gloucester, Wales, and New Forest) since the sample sizes from three kilns are small (five or fewer). We use the linear model function `lm()` to compute a multivariate analysis of variance with the numeric variables as the response variables and region as the explanatory variable:

```
> data(RBPottery)
> View(RBPottery)
> options(digits=3)
> RBP.manova <- lm(as.matrix(RBPottery[, 4:12])~Region,
  RBPottery)
> summary(RBP.manova)
Response Al2O3 :
```

```
Call:
lm(formula = Al2O3 ~ Region, data = RBPottery)

Residuals:
   Min      1Q   Median     3Q     Max
-3.241  -0.980    0.101  1.059   3.050

Coefficients:
                 Estimate Std. Error t value Pr(>|t|)
(Intercept)        16.941      0.317   53.48   < 2e-16 ***
RegionWales        -4.485      0.488   -9.19  6.9e-12 ***
RegionNew Forest    0.809      0.567    1.43     0.16
---
Signif. codes:  0 `***' 0.001 `**' 0.01 `*' 0.05 `.' 0.1 ` ' 1

Residual standard error: 1.49 on 45 degrees of freedom
Multiple R-squared:  0.711,     Adjusted R-squared:  0.698
F-statistic: 55.2 on 2 and 45 DF,  p-value: 7.68e-13
. . . results for remaining 8 variables omitted . . .
```

The results include an ANOVA test for each of the nine oxides, but only the one for Al2O3 is shown here. Recall that when categorical variables are included as explanatory variables, R codes them so that the first group (here Region Gloucester) is the intercept. In this case, the intercept is the mean percentage of aluminum oxide for ceramics from Gloucester. The second row of the Coefficients: table shows how ceramics from Wales differ from ceramics from Gloucester. They have about 4.5 percent less aluminum oxide. Next New Forest ceramics are compared to Gloucester ceramics and they have almost 1 percent more aluminum oxide. If you look at each of the oxides, you will see that there are significant differences for most of them. New Forest and Gloucester are not significantly different for titanium dioxide and none of them are different for barium oxide. We do not get direct comparisons between Wales and New Forest, but we are more interested in overall differences at this point.

To get an overall significance test of the differences between the regions, we use the manova() function:

```
> summary(manova(RBP.manova), test="Pillai")
         Df Pillai approx F num Df den Df Pr(>F)
Region    2    1.9     83.9     18     76 <2e-16 ***
Residuals 45
```

```
---
Signif. codes:  0 '***' 0.001 '**' 0.01 '*' 0.05 '.' 0.1 ' ' 1
> summary(manova(RBP.manova), test = "Roy")
          Df  Roy approx F num Df den Df Pr(>F)
Region     2 27.3      115      9     38 <2e-16 ***
Residuals 45
---
Signif. codes:  0 '***' 0.001 '**' 0.01 '*' 0.05 '.' 0.1 ' ' 1
```

There are four different indices for testing the significance of MANOVA: Pillai's trace (`test = "Pillai"`, the default), Wilk's lambda (`test = "Wilks"`), Hotelling–Lawley's trace (`test = "Hotelling-Lawley"`), and Roy's largest root (`test ="Roy"`). In this case all four indicate significant differences between the group centroids although only two are shown above. Rencher and Christenson recommend Pillai if the sample sizes are variable, the covariance matrices between groups are different, and the variables are not highly correlated (2012: 190). These are conditions that would be common in archaeological data. Wilks also performs well unless the covariance matrices are very different. Roy is better if the variables are highly correlated. There are some modest positive and negative correlations, but Roy and Pillai agree that we can reject the null hypothesis of no difference between the regions.

Here we are looking at ceramic composition. Another interesting application of MANOVA involves morphological measurements of artifact types from multiple locations or time periods. This is the approach taken in analyses of object shape called geometric morphometrics, which involves measuring landmark positions on objects or identifying multiple points along a curve to analyze and compare shape. We will not explore morphometrics in detail, but it generally involves principle components analysis (Chapter 12) followed by MANOVA. The R packages `geomorph`, `Momocs`, `Morpho`, and `shapes` provide the necessary functions. We now know that ceramic composition is different over the three regions, but we would like to know how they are different and that takes us to descriptive (canonical) discriminant analysis.

11.2 DESCRIPTIVE (CANONICAL) DISCRIMINANT ANALYSIS

The MANOVA results indicate that there are significant differences between the group means for the three regions. It would be useful to be able to visualize those differences to see how distinct the groups are. Do they form separate clusters with empty space in between, or do they form overlapping clusters? With two or three variables, we can just plot the data, but with nine, that is impossible. Descriptive or canonical discriminant analysis identifies linear combinations of the variables that provide the maximum separation of the groups.

Imagine a nine-dimensional plot of the three regions with the group centroids identified. The goal is to place a single line through the grand centroid (the mean on all variables for all of the ceramics regardless of region) and then orient that line so that when we project the group means to the line, the groups will be more spread out than they are for any other line. If there are only two groups, there is only one line. If there are three groups, we can place a second line that also runs though the grand centroid and is orthogonal (at a 90° angle) to the first line and then rotate that line until it provides the greatest separation between the groups that is not accounted for by the first line. These lines are the canonical variates and there will be one fewer than the number of groups (or the number of variables, whichever is less).

To compute the canonical variates (also called canonical discriminant functions), we use the candisc() function in package candisc to install that package (Friendly and Fox, 2016):

```
> library(candisc)
> RBP.can <- candisc(RBP.manova)
> RBP.can

Canonical Discriminant Analysis for Region:

  CanRsq Eigenvalue Difference Percent Cumulative
1  0.965       27.3       11.7    63.7       63.7
2  0.940       15.6       11.7    36.3      100.0

Test of H0: The canonical correlations in the
current row and all that follow are zero

  LR test stat approx F num Df den Df Pr(> F)
1       0.0021      454      4     88 <2e-16 ***
2       0.0604      700      1     45 <2e-16 ***
---
Signif. codes:  0 '***' 0.001 '**' 0.01 '*' 0.05 '.' 0.1 ' ' 1
```

The output summarizes the two canonical vectors and tests their statistical significance. The test assumes that the data follow a multivariate normal distribution.

Both are statistically significant. The canonical R-square values ("CanRsq" column) measures how well each canonical variate separates the groups. The eigenvalue is a measure of the magnitude of that canonical variate. Since there are three groups, there will be (groups − 1) = 2 eigenvalues greater than 0 and 2 eigenvectors associated with them. The "Percent" column indicates that 63.7 percent of the separation is provided by the first canonical variate and the remaining 36.3 percent by the second. The likelihood ratio tests for both variates are significant, indicating that the region group means for each canonical variate are significantly different. We can get more details from summary():

```
> summary(RBP.can)

Canonical Discriminant Analysis for Region:

  CanRsq Eigenvalue Difference Percent Cumulative
1 0.9646      27.26      11.71   63.68      63.68
2 0.9396      15.55      11.71   36.32     100.00

Class means:

              Can1    Can2
Gloucester  -1.423  -4.009
Wales       -4.042   4.454
New Forest   9.597   1.694

 std coefficients:
           Can1         Can2
Al2O3    0.77136   -0.49514
Fe2O3   -1.08374   -0.47129
MgO     -0.31396    0.59888
CaO     -0.10455   -0.73799
Na2O     0.16144   -0.25820
K2O     -0.14251    0.18544
TiO2     0.48386   -0.02808
MnO     -0.11231    0.17444
BaO     -0.03427    0.42212
```

The first table is the same table of eigenvalues. The "Class means" table shows the mean for each region on each of the canonical variates. Notice that Gloucester and Wales have negative values on the first canonical variate while New Forest is well away from them with a positive value. On the second canonical variate, Gloucester and Wales are split between positive and negative while New Forest is in the middle. These values can be used to plot the locations of the regions in the canonical variate space.

The "std coefficients" are the weights that we use to compute the canonical scores for the observations once the original variables have been converted to standard scores. These scores provide some indication of how important each variable is in defining the canonical variates. Notice that Al2O3, Na2O, and TiO2 have positive coefficients so the scores for ceramics that have more than the average amount of those oxides will tend to have larger positive values, and ceramics that have more than the average amount of the other oxides will tend to have larger negative values. On the second variate, the positive values are for MgO, K2O, MnO, and BaO so ceramics with more than average amounts of those oxides will tend to have larger positive values. The candisc() function also computes "raw" coefficients but these are not as easily interpreted. We can also get the structure coefficients:

```
> coef(RBP.can, type="structure")
         Can1    Can2
Al2O3   0.577  -0.644
Fe2O3  -0.871  -0.443
MgO    -0.738   0.607
CaO    -0.373  -0.850
Na2O   -0.502  -0.450
K2O    -0.747   0.284
TiO2    0.500  -0.335
MnO    -0.694   0.308
BaO    -0.104  -0.102
```

The structure coefficients show the correlations between each variable and each canonical variate. On the first canonical variate, Fe2O3, MgO, K2O, and MnO have relatively large negative correlations so that changes in those oxides should be reflected in the first variate. On the second canonical variate, CaO has a large negative correlation. Al2O3 and MgO have moderately large positive correlations. None of the other oxides have correlations over .6 (positive or negative). We can visualize these differences better with a biplot (Figure 49):

```
> plot(RBP.can, main="Romano-British Pottery Regions -
  Canonical Variates")
Vector scale factor set to 7.447
```

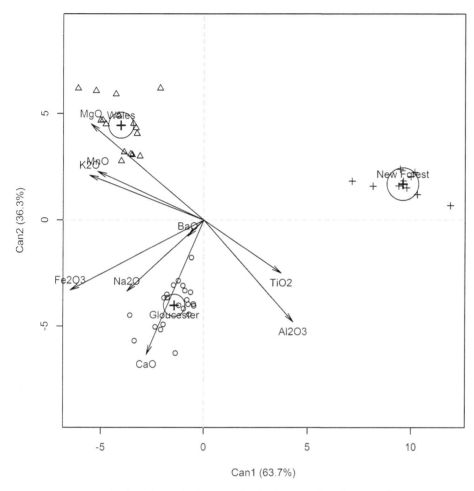

FIGURE 49 Biplot of canonical variates for the Romano-British pottery by region.

A biplot shows two sets of information on a single plot, usually the rows and the columns of a data matrix. Once you get accustomed to them, they are very informative and they are the standard way of displaying canonical variates, principle components (Chapter 12), and correspondence analysis (Chapter 13). The different groups are represented by different symbols and colors. Each group centroid is identified by a large plus sign with a group label. The circles around the centroids indicate the 95 percent confidence limits for the centroids (not the data points). The three centroids are very well separated. The points are the individual ceramics and the arrows represent the variables. The arrows originate at the origin (0, 0) on the graph. If we think of the points as being plotted in nine dimensions with a plane defined by the two canonical variates centered at the grand centroid, the arrows represent the projections or shadows of each axis on that plane. The angle between the arrow and the canonical variate axes reflect its correlation with that canonical variate. All but two oxides had negative correlations with the first variate and they all pointing to the left. The oxides that had larger, negative correlations are closer to the horizontal axis. Al2O3 and TiO2 had positive correlations and they are pointing to the right. CaO had a large negative correlation with the second variate and it points down and is closer to the vertical axis.

The lengths of the arrows reflect the sum of the squared correlations. For Fe2O3 that is $(-0.871)^2 + (-0.443)^2 = .9553$ while for Na2O it is $(-0.502)^2 + (-0.450)^2 = 0.4545$ and you can see the difference in the lengths of their arrows. BaO has small correlations with both variates and its arrow is very short. It is clear that K2O and MnO are correlated with one another because their arrows form a small angle (their correlation is .60) and that both of them have negative correlation with Al2O3, which is pointing in the opposite direction (–.50 and –.52). Since the biplot collapses nine dimensions into two, it will not reflect the individual correlations between variables perfectly. Note on the R Console "Vector scale factor set to 7.447" just means that the lengths of the arrows have been multiplied by that amount to scale them to fit on the plot.

If you want to construct other kinds of plots with the canonical discriminant scores, you can add them to your data frame as follows:

```
> RBPottery <- data.frame(RBPottery, RBP.can$scores[, -1])
> View(RBPottery)
> colnames(RBPottery)
 [1] "ID"    "Kiln"   "Region"    "Al2O3"   "Fe2O3"   "MgO"     "CaO"
     "Na2O"
 [9] "K2O"   "TiO2"   "MnO"       "BaO"     "Can1"    "Can2"
```

Don't forget to save the file if you are planning to use it again. Finally, we can plot the groups by their canonical coordinates with 95 percent confidence ellipses around each group (Figure 50):

```
> scatterplot(Can2~Can1 | Region, RBPottery, smoother=FALSE,
+     asp=1, reg.line=FALSE, ellipse=TRUE,
+     levels=.95, legend.coords="bottomright")
```

These ellipses represent 95 percent confidence ellipse for the data points in each region. The asp=1 argument ensures that the horizontal and vertical axes are scaled equally so that horizontal distances are the same as vertical distances. Notice that these ellipses are not circles. The canonical variates are uncorrelated with one

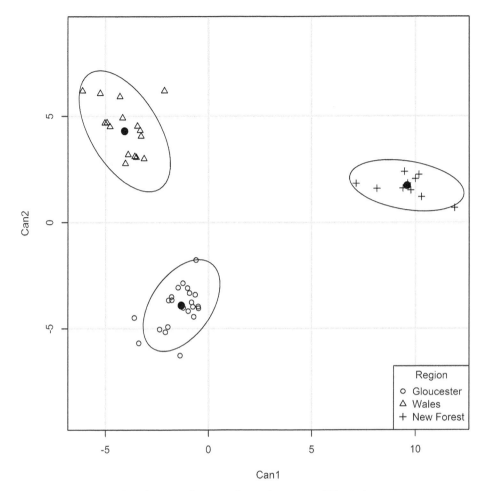

FIGURE 50 Plot of canonical variates for Darl, Ensor, and Travis dart points.

another and are shown on the same scale so the confidence ellipses for the centroids are circles, but the ceramics within a group may show covariance between the canonical variates. Wales ceramics show a moderate negative covariance (−.429), while Gloucester ceramics show a moderate positive covariance (.426) and New Forest shows less covariance (−0.279).

11.3 PREDICTIVE DISCRIMINANT ANALYSIS

Predictive discriminant analysis allows us to build functions that let us predict to what group an observation belongs. The predictive functions provide the probability that an observation belongs to each of the groups we have defined. Linear discriminant analysis constructs a linear function using a pooled covariance matrix for all of the groups (function lda() in package MASS). If the group covariance matrices are different from one another, quadratic discriminant analysis uses separate covariance matrices (function qda() in package MASS). Getting good results requires having enough data to make an accurate estimate of this matrix. Recommended sample sizes for a pooled covariance matrix are usually in the range of three to five times the number of variables.

The Romano-British glass data on major and minor elements (RBGlass1) has 105 observations for 11 elements. For two groups, there is a single discriminant function since once we know the probability of membership in the first group, we can subtract it from 1 to get the probability of membership in the other group. Discriminant analysis assumes that any specimen we are trying to place into a group belongs to one of them. That is none of the specimens belong to another unknown group. We can construct a predictive function using the 11 numeric variables to predict site using the lda() function in the MASS package (Box 13):

```
> data(RBGlass1)
> library(MASS)
> (RBGlass1.lda <- lda(Site~., RBGlass1, prior=c(.5, .5)))
Call:
lda(Site ~ ., data = RBGlass1, prior = c(0.5, 0.5))

Prior probabilities of groups:
Leicester Mancetter
      0.5        0.5


Group means:
            AL    FE    MG   CA   NA    K     TI      P    MN     SB     PB
LEICESTER 2.38 0.696 0.548 6.59 18.2 0.707 0.1000 0.117 0.273 0.2592 0.0315
MANCETTER 2.47 0.476 0.533 7.19 17.2 0.720 0.0804 0.139 0.414 0.0941 0.0252


Coefficients of linear discriminants:
        LD1
Al    4.295
Fe   -4.090
Mg   -4.835
Ca   -0.105
Na    0.147
```

```
K      1.069
Ti   -50.188
P     42.258
Mn     3.013
Sb     4.163
Pb    15.978
```

The lda() function takes either a numeric matrix of variables and a grouping variable as the first two arguments or a formula with the grouping variable on the left and the numeric variables on the right. The ". " on the right of the tilde (~) indicates that we want to use all of the variables that are not on the left side of the tilde (here only Site), which saves some typing.

We set the prior probabilities to .5 for each site. The prior probabilities are used in predicting group membership. If we do not specify prior probabilities, the function uses the proportion of each type. For these data, 59 specimens come from Leicester and 46 come from Mancetter, but we do not know if this reflects greater glass production at Leicester or differences in excavation and sampling at the sites. Making the prior probabilities .5 simply reflects our ignorance about future samples by assuming that each site has an equal probability.

The printed output of the function includes summary statistics showing the group means for each variable and the linear discriminant function coefficients. These are the coefficients that will be used to compute the linear discriminant scores for each specimen. The size of the coefficients is not a direct indication of the importance of each element in discriminating between the two sites. To compute the score, the raw data must be centered (subtract the column mean from each observation). Then the centered values are multiplied by the coefficients. The size of the coefficients reflect both the ability of that element to separate the groups and the variance in that element. As a result, some elements that do not appear to show much separation (e.g., Ti, P) and elements that show more separation have small coefficients (e.g., Ca, Na). We can also plot the results:

```
> plot(RBGlass1.lda)
> title(main="Romano-British Glass, Major and Minor
  Elements")
```

These commands produce two histograms representing the linear discriminant score for each specimen by site (Figure 51). We have to add the title using the title() function since the special version of plot() used for lda objects does

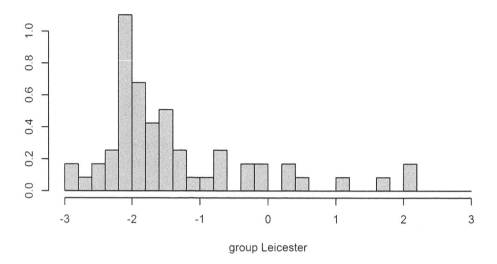

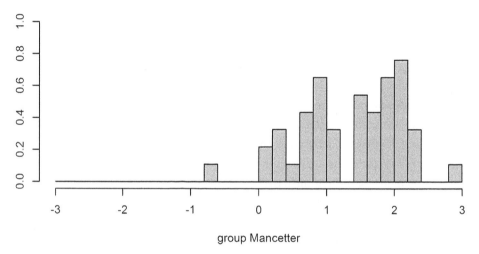

FIGURE 51 Histograms of discriminant analysis scores for Romano-British glass from two sites.

not support the main= argument. It is clear that the groups are distinct, but that there is also some overlap. You can see that most of the Leicester glass has negative scores and most of the Mancetter glass has positive scores. To see exactly how successful the discriminant function is in predicting site we use the predict() function on the output from lda():

```
> RBGlass1.prd <- predict(RBGlass1.lda)
> RBGlass1.out <- with(RBGlass1.prd, data.frame(Site=
+    RBGlass1$Site, Predict=class, posterior, x))
```

```
> RBGlass1.out[c(1, 6, 102, 103), ]
          Site    Predict Leicester Mancetter    LD1
1    Mancetter Mancetter   0.00518  0.994820   1.929
6    Mancetter Leicester   0.87449  0.125515  -0.712
102  Leicester Mancetter   0.29771  0.702291   0.315
103  Leicester Leicester   0.99961  0.000387  -2.882
```

The object RBGlass1.prd is a list with three parts. The first part, RBGlass1.prd$class, is a vector with the predicted class membership for each observation. The second part, RBGlass1.prd$posterior, is a matrix showing the posterior probabilities. There is a column for each group and a row for each specimen. Each row sums to 1.0 since discriminant analysis assumes each point belongs to one of the two sites. In each row, the column with the higher percentage is the group to which that row is assigned. The third part, RBGlass1.prd$x, is a vector containing the discriminant function scores. These are the values on the x-axis of the histograms (Figure 51). The print() function just prints each element of the list separately which is not very helpful so we create a data frame by combining Site from RBGlass1 with the three parts of RBGlass1.prd.

We just print out rows 1, 6, 102, and 103 of the data frame, but you can see all of the results in a window with View(RBGlass1.out). The first column shows from which site the specimen came. The second column ("class") shows from which site it was predicted to belong. Then the posterior probabilities of belonging to each group. Finally, the linear discriminant score. Row 1 is from Mancetter and is correctly predicted as coming from Mancetter since the probability is .99. Row 6 is from Mancetter but incorrectly predicted as coming from Leicester because the probability is .87 that it comes from there. You can see this specimen on the bottom histogram as the leftmost bar in Figure 51. Row 102 is from Leicester but is incorrectly predicted as coming from Mancetter because the probability is .70 that it came from there. Finally, row 103 is from Leicester and is correctly predicted as coming from Leicester with a probability of 1.0. The last column is the linear discriminant score and it is this value that is plotted on the histograms.

To see how accurate the classifications are, we use a confusion table, which is just a cross-tabulation of the actual site against the predicted site. The counts along the diagonal of that table are the points that were correctly classified while the counts off the diagonal are the points that were incorrectly classified:

```
> confusion <- xtabs(~Site+Predict, RBGlass1.out)
> addmargins(confusion)
          Predict
Site           Leicester Mancetter    Sum
  Leicester           52         7     59
  Mancetter            1        45     46
  Sum                 53        52    105
> sum(diag(confusion))/sum(confusion)*100
[1] 92.4
```

The confusion table shows us where glass specimens came from and how they were classified. The first row shows that 52 specimens from Leicester were correctly classified as coming from Leicester, but seven were misclassified as coming from Mancetter. The second row shows that 45 specimens from Mancetter were correctly classified as coming from Mancetter and only one specimen was misclassified as coming from Leicester. The last line tells us that 92 percent of the points are correctly classified ((52 + 45)/105*100 = 92.4). That is not perfect, but it is substantially better than we would do by chance (about 50 percent correct). The diag() function extracts the diagonal values from a matrix, here that is 52 and 45.

There is a problem, however, since we used the same data to build the classification function and to test it. This is the same overfitting problem we encountered in Chapter 10 with logistic regression. As a result, the predictions are almost certainly overly optimistic and our accuracy with new glass specimens will probably be less. To get an idea how overly optimistic, we need to use different data to create and test the discriminant functions. We could divide the data into a training set to create the discriminant functions and a test set to test them, but our sample size is already small. Alternatively we could use a form of cross validation called "leave-one-out" classification. This procedure removes the first observation, computes the discriminant functions using the rest, and then predicts the group for the first observation. Then the second observation is removed, new discriminant functions computed, and the second observation is predicted. Since we have 105 glass specimens, we do this 105 times using 104 specimens to predict the one left out. Fortunately lda() can do this automatically:

```
> RBGlass1.prd2 <- lda(Site~., RBGlass1, prior=c(.5, .5),
  CV=TRUE)
> RBGlass1.out2 <- with(RBGlass1.prd2, data.frame(Site=
+    RBGlass1.out$Site, Predict=class, posterior,
+    LD1=RBGlass1.prd$x))
```

```
> confusion <- xtabs(~Site+Predict, RBGlass1.out2)
> addmargins(confusion)
            Predict
Site        Leicester    Mancetter      Sum
  Leicester        49           10       59
  Mancetter         4           42       46
  Sum              53           52      105
> sum(diag(confusion))/sum(confusion)*100
[1] 86.7
```

When we use CV=TRUE with lda(), the returned information is different. Since lda() executed 105 linear discriminant analyses, we only get the predicted group and the posterior probabilities. We do not get x, the matrix of discriminant scores. In other words, using lda() with CV=TRUE is more like using lda() followed by predict(). To emphasize that, we called the object RBGlass1.prd2 instead of something like RBGlass1.lda2. Then we create a new output data frame with the results called RBGlass1.out2 preserving the LD1 column from the original analysis. With leave-one-out cross-validation, our percentage of correctly predicted point types has dropped from 92 to 87 percent. The lower figure is a more realistic estimate of our accuracy in predicting a manufacturing site for new specimens. We can easily list the incorrect predictions:

```
> errors <- subset(RBGlass1.out2, subset=Site != Predict)
> nrow(errors)
[1] 14
> head(errors, 5)
        Site    Predict Leicester Mancetter      LD1
5  Mancetter  Leicester    0.6145    0.3855    0.123
6  Mancetter  Leicester    0.9315    0.0685   -0.712
9  Mancetter  Leicester    0.5202    0.4798    0.258
18 Mancetter  Leicester    0.5209    0.4791    0.143
25 Leicester  Mancetter    0.0218    0.9782    0.411
```

This saves the 14 errors as an object called errors. For rows 9 and 18, the posterior probabilities were split evenly.

Linear discriminant analysis for three or more groups is exactly the same except that there will be more scores and more posterior probabilities. With three or more groups, R will change the plot from a histogram to a scatterplot of the first two discriminant scores.

One of the assumptions in linear discriminant analysis is that the groups have the same covariance matrix. If they do, the shape and orientation of the group confidence ellipses should be approximately the same in plots like the one in Figure 50. Even if the ellipses are similar in two dimensions, the within group covariance matrices could still be different. Box's M test can be used to test the null hypothesis that the covariance matrices are equal, but it is known to be very conservative meaning that it will reject the null hypothesis that the covariance matrices are equal even if the differences are too small to affect the results. The test is available as boxM() in the biotools package.

The qda() function in the MASS package performs a quadratic discriminant analysis, which uses separate covariance matrices. If you run Box's M, you will discover that the covariance matrices for Leicester and Mancetter are not equal. Then if you repeat the analysis using qda() so that you can use separate covariance matrices, you will discover that qda() does not provide better predictions of group membership for these data so the classification errors are not a result of using the pooled covariance matrix.

Another consideration with discriminant analysis is whether some of the observations are outliers; that is, they are misclassified and really belong to a group not included in the analysis. This applies to the original observations and to new observations that we classify using the discriminant functions. Evaluating outliers involves a third probability (after the prior and posterior probabilities) called typicality. This is the probability that an observation with the observed values would be a member of a particular group. It is a measure of how far from the group centroid the observation lies. In Figure 50, imagine there were samples with linear discriminant scores greater than 4 or less than –4. These specimens would be outside the range of the others and we would wonder if these specimens were a result of measurement error or glass imported from another source.

We have two ways to measure typicality, one using the linear discriminant functions and one using the original data. In either case we use the Mahalanobis D^2 as the distance measure. The only difference is whether we use the within groups covariance matrix or we modify that matrix by weighting the variables using the linear discriminant functions. There is disagreement on which method is more appropriate (Huberty and Olejnik, 2006: 289–290). The probability distribution of distances based on the linear discriminant functions is known and this is the approach used by SPSS® (IBM Corp, 2013). When the original data are used to estimate the covariance matrix, there is disagreement over what the distribution function should be. The standard rule of thumb has been to use Chi-square with the degrees of freedom equal to the number of numeric variables. Function `typprob()` in package `Morpho` can be used to compute typicality probabilities.

R has a number of other methods for supervised classification including recursive partitioning or regression trees (package `rpart`), neural networks (package `nnet`), and support vector machines (package `e1071`). Venables and Ripley (2002) provide a nice introduction to these methods. Ensemble methods that combine multiple models to improve prediction include bootstrap aggregating (`bagging`, package `ipred`) and random forests (package `randomForest`).

BOX 13 LINEAR DISCRIMINANT ANALYSIS USING `lda()`

```
lda(x, grouping, prior = proportions, tol = 1.0e-4,
    method, CV = FALSE, nu, ...)
lda(formula, data, ..., subset, na.action)
```

Linear discriminant analysis is used to identify separation between known groups based on a linear combination of numeric variables. There are two ways to specify the analysis using the `lda()` function, which is included in package MASS. The first is to provide a numeric matrix or data frame as `x=` and then a `grouping=` variable, usually a factor. The second is to use the formula specification where the grouping variable is on the left and the variables are on the right.

With either method, you can specify the prior probabilities using `prior=`. The default is to set the prior probabilities equal to the number of observations in each group divided by the total number of observations. This assumes that sampling across groups was random. When the observations come from groups that were sampled independently, the sample sizes may not reflect the prior probabilities accurately. If in doubt, give each group equal prior probability (e.g., `prior=rep(1/g, g)` where g is the number of groups).

The `CV=TRUE` argument runs the linear discriminant analysis n times where n is the number of observations. For each run, one observation is removed and the remaining $n - 1$ observations are used to compute the linear discriminant analysis and predict the group membership of the removed observation. When this argument is set, the object returned includes the predicted membership of each observation and the posterior probabilities of membership in each group. The discriminant function coefficients and scores are not returned (since there would be n different versions). When CV=TRUE, the `plot()` and `predict()` functions will not work.

The other arguments are not often used as they relate to technical details of the method. The `method=` argument allows changing the estimators for the mean and variance. Setting this to `method="cov.mve"` will use robust estimates. The function returns a list including the prior probabilities, the number in each group, the means for each group, the discriminant function coefficients, and the number of observations.

There are special `plot()` and `predict()` functions for the objects returned by `lda()`. The `plot()` function produces histograms when there is a single discriminant function, a scatterplot when there are two functions, and a pairs plot when there are three or more. The `predict()` function returns a list with three parts: `class`, `posterior`, and `x`. The first is the predicted group membership, the second is a matrix of posterior probabilities, and the third is a matrix of discriminant function scores.

Table 12 *Functions introduced in Chapter 11*

Function	Package	Description
aggregate	stats	Split data into subsets and run a function on each
as.matrix	base	Convert object to a matrix
candisc	candisc	Canonical discriminant analysis
diag	base	Extract the diagonal from a matrix
dim	base	Show the dimensions (rows, cols, etc.) of an object
HotellingsT2Test	DescTools	Hotelling's T2 test
lda	MASS	Linear discriminant analysis
manova	stats	Multivariate analysis of variance
qda	MASS	Quadratic discriminant analysis
title	graphics	Add labels to a plot

Note: Packages `base`, `datasets`, `graphics`, `grDevices`, `methods`, `stats`, and `utils` are automatically loaded when R starts.

12

Principal Components Analysis

Principal components analysis and factor analysis are related, but distinct, methods for analyzing the structure of multivariate data. In Chapter 11, we identified linear combinations of variables that would separate known groups. If we suspect there are groups in the data or that the variables are related to one another, principal components may help us to identify those patterns.

Principal components analysis looks for a way to simplify the dimensionality of the data. If we have only two variables (e.g., length and width), we can display their relationship with a simple scatterplot of length against width that indicates if the variables are correlated with one another or if there are distinct clusters of observations. If there are three variables (add thickness for example), we can display a 3-D representation that can be rotated to look for patterns in the data. After three variables, there is no simple way to display the data. One approach is to find a way of projecting the data into a smaller number of dimensions just as a shadow is a two-dimensional projection of a three-dimensional object. That projection will result in the loss of information so we would like to find the projection that captures as much detail as possible. Principal components analysis does this by identifying the direction of maximum covariance (or correlation) in the data. The first component identifies that direction. The second component finds the next largest direction of covariance (or correlation) subject to the constraint that it must be orthogonal (at a right angle or uncorrelated) with the first dimension. If the data are highly correlated, we may be able to accurately summarize many variables in a few dimensions. Principal components analysis tells us about the structure of the data and provides us with a way of displaying the observations in a reduced number of dimensions. Sometimes that can help us to see clustering in the data that might indicate distinct artifact types (Christenson and Read, 1977; Read, 2007).

While principal components focus primarily on summarizing multivariate data, factor analysis has a different goal. Factor analysis assumes that the data are the product of unobserved (or latent) factors. The correlations between variables provide the evidence of these latent factors. Using the example of length and width, we might argue that the correlation between length and width is "caused" by a latent variable called "size." Factor analysis is used widely in psychology where the performance on tests is assumed to be caused by qualities of the human mind that are not directly observable. The goal in factor analysis is to discover these latent variables, describe or define them, and possibly use them as variables in further analyses. Factor analysis is not used widely in archaeology although it was one of the first multivariate methods to be used to solve an archaeological problem. Lewis and Sally Binford used factor analysis on Mousterian artifact assemblages and argued that the factors they identified from the correlations between various tool types were the result of Neanderthals using sets of tools in different activities (Binford and Binford, 1966). Lewis Binford continued to explore the technique with data from seven Lower Paleolithic Acheulean sites (Binford, 1972). After those publications, factor analyses were relatively common in archaeology for 10–15 years, but the technique has largely been replaced by other methods, primarily correspondence analysis (Chapter 13).

Some of the confusion between the two methods comes from the fact that principal components analysis can be used to get initial estimates for the iterative process of identifying factors. Also principal components can be rotated if we want to provide simple descriptions of the components rather than treat them simply as a coordinate system for displaying the data (Dunteman, 1989; Jackson, 2003; James et al., 2013; Jolliffe, 2002; Rencher and Christensen, 2012).

The steps in principal components analysis are to identify a set of numeric variables. These can include dichotomous variables, but not categorical variables unless they are recoded as dichotomous variables (i.e., dummy variables). Then compute a correlation matrix (or under some circumstances a covariance matrix). The correlation matrix is analyzed to identify the directions of maximum correlation by extracting eigenvalues and eigenvectors. The eigenvalues are the variances of the principal components. Since each successive component captures less variance, the first eigenvalue is the largest and each successive eigenvalue is less than the preceding one. A plot of the decreasing eigenvalues is called a scree plot. Completely random data will have a nearly horizontal scree plot. The eigenvectors are also referred to as the principal component loadings. The loadings can be used to identify which variables are well represented by each component and they can be used to compute principal component scores for each observation in the new spatial representation. This new space has the same number of dimensions as the original but each successive dimension contributes less information so we can drop some of them without losing too much information about the structure of the data.

Principal components analysis involves at least three decisions after you have decided what variables to include in the analysis. The first is whether to use the correlation matrix or the covariance matrix. The second is how many components to use, and the third is whether to rotate the axes of the components to make it easier to interpret the results.

Principal components can be extracted from a covariance matrix or a correlation matrix. The covariance matrix retains the units of measurement and differences in the variances among the variables. As a result, all of the variables should be measured on the same scale. In the hand axe data set (Handaxes) for example, all variables are measured in millimeters. In addition, the variables should have comparable variances. If they do not, the biggest variances will dominate the results. For the hand axes, the variance for length is 673 while the variance for thickness measured 1/5 of the length from the tip (T1) is 21. if we use the covariance matrix, length will influence the results much more than T1. If we consider the variables to be equally important in measuring size and shape, then the analysis should use the correlation matrix. If the variables are measured in different units (e.g., millimeters, square millimeters, and grams), the correlation matrix should be used. The main drawback to using the correlation matrix is that the various tests of significance used for principal components analysis apply only when the covariance matrix is used (Jackson 2003: 98–102; Jolliffe 2002: 49–56), but we are usually more interested in visualizing the data than in testing the statistical significance of the principal components.

The number of components to use depends primarily on the goals of the analysis. A standard rule of thumb, borrowed from factor analysis, is to select eigenvalues greater than 1 (assuming the correlation matrix is used) or to use a change in the slope of the scree plot. Another approach is to compare the scree plot to randomized data to see at what point the eigenvalues are comparable to the values produced by randomized data. The goals of the analysis should be taken into account. If the goal is to analyze correlations between variables, then components with eigenvalues greater than one are explaining the variability of more than one variable while components with eigenvalues below one are explaining less than one variable. But if the goal is to summarize the variability in the data along major dimensions, correlations may simply reflect redundancy in measurement. For example, artifact size is not more important because many different measurements of an artifact reflect size in some way. The correlations between the variables reflect the difficulty in measuring shape without also measuring size. An eigenvalue below one could indicate that a part of a single variable is the only one that captures an important aspect of shape.

The same can happen with other kinds of data. In compositional data, the goal is to separate artifacts by composition. A cluster of correlated elements might provide that separation, but it is also possible that a single element could do so.

The conclusion is that you should use the rules of thumb with some caution depending on what you are trying to accomplish. The best situation will be one in which you have external criteria that help you identify the right number of components. For displaying the data, it is difficult to work with more than two or three components.

Rotation involves spinning the components to a different orientation. Rotation is used in factor analysis to improve the interpretability of the components. Components are easier to interpret if the distribution of the squared loadings is bimodal. This just means that the component has a few variables with large loadings (positive or negative), which can be used to interpret the component while the rest of the variables have small loadings. Rotation is not necessary when using principal components as a reduced set of axes for examining the data. However, it might make sense if the data are size standardized before extracting principal components. That could be accomplished by dividing the variables by the geometric mean as described in Chapter 6. Rotation might then make it easier to define the shape components in the data.

When the principal components are first extracted, the directions of the components are uniquely defined in terms of the amount of variance they account for in the original data (except for reflection), but rotating the components loses that information. There are several rotation methods that give somewhat different results and while some methods preserve the orthogonal structure (i.e., the fact that the components are uncorrelated), other methods allow the components to become correlated with one another. Also, rotation is defined for a specific number of components. If you decide to rotate the components, you should use the `principal()` function in package `psych` since it provides better support for rotating components.

The results of principal components analysis are generally presented in a biplot like the one we saw in Chapter 11 that shows the relationships between the variables and the distribution of observations on the same plot.

The base functions for computing principal components in R are `princomp()` and `prcomp()`. They will usually produce almost identical results although they use different computational methods to extract the components. While `princomp()` uses the traditional method of extracting eigenvectors from a correlation or covariance matrix, `prcomp()`, extracts the vectors from a rectangular matrix using singular value decomposition. The manual pages recommend `prcomp()` as being numerically more accurate. This probably only matters if the variables are very highly correlated or the number of cases is fewer than the number of variables, but to keep things simple, we will use the recommended function (Box 14):

```
> library(archdata)
> data(Handaxes)
> options(digits=3)
> Handaxes.pca <- prcomp(Handaxes[, -1], scale.=TRUE)
> Handaxes.pca
Standard deviations:
[1] 2.060 1.088 0.753 0.741 0.525 0.315 0.283

Rotation:
        PC1      PC2     PC3     PC4     PC5      PC6      PC7
L   -0.392   0.3230  -0.354  0.3384  -0.481   0.5017   0.1390
L1  -0.332  -0.5386  -0.243  0.4712  -0.131  -0.5454   0.0655
B   -0.441   0.2357   0.261  0.1521   0.124  -0.0750  -0.7983
B1  -0.384  -0.4253   0.322  0.1108   0.479   0.5190   0.2390
B2  -0.361   0.5351   0.333  0.0161   0.142  -0.4137   0.5303
T   -0.363   0.0565  -0.671 -0.4932   0.407  -0.0635  -0.0268
T1  -0.363  -0.2822   0.287 -0.6201  -0.567  -0.0265   0.0076
> summary(Handaxes.pca)
Importance of components:
                          PC1    PC2     PC3     PC4     PC5     PC6     PC7
Standard deviation      2.060  1.088  0.7534  0.7406  0.5253  0.3148  0.2835
Proportion of Variance  0.606  0.169  0.0811  0.0784  0.0394  0.0142  0.0115
Cumulative Proportion   0.606  0.775  0.8566  0.9349  0.9744  0.9885  1.0000
> Handaxes.pca$sdev^2  # Variances or Eigenvalues
[1] 4.2437 1.1848 0.5677 0.5485 0.2759 0.0991 0.0803
```

First, we need to load the archdata package and select the Handaxes data set. Then we compute the principal components. By using the scale.=TRUE argument, we are standardizing the variables so that differences in scale do not affect the results. This is equivalent to extracting the principal components using the correlation matrix.

First look at the table labeled "Rotation." This is more commonly called the factor or component loadings table. There are seven columns because there are seven variables. The number of components is usually equal to the number of variables or one less than the number of cases, whichever is less. If some of the variables can be predicted exactly by a linear combination of the other variables, the number of components is reduced for each of those predictable variables. For example, if the variables were the percentages of artifacts in a set of assemblages and they summed to 100 on each row, the last variable would be a perfect linear combination of the others.

Now look at the column labeled "PC1." Note that all of the loadings are negative. When the observations represent measurements of an object, the first principal component usually represents variation in the size of the object. As a result, all of the variables have the same sign unless some variables are unrelated to size (e.g., ratios between variables). The direction of the principal component is arbitrary so the signs could all be negative (as in this case) or all positive. The signs can be flipped by multiplying the component by –1 without affecting the results.

The loadings are like regression coefficients in that we multiply the variables by these coefficients to create principal component scores for each hand axe. These loadings give us a general idea of which variables are important in describing each of the components. The PC1 loadings range from –0.33 to –0.44. Because the loadings are negative, larger hand axes have negative scores on the first component and smaller hand axes have positive scores. In the second column, PC2, L1 (distance from the butt to the location of the maximum breadth) and B1 (breadth measured at 1/5 of the length from the tip) have larger negative loadings and B2 (breadth measured at 1/5 of the length from the butt) has a larger positive loading. Hand axes broader at the tip (cleaver shaped hand axes) will have negative scores and hand axes broader closer to the butt (triangular hand axes) will have positive scores. The third and fourth components seem to emphasize thickness. While it is useful to examine the loadings to understand what the different components seem to be measuring, the components are extracted without any consideration of your ability to interpret them.

The "Importance of components" section shows the standard deviations for each component. Principal components analysis identifies the direction of maximum covariance or correlation for the first component. Since we standardized the variables, each variable has a standard deviation (and variance) equal to 1. The total variance in the data is $7 \times 1 = 7$ since there are seven variables. The table does not show the variances directly but they are simply the square of the standard deviations as shown in the last command. The standard deviation of the first component is 2.06 so the variance is 4.2 out of a total variance of 7. The first component explains about 60.6 percent of the variation in the standardized values. This component is clearly describing hand axe size. The second component has a variance of 1.18 and explains about 16.9 percent of the variance so together they explain 77.5 percent. That means that we can describe over 75 percent of the variation in the data with just two of the seven components. Adding the third and fourth components, increases the percentage to 93.5 percent. Together the last three components account for only 6.5 percent of the total variance. We can visualize these numbers with a screeplot (Figure 52):

Furze Platt Handaxes

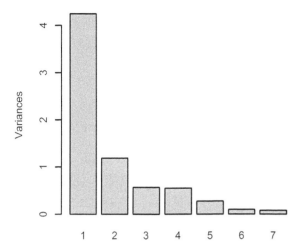

FIGURE 52 Scree plot for the hand axe measurements.

```
> names(Handaxes.pca$sdev) <- 1:7
> plot(Handaxes.pca, main="Principal Components for Furze
  Platt Hand Axes")
```

The plot shows that the first principal component dominates the other six. Only the first two principal components have variances (eigenvalues) greater than 1. Together they describe the size and one aspect of shape in the data. The names() command is not essential, but without it the components are not labeled.

The results of a principal component analysis are often displayed with a biplot that shows the observations and the variables on a single plot:

```
> biplot(Handaxes.pca, xlabs=rep("*", nrow(Handaxes)), pc.biplot=TRUE)
```

Figure 53 shows a biplot for the first two principal components following Gabriel and Odoroff (1990). The default for biplot() is to label each observation with its row name, but with a large number of points that becomes illegible so we are using an asterisk to mark each point with xlabs=rep("*", nrow(Handaxes)). Try running the command after removing the xlabs= argument to see how unreadable the plot becomes.

A biplot shows both columns (variables) and rows (observations) on a single plot. Since it represents multidimensional data in two dimensions, it is an approximation and various scaling methods can be used. Looking at the variables, the arrows are all pointing to the left since the loadings on the first component were all negative.

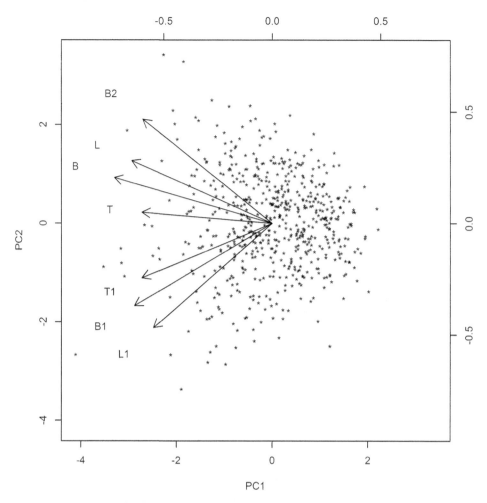

FIGURE 53 Biplot for the first two principal components for the hand axe data.

The axis scales for the variables are along the top and right side of the plot, but these values refer to the scaled values not the exact values of the loadings. For the second component L1, B1, and T1 shown in the lower left quadrat since they have negative loadings on the first and second components. L1 is lower than the other two because it has the most negative loading on the second component. In the upper left quadrat are T, B, L, and B2. The largest loading on the first component is B and it extends the farthest to the left. The largest loading on the second component is B2 and it is located closest to the top of the biplot.

The plot displays the hand axes in terms of two dimensions instead of seven. The first dimension reflects the size of the hand axe so that large hand axes are on the left and small ones are on the right. The second dimension (PC2, the y-axis) reflects shape ranging from triangular at the top to cleaver shape toward the bottom.

The lengths of the vectors reflect the communality of each variable, how well the first two components describe that variable. Longer arrows indicate that the variable is well described in the first two dimensions.

In addition to the loadings, principal components analysis produces scores for each observation in the reduced space. These scores are used to place the asterisks on Figure 53. The distances between points on the plot approximates their Mahalanobis distance. Mahalanobis differs from simple Euclidian distance by taking covariance between the variables into account. We will discuss it in more detail in Chapter 14 on distances and scaling.

The biplot also shows that the variables tend to form two groups. Notice that if we rotated the axes clockwise about 45°, each cluster would be adjacent to an axis so that they would have large values on one axis and small values on the other axis. This is exactly what rotation would accomplish. If we take this path, we no longer have a component that expresses size, instead both components express size and an aspect of hand axe shape.

These groupings of the variables change if we plot the second and third components (leaving out the size component):

```
> biplot(Handaxes.pca, choices=2:3, xlabs=rep("*", nrow(Handaxes)),
+    pc.biplot=TRUE)
```

Figure 54 shows a view of the data looking down though the first component so that we are looking at only shape variation. The interpretation of the second component (PC2, x-axis) is the same as before, but now cleaver-shaped hand axes are on the left side of the plot. The third component (PC3, y-axis) is primarily affected by hand axe thickness with thicker hand axes on the bottom of the plot and thinner ones toward the top. Also note that the variables spread all around the plot and this reflects the shape difference along the second and third components.

Figure 55 summarizes the hand axe sizes and shapes in terms of the first two principal components. Hand axes 2, 225, 332, and 333 were selected for being approximately in the middle of each of the four quadrants beginning in the upper left and proceeding clockwise. The outline is drawn using the two length and three breadth measurements and assuming the hand axe is symmetrical, but this is as close as we can get to a two-dimensional representation with only five measurements (the two thickness measurements are not used). The first component (left versus right) clearly relates to size and the second component (bottom versus top) represents the shape range from cleaver shaped to triangular, ignoring size.

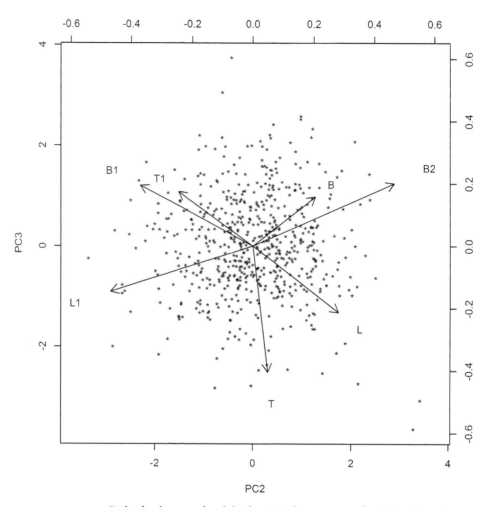

FIGURE 54 Biplot for the second and third principal components for the hand axe data.

One question we might ask is whether there is evidence of distinct groups in the data that might suggest that the sample of hand axes consists of several distinct types. There are not clearly separated groups, but there are some small clusters that might be worth exploring further. The biplot provides a rich depiction of the results, but it takes some practice to get the most out of it.

There are two ways to standardize component loadings and scores. The prcomp() function standardizes the loadings so that the sum of the squares in each column is equal to 1:

```
> colSums(Handaxes.pca$rotation^2)
PC1 PC2 PC3 PC4 PC5 PC6 PC7
  1  1  1  1  1  1  1
```

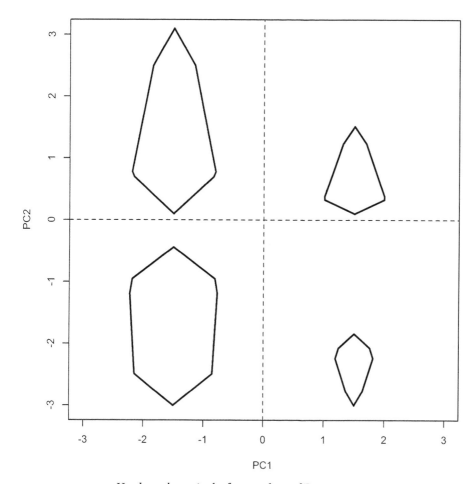

FIGURE 55 Hand axe shapes in the four quadrats of Figure 52.

All seven components are the same. Other versions of principal components standardize the loadings so that the sum of the squared loadings equals the variance of the component:

```
> Handaxes.str <- sweep(Handaxes.pca$rotation, 2, Handaxes.
  pca$sdev, "*")
> Handaxes.str
       PC1     PC2     PC3     PC4     PC5      PC6      PC7
L   -0.81   0.352 -0.27   0.251 -0.253   0.1579   0.0394
L1  -0.68  -0.586 -0.18   0.349 -0.069  -0.1717   0.0186
B   -0.91   0.257   0.20   0.113   0.065 -0.0236  -0.2263
B1  -0.79  -0.463   0.24   0.082   0.251   0.1634   0.0677
B2  -0.74   0.582   0.25   0.012   0.075 -0.1302   0.1503
```

```
T  -0.75  0.061 -0.51 -0.365  0.214 -0.0200 -0.0076
T1 -0.75 -0.307  0.22 -0.459 -0.298 -0.0084  0.0022
> colSums(Handaxes.str^2)
  PC1   PC2   PC3   PC4   PC5   PC6   PC7
4.244 1.185 0.568 0.549 0.276 0.099 0.080
```

The sweep() function takes a matrix and applies a function to the rows or columns of the matrix. In this case, the seven standard deviations are multiplied down the columns. The first standard deviation down the first column, the second standard deviation down the second column, etc. Now the sum of the squared values equals the variance (eigenvalue) for that component.

The result is a structure matrix. The loadings are now equal to the correlation between each of the variables and the principal components. For example, the correlation between length and the first component is –0.81. This shows more clearly that all seven variables are strongly correlated with the first component. The second component contrasts L1 (distance from the butt to the maximum breadth) and B1 (width 1/5 of the length from the tip), which have negative correlations to B2 (breadth 1/5 of the length from the butt), which has a positive correlation. Components 3 and 4 describe variation in thickness.

If you square the structure loadings and sum across the components, you get the communality. If we sum across all seven columns, the communalities will be 1, because seven components describe all of the variability in the variables, but if we sum only the first two columns we get the communality for the first two components. The communality ranges from 0 to 1, with 1 indicating that the variable is perfectly represented by the two components and 0 indicating that the variable is perpendicular to the first two components and is not represented at all.

```
> rowSums(Handaxes.str[, 1:2]^2)
   L   L1    B   B1   B2    T   T1
0.78 0.81 0.89 0.84 0.89 0.56 0.65
```

The communalities for B (.89), B2 (.89), B1 (.84), and L1 (.81) are the largest. Over 80 percent of the variability in these variables are explained by the first two components. T (.56) is the smallest while L (.78) and T1 (.65) are in the middle.

Likewise there are two ways of standardizing principal component scores, one setting the variance of the scores to the variance of the loading and the other setting all of the variances to 1. The scores are stored as a matrix, x in the list returned by prcomp(). The prcomp() function sets the sum of the squared loadings to 1 and the variances of the scores equal to the eigenvalues:

```
> rowSums(Handaxes.pca$rotation^2)
 L L1  B B1 B2  T T1
 1  1  1  1  1  1  1
> apply(Handaxes.pca$x, 2, var)
  PC1   PC2   PC3   PC4   PC5   PC6   PC7
4.244 1.185 0.568 0.549 0.276 0.099 0.080
```

You can convert the scores to equal variances using the scale() function. The command Handaxes.scr <- scale(Handaxes.pca$x[, 1:2]) would standardize the first two principal component scores. If you use the principal component scores in a cluster analysis you may want the variables to have equal weight. In that case you need to standardize the scores produced by prcomp(). Only standardize the larger components. The smaller components are likely to be noise and should not be included.

Several R functions provide factor analysis (Kim and Mueller, 1978a, 1978b; Rencher and Christensen, 2012). Factor analysis assumes that variables that cannot be directly observed cause the correlations between the observed variables. The factanal() function computes a maximum likelihood estimate of the factors and the psych package has function fa(), which provides several exploratory factor analysis methods as well as a variety of rotation techniques. As indicated at the beginning of the chapter, these are used to construct latent variables. In archaeology, they were used primarily to analyze artifact assemblages, but currently assemblages are usually analyzed with correspondence analysis (Chapter 13).

BOX 14 PRINCIPAL COMPONENTS WITH prcomp()

```
prcomp(x, retx = TRUE, center = TRUE, scale. = FALSE,
       tol = NULL, ...)
prcomp(formula, data = NULL, subset, na.action, ...)
```

Function prcomp() constructs principal components using singular value decomposition of the rectangular data matrix. This approach is recommended over the traditional eigen analysis of a correlation or covariance matrix (available through princomp()). The analysis may be specified by numeric matrix or data frame or using a formula with nothing on the left side of the tilde.

The default arguments for `prcomp()` return principal component scores (`retx=TRUE`), subtract the column mean from each variable (`center=TRUE`), but do not divide by the standard deviation (`scale.=FALSE`). All of the components are retained (`tol=NULL`). This is equivalent to performing the analysis on the covariance matrix. Standardizing the variables to have a mean of 0 and a standard deviation of 1 (`center=TRUE`, `scale.=TRUE`) is equivalent to performing the analysis on the correlation matrix and is preferred if the variables are measured on different scales or have substantial differences in variance.

The function returns a list of five parts. The first part, `sdev`, provides the standard deviations of the principal components. Squaring these gives the variances that are equivalent to the eigenvalues. The second part, rotation, provides the principal component loadings. These are standardized so that the sum of the squared values in each column equals 1. The next two parts provide the means (`center`) and the standard deviations (`scale`) of the original data. The last part, x, provides the principal component scores standardized to have standard deviations equal to the principal components (i.e., equal to the values in `sdev`). Using `plot()` with a `prcomp` object displays a scree plot of the eigenvalues (variances) of the principal components. Using `biplot()` with a `prcomp` object returns a biplot. There are options to change the labeling of the points (the default is to use row numbers or names) and the scaling of the plot. There is also a version of `predict()` for `prcomp` objects that will compute the principal component scores for observations that were not included in the analysis.

Table 13 *Functions introduced in Chapter 12*

Function	Package	Description
biplot	stats	Draw a biplot showing rows and columns
fa	psych	Exploratory factor analysis
factanal	stats	Maximum-likelihood factor analysis
prcomp	stats	Principal components by SVD
principal	psych	Principal components with rotation
princomp	stats	Principal components by eigenvalue extraction
sweep	base	Apply a function and value across rows or columns

Note: Packages `base`, `datasets`, `graphics`, `grDevices`, `methods`, `stats`, and `utils` are automatically loaded when R starts.

13

Correspondence Analysis

Correspondence analysis provides a way to summarize categorical data in a reduced number of dimensions (Clausen, 1998; Greenacre, 2007). In that sense, it is very similar to principal components analysis. Principal components is an asymmetrical analysis. We use the correlations (or covariances) between the variables as a summary of the structure in the data. The principal components represent a way of describing the correlation matrix in fewer components than variables. The analysis is asymmetrical because we focus on the relationships between variables and use the principal components to compute scores for each of the observations in the new, reduced space.

In correspondence analysis, the data usually consist of counts of different kinds of things. They could be different artifact types from a variety of sites, strata, or features or they could be different elements in the composition of artifacts. Correspondence analysis is a symmetrical analysis because we adjust the data matrix by both the rows (observations) and the columns (variables) before conducting the analysis. As a result, we can project the observations into the space defined by the variables (as with principal components) or the variables into the space defined by the observations. We can also create biplots summarizing both views.

The adjustment of the data matrix is simply a modification of the Chi-square test that we covered in Chapter 9. In the Chi-square test we compute an expected value for a particular cell by multiplying the row sum by the column sum and dividing by the total sum. The difference between the observed and expected values is squared and divided by the expected value to get the Chi-square contribution for that cell. The sum of all the Chi-square contributions is the total Chi-square value that we use to see if the observed counts are significantly different from what we would expect by chance.

To perform a correspondence analysis, we modify that procedure slightly. First, we divide every value in the table by the sum of all the entries so that each cell represents the proportion of the total found in that cell. Then we compute the expected proportions using the row and column sums of the table of proportions. Finally, we subtract the expected proportion from the observed proportion and divide by the square root of the expected proportion. This gives us a table of Chi-square residuals (called Pearson residuals in the output from the `chisq.test()` function). In correspondence analysis, they are referred to as standardized residuals, but do not confuse these with the standardized residuals in the output from the `chisq.test()`, which are based on a different formula (Agresti, 2007: 38). Correspondence analysis involves a singular value decomposition of these standardized residuals. The structure that we are trying to represent in the analysis is not the correlation between variables but the deviations from the expected values (residuals). As with principal components analysis, we want to represent that structure in a few dimensions and we may be interested in explaining those dimensions in terms of cultural or temporal processes.

There are several packages that provide correspondence analysis in R. We will use package `ca` (Nenadic and Greenacre, 2007), which was developed by Michael Greenacre to supplement his book, *Correspondence Analysis in Practice,* second edition (2007).

We will use the `Olorgesailie.sub` data set to illustrate correspondence analysis. This is the data on several Lower Paleolithic localities at Olorgesailie described in Glynn Isaac (1977). Load data set and view it and the variable labels with the following commands:

```
data(Olorgesailie.sub)
View(Olorgesailie.sub)
View(attr(Olorgesailie.sub, "Variables"))
```

The first two data columns identify the vertical (`Strat`) and horizontal (`Locality`) position of each assemblage. Current estimates are that the lower unit is about 992,000 years old, the middle unit is about 800,000–900,000 years old, and the upper unit is about 662,000 years old (Potts, 2011). The remaining columns (3 through 18) represent different artifact types. The `Variables` attribute provides a more complete name for each type.

First, we should look at the basic counts for the artifact types and the assemblages:

```
> sum(Olorgesailie.sub[,3:18])
[1] 2244
> colSums(Olorgesailie.sub[,3:18])
HA PHA CHA   CL KN BLCT PAT  CH  CS LFS  CB OLT SSS SSNP OST  SP
30 499  83  286 58   81  25  75  15  94  58  71 558  256  15  40
> rowSums(Olorgesailie.sub[,3:18])
L1 L2 L3 L4  L5 M1a M1b M2a M2b M3 M4 M5 M6  M7  M8 M9  U1 U2 U3
61 68 55   1 219 198  50 103 581 77 78 211 30 112 147 22 147 64 20
```

There are 2,244 artifacts distributed among 16 types with counts ranging from 15 for other small tools (OST) and core scrapers (CS) to 558 for simple small scrapers

(SSS). The 19 assemblages range in size from 1 for L4 (Lower, FB/HL) to 581 for M2b (Middle DE/89B-I) so there are substantial size differences between the types and the assemblages. In terms of proportions, other small tools (OST) make up 0.0067 (15/2,244) of the combined assemblages while simple small scrapers (SSS) are 0.2487 (558/2,244). The L4 assemblage makes up less than 0.0004 (1/2,244) of the combined assemblages while M2b is 0.2589. These row and column proportions are called "**masses**" in correspondence analysis.

Now compute the Chi-square value for the table:

```
> Olor.chi <- chisq.test(Olorgesailie.sub[,3:18], simulate.p.
  value=TRUE)
> Olor.chi

        Pearson's Chi-squared test with simulated p-value (based on 2000
        replicates)

data:  Olorgesailie.sub[, 3:18]
X-squared = 1717.1, df = NA, p-value = 0.0004998
```

The Chi-square value is very large, 1717 with a *p*-value of .0005. More useful is to look for patterns of deviation from the expected values:

```
> View(round(Olor.chi$residuals, 2))
> quantile(Olor.chi$residuals, probs=c(0, .025, .975, 1))
        0%       2.5%      97.5%       100%
-9.606998  -4.071413   5.915937  10.188056
```

The first command displays the residuals and the second shows the values of the 0.025 and 0.975 quantiles to make it easier to identify extreme values. In this case, only 2.5 percent of the residuals are larger than 5.92 and only 2.5 percent are smaller than −4.07. We can also list the most extreme residuals with a few commands:

```
> residuals <- as.data.frame.table(Olor.chi$residuals)
> residuals <- residuals[order(abs(residuals$Freq),
  decreasing=TRUE), ]
> head(residuals)
    Var1 Var2      Freq
28   M2b  PHA 10.188056
53    M8  CHA 10.105115
237  M2b  SSS -9.606998
66   M2b   CL  8.593781
233   L5  SSS  7.526618
289   L4   SP  7.356482
```

This converts the 16 × 19 table of residuals to a data frame with a row for each cell (304) and sorts them by absolute value using the `order()` function. Of the six most extreme values, three come from assemblage M2b, which has many more pick-like hand axes (PHA) and cleavers (CL), but fewer simple small scrapers (SSS) than would be expected by chance. Assemblage M8 has many more chisel hand axes (CHA) than expected. Correspondence analysis will try to summarize these patterns in a few dimensions.

If we divide the Chi-square value by the total sample size, we get the Phi-square measure of association (Chapter 9), which is called the "**total inertia**" in correspondence analysis. The command `Olor.chi$statistic/sum(Olor.chi$observed)` produces the value 0.765. Since our table has 19 rows and 16 columns, the maximum possible value of Phi-square is 15 (the smaller of rows – 1 or columns – 1) so this does not reflect a very large deviation from the expected values. In correspondence analysis the **masses** are the proportions of the rows or columns and the **inertias** are the Chi-square distances (standardized by the sample size). Now we are ready to compute a correspondence analysis for the Olorgesailie assemblages. Install the `ca` package (Box 15) and then load it:

```
> install.packages("ca")
> library(ca)
> options(digits=2, scipen=5)
> Olor.ca
```

```
Principal inertias (eigenvalues):
            1         2         3         4         5         6         7
Value       0.376144  0.119925  0.070236  0.053028  0.030946  0.029602  0.023563
Percentage  49.16%    15.67%    9.18%     6.93%     4.04%     3.87%     3.08%
            8         9         10        11        12        13        14
Value       0.018467  0.016749  0.012203  0.005712  0.003544  0.003002  0.001569
Percentage  2.41%     2.19%     1.59%     0.75%     0.46%     0.39%     0.21%
            15
Value       0.000489
Percentage  0.06%
```

```
Rows:
          L1     L2     L3     L4       L5     M1a    M1b     M2a     M2b    M3
Mass      0.027  0.030  0.025  0.00045  0.098  0.088  0.022   0.046   0.26   0.034
ChiDist   1.293  1.194  1.109  7.42294  0.842  0.634  1.105   0.967   0.82   0.600
Inertia   0.045  0.043  0.030  0.02455  0.069  0.035  0.027   0.043   0.17   0.012
Dim. 1    1.774  1.084  1.210  -0.74794 1.122  0.852  -0.571  -1.040  -1.23  0.622
Dim. 2    1.043  0.315  0.700  1.48439  0.034  0.490  -0.810  0.706   0.75   0.077
```

	M4	M5	M6	M7	M8	M9	U1	U2	U3
Mass	0.035	0.094	0.013	0.050	0.066	0.0098	0.066	0.029	0.0089
ChiDist	0.976	0.586	1.050	0.972	0.986	1.0731	0.402	0.913	1.7032
Inertia	0.033	0.032	0.015	0.047	0.064	0.0113	0.011	0.024	0.0259
Dim. 1	-0.356	0.617	0.276	-1.154	-0.216	1.0863	0.392	1.290	1.2940
Dim. 2	-2.020	-0.265	-2.194	-1.182	-2.587	0.4884	0.239	0.148	1.5194

Columns:

	HA	PHA	CHA	CL	KN	BLCT	PAT	CH	CS
Mass	0.013	0.222	0.037	0.127	0.026	0.036	0.0111	0.033	0.0067
ChiDist	1.470	0.661	1.581	0.881	0.916	0.891	0.6763	0.615	1.8725
Inertia	0.029	0.097	0.092	0.099	0.022	0.029	0.0051	0.013	0.0234
Dim. 1	0.014	-0.993	-0.146	-1.265	-1.158	-0.047	-0.2645	0.118	0.8038
Dim. 2	-2.462	0.043	-4.316	0.701	0.287	-1.331	0.1928	0.492	1.0128

	LFS	CB	OLT	SSS	SSNP	OST	SP
Mass	0.042	0.026	0.032	0.249	0.114	0.0067	0.018
ChiDist	0.501	1.109	0.778	0.734	0.906	2.0330	1.490
Inertia	0.011	0.032	0.019	0.134	0.094	0.0276	0.040
Dim. 1	-0.589	1.111	-0.154	1.125	1.215	0.4655	-0.459
Dim. 2	0.149	-0.643	0.058	0.071	0.747	0.8064	0.514

After installing and loading the ca package, we set significant digits to two and scipen to five. That will reduce the number of decimal places printed and discourages R from using scientific notation for small numbers. By default, ca() extracts as many dimensions as possible (here 15, the smaller of rows – 1 or columns – 1), but it only prints out summaries for the first two. The **principal inertias** are listed first. These are the squares of the singular values (stored in Olor.ca as sv). If you square these values and sum them (sum(Olor.ca$sv^2)), you will get the Phi-square that we computed earlier from the Chi-square test (0.765). The first two dimensions account for about 65 percent of the inertia. The next two dimensions add 9 and 7 percent respectively. They may be worth exploring since the expected percentage for a dimension is 1/15 (6.7 percent).

The next section of the output summarizes the rows. "Mass" is the proportion of the artifacts and "ChiDist" is the square root of the Phi-square for that row. It measures how the proportions of the various artifact types in that row differ from the proportions for all of the assemblages combined. Look through the distances to identify assemblages that have large distances. The very small assemblage (L4 with a single artifact) has the largest distance by far (7.4). The next largest is U3 (1.7).

The "Inertias" are the distances squared times the mass (Phi-square times the mass). The sum of this row equals the **total inertia**. Although the distance value for L4 was large, the inertia is small because the mass is so small. The same holds for

U3. Since total inertia is distributed over 19 assemblages, the "expected" inertia for an assemblage is 0.7652/19 = 0.0403. Inertias for L4 and U3 fall below this threshold while the inertia for L5 is moderately higher (0.069) and M2b is much higher (0.17).

Using U3 as an example, we can compute these measures directly from the original data and the Chi-square table:

```
> Total <- sum(Olorgesailie.sub[, 3:18])    # Total artifacts
> Row <- sum(Olorgesailie.sub["U3", 3:18]) # Artifacts in assemblage U3
> Chi <- sum(Olor.chi$residuals["U3", ]^2) # Chi square for assemblage U3
> Row/Total                 # Mass
[1] 0.0089
> sqrt(Chi/Row)             # ChiDist
[1] 1.7
> (Chi/Row)*(Row/Total)   # Inertia (or Chi/Total)
[1] 0.026
```

"Dim. 1" and "Dim. 2" are the coordinates for the first two dimensions extracted from the table. They are analogous to the principal component scores from Chapter 12.

Now look at the summary for the columns. Looking at the masses, it is clear that simple small scrapers (SSS, 25 percent) and pick-like hand axes (PHA, 22 percent) are the most common types. None of the types have Chi-square distances as large as the L4 assemblage did. The largest distances are for other small tools (OST) and core scrapers (CS). Since total inertia is distributed over 16 assemblages, the "expected" inertia for an assemblage is 0.7652/16 = 0.0478. The inertia for simple small scrapers (SSS) is much larger than this (0.13) and the inertias for pick-like hand axes (PHA), chisel hand axes (CHA), cleavers (CL), and small scrapers, nosed point (SSNP) are all about twice the expected value. To illustrate the computation of the values for SSS, we need to slightly modify the code for the row values:

```
> Total <- sum(Olorgesailie.sub[, 3:18])
> Row <- sum(Olorgesailie.sub[, "SSS"])
> Chi <- sum(Olor.chi$residuals[, "SSS"]^2)
> Row/Total                 # Mass
[1] 0.25
> sqrt(Chi/Row)             # ChiDist
[1] 0.73
> (Chi/Row)*(Row/Total)   # Inertia (or Chi/Total)
[1] 0.13
```

In addition to the results produced by the print() function, we can get an alternate presentation of the results using summary(Olor.ca). The two reports complement one another so it will usually be worthwhile to print out both. Instead of simply listing the principal inertias and their percentages, the second set of results provides a histogram and cumulative percentages so we can easily see that the first two dimensions explain almost 65 percent of the variation in the table while adding the third and fourth dimensions would give us almost 81 percent. The summaries for the rows and columns compactly provide a great deal of information. The numeric columns are presented as per mills (values are multiplied by 1,000 and rounded). Once this is taken into account, it is clear that the 27 for L1 mass is really 0.027, which is what we had with the `print()` results:

```
> summary(Olor.ca)

Principal inertias (eigenvalues):

 dim    value       %    cum%     scree plot
  1    0.376144   49.2   49.2     ************
  2    0.119925   15.7   64.8     ****
  3    0.070236    9.2   74.0     **
  4    0.053028    6.9   80.9     **
  5    0.030946    4.0   85.0     *
  6    0.029602    3.9   88.9     *
  7    0.023563    3.1   91.9     *
  8    0.018467    2.4   94.3     *
  9    0.016749    2.2   96.5     *
 10    0.012203    1.6   98.1
 11    0.005712    0.7   98.9
 12    0.003544    0.5   99.3
 13    0.003002    0.4   99.7
 14    0.001569    0.2   99.9
 15    0.000489    0.1  100.0
       --------   -----
Total: 0.765178  100.0
```

```
Rows:
      name  mass  qlt  inr    k=1  cor  ctr    k=2  cor  ctr
1  |   L1 |   27  785   59 | 1088  707   86 |  361   78   30 |
2  |   L2 |   30  318   57 |  665  310   36 |  109    8    3 |
3  |   L3 |   25  496   39 |  742  448   36 |  242   48   12 |
4  |   L4 |    0    9   32 | -459    4    0 |  514    5    1 |
5  |   L5 |   98  667   90 |  688  667  123 |   12    0    0 |
6  |  M1a |   88  751   46 |  523  680   64 |  170   72   21 |
```

```
 7 |  M1b |  22  165  36 | -350 100    7 | -281   65   15 |
 8 |  M2a |  46  499  56 | -638 435   50 |  244   64   23 |
 9 |  M2b | 259  958 225 | -754 855  391 |  261  103  147 |
10 |   M3 |  34  406  16 |  381 404   13 |   27    2    0 |
11 |   M4 |  35  563  43 | -218  50    4 | -699  513  142 |
12 |   M5 |  94  442  42 |  379 417   36 |  -92   25    7 |
13 |   M6 |  13  550  19 |  169  26    1 | -760  524   64 |
14 |   M7 |  50  707  62 | -708 530   66 | -409  177   70 |
15 |   M8 |  66  843  83 | -132  18    3 | -896  825  438 |
16 |   M9 |  10  410  15 |  666 385   12 |  169   25    2 |
17 |   U1 |  66  400  14 |  240 357   10 |   83   43    4 |
18 |   U2 |  29  754  31 |  791 751   47 |   51    3    1 |
19 |   U3 |   9  313  34 |  794 217   15 |  526   95   21 |

Columns:
        name mass  qlt  inr    k=1 cor ctr    k=2 cor ctr
 1 |   HA |  13  336  38 |    9   0    0 | -853  336   81 |
 2 |  PHA | 222  850 127 | -609 849  219 |   15    1    0 |
 3 |  CHA |  37  897 121 |  -89   3    1 | -1495 894  689 |
 4 |   CL | 127  851 129 | -776 775  204 |  243   76   63 |
 5 |   KN |  26  613  28 | -710 601   35 |   99   12    2 |
 6 | BLCT |  36  268  37 |  -29   1    0 | -461  267   64 |
 7 |  PAT |  11   67   7 | -162  58    1 |   67   10    0 |
 8 |   CH |  33   90  17 |   72  14    0 |  170   77    8 |
 9 |   CS |   7  104  31 |  493  69    4 |  351   35    7 |
10 |  LFS |  42  529  14 | -361 519   15 |   51   11    1 |
11 |   CB |  26  418  42 |  681 378   32 | -223   40   11 |
12 |  OLT |  32   15  25 |  -94  15    1 |   20    1    0 |
13 |  SSS | 249  885 175 |  690 884  315 |   25    1    1 |
14 | SSNP | 114  758 122 |  745 677  168 |  259   82   64 |
15 |  OST |   7   39  36 |  286  20    1 |  279   19    4 |
16 |   SP |  18   50  52 | -281  36    4 |  178   14    5 |
```

But there are new columns as well. The "qlt" (**Quality**) column reflects how well the dimensions extracted represent the row or column. This is based on the squared correlation so the range is from 0 to 1, converted to per mills so from 0 to 1,000, and is analogous to communality in principal components. Assemblage L1 has a quality of 785, suggesting that it is reasonably well represented, but not as well as Mb2, which has a quality of 958. Assemblage L4 is very poorly represented with a quality of 9. For the artifact types, the quality values indicate that chisel hand axes (CHA), pick-like hand axes (PHA), and simple scrapers, small (SSS) are well represented in two dimensions, but other large tools (OLT), other small tools (OST), and spheroids (SP) are not. The next column, "inr", is **relative inertia** per mill. These are the same inertias listed in the print() output, but they have been divided by the sum of the inertias, multiplied by 1,000 and rounded to an integer value to create the per mill value.

The "k=" columns are the coordinates for the first two dimensions. The print() command produces **standard coordinates** while the summary() command produces **principal coordinates**. Principal coordinates are simply standard coordinates that have been multiplied by their respective singular value (e.g., Olor.ca$rowcoord[,1] * Olor.ca$sv[1]) and converted to per mills.

Greenacre (2007) refers to standard coordinates as projections of vertices and the principal coordinates as projections of profiles. This has similarities to principal components where we distinguished between loadings (for the variables, analogous to projections of vertices) and scores (for the observations, analogous to projections of profiles). Since correspondence analysis is symmetrical, we can project rows in the space defined by columns (typical for principal components) or we can project columns in the space defined by the rows.

The "cor" (**Correlation**) columns for each dimension reflect the squared correlations with that row. Greenacre (2007) refers to these values as relative contributions or squared cosines. A value of 1,000 would indicate that the dimension captured the variability of that row (or column) perfectly. The sum of the "cor" columns over the dimensions gives us the value for the "qlt" (quality) column, which was discussed previously.

The "ctr" (**Contribution**) columns show how the rows or columns contribute to the definition of each dimension. Assemblage M2b is the major contributor to the first dimension and M8 is the major contributor to the second dimension. For the columns' simple scrapers, small (SSS) is the major contributor for the first dimension and chisel hand axes (CHA) is the major contributor for the second dimension.

The ca package provides a number of different plots to help interpret the results of the analysis. To get a symmetric plot that includes the rows and columns scaled to fit together, we use the defaults. This works well for small- to moderate-sized data sets, but becomes unwieldy for larger ones:

```
> plot(Olor.ca)
```

Figure 56 shows that the artifact types are stretched out along the first dimension except for three types that extend down along the second dimension. Cleavers (CL), knives (KN), and pick-like hand axes (PHA) are on the left side of the plot and

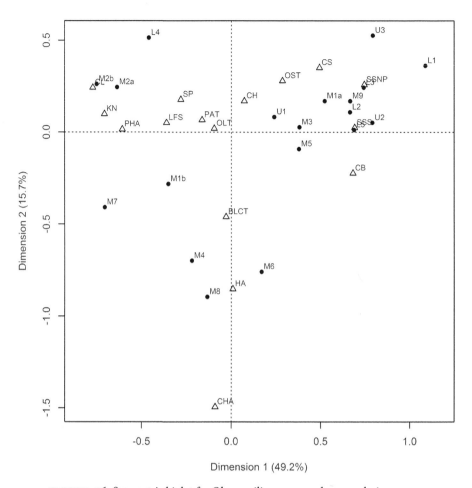

FIGURE 56 Symmetric biplot for Olorgesailie correspondence analysis.

small scrapers, simple (SSS) and small scrapers, nosed point (SSNP) are on the right side. This suggests that the major axis of assemblage variability is between large and small tools, an observation made previously by Kleindienst (1961) and Isaac (1977). The assemblages cluster in three, or possibly four, groups. Assemblages that fall along a temporal sequence will often form an arch or horseshoe in a plot like this (Chapter 17), but that does not seem to be the case here. Using the initial letter (L, M, U) as a rough chronological indicator shows that the lower and upper assemblages are intermixed in the upper right quadrant (except for the tiny L4 assemblage). The middle assemblages spread across the entire range of the first dimension.

In general, assemblages close to a type should have more than expected amounts of that type. This will not hold invariably since we have collapsed multiple dimensions

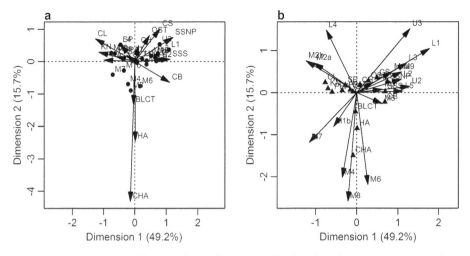

FIGURE 57 Row (a) and column (b) principal biplots for Olorgesailie correspondence analysis.

into two and the position of an assemblage is based on all of the types, not just those nearby. For example, in the upper left corner of the figure assemblage M2b is very close to CL (Cleavers) and the Chi-square residual was 9. It is also close to KN (Knives) and PHA (Pick like hand axes) and it had residuals of 5 and 10 respectively. L5 is practically on top of SSS (Small scrapers simple) and its Chi-square residual was 8. M8 had a residual of 10 with CHA (Chisel hand axes). It is not that close to the CHA point although it is closer than any other assemblage.

We can also create asymmetric plots that show the rows or columns in the space defined by the other. To plot the assemblages (rows) in the space defined by the artifact types (columns), we specify "rowprincipal" as the map (Figure 57a):

```
> plot(Olor.ca, map="rowprincipal", arrows=c(FALSE, TRUE))
```

The arrows command is not essential, but it produces a biplot that resembles those in principal components analysis and it emphasizes that we are defining the space using the artifact types as the axes (like we used the measurements length, width, and so on to define the space for the Furze Platz hand axes). The assemblages lie within the area defined by the arrows except for L4, which is hard to see because it is overprinted with SP (spheroids). This is because L4 consists of a single spheroid (the arrow pointing at about 11 o'clock). Since 100 percent of the assemblage is spheroids, L4 lies on the end point of the axis. You cannot expect to read percentages directly from the graph in most cases since we have collapsed 16 dimensions into two.

We can also plot the artifact types (columns) in the space defined by the assemblages (rows) (Figure 57b):

```
> plot(Olor.ca, map="colprincipal", arrows=c(TRUE, FALSE))
```

Note that L4 and SP are no longer superimposed. Although the only artifact in L4 is a spheroid, only a small percentage of the spheroids are found in L4 (2.5 percent). Most of the spheroids come from M2a and M2b (20 percent in each) and SP lies on those axes.

We can use plot3d(Olor.ca) to get an interactive 3-D window with the types and sites plotted that can be rotated and zoomed (load library(rgl) first). If you run this command you will be able see three dimensions. You will want to drag a corner of the window with the left mouse button to make the window bigger. L4 is not well-represented in the first two, but in the third dimension it is far from the other sites. Dragging with the left mouse button rotates the view and dragging with the right button (or using the wheel) zooms in and out.

We might wonder how much of an effect very large or very small samples have on the results. The print() and especially the summary() output give us a good indication. The very small assemblage L4 is not well described by the first two dimensions, suggesting that it has not influenced the results to any substantial degree. The very large sample, M2b, is less clear. It is well described by the first two dimensions and it has the largest contribution value for the first dimension so that we might wonder if it has dominated the results at the expense of other interesting patterns. Fortunately, we can easily answer these questions by computing the correspondence analysis leaving out these two assemblages and then plotting them in the space defined without them:

```
> Olor.ca2 <- ca(Olorgesailie.sub[,3:18], suprow=c(4, 9))
> plot(Olor.ca2)
```

Initially, this plot looks dramatically different (Figure 58). Part of the difference is that L4 is now plotted far away from the rest of the assemblages, which compresses the rest of the plot. Second, the first axis has flipped so that the larger tools are now on the right side of the plot and the small tools on the left. The second axis is similar to the original but there are clearly differences. Assemblage M2b is characterized by higher than expected numbers of pick-like hand axes (PHA), cleavers (CL), and knives (KN), and these types are all plotted close together in the original analysis. Now cleavers are high on the second dimension while pick-like hand axes and knives are low on that dimension and they are closer to the hand axes (HA), chisel hand axes (CHA), and broken large cutting tools (BLCT).

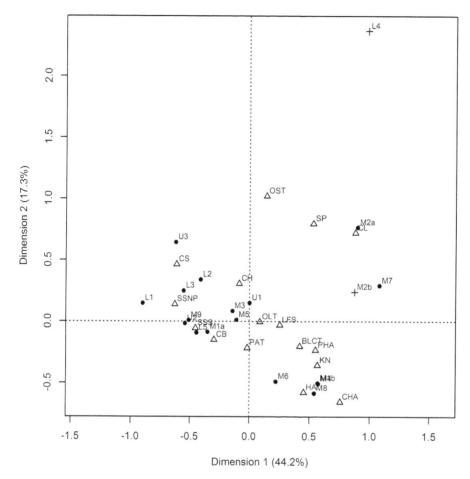

FIGURE 58 Symmetric biplot of Olorgesailie data excluding L4 and M2b.

Despite the apparent differences, the correlation between the two first dimensions is very high (−0.99) and the correlation between the two second dimensions is relatively high (0.68):

```
> cor(Olor.ca$rowcoord[,1], Olor.ca2$rowcoord[,1])
[1] -0.99
> cor(Olor.ca$rowcoord[,2], Olor.ca2$rowcoord[,2])
[1] 0.68
```

There are still three clear groups of assemblages and the large tool/small tool dichotomy is clearly apparent although it now ranges from the upper left to the lower right of the plot. So L4 and M2b had little influence on the first dimension, but substantially more on the second. If you look at the changes in the quality (qlt) and correlation (cor) columns you will see the differences. Which version is superior will depend on the degree to which the results "make sense" in terms of other information we have about the sites.

We could also explore the possibility of reducing the sample size of M2b by sampling down to the size of the next largest assemblage:

```
> Olor2 <- Olorgesailie.sub[, 3:18]
> Olor2["M2b",] <- round(Olor2["M2b",]/581*219, 0)
> Olor2.ca <- ca(Olor2)
> plot(Olor2.ca)
```

These commands create a copy of Olorgesailie (just the artifact columns) and then adjusts M2b downward from a total sample of 581 to 219 (the size of assemblage L5), resulting in a plot that is quite similar to the one where L4 and M2b were removed. Since the assemblage size probably relates more to how long the site was excavated, how much of it was excavated, and the deposition rate than it does to the cultural activities that occurred at the site, eliminating very small and very large assemblages (or at least reducing their influence) will probably produce results that are more interpretable. Correspondence analysis uses Chi-square distances, which reduces the influence of large samples and boosts the influence of small samples, but very large samples can still warp the results, making interpretations more difficult.

The correspondence analysis suggests that a large part of the variability in the Olorgesailie assemblages is a difference between assemblages dominated by large tools and those dominated by small tools, but it does not tell us why. Behavior, erosional processes, and other factors could be important. We can display the differences using a standard type of display used by archaeologists to order assemblages chronologically even though chronology does not seem to explain this pattern. The package plotrix has an implementation of the battleship plot that we will use more in Chapter 17. We used the package in Chapter 5 so you should already have it installed.

```
> library(plotrix)
> rows <- order(Olor.ca$rowcoord[, 1])
> cols <- order(Olor.ca$colcoord[, 1])
> props <- prop.table(as.matrix(Olorgesailie.sub[, 3:18]), 1)
> dev.new(width=12, height=8)
> battleship.plot(props[rows,cols], main=
+    "Olorgesailie Assemblages",    y")
```

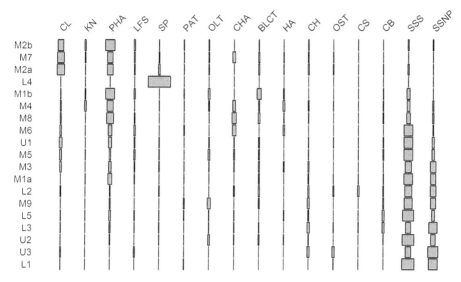

FIGURE 59 Battleship plot with rows and columns ordered by the first dimension in the correspondence analysis for the Olorgesailie assemblages.

We use the `order()` function to order the assemblages (rows) and the artifact types (columns) by their first dimension scores (the "Dim. 1" rows in the output). Then we convert artifact counts to a table of row proportions. The fifth command opens a rectangular plot window instead of the normal square one and the last command produces the battleship plot. Figure 59 shows the results. The large tool assemblages are on the upper left and the small tool assemblages are in the lower left. There is no clear break between them with a number of assemblages falling in the middle.

Correspondence analysis is widely used in ecology and community studies. In addition to simple correspondence analysis, there are expansions including multiple correspondence analysis on categorical variables, joint correspondence analysis on categorical variables, detrended correspondence analysis to remove curvature in the first 2 dimensions (Chapter 17), canonical correspondence analysis to include numeric explanatory variables, and co-correspondence analysis to compare two sets of variables from the same sites. There are several implementations in R including `ca()` and `mjca()` in ca (Nenadic and Greenacre, 2007), `corresp()` and `mca()` in MASS (Venables and Ripley, 2002), `decorana()` and `cca()`, in vegan (Oksanen, et al, 2016), `cca()` in ade4 (Dray and Dufour, 2007), `CA()` and `MCA()` in FactoMineR (Le et al., 2008), anacor() in anacor (de Leuw and Mair, 2009), and coca() in cocorresp (Simpson, 2009).

BOX 15 CORRESPONDENCE ANALYSIS WITH ca() IN PACKAGE ca

```
ca(obj, nd = NA, suprow = NA, supcol = NA,
   subsetrow = NA, subsetcol = NA, ...)
```

```
ca(formula, data, ...)
```

The first argument (obj=) accepts tables, matrices, and data frames that resemble tables. Data frames can also be used with the formula method where two variables are on the right side of the formula.

The default analysis is to use all rows and columns of the data in the analysis and to extract all of the dimensions (one less than the number of rows or columns, whichever is less). The nd= argument sets the number of dimensions to extract (usually two, but more may be helpful in some cases). The suprow= and supcol= arguments take index numbers of rows or columns that should be passive. These supplementary rows or columns are not included in the analysis, but the results are used to estimate coordinates for them so that they appear on plots. The subsetrow= and subsetcol= arguments are used to specify the indices of rows and columns that should be included in the analysis so that only a portion of the table is analyzed.

The function returns a list of 16 elements. The singular values (sv) come first followed by the number of dimensions (nd) if the nd= argument was used. Then the names, masses, Chi-square distances, inertias, coordinates, and indices of supplementary points for the rows (rownames, rowmass, rowdist, rowinertia, rowcoord, rowsup) and for the columns (colnames, colmass, coldist, colinertia, colcoord, colsup). The last elements are a copy of the original data table stored as a matrix (N) and the call used for the function (call).

The ca() function returns a ca object that has print(), summary(), plot(), and plot3d() methods. The plotting functions have numerous options. See ?plot.ca and ?plot3d.ca for more information.

Table 14 *Functions introduced in Chapter 13*

Function	Package	Description
anacor	anacor	Simple and canonical correspondence analysis
battleship.plot	plotrix	Create a battleship plot
ca	ca	Correspondence analysis
CA	FactoMineR	Correspondence analysis
cca	vegan	[Partial] [constrained] correspondence analysis
cca	ade4	Canonical correspondence analysis
coca	cocorresp	Fit co-correspondence analysis ordination models
corresp	MASS	Correspondence analysis
decorana	vegan	Detrended correspondence analysis
mca	MASS	Multiple correspondence analysis
MCA	FactoMineR	Multiple correspondence analysis
mjca	ca	Multiple and joint correspondence analysis
order	base	Return an index used to re-order a matrix or data frame

Note: Packages `base`, `datasets`, `graphics`, `grDevices`, `methods`, `stats`, and `utils` are automatically loaded when R starts.

14

Distances and Scaling

We have discussed the concepts of multivariate spaces and distances in earlier chapters. With discriminant analysis, we created a space that separated groups of observations. With principal components, we defined a multivariate space for the observations in fewer dimensions while losing the least amount of information. With correspondence analysis, we displayed observations and variables in terms of their Chi-square distances. This chapter is the first of two that focus on quantitative methods that start with a distance matrix and represent the distances between observations either in the form of a map (this chapter) or by grouping observations that are similar (Chapter 15). In both cases we generally start by computing a distance or similarity measure between pairs of observations.

The first part of the chapter describes different ways of defining distance and similarity. Different choices in the measurement of distance can have substantial influence on the results. The second part describes ways of analyzing distance matrices in order to represent them in the form of a map. If you have ever looked at a highway map, you may have noticed a triangular table of distances between major cities. What if you only had the table of distances? How would you go about reconstructing the map? Scaling methods were primarily developed in the field of psychology where data expressing perception or preferences are gathered directly in the form of a similarity matrix that reflects judgments regarding how similar pairs of stimuli are. In archaeology, the classic application is seriation, which attempts to represent variation in assemblages along a single dimension that may represent time (Chapter 17). The third part of the chapter illustrates how to compare two distance matrices. For example, if we have sites located in a region and collections of ceramics from those sites, how do we compare the geographic distances to ceramic assemblage distances?

14.1 DISTANCE, DISSIMILARITY, AND SIMILARITY

The term **distance** refers to a numeric score that indicates how close or far two observations are in terms of a set of variables. Larger distances mean the observations are less similar to one another. **Dissimilarity** measures are larger when two objects are more distant or different from one another. **Similarity** measures are larger when two objects are more like one another. For a series of characteristics or traits, a count of the number of traits common to both objects is a similarity measure. If we subtract the number of traits in common from the total number of traits, we have a dissimilarity measure. Any dissimilarity measure can be converted into a similarity measure by subtracting it from the largest possible value and vice versa. The broader term **proximity** refers to measures of similarity and dissimilarity.

The terms dissimilarity and distance are routinely used interchangeably, but **distances** should satisfy three requirements that are not necessarily imposed on dissimilarities. The first requirement is that the distance between two objects is not zero, unless they are identical to one another. The second is that the distance from one object to another is the same as the distance from the second to the first (symmetry). Finally, for any three objects the distance from the first to the third can never be greater than the sum of the distances from the first to the second plus the distance from the second to the third (the triangle inequality). In concrete terms, if I am traveling to a particular city and I decide to visit another city on the way, the total distance traveled cannot be less than (but it could be equal to) the distance traveling directly to my original destination.

There are many ways of measuring dissimilarity or distance. A recent article examined 45 measures and classified them into eight families (Cha, 2007). Archaeologists generally use only a few including Euclidean distance, Manhattan distance, simple matching coefficient (symmetric binary), Jaccard coefficient (asymmetric binary), and Gower's coefficient. In addition, several other distance measures arise in the context of the multivariate methods we have already discussed such as Mahalanobis and Chi-square distances. Also angular distances (cosine similarity, related to the Pearson correlation coefficient). In studying large-scale regional phenomena, great circle distances, the shortest distance between two points on a sphere, become important. The appropriate measure of distance is closely related to the kind of variables we are using.

14.1.1 Distances for Continuous and Discrete Metric Data

Euclidean distance is simply the straight line distance between two points (observations). We take the square root of the sum of the squares of the differences between two observations over all the variables. Euclidean distance will be appropriate whenever the variables consist of numeric measurements. This includes presence/absence or dichotomous variables and it can include rank or ordinal variables.

Manhattan distance (also called city block distance) takes the sum of the absolute values of the differences between two observations over all the variables. Instead of the straight line distance, this is the distance we travel if we are restricted to walking along city blocks and assuming we cannot cut diagonally across a block. If the coordinates of one point are (0, 0) and the coordinates of a second point are (1, 1), the Euclidean distance is 1.414 while the Manhattan distance is 2.

Both Euclidean and Manhattan distance measures are part of a family called **Minkowski** distances. Minkowski distances are defined as follows:

$$D_{ij} = \left(\sum \left| x_{ik} - x_{jk} \right|^p \right)^{1/p}$$

where D_{ij} is the distance between rows i and j in the data matrix; x_{ik}, x_{jk} are the observations on rows i and j for column k; and p is an integer that defines the specific Minkowski distance.

When p is 1, the distance is Manhattan; when it is 2, the distance is Euclidean; and when it is infinity, the distance is Chebyshev or maximum.

When the data are discrete counts, two variants of Manhattan distance are common. In ecology and biology, the Bray–Curtis dissimilarity measure is used to compare different sites based on the counts of various taxa at each site. In archaeology, the Brainerd–Robinson Similarity coefficient is sometimes used to compare the similarity between two assemblages in terms of the percentages of different kinds of artifacts at each (Brainerd, 1951; Robinson, 1951). Since archaeological excavations rarely control the area or volume sampled from one site to another, percentages are usually used instead of counts. Subtracting the Manhattan distance between two assemblages from 200 gives a similarity measure that ranges from 200 (identical) to 0 (no overlapping types). While distances between artifact measurements (e.g., hand axes or projectile points) almost always utilize Euclidean distance, assemblages are better described using Manhattan distance.

To see why, imagine that we have four types and four assemblages. Assemblages A and D have a single type and assemblages B and C each have an even split between two types. Assemblage A has no types in common with C or D and assemblage B has no types in common with C or D. The following code creates the assemblages and two distance matrices:

```
> A <- c(100, 0, 0, 0)
> B <- c(50, 50, 0, 0)
> C <- c(0, 0, 50, 50)
> D <- c(0, 0, 0, 100)
> ABCD <- rbind(A, B, C, D)
> colnames(ABCD) <- paste0("Type", 1:4)
> ABCD
    Type1  Type2  Type3  Type4
A    100      0      0      0
B     50     50      0      0
C      0      0     50     50
D      0      0      0    100
> dist(ABCD, method="euclidean")
     A    B    C
B   71
C  122  100
D  141  122   71
> dist(ABCD, method="manhattan")
     A    B    C
B  100
C  200  200
D  200  200  100
```

The matrices illustrate the problems with Euclidean distance on data that consists of proportions or percentages of different artifact types by assemblage. Assemblages A and B have one type in common and their Euclidean distance is 71. Assemblages A and C have no types in common and their Euclidean distance is 122. Assemblages A and D also have no types in common, but their Euclidean distance is 141. In addition, B and C have no types in common, but their Euclidean distance is 100. In this simple example, two assemblages that have no types in common can have Euclidean distances of 100, 122, or 141! Generally we would expect that two assemblages with no types in common should have the same distance regardless of the percentages of those types. In contrast the Manhattan distances between A and B and between C and D are 100 since each pair shares one type. The distances between A and C, A and D, B and C, and B and D are all 200. If your assemblages are based on proportions or percentages, Manhattan distances are likely to give better results.

Creating a distance matrix based on artifact measurements that represent the interesting patterns in the data requires some careful thought, especially if the variables differ in magnitude or scale. For example, the hand axes data set has length, breadth, and thickness measurements. These are all measured on the same scale, but they differ substantially in magnitude. Length ranges from 69 to 242 mm, breadth ranges from 34 to 123 mm, and thickness from 20 to 69 mm. If we compute Euclidean distances using these three measures, length will contribute the most to the distances so any analyses we perform on the distance matrix will reflect length more than breadth or thickness. The problem is even greater if we include variables measured on different scales. The dart points data set included a measure of weight in grams. Counts of flakes or angles of various parts of the artifact would be other examples of numeric variables measured on different scales.

Several methods can be used to reduce size effect between variables (Chapter 6). One is to standardize the variables before computing the distance matrix. Then all of the variables will have a mean of zero and a standard deviation of 1. This eliminates the unit of measurement (cm, mm, gm, direction, etc.) and differences in magnitude so that each variable is weighted equally.

Another approach is to take the logarithm (base 10 or base e). Logarithms are undefined for zeros so the usual approach is to add a small number to the zeros (e.g., 0.05). Alternatively adding 1 to every value produces transformed variables that have a minimum value of 0 when the original value was zero. Use of log transforms is relatively common, especially in compositional analysis. They reduce the differences in magnitude between the variables, but they do not eliminate them and they do not eliminate differences in the unit of measurement although this is usually not an issue for compositional data since the variables are measured in the same units.

The rows may also exhibit size differences (Chapter 6). For archaeological assemblages, it is common to remove size by converting the counts to percentages or proportions. This assumes that assemblage size is not related exclusively to the cultural activities that produced the deposit. In fact, deposition rates, excavation budgets, and other exogenous factors usually affect assemblage size. However, for well-defined, rapidly sealed deposits that have been completely excavated (graves, structures, especially burned structures, shipwrecks, and potentially other feature types), assemblage size may be meaningful. Combining measurements into new variables by computing ratios is another approach to eliminating the size effect. Dividing each variable by the geometric mean is another approach. For compositional data, including artifact assemblages, dividing the variables by the last (or some other) variable has been recommended to remove the effects of closure that results from converting to percentages, per mills, ppm, or ppb (Aitchison, 1986).

Still another consideration is whether to measure distance using the space defined by the variables that may include correlated variables or to convert to an orthogonal representation of that space by computing principal component scores to use in the analysis instead of the original variables. A decision must also be made regarding how to weight those scores (equally or by eigenvalue, Chapter 12). Alternatively

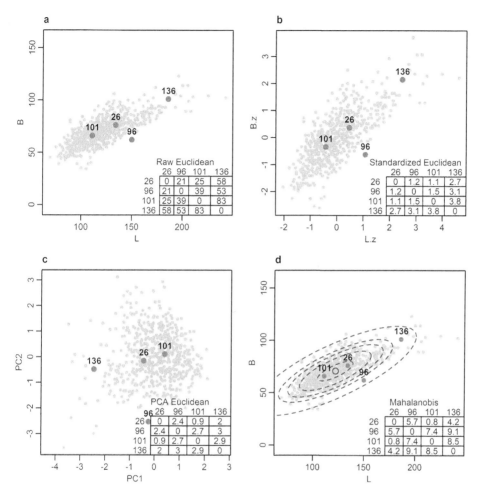

FIGURE 60 Four ways of measuring distances: (a) raw Euclidean; (b) standardized Euclidean; (c) principal components Euclidean; and (d) Mahalanobis distance.

Mahalanobis distances, which take covariance into account, can be useful if the data can be described by a single covariance matrix.

As an example Figure 60a–d shows four different ways of computing distance between the Furze Platt hand axes based on their length and breadth. Figure 60a plots the hand axes by length and breadth and shows the distances between four hand axes based on Euclidean distance. Figure 60b shows the same information after standardizing the variables so that length and breadth each have a mean of 0 and a standard deviation of 1. This change accentuates the vertical distance in comparison to the first plot. Figure 60c uses principal components to remove the correlation between length and breadth. The net effect is to pull hand axe 96 farther away from the center and push 136 toward the center. Finally, Figure 60d shows the original values with a probability

Table 15 *Rank order of distances for different measures of distance*

	26/96	26/101	96/101	96/136	26/136	101/136
Raw	1	2	3	4	5	6
Standardized	2	1	3	5	4	6
PCA	3	1	4	6	2	5
Mahalanobis	3	1	4	6	2	5

ellipse at .2, .6, .8, .9, and .99 to approximate Mahalanobis distance. Since 101, 26, and 136 lie along the line representing the covariance between length and breadth, they are considered closer together than to 96, which is perpendicular to that line. In fact, the distances are very similar to those based on the principal components.

Table 15 summarizes the differences between the methods. With the raw data, the distance between hand axes 26 and 96 is the smallest. Standardizing the variables makes it the second smallest distance and with principal components and Mahalanobis, it is in third place. The distance between hand axes 26 and 101 is the second smallest for the raw data, but the smallest for the other three methods. The distance between hand axes 96 and 136 is in fourth place for the raw data, fifth place for the standardized data, and last place (largest) for principal components and Mahalanobis distances. Note that the order of the distances for principal components and Mahalanobis is the same. Either of these measures removes scale differences between the measurements and removes the effects of correlation between the measurements. It is important to consider these issues while preparing to analyze the data and very important to indicate what those decisions were in publication.

14.1.2 Distances for Dichotomous Data

The **simple matching coefficient** (symmetric binary) and the **Jaccard coefficient** (asymmetric binary) are appropriate for dichotomous data. The difference between the two is how they treat cases where both observations have zeros on a particular variable. When both observations score as present for a variable, we want to count that as an indication of similarity. But how do we count observations that score as absent for both observations? The symmetric coefficient gives joint presence and joint absence equal weight while the asymmetric coefficient counts only joint presence. The nature of the dichotomous variable may help to make this decision. For example, if we code ceramics as grit-tempered or bone-tempered, or paint as red or white, we probably want to use a symmetric coefficient since the 1 and 0 codes are just arbitrary designations for two different characteristics. If the dichotomy refers to the presence of a rare artifact type (in a grave for instance), then we may not want to count the absence of that type as the same kind of information as the presence of that type. In this case, the asymmetric coefficient seems more appropriate. The value for both coefficients ranges from 0 to 1.

We can include categorical variables by converting each variable into k dichotomous variables where k is the number of categories. For example `color=c("red",` `"green",` `"blue")` becomes three variables: `color.red`, `color.green`, and `color.blue` so that red is coded as (1, 0, 0), green as (0, 1, 0), and blue as (0, 0, 1). These are sometimes referred to as indicator variables.

Most distance measures assume that all of the variables are of the same type (all numeric or binary or categorical). The exception, Gower's coefficient, combines numeric, dichotomous, categorical, and ordinal variables into a single distance measure (Gower, 1971). Numeric and ordinal variables are measured with a Manhattan distance that is divided by the range of the distances so that each ranges from 0 to 1. Dichotomous variables can use either the symmetric or asymmetric coefficients and categorical variables count cases where both observations (rows) are in the same category. All of the variables are standardized so that they range from 0 to 1 and all of the distances coefficients are summed and divided by the number of variables.

R includes a basic function, `dist()`, for computing distance matrices that will work in many circumstances. Of the measures we have discussed, it includes Euclidean distance, asymmetric binary (Jaccard), and Manhattan. Several other rarely used measures are also included (Canberra, Maximum, and any Minkowski distance by specifying p). Canberra is a weighted form of the Manhattan distance. The `cluster` package has a distance function called `daisy()` that computes the Gower measure as does `gower.dist()` in package `StatMatch`. There are other distance functions that you may find useful for particular purposes. Mahalanobis distance matrices can be computed with functions in several packages: `distance()` in package `ecodist`, `mahalanobis.dist()` in package `StatMatch`, and `D2.dist()` in package `biotools`. Great circle distance matrices can be computed from latitude/longitude data with `distm()` in package `geosphere`.

14.2 MULTIDIMENSIONAL SCALING

Multidimensional scaling takes a distance or dissimilarity matrix and returns a set of coordinates (usually two or three) that approximate the distances between the original observations. It is used to visualize similarity and difference between observations. There are basically two approaches to multidimensional scaling, metric and non-metric, depending on whether we consider the distances to be interval scale data or ordinal scale data. Metric multidimensional scaling is exact in the sense that the best fit can be directly determined whereas non-metric multidimensional scaling involves improving on an initial configuration so that multiple runs with different initial configurations can lead to different results.

The classical version of metric multidimensional scaling is also called principal coordinates analysis and is available in R using the function `cmdscale()`. Non-metric multidimensional scaling is available using the function `isoMDS()` in the MASS package. Other implementations include functions `monoMDS()` and `metaMDS()` in package `vegan` and functions `nmds()` and `bestnmds()` in package `labdsv`.

We can illustrate these methods with the `Acheulean` data from the `archdata` package. This data comes from a paper by Lewis Binford (1972) based on Maxine Kleindienst's analysis of Acheulean assemblages in Africa (1961, 1962), which was

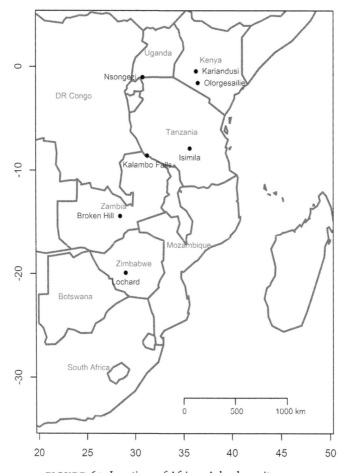

FIGURE 61 Locations of African Acheulean sites.

also analyzed by Isaac (1977). Binford presents the percentages for 12 tool types at 32 assemblages from seven sites (including Olorgesailie). The locations of the sites are shown in Figure 61.

To create the Acheulean data frame, the percentages in the published tables have been converted back to counts by dividing by 100 and multiplying by the total number of tools. The different assemblages from each site are combined. In addition, the approximate latitude and longitude for each site are included. The largest assemblage is Kalambo Falls with 1,349 artifacts and the smallest is Broken Hill (Kabwe) with 94. Before computing a distance matrix, we need to convert the counts to percentages to remove assemblage size from the analysis:

```
> data(Acheulean)
> Acheulean.pct <- Acheulean[, -(1:2)]/rowSums(Acheulean[, -(1:2)]) * 100
> print(Acheulean.pct, digits=2)
                HA   CL   KN  FS     D    CS     P    CH    SP  OLT    SS   OST
Olorgesailie  21.7 10.6  6.4 1.9  0.55  1.21  0.33   3.5  5.73 0.66  23.5  24.0
Isimila       30.0 25.4  3.7 3.4  0.73  3.66  1.95   7.6  2.07 1.83  12.0   7.8
Kalambo Falls 25.0 19.6  4.4 7.1  0.59  9.19  1.33   5.1  0.44 1.26  22.5   3.6
Lochard       24.1  7.0  1.6 1.1  6.42  0.53  0.00  17.1  1.60 4.28  24.6  11.8
Kariandusi    39.5 16.8 14.1 6.9  0.90  1.50  2.10   1.8  1.50 2.40   5.1   7.5
Broken Hill    1.1  8.5  1.1 1.1  0.00  1.06  0.00   4.3 26.60 0.00  37.2  19.1
Nsongezi       7.9  9.9  1.0 4.7  0.52 14.66  0.52   9.9  0.00 5.24   8.9  36.6
> View(attr(Acheulean, "Variables"))
```

By combining multiple assemblages from different sites, we have collapsed a great deal of potentially interesting variability, but here we are looking for broad geographic differences. Now we compute the distance matrix using Manhattan distances:

```
> Acheulean.dst <- dist(Acheulean.pct, method="manhattan")
> print(Acheulean.dst, digits=2)
      Olorgesailie Isimila Kalambo Falls Lochard Kariandusi
  Broken Hill
Isimila            68
Kalambo Falls      57      41
Lochard            53      69       65
Kariandusi         82      49       63      93
Broken Hill        71     122      113      94        143
Nsongezi           80      94       95      94        114        110
```

By default dist() only stores the lower triangle of the distance matrix. By modifying the command to print(Acheulean.dst, upper=TRUE, diag=TRUE) you can get the full symmetric matrix. The distance matrix for the Acheulean assemblages is based on 12 artifact types (so 12 dimensions). We can explore the possibility that the distances could be well-approximated in fewer dimensions using metric and non-metric multidimensional scaling. Both methods produce a set of coordinates that attempt to reconstruct the observed distances. The coordinates should not be unique because if they are rotated or reflected, they will still produce the same distance matrix. Plotting the coordinates gives us a map of the relationships between assemblages that may help us to better understand assemblage variability, but it is a map without a north arrow. The positions of the points with respect to one another are constant, but not direction.

Metric scaling is based on an eigen analysis of the distance matrix so the result is exact except for rotations and reflections of the coordinates. We can run classical scaling using the function cmdscale() (Box 16):

```
> options(digits=3)
> cmdscale(Acheulean.dst, k=1, eig=TRUE)$GOF
[1] 0.553 0.553
> cmdscale(Acheulean.dst, k=2, eig=TRUE)$GOF
[1] 0.792 0.792
> cmdscale(Acheulean.dst, k=3, eig=TRUE)$GOF
[1] 0.901 0.901
```

The cmdscale() function has several arguments that will return additional information. The default is to return coordinates for each point for two dimensions. We want to see how the goodness of fit (GOF) changes as we increase the number of dimensions. The maximum possible value is 1. To get the goodness of fit value, we need to retain the eigenvalues with eig=TRUE. We run the analysis three times specifying k = 1, 2, and 3 dimensions and displaying the GOF value. There are two GOF values that represent different ways of calculating the index when some of the eigenvalues are negative. When the eigenvalues are all positive, the two values will be the same as they are here, but generally they will be very close. With one dimension, we are capturing 0.55 (55 percent) of the sum of the eigenvalues. With two dimensions, we get 0.79 and with three dimensions that increases to 0.90. We will use the default value of two dimensions for this example to keep things simple, but three dimensions would fit the data better. Now run the analysis again removing eig=TRUE and save the results:

```
> Acheulean.pco <- cmdscale(Acheulean.dst)
> cor(Acheulean.dst, dist(Acheulean.pco))
[1] 0.971
```

The second command computes the correlation coefficient between the original distances and the distances computed from the coordinates that cmdscale()

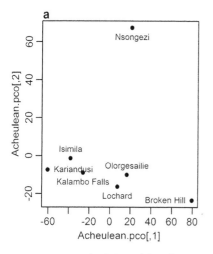 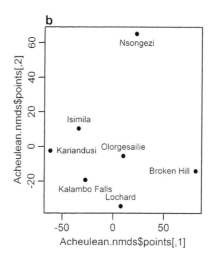

FIGURE 62 Metric (a) and non-metric (b) multidimensional scaling of Acheulean sites.

returned. The fit is very good. Now we can plot the sites by the coordinates (Figure 62a):

```
> plot(Acheulean.pco, pch=16)
> text(Acheulean.pco, rownames(Acheulean), cex=.75,
+    pos=c(3, 3, 1, 1, 4, 2, 1))
```

Note the use of the pos= argument to put the label below (1), left (2), above (3), or right (4) of the point. If you start with pos=c(1, 1, 1, 1, 1, 1, 1), you can rerun the plot command a few times and change the value for particular sites until none overlap or are truncated by the axes. You can get the order of the sites with rownames(Acheulean).

You can see that Kariandusi, Nsongezi, and Broken Hill anchor the corners of a triangle with the remaining sites falling along the line between Kariandusi and Broken Hill. In fact, the first dimension (the x-axis) describes the data well except for Nsongezi. It would be useful to look at the data after ordering the sites by the first dimension:

```
> round(Acheulean.pct[order(Acheulean.pco[, 1]), ])
```

	HA	CL	KN	FS	D	CS	P	CH	SP	OLT	SS	OST
Kariandusi	40	17	14	7	1	1	2	2	1	2	5	7
Isimila	30	25	4	3	1	4	2	8	2	2	12	8
Kalambo Falls	25	20	4	7	1	9	1	5	0	1	22	4
Lochard	24	7	2	1	6	1	0	17	2	4	25	12
Olorgesailie	22	11	6	2	1	1	0	4	6	1	23	24
Nsongezi	8	10	1	5	1	15	1	10	0	5	9	37
Broken Hill	1	9	1	1	0	1	0	4	27	0	37	19

The sites at the top of the table are those on the left size of Figure 62a. They are dominated by large tools including hand axes (HA) and cleavers (CL) while those at the bottom of the table are dominated by side scrapers (SS) and other small tools (OST). This is very similar to the pattern we found among the assemblages at Olorgesailie in Chapter 13. Nsongezi is distinctly different in the high percentage of core scrapers (CS).

We can repeat the analysis using Kruskal's non-metric multidimensional scaling using the isoMDS() function in the MASS package. Non-metric scaling begins with a starting configuration and then iterates toward a solution that minimizes stress (a measure of how well the new coordinates reconstruct the original distances).

The final configuration is shown in Figure 62b.

```
> library(MASS)
> Acheulean.nmds <- isoMDS(Acheulean.dst)
initial  value 5.341900
. . . deleted . . .
final  value 0.812263
converged
> Acheulean.nmds
$points
                  [,1]   [,2]
Olorgesailie     10.03  -5.38
Isimila         -33.92  10.35
Kalambo Falls   -27.08 -19.27
Lochard           7.69 -34.44
Kariandusi      -61.92  -2.39
Broken Hill      82.25 -14.01
Nsongezi         22.96  65.14

$stress
[1] 0.812

> plot(Acheulean.nmds$points, pch=16)
> text(Acheulean.nmds$points, rownames(Acheulean), cex=.75,
+      pos=c(3, 3, 1, 3, 4, 2, 1))
```

Non-metric scaling involves iteration from a starting configuration to minimize stress, a measure of the deviation of the distances computed from the estimated points from the observed distances. The isoMDS() function uses the results of `cmdscale()` as the starting configuration so it will always return the same results. In some cases, that may not be the best possible solution. For these data, the stress value for the principal coordinates solution was 5.34 and it took between 35 and 40 iterations to converge on a final result with a stress value of 0.81. Asking for three dimensions using `isoMDS(Acheulean.dst, k=3)` reduces stress to 0.003. However, with seven sites, we have 21 distances and three dimensions involves estimating 21 (3×7) coordinates. Generally we need to have more than $2k + 1$ points where k is the number of dimensions and preferably several more. Three dimensions requires $2 \times 3 + 1 = 7$ points so we need at least eight sites. It is mathematically possible to get results with seven points, but they will not be stable. Also the Pearson and Spearman correlations between the distances based on two dimensions and the original distances are very good (0.97, 0.98). Comparing Figures 62a and 62b, it is clear that the main difference between the two was to push pairs of assemblages apart on the y-axis so that Isimila/Kalambo Falls and Olorgesailie/Lochard are farther apart.

Because non-metric scaling uses iteration to improve a starting configuration, it can end up in a local minimum. This is the best solution given the starting configuration, but not necessarily the solution with the lowest stress. Fortunately, the `vegan` package has a version of non-metric multidimensional scaling that can check various randomly selected starting configurations and pick the best one. Install the package and then run the following code:

```
> library(vegan)
> set.seed(42)
> Acheulean.nmds2 <- metaMDS(Acheulean.dst, trace=0)
> Acheulean.nmds2$stress
[1] 0.0079
> cor(Acheulean.dst, dist(Acheulean.nmds2$points))
[1] 0.968
> cor(Acheulean.dst, dist(Acheulean.nmds2$points),
  method="spearman")
[1] 0.978
> plot(Acheulean.dst, dist(Acheulean.nmds2$points))
```

By default `metaMDS()` tries 20 different starting configurations and returns the one with the smallest stress value. The output indicates a stress value of 0.0079, which initially seems much smaller than 0.81 value from `isoMDS()`, but the latter value is percent stress so we need to multiply by 100 (0.79) to get a comparable value.

The stress is slightly smaller (0.79 versus 0.81). The Pearson and Spearman correlations between the original distances and the fit is about the same as for both results, 0.97 and 0.98. The results are essentially identical.

We can also plot the function that is used to map the original distances to the new distances (called a Shepard plot):

```
> Acheulean.shp <- Shepard(Acheulean.dst, Acheulean.
  nmds$points)
> plot(Acheulean.shp, xlab="Manhattan Distances",
  ylab="Scaled Distances")
> with(Acheulean.shp, lines(x, yf, type="S"))
```

The plot shows the non-decreasing (monotone) relationship between the original and fitted distances as a step function (Figure 63). The points all fall very close to the line indicating a very good fit.

One of the goals in multidimensional scaling can be to identify the "meaning" of the dimensions produced by the analysis. We have already compared the original and fitted distances, but we can also look for correlations between the original variables and the coordinates for each dimension:

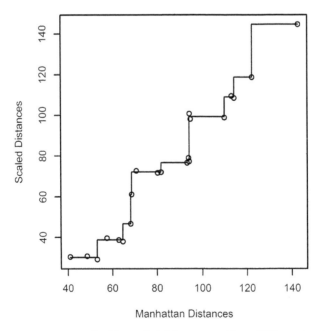

FIGURE 63 Shepard plot for non-metric multidimensional scaling of Acheulean data.

```
> cor(Acheulean.pct, Acheulean.nmds$points)
        [,1]    [,2]
HA  -0.9473 -0.2854
CL  -0.7035  0.0598
KN  -0.7133 -0.1312
FS  -0.7047  0.2557
D   -0.0471 -0.4567
CS  -0.0168  0.7488
P   -0.8613  0.1269
CH   0.1639 -0.0448
SP   0.7781 -0.2460
OLT -0.1583  0.4896
SS   0.7563 -0.5799
OST  0.5879  0.7070
> cor(Acheulean[, 1:2], Acheulean.nmds$points)
        [,1]   [,2]
Lat   -0.408  0.643
Long  -0.680  0.136
```

The correlations show that the first dimension has moderate to high correlations (outside the range of –0.5 to 0.5) for eight of 12 artifact types. Hand axes, cleavers, knives, flake scrapers, and picks have high negative correlations while spheroids, side scrapers, and other small tools have positive correlations. The second dimension has only three moderate to high correlations. It contrasts core scrapers and other large tools (positive correlations) with small scrapers (negative correlation). Ngsongezi has relatively high percentages of core scrapers and other large tools and a low percentage of side scrapers which explains why it is located at the top of the plot in Figures 62a and 62b.

The second command looks at correlations between latitude and longitude by the coordinates. The first axis has a moderate negative correlation for longitude and the second axis has a moderate correlation for latitude. This suggests that there may be geographic differences in assemblage variability.

While we can perform a similar analyses on these assemblages using correspondence analysis, the main advantage of multidimensional scaling is that gives us the opportunity to explore how the patterning in the data is affected by different ways of measuring distance and in considering how those patterns change between metric and non-metric analyses.

14.3 COMPARING DISTANCE MATRICES – MANTEL TESTS

The Acheulean data set includes the approximate latitude and longitude for each site. We can test the hypothesis that differences between the stone tool assemblages are based on geographic factors by comparing the assemblage distances to the geographic distances. We already have the assemblage distance matrix (`Acheulean.dst`) so we only need to create a matrix of geographic distances. The `distm()` function in the package `geosphere` computes great circle distance matrices using one of several functions. We will use the Vincenty ellipsoid function, which adjusts for the fact that the earth is not a perfect sphere. The `distm()` function returns a symmetric matrix of distances in meters, but the `dist()` function returns a lower triangular matrix (just the part below the diagonal) so we use `as.dist()` to make the conversion. We divide the distances (which are in meters) by 1,000 to convert to kilometers. Finally we add the `Labels` attribute with the site names, something that `dist()` does automatically.

```
> library(geosphere)
Loading required package: sp
> Acheulean.gd <- as.dist(distm(Acheulean[,2:1],
+     fun = distVincentyEllipsoid)) / 1000
> attr(Acheulean.gd, "Labels") <- c("Olor", "Isimila",
+   "K Falls", "Lochard", "Karian", "Brk Hill",
+   "Nsongezi")
> round(Acheulean.gd)
     Olor Isimila K Falls Lochard Karian Brk Hill
```

	Olor	Isimila	K Falls	Lochard	Karian	Brk Hill
Isimila	705					
K Falls	967	488				
Lochard	2184	1508	1275			
Karian	127	827	1059	2294		
Brk Hill	1672	1064	713	611	1769	
Nsongezi	634	930	839	2098	613	1504

In Figures 62a and 62b Nsongezi is far from the other sites, but it is not separated geographically to nearly the same degree. The following commands will plot the two sets of distances along with the least squares regression line (Figure 64):

```
> plot(Acheulean.gd, Acheulean.dst, pch=16)
> abline(lm(Acheulean.dst~Acheulean.gd))
> cor.test(Acheulean.gd, Acheulean.dst,
  alternative="greater")

    Pearson's product-moment correlation

data:  Acheulean.gd and Acheulean.dst
t = 0.5, df = 20, p-value = 0.3
```

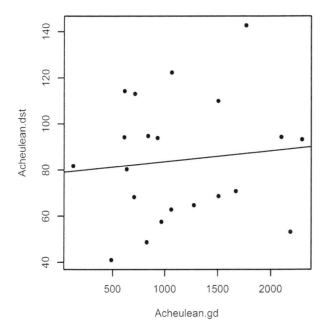

FIGURE 64 Plot of geographic distance and assemblage distance for the Acheulean sites.

```
alternative hypothesis: true correlation is greater than 0
95 percent confidence interval:
 -0.274  1.000
sample estimates:
  cor
0.107
```

We use the `cor.test()` function to estimate the correlation (.107) and its significance (p = .3), but this test overestimates the significance since we have 21 distances, that are based on only seven observations. Notice that this is a one-tailed test since we do not expect the correlation to be negative. That would imply that sites farther away are more similar to one another than sites nearby. Since we do not reject the null hypothesis that geographic distance is unrelated to assemblage distance, the overestimate just means that the true p-value is even larger (less likely to be significant).

Just for the purposes of illustration we can use the Mantel test to test the significance of an association between two distance matrices. The Mantel test does this by permuting the rows and columns of the two matrices and computing the correlation for each pair. If the correlation is significant, it should be larger than all but the largest 0.05 permutations. There are several implementations of the

Mantel test in R, but we will use the `mantel()` function in the `vegan` package (Box 17):

```
> library(vegan)
> set.seed(42)
> Acheulean.man <- mantel(Acheulean.gd, Acheulean.dst)
Set of permutations < 'minperm'. Generating entire set.
> Acheulean.man

Mantel statistic based on Pearson's product-moment
  correlation

Call:
mantel(xdis = Acheulean.gd, ydis = Acheulean.dst)

Mantel statistic r: 0.107
   Significance: 0.4

Upper quantiles of permutations (null model):
  90%    95% 97.5%    99%
0.343 0.455 0.558 0.606
Permutation: free
Number of permutations: 999
```

We are using 999 permutations to evaluate the correlation between Manhattan distances for the Acheulean assemblages and the geographic distances. The Mantel statistic r is just the Pearson's correlation that we computed with `cor.test()`. The function will also work with Spearman or Kendall correlations. The upper quantiles of the permutations show that to reject the null hypothesis at the .05 level of significance (95 percent quantile), we would need a correlation coefficient of more than .455. The correlation value for each of the 999 permutations is stored as `perm` in the object returned by `mantel()`, which we saved as `Acheulean.man`.

Previous investigations of Lower Paleolithic assemblages have concluded that geographic differences are small to non-existent, which agrees with our conclusions here. To strengthen this conclusion, we should continue to analyze the data by splitting out assemblages from each site that are roughly comparable in age. We also need more sites.

It is also possible to construct a partial Mantel test by comparing two matrices controlling for a third matrix using `mantel.partial()` in package `vegan`. For example, if we had age estimates for the sites, we could create a distance matrix based on the difference in ages between sites and test for a significant association between age and assemblage variability after controlling for geographic distance.

BOX 16 MULTIDIMENSIONAL SCALING WITH `cmdscale()`
IN PACKAGE `stats` AND `isoMDS()` IN PACKAGE MASS

```
cmdscale(d, k = 2, eig = FALSE, add = FALSE, x.ret = FALSE)
isoMDS(d, y = cmdscale(d, k), k = 2, maxit = 50,
  trace = TRUE, tol = 1e-3, p = 2)

Shepard(d, x, p = 2)
```

Function `cmdscale()` performs classical metric multidimensional scaling also known as principal coordinates analysis using a distance matrix (such as that returned by `dist()`). The function computes coordinates that produce distances similar to those in the distance matrix assuming that the distances are metric (e.g., the distance between 1 and 3 is twice the distance between 1 and 2). The result is unique except for rotation and reflection. By default, the coordinates for two dimensions are returned. Optionally, more dimensions (or only one) can be specified using the `k=` argument.

In addition, three arguments can be set to return additional information. Setting `eig=TRUE` will return the eigenvalues computed during the analysis, which can be used to gauge the importance of each dimension. In addition two GOF (goodness of fit) values are also provided. They range from 0 to 1, with 1 representing a perfect fit to the distances. The differences relate to how negative eigenvalues are handled and the two values will not usually be very different. Less commonly used settings include `add=TRUE`, which adds a constant to the distances so that they will be Euclidean, and `x.ret=TRUE`, which returns a doubly centered symmetric distance matrix.

Function `isoMDS()` performs Kruskal's non-metric multidimensional scaling using a distance matrix (such as that returned by `dist()`). The function computes coordinates that produce distances whose rank order is approximately the same as the original distances (e.g., the distance between 1 and 3 is more than the distance between 1 and 2, but not necessarily exactly twice the distance). The result is based on iteration of an initial configuration to a minimum stress value, which could be a local minimum so that different starting configurations can give different results. The default starting configuration for `isoMDS()` is taken from `cmdscale()`, but a configuration can be provided using the `y=` argument.

The default analysis returns coordinates for two dimensions (`points`) and a stress value (`stress`). Messages regarding the initial and final stress values are also provided. Setting the `k=` argument requests more dimensions (or only one) and setting `trace=FALSE` turns off the messages. Less commonly used settings include `maxit=`, which changes the number of iterations (if convergence is not reached within the default of 50), `tol=`, which sets the tolerance for convergence, and p=, which changes the configuration space for the analysis.

The `Shepard()` function returns a list of three vectors to plot a monotonic step function (`yf`) between original distances (`x`) and the distances computed from the scaling results (`y`).

Other implementations include functions `monoMDS()` and `metaMDS()` in package `vegan` and functions `nmds()` and `bestnmds()` in package `labdsv`. These functions have the option to automatically generate multiple starting configurations to reduce the possibility that the final configuration is a local minimum.

BOX 17 MANTEL TESTS USING `mantel()` IN PACKAGE `vegan`

```
mantel(xdis, ydis, method="pearson", permutations=999,
strata = NULL, na.rm = FALSE, parallel = getOption("mc.
cores"))
```

Function `mantel()` finds the Mantel statistic, a correlation between two dissimilarity matrices. The significance of the statistic is evaluated by permuting rows and columns of the first dissimilarity matrix. The function takes two distance matrices (`xdis=` and `ydis=`). The default analysis is to compute the Pearson correlation between the matrices and generate a *p*-value for that correlation by permuting the rows and columns of the first dissimilarity matrix 999 times.

The `method=` argument allows the correlation statistic to be set to `"pearson"` (the default), `"spearman"` or `"kendall"`. The `permutations=` argument allows increasing or decreasing the number of permutations. The `strata=` argument allows specifying blocks of observations as members of a particular stratum to restrict permutation to observations within each of the strata. Missing values are controlled by `na.rm=` and `parallel=` controls the use of multiple CPU cores in your computer with the parallel package if you are working on very large matrices.

The function returns an object of class mantel, which consists of a list with seven elements. The `call`, `method`, `permutations`, and `control` elements provide information about the analysis and how it was performed. The `statistic` is the correlation between the matrices and the `significance` is the *p*-value. The `perm` vector includes the correlation values for all of the permutations. It can be used to look at the distribution of the correlation values using `hist()` for example. Other implementations of the Mantel test are available in packages `ade4`, `ape`, `biotools`, and `ecodist`.

Table 16 *Functions introduced in Chapter 14*

Function	Package	Description
as.dist	stats	Convert symmetrical matrix to a distance object
bestnmds	labdsv	Use iterations of nmds and select best configuration
cmdscale	stats	Classical metric multidimensional scaling
D2.dist	biotools	Compute squared generalized Mahalanobis distance matrix
daisy	cluster	Compute distance matrix
dist	stats	Create a distance matrix
distance	ecodist	Compute distance matrix, including Mahalanobis
distm	geosphere	Compute geographical distances
distVincentyEllipsoid	geosphere	Compute great circle distances
gower.dist	StatMatch	Compute Gower distance matrix
isoMDS	MASS	Kruskal's non-metric multidimensional scaling
mahalanobis.dist	StatMatch	Compute Mahalanobis distance matrix
mantel	vegan	Compute Mantel test
mantel.partial	vegan	Partial Mantel test of three matrices
metaMDS	vegan	Non-metric scaling with multiple starts
monoMDS	vegan	Perform non-metric multidimensional scaling
nmds	labdsv	Perform non-metric multidimensional scaling using isoMDS
Shepard	MASS	Compute MDS results for a Shepard diagram

Note: Packages `base`, `datasets`, `graphics`, `grDevices`, `methods`, `stats`, and `utils` are automatically loaded when R starts.

15

Cluster Analysis

Cluster analysis includes a number of techniques for combining observations into groups based on one or more variables. Clustering is unsupervised classification since we do not have any information about how many groups or how they should be defined. The groups can be formed in five ways. First, we can start with all of the objects and divide them into two groups and then we can subdivide each of those groups. For example, we can separate the ceramics that have shell temper from those that have sand temper. We could divide each of those groups by the shape of the pot by separating jars from bowls. Then we could look at each of those groups and divide them by decorative techniques, such as painting, cord-marking, or incising. This is a common way of approaching artifact typology for ceramics. A second way of forming groups is to use a "type specimen." One or more artifacts is used to identify distinct types. Then artifacts are placed with the type specimen they most closely resemble. New projectile points are classified by comparing them to established descriptions of existing types. If the specimen does not match any of the known types, a new one can be defined. Third, we can divide the specimens into groups so that each group is relatively homogeneous. This approach is similar to the type specimen approach, but we do not identify type specimens in advance although we do have to decide how many groups seem reasonable. Fourth, we could start with all of the objects and find the two that are most similar. Then the next two and so on. This process includes adding a third specimen to an existing pair and to combining two pairs into a larger group. The process continues until there is only one group. This approach requires very careful operational definitions of what "similar" means and how it is to be measured. Until computers became widely available, archaeologists rarely used this approach. Finally, we could use a distance measure (rather than a single variable) to divide the collection into more and more groups. This approach is a logical combination of the first and the third approaches, but it is very difficult to operationalize and very computer-intensive if there are many variables and many observations so it is rarely used.

In technical terms, the five approaches are described as **monothetic divisive, type specimen, k-means, polythetic agglomerative** (or hierarchical), and **polythetic divisive**. **Monothetic divisive** means that each division of the objects into groups is based on a single criterion. In the example above we first divided the ceramics on the basis of temper, then by vessel form, and then by decoration. At each stage, we must decide which variable to use to subdivide the group. We also must decide where to stop the process and that determines how many groups we have created.

The **type specimen** approach involves a historical element. We identify a distinctive artifact (or fossil, or species) and then compare newly discovered specimens to the type specimens. The result of the analysis is that new specimens are assigned to an existing type or used as the basis for a new type.

k-**means** is analogous, but avoids the historical element. All of the specimens are examined simultaneously. We decide in advance how many groups there will be (the k in k-means) and then group objects around the k-means (centroids). When humans do this, they use their professional judgment to decide what characteristics are most important when comparing new specimens to the type specimens. With computers, we need to be more specific. For each object, we compare its distance to the centroid of each of the k groups and we place it in the closest group. The procedure needs starting centroids and if there is no prior information, we can use randomly selected centroids. As a result, k-means does not necessarily produce the same classification each time. We usually run multiple analyses using different randomly selected initial centroids each time and select the best one. In k-means, the centroid of the group changes as we add object since it is defined by the mean values of all the objects in the group. Whereas the monothetic divisive method is based on a single characteristic at a time, k-means combines all of the attributes into a single distance measure.

Polythetic agglomerative is the opposite of the first approach. We combine all of the attributes into a single distance measure (just like with k-means) and we combine pairs of objects (or objects with groups, or groups with groups) until everything is combined into one group. The process can be represented as a tree or dendrogram that shows what has been combined at each stage. As with monothetic divisive, we have to make a decision about where to stop the process and we do that by deciding where to cut the dendrogram.

Finally, **polythetic divisive** involves finding the optimal sequence of splits based on all of the variables so we move from a single group to each object in its own group. The number of possible splits grows very rapidly with the number of objects being clustered. As a result, there are only a few implementations of this process and they will work only for small data sets. Some divisive methods overcome this limitation by combining the variables (e.g., principal components) and then splitting on the composite variable to reduce the computational burden. This approach has rarely been used on archaeological data sets.

Computer-based cluster analysis began in the late 1960s and early 1970s as computers became more readily available (Hodson, 1971; Doran and Hodson, 1975). There are a number of good introductions to cluster analysis by archaeologists (Aldenderfer and Blashfield, 1984; Baxter, 1994, 2003; Doran and Hodson, 1975; Shennan, 1997), and by non-archaeologists (Everitt et al, 2011; James et al, 2013; Rencher and Christenson, 2012; Venables and Ripley, 2002).

Archaeologists have different reasons for grouping observations (artifacts, features, sites, etc.). Grouping can be seen as a form of measurement since we end up with a new categorical variable representing group membership. For example, we might group graves by grave goods to see if some groups are more likely to be found with adult or juvenile internments, with male or female internments, within higher or lower social strata, or with internments found in different parts of the site. Likewise we might want to see if artifacts grouped by their size and shape are distributed vertically or horizontally within a site or across different sites in a region. In these cases, we divide the graves or the artifacts into groups and then look at how those groups vary in terms of criteria that were not used in defining the groups in the first place. The value of the groups comes from the fact that they help us to identify potentially significant patterns in the archaeological record.

Alternatively, grouping can be seen as a way of identifying "real" clusters in multidimensional space. These groups may be explained by reference to cultural, functional, raw material, or temporal differences. They may be an unconscious or unintended consequence of cultural processes or a result of non-human formation processes. Alternatively they could represent a conscious effort to create cultural or functional types by the people who produced those artifacts or features. It will usually not be easy to distinguish between these alternatives. It is also not easy to answer the statistical question regarding whether the groups represent a purely arbitrary division of the observations or non-random clusters in multidimensional space, but it is sometimes possible.

Performing a cluster analysis involves making decisions about which method to use and how to implement it. R does not make this easier by providing a limited number of choices. There are numerous packages providing many different approaches to cluster analysis. It is usually advisable to try several different approaches and compare them to one another and to external criteria. In this chapter, we will describe the two methods used most commonly in archaeological research: *k*-means partitioning and hierarchical (polythetic agglomerative) clustering.

15.1 *K*-MEANS PARTITIONING

K-means divides the data into the number of groups specified by the investigator. It has the advantage of being very fast since the distance between each pair of rows does not have to be calculated, just the distances of each row to each of the *k* group centroids. The centroid of the group is the just mean values for all of the measurements for all of the current members of the group. *K*-means allocates objects to *k* groups in such a way that the sum of the squared Euclidean distances between each point and the group to which it is assigned is minimized. On each iteration, observations are assigned to the closest centroid. Then the centroids are recomputed based on the assignments and each observation is re-evaluated to see if it now lies closer to a different centroid.

When *k*-means is started by letting the function choose the initial centroids randomly, repeated runs do not necessarily produce the same results, especially if there are many variables or the data do not fall into distinct groups. There is a method for picking starting centroids that does better than random choice that is used in a number of statistical packages, but it can still fail to find the optimal solution (Arthur and Vassilvitskii, 2007). As a result, it is common to generate multiple runs and select the one with the smallest total within group sum of squares. *K*-means can also be affected by rows with extreme values so it may be advantageous to screen the data for outliers before proceeding. If there are outliers, they can be eliminated or a robust version of *k*-means, called partitioning around medoids (`pam()` in package `cluster`), can be used instead (Maechler, et al., 2014). Before using *k*-means, you will have to decide if you need to weight the variables (Chapter 14) since the procedure uses Euclidean distances.

To illustrate *k*-means, we will replicate a pilot study of British hand axes using the Furze Platt hand axe data. The original study by Hodson used a random sample of 500 hand axes from Roe's data set (Hodson, 1971; Roe, 1964, 1968, 1981). Following Roe, Hodson uses one size measurement (length or *L* in the `Handaxes` data set) and four shape measurements: breadth/length (`B/L`) ratio, Thickness/Breadth ratio (`T/B`), breadth 1/5 from the top divided by breadth 1/5 from the base (`B1/B2`), and length measured from the base to the point of maximum breadth divided by the overall length (L1/L). Roe used the last of these measures to divide the artifacts into three shape groups:

1. Cleavers if L1/L > 0.55
2. Ovate hand axes if $0.35 \leq$ L1/L ≤ 0.55
3. Pointed hand axes if L1/L < 0.35

He described hand axe assemblages in terms of a tripartite scatterplot that showed B1/B2 against B/L for each of the three groups. We can summarize the approach by creating the necessary variables and then using coplot():

```
> Roe <- with(Handaxes, data.frame(L, B_L=B/L, T_B=T/B, B1_
  B2=B1/B2, L1_L=L1/L))
> Roe$Shape <- factor(ifelse(Roe$L1_L > .550, "Cleaver",
+   ifelse(Roe$L1_L < .35, "Pointed", "Ovate")))
> save(Roe, file="Roe.RData")
> coplot(B1_B2~B_L | Shape, Roe, rows=1, show.given=FALSE,
+   xlab=c("B/ L", "Shape: Cleaver, Ovate, Pointed"),
+   ylab="B1/ B2")
```

Figure 65 shows the plot that closely resembles Roe's Group 1 assemblages (1968). Roe's shape groups represent a monothetic divisive, partitioning of the hand axes since he uses a single variable to divide the sample into three groups. In contrast, Hodson was interested in forming polythetic groups based on all five variables. We can create a new data frame to repeat Hodson's analysis:

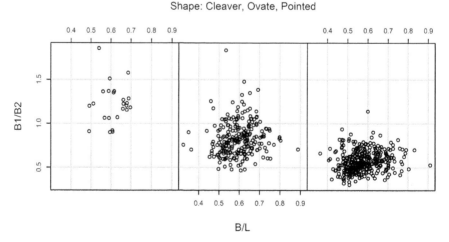

FIGURE 65 Tripartite plot of Furze Platt hand axes based on Roe (1964).

```
> Hodson <- with(Roe, data.frame(logL = log10(L), logB_
  L = log10(B_L),
+   logT_B = log10(T_B), logB1_B2 = log10(B1_B2), logL1_
  L = log10(L1_L)))
> str(Hodson)
'data.frame':   600 obs. of   5 variables:
 $ logL     : num 2.13 2.35 2.3 2.2 2.24 ...
 $ logB_L   : num -0.229 -0.335 -0.28 -0.309 -0.189 ...
 $ logT_B   : num -0.285 -0.185 -0.364 -0.324 -0.293 ...
 $ logB1_B2 : num 0.05704 -0.27963 -0.26824 -0.37358 0.00955 ...
 $ logL1_L  : num -0.288 -0.645 -0.589 -0.645 -0.363 ...
> save(Hodson, file="Hodson.RData")
```

This creates and saves a new data frame with the five log base 10 transformed variables. Now we can try a simple k-means cluster analysis (Box 18):

```
> options(digits=7)
> set.seed(42)
> Hodson.km <- kmeans(Hodson, 3)
> Hodson.km$tot.withinss
[1] 16.39984
> table(Hodson.km$cluster)

  1   2   3
147 180 273
```

We ask for three clusters and kmeans() returns a list with nine elements. The first element (Hodson.km$cluster) indicates to which cluster each hand axe belongs. The second element (Hodson.km$centers) gives the centroids (means for each variable) for each cluster. The next four elements show the distributions of the sums of squares. The sum of the squared deviations of each of the 600 hand axes from the grand mean is the total sum of squares (totss). The sum of squared deviations of each hand axe from its group mean is the within group sum of squares, one for each group (withinss). The total within sums of squares is the sum of the within group sum of squares (tot.withinss = sum(withinss)) and the between sum of squares is the difference between the total sum of squares and the total within group sum of squares (betweenss = totss-tot.withinss). When every hand axe is in its own group (600 groups), then the total within group sum of squares is 0. When all 600 hand axes are in one group, the total within group sum of squares is equal to the total sum of squares. As we increase the number of groups, the total within group sum of squares will decrease. The remaining parts in the list include `size`, the number of observations in each group; `iter`, the number of iterations; and `ifault`, an error code if there was a problem with the analysis.

Our total within group sum of squares is 16.4. But we used only a single start in the analysis so we don't really know if that is the smallest possible value. We can run the analysis many times to see how variable the results can be:

```
> set.seed(42)
> table(replicate(1000, kmeans(Hodson, 3)$tot.withinss))

16.3964339241825 16.3992506995331 16.3998434394056 16.4000411793034
             657               60              277                5
17.7834288476554
               1
```

This runs the `kmeans()` function 1,000 times and tabulates the results. The smallest value for the total within sum of squares is 16.39643, which is smaller than 16.39984 so we did not have the minimum value. It is possible that with more than 1,000 replications we could get even smaller, but the smallest four values range from 16.39 to 16.40 so they are very close and the differences between them are probably minor. Notice that the smallest value occurs 657 times out of 1,000 so 66 percent of the time the smallest value is identified. Our result is the third smallest and it occurs 277 times out of 1,000. We can tell `kmeans()` to run the analysis multiple times and pick the best result:

```
> set.seed(42)
> Hodson.km2 <- kmeans(Hodson, 3, nstart=25)
> Hodson.km2$tot.withinss
[1] 16.39643
> Hodson.km2$size
[1] 173 275 152
```

Now we get the smallest value for the total within sum of squares and the distribution of the hand axes into the three groups is slightly different from our first run:

```
> xtabs(~Hodson.km$cluster+Hodson.km2$cluster)
                  Hodson.km2$cluster
Hodson.km$cluster    1    2    3
                1    0    0  147
                2  173    7    0
                3    0  268    5
```

Our original cluster 1 is now cluster 3 and that cluster includes 5 hand axes that were originally placed in cluster 3. Original cluster 2 is now cluster 1 but 7 hand axes that were in the original cluster 2 are now in the new cluster 2. Original cluster 3 is now cluster 2 except for 5 hand axes that joined new cluster 3. That probably seems confusing, but the cluster numbers are completely arbitrary. Two sets of results are the same all the cell values in each row and column are zero except for one cell. Here, there are only 7 + 5 = 12 hand axes that have moved out of 600 (2 percent). How do these groups compare to the original partition that Roe made using only one of these variables:

```
> xtabs(~Roe$Shape+Hodson.km2$cluster)
          Hodson.km2$cluster
Roe$Shape     1    2    3
   Cleaver    0    0   24
   Ovate      0  110  127
   Pointed  173  165    1
```

There is a clear connection between the two groupings. Our cluster 1 includes only hand axes that Roe classified as pointed and all of the cleavers are in cluster 3, but that cluster includes 1 pointed hand axe and about half of the ovate hand axes with the other half falling into group 2, which includes half of the pointed hand axes. We can compare the two groupings in terms of their descriptive statistics using aggregate():

```
> print(aggregate(.~Shape, Roe, mean), digits=3)
     Shape     L    B_L    T_B  B1_B2   L1_L
1  Cleaver   117  0.612  0.562  1.224  0.621
2   Ovate    119  0.598  0.566  0.830  0.418
3  Pointed   124  0.579  0.541  0.574  0.273
> Cluster <- Hodson.km2$cluster
> print(aggregate(.~Cluster, Roe[, 1:5], mean), digits=3)
   Cluster    L    B_L    T_B  B1_B2   L1_L
1        1  133  0.566  0.516  0.498  0.238
2        2  117  0.587  0.573  0.662  0.339
3        3  119  0.613  0.553  1.002  0.475
```

Cleavers have large values for B1_B2 and L1_L since their maximum breadth is closer to the tip of the artifact and they tend to be shorter. Ovate hand axes are more symmetrical in that the point of maximum breadth is toward the middle (L1_L) and the ratio of the breadth near the tip to the breadth near the base approaches 1 (B1_B2). Pointed hand axes have a maximum breadth near the base (low values of L1_L) and a breadth near the tip that is about half the breadth near the base (B1_B2). The clusters formed by *k*-means are generally similar, but *k*-means tends to form groups that are approximately equal in size unlike Roe's classification, which put only 24 hand axes in the cleaver group and more than half in the pointed group.

We can visualize the groups using principal components:

```
> Hodson.pca <- prcomp(Hodson, scale.=TRUE)
> biplot(Hodson.pca, pc.biplot=TRUE, xlim=c(-4, 4),
  ylim=c(-4, 4),
+       xlabs=Hodson.km2$cluster, cex=.7)
```

Figure 66 shows that the three groups are arranged in vertical bands along the first principal component. Because there are so many points, it can be hard to see the vector labels, but logB1_B2 and logL1_L are superimposed pointing to the right. The logL vector is pointing to the left and down, but it is short, indicating

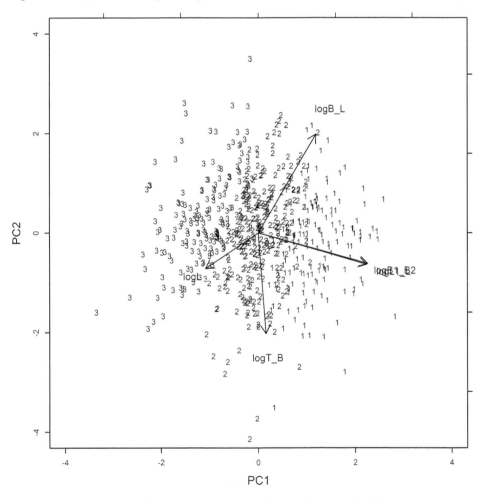

FIGURE 66 Biplot of Furze Platt hand axes with three clusters defined by k-means.

that it is not well represented by the first two components. The other two variables, `logT_B` and `logB_L` point down and up respectively so they do not seem to play much of a role in defining the groups.

The three clusters seem to represent variation in shape, but perhaps the data would be better expressed by more than three clusters. Also we would like to know if the clusters represent distinct point clouds or if we have just chopped them along a continuum.

15.1.1 Number of Clusters and Cluster Separation

We used three groups because of a previous study that used three groups, but we could reconsider if that is the best number of groups. One rule of thumb involves looking at a scree plot that shows how the total within sum of squares increases as the number of clusters decreases. As the number of clusters decreases, the total within cluster sum of squares will increase. If there is a natural number of clusters in the data, we should see a jump in the total within cluster sum of squares when we reduce the number of clusters. In addition, we can compare the observed data to randomized data to see how both sets behave as the number of clusters decreases. The randomized data has all of the same values as the observed data, but each column (variable) is randomized so that any correlations between variables are eliminated. The following code creates a scree plot:

```
> set.seed(42)
> y <- sapply(2:25, function(k) kmeans(Hodson, k,
  nstart=25)$tot.withinss)
> plot(2:25, y, type="b", ylab="Total Within Sum of Squares",
+      xlab="Number of Clusters")
```

A scree plot shows how the total within cluster sum of squares changes as the number of clusters decreases. The first command uses the `sapply()` function to run the `kmeans()` function 24 times (2 to 25 clusters), picking the best result from 25 starts at each cluster level. The second function plots the results and labels the axes. Now we add randomized data to the plot:

```
> set.seed(42)
> yr <- sapply(2:25, function(k) kmeans(sapply(Hodson,
+      sample), k, iter.max=20, nstart=10)$tot.withinss)
> lines(2:25, yr, lty=2)
```

The first command is a bit complicated since it uses `sapply()` twice. The `sapply(Hodson, sample)` command runs the `sample()` function on each column in the `Hodson` data frame. By default, `sample()` draws a random sample that includes all of the original values in a random sequence (i.e., a random permutation of the original data). Compare the results of `cor(Hodson)` and `cor(sapply(Hodson, sample))` to see how the correlation structure of the original data disappears. The rest of the first command computes the total within cluster sum of squares for cluster sizes from 2 to 25 using the randomized data. The only difference is an increase in the `iter.max=` value from the default value of 10 to 20. Running the command initially produced a warning that for some cluster sizes *k*-means did not converge within 10 iterations. The `lines()` function plots a dashed line for the randomized data. To see how much variation there is from one randomized data set to another, run these two commands five times to get five randomized lines (do not include `set.seed(42)`). Then add a legend to finish the plot (Figure 67):

```
> legend("topright", c("Original Data", "Randomized Data"),
+        lty=1:2, pch=c(1, NA))
```

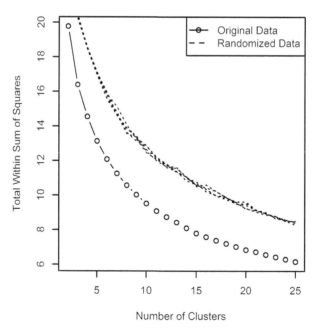

FIGURE 67 Scree plot for Furze Platt hand axes showing original data and five sets of randomized data.

The figure suggests that there is no obvious number of clusters. The total within cluster sum of squares increases gradually as the number of clusters decreases, but does not show a jump that would suggest the number of clusters.

There is a substantial literature on how to determine how many groups should be used in cluster analysis. Function NbClust() in package NbClust provides indices for 30 different methods of determining the optimal number of clusters in a data set (Charrad et al., 2014; and the 36 references in the package documentation). By default NbClust() computes 26 of the 30 (the other four are computationally intensive). Install the package and then type the following commands:

```
> library(NbClust)
> oldp <- par(no.readonly=TRUE)
> par(ask=TRUE)
> set.seed(42)
> nclust <- NbClust(Hodson, method="kmeans")
 . . . informational messages deleted . . .
*******************************************************
* Among all indices:
* 9 proposed 2 as the best number of clusters
* 8 proposed 3 as the best number of clusters
* 1 proposed 4 as the best number of clusters
* 3 proposed 9 as the best number of clusters
* 1 proposed 14 as the best number of clusters
* 1 proposed 15 as the best number of clusters
          ***** Conclusion *****
 * According to the majority rule, the best number of
 clusters is  2
*******************************************************
> nclust$Best.nc[1, ]
       KL          CH Hartigan     CCC Scott     Marriot TrCovW
        3           2        3       2     3           9      3
   TraceW Friedman    Rubin  Cindex     DB Silhouette   Duda
        3        9        9       3      2           2      2
  PseudoT2    Beale Ratkowsky    Ball PtBiserial  Frey McClain
        2        2        4       3      3           1      2
     Dunn   Hubert  SDindex  Dindex   SDbw
       14        0        2       0     15
> par(oldp)
```

The first command sets the graphical parameter ask=TRUE since NbClust() produces two plots in rapid succession. This tells R to wait for you to press Enter or click on the plot window to get each plot. The analysis will take a minute or two since the function has to run 26 different tests for 2 to 15 clusters. The Hubert and the D index are shown in the two plots and they come to the same conclusion we did with the scree plot that there is no distinct knee or bend, indicating how many clusters there are in the data. Then we get a summary of the results indicating two or three clusters as the best number. The results of the analysis are stored in a list called nclust. The nclust$Best.nc[1,] command summarizes the suggested number of clusters for each of the methods.

In addition to finding out how many clusters seem to characterize the data, we would also like to know how well-separated the clusters are. Do they form separate groups in multidimensional space or have we just divided the space up in a more or less arbitrary manner? The answer to that question is increasingly difficult to answer as the number of dimensions increases. The disagreement regarding the number of clusters suggests that there are not compact, well-separated groups. The package cluster gives us some tools for answering this question.

Silhouette plots provide an indication of how well the clusters are separated from one another. The plot is constructed by taking each observation and computing the average distance of that observation to all of the other observations in the same cluster. Then we compute the average distance of that observation to all of the other observations in the nearest cluster. If the clusters are well separated, the average distances within a cluster will be smaller than the average distances to observations in the neighboring cluster. For each observation, an index is computed that ranges from 1 (the observation belongs to a cluster where all of the observations are identical so the within cluster distances are 0) to negative when the average distances to the observations in the neighboring cluster are smaller than the average distances to observations within the same cluster.

This will be simpler to understand if we use an example with well-separated clusters. The following commands generate three clusters and plot them:

```
> set.seed(7)
> n <- 15
> s <- .35
> x <- c(rnorm(n, 3, s), rnorm(n, 2, s), rnorm(n, 5, s))
> y <- c(rnorm(n, 3, s), rnorm(n, 5, s), rnorm(n, 4, s))
> g <- rep(1:3, each=n)
> Ex <- data.frame(g, x, y)
> plot(y~x, Ex, xlim=c(1, 6), pch=as.character(Ex$g),
    las=1, asp=1)
```

The three clusters are created by drawing from a random normal distribution with centers at (3, 3), (2, 5), and (5, 4). The standard deviation for all three distributions is .35 (Figure 68). The clusters are quite distinct and k-means has no difficulty finding them. The next commands compute the clusters using k-means and then produce a silhouette plot (Figure 69a):

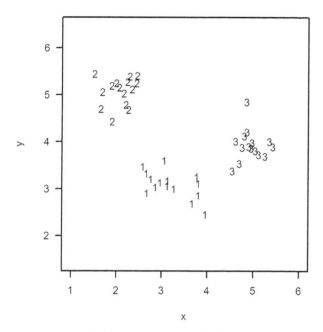

FIGURE 68 Three well-separated clusters.

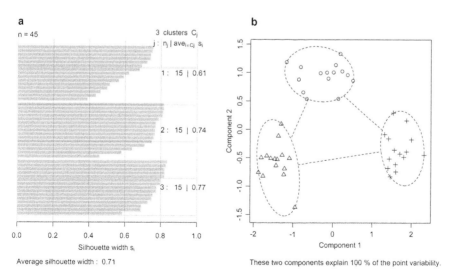

FIGURE 69 Silhouette plot (a) and clusplot (b) for well-separated clusters.

```
> set.seed(42)
> Ex.km <- kmeans(Ex[,-1], 3, nstart=5)
> xtabs(~Ex$g+Ex.km$cluster)
     Ex.km$cluster
Ex$g  1  2  3
   1 15  0  0
   2  0  0 15
   3  0 15  0
> library(cluster)
> plot(silhouette(Ex.km$cluster, dist(Ex[,-1])),
+    main="Silhouette Plot of Well Separated Clusters")
> grid(col="black")
```

After running kmeans(), we produce a cross-tabulation of the original and *k*-means groups. The group numbers are not the same, but each of the original groups is identified perfectly since each row and each column in the table has a single non-zero entry. In Figure 69a the cluster numbers refer to the numbers returned by kmeans(). The silhouette plot shows that the average silhouette width is 0.71. Observations in a cluster are overwhelmingly closer to observations in their cluster than they are to observations in the nearest neighboring cluster. Each horizontal bar in the figure is a single observation and the average width for each cluster ranges from 0.61 to 0.77. No values are negative.

Cluster 1 has the lowest average silhouette width. If you look at Figure 68, you can see that group 1 is a little more dispersed than the other groups. That is why the index values are smaller. None of the observations have negative values and none is close to zero. On Figure 68, group 2 is farther from the other two groups. This is cluster 3 in Figure 69a and it has the larger index values.

Another way of visualizing cluster separation is a clusplot, which plots the first two principal components and identifies the clusters with ellipses. The distances between ellipses provides an indication of the separation between the groups:

```
> clusplot(Ex[,-1], Ex.km$cluster, col.clus="black", lty=2,
+    main="Clusplot - Well Separated")
```

Figure 69b shows the first two principal components. Since there are only two variables, the two components explain 100 percent of the point variability. With more variables, this would not be the case and clusters separated in higher dimensions might appear to overlap. Each cluster is identified by a symbol and the members of a cluster are surrounded by an ellipse that contains the points. The plot characters are 1, 2, and 3 so group 1 is a circle, group 2 is a triangle, and group 3 is a plus sign. Lines show the separation between the ellipses.

Now that we have ways of looking at cluster separation, we can generate a silhouette plot and a clusplot for the hand axes:

```
> Groups <- Hodson.km2$cluster
> plot(silhouette(Groups, dist(Hodson)),
+       main="Silhouette Plot of Furze Platt Hand Axes")
> grid(col="black")
```

Figure 70a shows that the hand axe groups are not well-separated. The average silhouette width is only 0.22 (compared to 0.71 for the well-separated groups in Figure 69). There are a few negative values. The clusplot supports this conclusion:

```
> clusplot(Hodson, Groups, col.clus="black", lty=2, cex=.75,
+       main="Clusplot - Furze Platt Hand Axes")
> legend("topright", paste0("Group ", 1:3), pch=1:3)
```

The first two principal components explain only 68 percent of the variance so there may be additional separation in other dimensions, but Figure 70b shows overlap in the groups. The ellipses for groups 1 (pointed hand axes) and 3 (cleavers and some ovate hand axes) are separated, but group 2 (ovate and pointed hand axes) overlaps. Our conclusion must be that the three groups we have constructed from the Furze Platt hand axes have divided them into three groups that are not well separated. The utility of the groups would have to be demonstrated by showing that they are distinct in terms of information not included here, such as raw material,

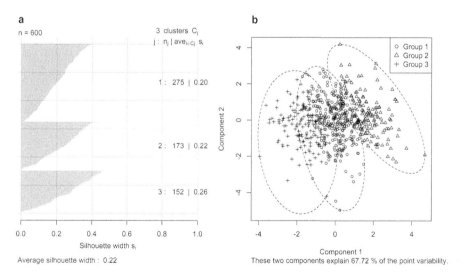

FIGURE 70 Silhouette plot (a) and clusplot (b) of Furze Platt hand axes.

flaking pattern, breakage patterns, location within the site vertically or horizontally, or associations with features or other artifact types. In other words, the analysis is just beginning.

15.2 HIERARCHICAL CLUSTERING

Hierarchical clustering is an alternative to partitioning that starts with each observation representing a cluster and merging observations and clusters until we have combined everything into a single group. Hierarchical methods have the advantage that we can get results for all possible cluster sizes. They also provide a wider range of choices for distance measures and clustering methods. In fact, there are three sets of decisions to be made.

First, selection of the variables to be clustered and how to weight (or not weight) those variables (Chapters 6 and 14). For example, to weight the variables equally we would standardize them using `scale()` or replace them with principal component scores using `prcomp()` with `scale.=TRUE`. Variables with missing values can be included since the function that computes the distance matrix (`dist()`) will skip over them and adjust the distance to the number of variables used. Nevertheless, it may be advantageous to impute missing values using some of the approaches described in Chapter 7.

The second decision is how to compute distance (Chapter 14). Euclidian distance is the default and makes good sense for metric data. Manhattan distance may be more appropriate for assemblage data based on percentages. Symmetric and asymmetric binary is more appropriate for dichotomous data, and Gower is the only option if the variables include a mixture of numeric, dichotomous, ordinal, and categorical variables. Gower is not an option in `dist()`, but it is available using function `daisy()` in the `cluster` package.

The third decision is how to combine observations into clusters and clusters into bigger clusters. There are seven choices in `hclust()` (Box 19):

1. **Ward's method** creates clusters by minimizing the increase in the within cluster sum of squares. The method tends to construct relatively balanced clusters that are spherical in shape. There are two approaches in `hclust()`, `method="ward.D"`, and `method="ward.D2"` that are based on whether the Euclidean distances or their squares are used.
2. **Single linkage**, `method="single"`, adds an observation to a cluster if the distance from the observation to the nearest member of the cluster is less than

the distance to the nearest member of any other cluster. The method is the only one that can identify non-spherical clusters, but it often produces one large cluster that grows steadily.

3. **Complete linkage**, `method="complete"`, adds an observation to a cluster if the distance from the observation to the farthest member of the cluster is less than the distance to the farthest member of any other cluster. It tends to produce compact clusters of comparable size. This is the default method if you do not specify one of the others.

4. **Average linkage**, `method="average"`, combines clusters if the average of the distances between the members of that cluster is less than for any other cluster (also called unweighted pair group method with arithmetic mean [UPGMA]).

5. **McQuitty's method**, `method="mcquitty"`, is similar to average linkage except that the distance from an observation to a cluster is the weighted average of the distances to the clusters that make up the cluster (also called weighted pair group method with arithmetic mean [WPGMA]).

6. **Centroid**, `method="centroid"`, adds observations to a cluster if the distance to the centroid of the cluster is less than for any other cluster. The method is not widely used as it can produce reversals in the dendrogram because when two clusters are merged, the centroid shifts. Whereas the previous methods examine point-to-point distances, the centroid and median methods examine point-to-centroid (of the cluster) distances.

7. **Median**, `method="median"` is similar to the centroid method, but the centroid of the joined clusters is halfway between the centroids of the joined clusters. It also can produce reversals in the dendrogram.

The most commonly used methods are the first four with single linkage usually reserved for cases where linear-shaped clusters are expected. The heights (distances) for the first five methods increase with each cluster step.

To illustrate hierarchical cluster analysis we will use the Romano-British pottery data set, `RBPottery`. The data consist of the percentages of various oxides in pottery from five different kilns in three regions. We will use hierarchical cluster analysis to see if we can identify the regions and/or kilns using only the compositional data.

```
> data(RBPottery)
> RBPottery.dist <- dist(RBPottery[, 4:12])
> lbl <- paste0(abbreviate(RBPottery$Region, 1), "-",
+        abbreviate(RBPottery$Kiln, 1))
> RBPottery.hcl <- hclust(RBPottery.dist, method="ward.D2")
```

```
> plot(RBPottery.hcl, labels=lbl, hang= -1, cex=.75)
> rect.hclust(RBPottery.hcl, k=3)
> Groups <- cutree(RBPottery.hcl, k=3)
> table(RBPottery$Region, Groups)
              Groups
                1  2  3
  Gloucester  22  0  0
  Wales        0 16  0
  New Forest   0  0 10
```

The plot should look like Figure 71. It may look a little crowded on your screen. If you grab the left or right side of the plot window and drag, you can make the

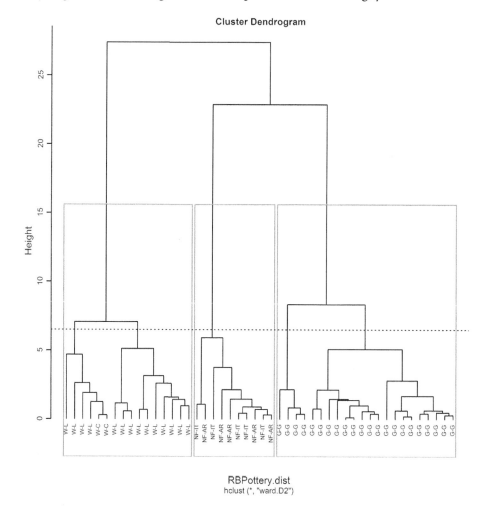

FIGURE 71 Hierarchical cluster analysis of Romano-British pottery.

window rectangular and the labels will spread out. After loading the data set, we compute a Euclidean distance matrix for the numeric variables (columns 4 through 12). We also create labels combining the `Region` and `Kiln` codes so we can easily see how well the clusters match the known locations. Then we use `hclust()` with method `ward.D2` to construct the hierarchical cluster analysis. We did not scale the variables so that oxides with larger percentages will have greater weight in determining the distances between specimens. The dendrogram shows how specimens were combined to form groups. Visually drawing a horizontal line at any height on the dendrogram allows us to see the cluster membership from 48 clusters to one cluster. For example a line at 10 on the `Height` scale divides the observations into three clusters, the number of regions. At about 6.5, there are five clusters, the number of sites (you could use `abline(h=6.5, lty=3)` to put a dotted line on the figure).

We use `rect.hclust()` to draw rectangles around the three-cluster solution. The labels do not identify individual specimens, but they do indicate region (G for Gloucester, NF for New Forest, and W for Wales) and kiln (AR for Ashley Rails, C for Caldicot, G for Gloucester, IT for Islands Thorns, and L for Lanedeyrn). It is clear that the ceramics from each region are correctly grouped, but that the kilns within a region are not grouped together. The last two commands use `cutree()` to cut the dendrogram at three groups and show which specimens belong to each group. Comparing the clusters to the known regions shows that Gloucester is group 1, Wales is group 2, and New Forest is group 3.

This example worked despite the fact that we suspect three of the oxide values are misprints in the published data (see the `RBPottery` manual page for details). Converting to standard scores would have increased the influence of those problem values. In other cases, the elements important for identifying compositional groups may be the less common elements. The results of the hierarchical cluster analysis were stored in `RBPottery.hcl`. This object contains the instructions for combining specimens into larger and larger groups:

```
> with(RBPottery.hcl, head(cbind(merge, round(height, 3)), 15))
        [,1]   [,2]    [,3]
 [1,]    -2     -5   0.127
 [2,]    -7    -20   0.210
 [3,]    -6    -22   0.293
 [4,]   -37    -38   0.301
 [5,]   -39    -45   0.318
 [6,]   -13    -14   0.374
 [7,]   -15    -16   0.390
```

```
[8,]     -3    -21   0.411
[9,]    -41    -42   0.440
[10,]    -9      3   0.484
[11,]   -19      7   0.575
[12,]   -23    -25   0.579
[13,]   -18      2   0.630
[14,]     8     10   0.638
[15,]   -26    -30   0.685
```

The first two columns indicate what is being combined at that step and the third column is the height (distance) at which they are being combined. If you want to trace the process, it will be easier if you label the dendrogram by row number (plot(RBPottery.hcl)). Here we just look at the first 15 rows (there are a total of 47 rows since there are 48 observations). The first row (step 1) tells us that observations 2 and 5 were combined to form the first cluster. Since they are preceded by a minus sign, these are observation numbers. The first 9 rows all involve combining two observations to form groups of 2. At row 10, observation 9 is combined with the cluster defined in row (step) 3. Since the 3 is a positive number, we know that it refers to a row in the clustering results not in the original data. So step 10 involves combining observation 9 with observations 6 and 22 (which were combined in step 3). Step 14 involves combining the groups formed in steps 8 and 10 (observations 3 and 21 with 9, 6, and 22). While this probably seems confusing, R is able use the information to draw the dendrogram. Also stored in RBPottery.hcl is a vector called order, which lists the order of the observations from left to right across the dendrogram.

In this case, we know which ceramics come from which region and how many regions are represented. Normally we would not have that much information so we would try different distance measures and different clustering methods. In this case, changing to Manhattan distances or changing the clustering method does not affect the results much. This consistency is an indication that the clusters are relatively well separated.

One way to evaluate the different choices is to use cophenetic correlation to see how well the dendrogram reproduces the relationships in the distance matrix (Shennan, 1997). The cophenetic distance between two observations is the dissimilarity at which the observations are first combined. When two observations are combined, it will be the distance between those two observations. When two clusters are combined, the distance between observations in different clusters will be the distance at which the clusters are joined. The function cophenetic() computes these distances from a hierarchical clustering object. The cophenetic correlation is just the Pearson correlation between the cophenetic distance matrix and the original distance matrix.

We can construct the cophenetic correlation for four common clustering methods, but we will copy RBPottery.dist to D first to save some typing since we will use the distance matrix eight times:

```
> D <- RBPottery.dist
> options(digits=3)
> cor(D, cophenetic(hclust(D, method="ward.D2")))
[1] 0.824
> cor(D, cophenetic(hclust(D, method="complete")))
[1] 0.772
> cor(D, cophenetic(hclust(D, method="average")))
[1] 0.869
> cor(D, cophenetic(hclust(D, method="single")))
[1] 0.829
```

All four provide the same classification results for three clusters and the cophenetic correlations are similar, but the value for complete linkage is the smallest and the value for average linkage is the largest for these data.

For k-means we constructed a scree plot by calculating the total within cluster sum of squares for a range of clusters. Hierarchical clustering essentially provides this information automatically so we can plot the change in height (a measure of the distance between clusters) and compare that to randomized data:

```
> plot(47:1, RBPottery.hcl$height, xlab="Number of Clusters",
+    ylab="Height", type="b")
> set.seed(42)
> RBPottery.hclr <- hclust(dist(sapply(RBPottery[, 4:12],
+    sample)), method="ward.D2")
> lines(47:1, RBPottery.hclr$height, lty=2)
> legend("topright", c("Original Data", "Randomized Data"),
  lty=1:2)
```

Figure 72 shows the scree plot compared to a single randomized data set. Notice how the height value jumps from three to two clusters. This suggests that the data fall into three clusters. We can also look at the results of NbClust() to see what it suggests as the best number of clusters for the data:

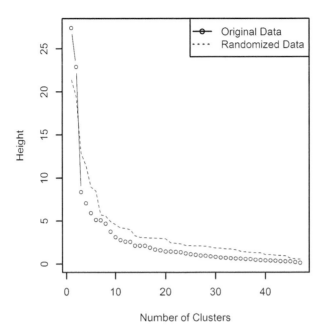

FIGURE 72 Scree plot for Romano-British Pottery data with hierarchical clustering.

```
> library(NbClust)
> oldp <- par(ask=TRUE)
> nclust <- NbClust(RBPottery[, 4:12], method="ward.D2")
. . . informational messages deleted . . .
*********************************************************
* Among all indices:
* 1 proposed 2 as the best number of clusters
* 14 proposed 3 as the best number of clusters
* 2 proposed 4 as the best number of clusters
* 1 proposed 5 as the best number of clusters
* 1 proposed 8 as the best number of clusters
* 1 proposed 10 as the best number of clusters
* 3 proposed 15 as the best number of clusters


        ***** Conclusion *****


* According to the majority rule, the best number of
  clusters is 3



*********************************************************
```

```
> nclust$Best.nc[1, ]
        KL          CH  Hartigan       CCC      Scott    Marriot    TrCovW
         3          15         3         3          3          3         3
    TraceW    Friedman     Rubin  Cindex                DB Silhouette      Duda
         3          10         3         5         15          3         4
   PseudoT2       Beale Ratkowsky      Ball PtBiserial         Frey   McClain
         4           8         3         3          3          1         2
      Dunn      Hubert   SDindex  Dindex       SDbw
         3           0         3         0         15
> par(oldp)
```

The result is substantial support for 3 clusters in the data and almost no support for 5 (the number of kilns). We can also use the silhouette plot and clusplot to see how well the clusters are separated:

```
> library(cluster)
> plot(silhouette(Groups, RBPottery.dist),
+    main="Silhouette Plot of Romano- British Pottery")
> grid(col="black")
> clusplot(RBPottery[, 4:12], Groups, col.clus="black", lty=2,
+    cex=.75, main="Clusplot - Romano- British Pottery")
> legend("topright", c("Gloucester", "Wales", "New Forest"),
+    pch=1:3)
```

Figure 73a shows that the average silhouette value is 0.6, which is not as high as the well-separated clusters in Figure 69a, but much higher than the hand axes in Figure 70a. The clusplot shows that New Forest is very distinct from the other two while Gloucester and Wales are closer to one another, but do not overlap in the first two principal components, which explain 67 percent of the variability (Figure 73b).

When we used k-means clustering, the centroids for each cluster were returned as part of the results. Those are not provided by the hierarchical clustering function since we need to specify the number of clusters to get the statistics. Earlier we used `cutree()` to save the classification results for three clusters as `Groups`. We can get the means with the `aggregate()` function:

```
> aggregate(RBPottery[, 4:12], list(Groups), mean)
  Group.1 Al2O3 Fe2O3  MgO   CaO   Na2O  K2O  TiO2     MnO     BaO
1       1  16.9  7.43 1.84 0.942 0.348 3.11 0.896 0.0717 0.0171
2       2  12.5  6.25 4.71 0.214 0.226 4.01 0.690 0.1386 0.0166
3       3  17.8  1.61 0.64 0.039 0.051 2.02 1.020 0.0032 0.0160
```

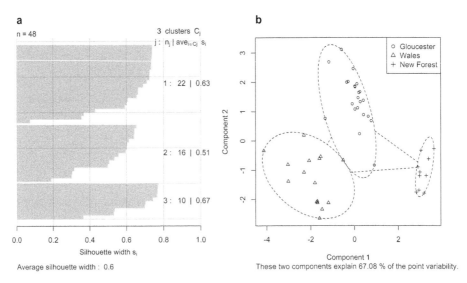

FIGURE 73 Silhouette plot (a) and clusplot (b) for Romano-British pottery.

This tells us how the regional groups differ from one another in terms of the mean percentages of the different oxides (1=Gloucester, 2=Wales, 3=New Forest). We could get more detailed statistics with numSummary() in package RcmdrMisc (Chapter 3).

15.3 OTHER METHODS

Most clustering procedures either partition the data or aggregate hierarchically. Among the partitioning methods, new approaches include the use of medoids rather than centroids to provide a more robust handling of extreme values. A medoid is the observation that has the minimum distance to all other members of the group. K-means identifies a point in space that is the mean for each of the variables for the members of a group (the centroid). An extreme value can drag the centroid into an area of empty space between the outlier and the other members of the group, but that cannot happen with a medoid. In addition to function pam() in package cluster, there is vegclust() in package vegclust (De Cáceres et al., 2010). Instead of assigning each specimen to a particular cluster, we can provide probabilities of membership like the ones we computed for discriminant analysis. This approach is called fuzzy clustering and implementations are available in packages cluster (fanny()), vegclust (vegclust()), and e1071(cmeans()) (Meyer et al., 2015). Model-based clustering methods assume the data represent a mixture of different multivariate distributions (often normal distributions). The data are partitioned by estimating the parameters of the unknown distributions. Package `mclust` is the primary implementation of this method (Fraley et al., 2012).

Divisive clustering is less well-represented. Package `cluster` has two divisive functions, `diana()` and `mona()`. The first implements a divisive hierarchical clustering algorithm for a distance matrix. As mentioned at the beginning of the chapter, the challenge is to reduce the task from considering all possible partitions. The procedure starts by finding the observation with the largest average distance in the distance matrix and using it to create a separate group of observations that are located closer to that observation. Groups are subdivided until each observation is its own group. The output of the function presents the results in reverse order so that the functions for producing dendrograms and cutting the tree will work. The second function implements monothetic divisive clustering of binary variables. At each stage, the variable with the maximal total association to the other variables is used to divide the group into two subgroups. These functions are described in detail in Kaufman and Rousseeuw (1990).

BOX 18 K-MEANS CLUSTERING WITH kmeans ()

```
kmeans(x, centers, iter.max = 10, nstart = 1,
    algorithm = c("Hartigan-Wong", "Lloyd", "Forgy",
  "MacQueen"),
    trace=FALSE)

fitted(object, method = c("centers", "classes"), ...)
```

This program performs *k*-means clustering of a data numeric matrix (x) into `centers=` clusters. If `centers=` a single number, then the data are partitioned into that many groups. If `centers=` a matrix, then it must have the same number of columns as the data and as many rows as the number of clusters desired. The matrix defines the centroids of the clusters at the start of the analysis.

K-means allocates objects to groups in such a way that the sum of the squared Euclidean distances between each point and the group to which it is assigned is minimized. On each iteration, observations are assigned to the closest centroid. Then the centroids are recomputed based on the assignments and the assignments of the observations are re-evaluated to see if they now lie closer to a different centroid. This process continues until the `iter.max=` value is reached or no observations are re-assigned. Since the initial centroids determine the results, it is possible for the algorithm to reach a local minimum for the total within sum of squares.

The default analysis uses the provided centers or a single randomly generated start using the Hartigan–Wong algorithm with trace off. It is wise to set `nstart=` to a number larger than the default value (e.g., 10, 20, or more) to make sure you have located the global minimum. If there is a warning that the algorithm did not converge within 10 iterations, increase `iter.max=` and run the analysis again.

The function returns a list of nine elements including an integer vector of the group assignments (`cluster`), a matrix of the cluster centers (`centers`), the total sum of squares (`totss`), a vector of the within cluster sum of squares for each cluster (`withinss`), the total within cluster sum of squares (the sum of the previous vector, `tot.withinss`), the between cluster sum of squares (`betweenss`), the number of observations in each cluster (`size`), the number of iterations needed for convergence (`iter`), and an integer value indicating a possible problem with the analysis (`ifault`).

There are `print()` and `fitted()` functions for `kmeans` objects. The `print()` function prints the cluster means, the cluster memberships, and between cluster sum of squares as a percentage of the total sum of squares. By default, the `fitted()` function returns a matrix of the same size as the input matrix with the observed values replaced by the means for the cluster to which they are assigned (`method="centers"`). When `method="classes"`, only the cluster assignments are returned.

BOX 19 HIERARCHICAL CLUSTERING WITH `hclust()`

```
hclust(d, method = "complete", members = NULL)
```

This program performs a hierarchical cluster analysis on a distance matrix. The analysis begins with n clusters where n is the number of observations. Each step reduces the number of clusters by one by combining observations and clusters until there is a single cluster ($n - 1$ steps). The process is determined by the method used for combining observations and clusters (`method=`). The choices for method are "ward.D", "ward.D2", "single", "complete", "average" (= UPGMA), "mcquitty" (= WPGMA), "median" (= WPGMC), or "centroid" (= UPGMC). The default analysis uses complete linkage ("complete"). Most of the methods produce compact clusters and relatively even cluster sizes. The single linkage method ("single") can identify linear clusters, but also tends to produce chaining (a single cluster that grows by accumulation).

The function returns a list with seven elements. The first, `merge`, is an $n - 1$ by 2 matrix, describing the merging of observations and clusters. Observations are identified by their row number in the original data preceded by a minus sign (–). Clusters are defined by their row number in the merge matrix without a minus sign. The second element, height, indicates the height (distance) at which the merge occurred. The order element indicates the order of the observations to be used in plotting the dendrogram and labels provides the label for each observation if they were present in the distance matrix.

Functions that work with hclust objects include cutree() , which will extract the cluster memberships for a particular number of clusters, plot(), which produces a dendrogram, rect.hclust(), which draws rectangles on a dendrogram showing the cluster branches, and identify(), which interactively identifies branches on a dendrogram. Also hclust objects can be converted to dendrogram objects with as.dendrogram() to use the more extensive functions for plotting and rearranging the branches on a dendrogram (e.g., plotting a horizontal dendrogram).

Table 17 *Functions introduced in Chapter 15*

Function	Package	Description
abbreviate	base	Abbreviate strings keeping them unique
as.dendrogram	stats	Create a dendrogram object
clusplot	cluster	Draw a clusplot of cluster separation
cmeans	e1071	Various clustering methods
cophenetic	stats	Cophenetic distances for hierarchical clustering
cutree	stats	Cut a dendrogram and provide cluster membership
daisy	cluster	Compute a dissimilarity matrix
diana	cluster	Divisive hierarchical clustering
fanny	cluster	Fuzzy clustering
hclust	stats	Hierarchical clustering
kmeans	stats	Preform *k*-means clustering
mclust	mclust	Model-based clustering
mona	cluster	Monothetic divisive clustering
NbClust	NbClust	Estimate the best number of clusters
pam	cluster	Partitioning of data around medoids
rect.hclust	stats	Identify groups on a dendrogram
rep	base	Repeat a value
silhouette	cluster	Draw a silhouette plot of cluster separation
vegclust	vegclust	Several clustering methods

Note: Packages base, datasets, graphics, grDevices, methods, stats, and utils are automatically loaded when R starts.

III

Archaeological Approaches to Data

16

Spatial Analysis

An integral aspect of archaeological data is that they come from particular places. We often want to examine the distribution of artifacts, sites, or features over space and R provides a number of tools for this purpose. We may also be interested in the direction or orientation of the object, house, or feature. This chapter will cover some of the basics, but there are specialized R packages for mapping and for analyzing gridded and point data. If most of your analysis involves spatial data it may be easier to use a geographic information system (GIS) package, but R can handle shape-files and other data structures that are produced by those packages and it provides extensive support for statistical analysis of spatial data. In this chapter we will cover directional statistics, creating simple distribution maps based on gridded or piece plotted data.

16.1 CIRCULAR OR DIRECTIONAL STATISTICS

Circular statistics include direction and orientation (Gaile and Burt, 1980; Jammalamadaka and Sengupta, 2001; Mardia and Jupp, 2000). If we are interested in the **direction** of something (for example burials or rock shelter openings), then we are using directional data. In general, this is recorded in degrees measured clockwise from north, but it can also include cyclical data where the cycle repeats daily, weekly, monthly, or yearly. In other cases, we are interested in the **orientation** of an elongated flake, blade, or bone fragment. Orientation can be defined as north/south or east/west so we are only using half of the circle since 0° and 180° or 90° and 270° are the same orientation. With bone fragments, for example, we usually cannot identify which end is the front and which is the back so we are working with orientation. With blades, we could define the platform end as the front in which case we could measure direction rather than orientation, but often only the orientation is recorded. The research question under consideration will help to make the decision between direction and orientation. Analytically, the first step with orientation data is to double each value and analyze it as directional data.

One of the problems with direction and orientation is that there are different ways of measuring. In trigonometry and calculus, we generally measure in radians rather than degrees (where 360° equals 2π (6.283185) radians), the starting direction is along the positive x-axis (3 o'clock), and we proceed around the circle in a counter-clockwise direction. Geographic direction is usually measured in degrees, starts at north (12 o'clock), and proceeds around the circle in a clockwise direction. This can make the display and analysis of directional data more complicated than it should be.

Just ignoring the fact that the data are directional is not a solution since standard descriptive statistics can be very misleading when applied to directional data. This is because directional data are two-dimensional, but since they lay on a circle we can describe them accurately with a single value (degrees or radians). But since they are on a circle, 359° and 1° are only 2 degrees apart on the circle, but subtracting them from one another gives us 358 or -358!

As an example, we will look at two directional variables in some data from the Ernest Witte site, a Late Archaic cemetery in Texas (Hall, 1981). The EWBurials data set includes 49 burials from Groups 1 (12) and 2 (37). Eight variables are included for each burial. Burials from Groups 1 and 2 that have missing values on any of these variables are not included. Two of the variables are directional, one indicating the direction of the internment as measured along the spinal column through the skull and the direction the individual is facing. First install and load package circular, which has functions for analyzing and plotting directional data (Agostinelli and Lund, 2013). Then open the data set and look at the structure:

```
> library(circular)
# Messages about the package redefining the sd() and var()
  functions
> options(digits=3)
> library(archdata)
> data(EWBurials)
> View(EWBurials)
> EWBurials$Direction
Circular Data:
Type = angles
```

```
Units = degrees
Template = geographics
Modulo = asis
Zero = 1.570796
Rotation = clock
 [1]  42  28 350 335   3 142 328 351 357 144  54  27  54  64  17  83
[17]  58  41 355  20  46  44  48   2   9  45 144 121 138 121  36 183
[33]  35  14  10  28  97  58  23 288  26 331  28 151   1 142 140  13
[49] 161
```

Direction and Looking are stored as class circular. They were created from numeric variables in degrees. For example, Direction is converted to class circular as follows:

```
> EWBurials$Direction <- circular(EWBurials$Direction,
+   units="degrees", template="geographics")
```

The circular() function lets us indicate that the circular data is measured in degrees and follows the conventions for geographic data (0 is north and degrees are measured clockwise). Package circular modifies some standard functions in R to handle circular data. We can start with some simple descriptive statistics:

```
> mean(EWBurials$Direction)
Circular Data:
Type = angles
Units = degrees
Template = geographics
Modulo = asis
Zero = 1.570796
Rotation = clock
[1] 42.1
> mean.default(EWBurials$Direction)
[1] 109
```

When we use the mean() function, R recognizes that the variable Direction is circular and uses the circular mean automatically. We can override that behavior by specifying mean.default() to get the arithmetic mean. The result is verbose, but it provides all of the information about what kind of circular data Direction is. The mean value is about 42° so the mean direction is approximately northeast. Note that this is very different from the arithmetic mean, which is 108.9 (approximately east by southeast). Clearly the arithmetic mean is very misleading. Now look at the results for `Looking`:

```
> mean(EWBurials$Looking)
Circular Data:
Type = angles
Units = degrees
Template = geographics
Modulo = asis
Zero = 1.57
Rotation = clock
[1] -132
> as.vector(mean(EWBurials$Looking)) + 360
[1] 228
> mean.default(EWBurials$Looking)
[1] 175
```

The mean is -132°, which we can get by going counter-clockwise from North (0°) or just add 360° to the mean to get 228° (Southwest). The arithmetic mean is 175° (South). The arithmetic mean is a misleading estimate of mean direction, but the circular mean can also be misleading. Consider the following examples:

```
> Example1 <- circular(c(0, 90, 180, 270), units="degrees",
+    template="geographics")
> as.vector(mean(Example1))
[1] NA
> Example2 <- circular(c(0, 90, 179, 270), units="degrees",
+    template="geographics")
> as.vector(mean(Example2))
[1] 89.5
```

In the first example, we take the four cardinal directions (North, East, South, and West) and the mean is NA (missing). That is because there is no mean direction, the four directional vectors point in opposite directions. The second example changes 180 to 179 and that is enough to give a mean direction of 89.5°. But practically speaking, there is no mean direction. We need a way to detect situations like this and that is to use **rho**, the mean resultant length of a vector of circular data:

```
> rho.circular(Example1)
[1] 4.33e-17
> rho.circular(Example2)
[1] 0.00436
```

If all of the directions are the same (e.g., 45, 45, 45, 45), then rho will be 1. When they are opposing one another (Example1), rho will be 0. In Example2, we can compute a mean, but the value of rho is close to 0, indicating that there is a great deal of variability in direction. Small values of rho indicate that direction is highly variable, so **circular variance** is defined as 1 – rho:

```
> var(Example1)
[1] 1
> var(Example2)
[1] 0.996
```

Circular standard deviation is also based on rho, but it is not the square root of the variance (sqrt(-2*log(rho))). We always need to check the value of rho or the variance to determine if the data have directionality. For Direction and Looking, the rho values are

```
> (Dir.rho <- rho.circular(EWBurials$Direction))
[1] 0.581
> (Look.rho <- rho.circular(EWBurials$Looking))
[1] 0.0845
```

Notice that the rho value for Direction (0.58 where 1 is the maximum possible value) is much larger than the rho value for Looking (0.08 where 0 is the minimum possible value). If we plot the data, it will be easier to see just how different the two means are (Figure 74a,b):

```
> dev.new(width=10, height=6)
> oldp <- par(mfrow=c(1, 2), mar=c(2.1, 1.1, 2.1, 1.1))
> plot(EWBurials$Direction, stack=TRUE, main="Direction")
> arrows.circular(mean(EWBurials$Direction), Dir.rho,
  length=.15, lwd=2)
> arrows.circular(circular(mean.default(EWBurials$Direction),
+    units="degrees", template="geographics"), Dir.rho,
+    length=.15, col="gray", lwd=2)
>
> plot(EWBurials$Looking, stack=TRUE, main="Looking")
> arrows.circular(mean(EWBurials$Looking), Look.rho,
  length=.15, lwd=2)
> arrows.circular(circular(mean.default(EWBurials$Looking),
+    units="degrees", template="geographics"), Look.rho,
+    length=.15, col="gray", lwd=2)
> par(oldp)
```

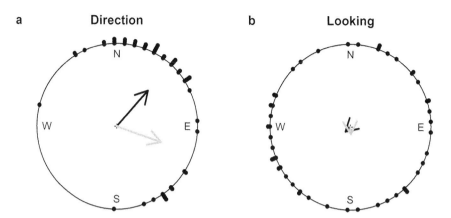

FIGURE 74 Plot of Ernest Witte burial direction (a) and looking (b) showing circular mean (black) and the arithmetic mean (gray).

These commands plot `Direction` and `Looking` around a circle. We use `dev. new()` to open a rectangular plot window since we are putting two plots side by side. The solid arrow is the circular mean. It is computed by treating all of the points as vectors originating at the center of the circle and finding the resultant vector. The length of the arrow is the length of that resultant vector (rho). The arithmetic mean is in gray and we have to convert it to circular data to add it to the plot. While most of the `Direction` values lie on the east side of the circle, the `Looking` values are all around and the difference in the rho values is clearly apparent from the lengths of the arrows. The plot suggests that there may be a bimodal distribution of burial `Direction`.

We can use the Rayleigh test to see if each group shows significant directionality for `Direction` and `Looking`. The null hypothesis is that the directions are randomly spread around the circle and the test statistic is the value of rho so the null hypothesis is that the value of rho is not significantly different from 0. Since there are two burial groups, we run the analysis on each group separately:

```
> aggregate(EWBurials[, 6:7], list(EWBurials$Group), mean)
  Group.1 Direction Looking
1       1     138.8    25.9
2       2      23.1  -143.8
> with(EWBurials, by(Direction, Group, rayleigh.test))
Group: 1

    Rayleigh Test of Uniformity
    General Unimodal Alternative
```

```
Test Statistic:   0.858
P-value:   0

------------------------------------------------------
Group: 2

     Rayleigh Test of Uniformity
     General Unimodal Alternative

Test Statistic:   0.848
P-value:   0
> with(EWBurials, by(Looking, Group, rayleigh.test))
Group: 1

     Rayleigh Test of Uniformity
     General Unimodal Alternative

Test Statistic:   0.398
P-value:   0.149

------------------------------------------------------
Group: 2

     Rayleigh Test of Uniformity
     General Unimodal Alternative

Test Statistic:   0.237
P-value:   0.126
```

The aggregate() function shows us the difference in the circular means for Direction and Looking by group. The Rayleigh test indicates that we can reject the null hypothesis of no directionality for Direction, but we cannot reject the null hypothesis for Looking. In the Rayleigh test, the alternate hypothesis is that the distribution is unimodal. As a result, the test can fail to detect non-uniform distributions that are multimodal. Several other tests are better at detecting multimodal distributions including range.circular(), kuiper.test(), rao.spacing.test(), and watson.test().

Rao's test for homogeneity lets us test for differences in direction between two groups:

```
> with(EWBurials, rao.test(split(Direction, Group)))

Rao's Tests for Homogeneity

    Test for Equality of Polar Vectors:

Test Statistic = 25.5
Degrees of Freedom = 1
P-value of test = 0

    Test for Equality of Dispersions:

Test Statistic = 0.0077
Degrees of Freedom = 1
P-value of test = 0.93

> with(EWBurials, rao.test(split(Looking, Group)))

Rao's Tests for Homogeneity

    Test for Equality of Polar Vectors:

Test Statistic = 0.0829
Degrees of Freedom = 1
P-value of test = 0.773

    Test for Equality of Dispersions:

Test Statistic = 0.278
Degrees of Freedom = 1
P-value of test = 0.598
```

The results indicate that mean Direction is different between the groups. The first Rao test (test for equality of polar vectors) indicates that these differences are statistically significant, but the second Rao test (test for equality of dispersions) indicates that the two groups have similar dispersion of values around their mean directions. For Looking neither test is significant. The mean directions are very different between the groups, but the Rayleigh test indicated that Looking was essentially random for both groups. We can plot both groups on wind rose plots to show the difference (Figure 75a,b):

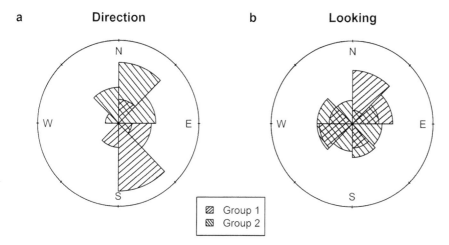

FIGURE 75 Wind rose plots of Ernest Witte burial direction and looking by group.

```
> dev.new(width=10, height=6)
> oldp <- par(mfrow=c(1, 2), mar=c(2.1, 1.1, 2.1, 1.1))
> with(EWBurials, rose.diag(Direction[Group==1], bins=8,
+   prop=1, density=12, angle=40, lwd=1))
> with(EWBurials, rose.diag(Direction[Group==2], bins=8,
+   prop=1, density=12, angle=130, lwd=1, add=TRUE))
> title(main="Direction")
> legend("topleft", c("Group 1", "Group 2"), density=24,
  angle=c(40, 130))
>
> with(EWBurials, rose.diag(Looking[Group==1], bins=8,
+   prop=1, density=12, angle=40, lwd=1))
> with(EWBurials, rose.diag(Looking[Group==2], bins=8,
+   prop=1, density=12, angle=130, lwd=1, add=TRUE))
> title(main="Looking")
> par(oldp)
```

We use crosshatching to make it easier to see the overlap between the two groups. The `circular` package also provides functions to correlate two circular variables, compute linear regressions, produce kernel density plots and other kinds of plots.

16.2 MAPPING QUADRAT-BASED DATA

One of the best ways to describe spatial data is to produce maps showing where artifacts and features are located. Simple excavation unit maps are easily produced in R using the base graphics functions. For example, the data set `BarmoseI.grid` contains the coordinates for the southwest corner of 107 excavated squares at Barmose I, a Maglemosian site used by Blankholm to illustrate several spatial analysis methods (1991). The data frame consists of three variables, `East`, `North`, and `Debitage` (the number of flakes in that square). We will use this data to show several ways of displaying count or density data from a set of grid squares.

First, we can make a simple plot of the excavation units displaying the number of flakes in each unit. The first step is to use the `plot()` function to create an empty plot with axes and titles. Then we use the `text()` function to print the numbers in the center of each unit:

```
> data(BarmoseI.grid)
> box <- with(BarmoseI.grid, c(min(East), max(East)+1,
+    min(North), max(North)+1))
> plot(NA, xlim=box[1:2], ylim=box[3:4], xlab="East",
+    ylab="North", main="Debitage", type="n", asp=1)
```

The first command figures out the dimensions of the entire excavation unit, which is the minimum value of East to the maximum value of `East` + 1 and the minimum value of `North` to the maximum value of `North` + 1. We save the results as box to set the plotting range. Then the plot command uses NA for the data since we just want to set up the plot with the *x* and *y* limits, *x* and *y* labels, and a title. The `type="n"` argument specifies that no data should be plotted and `asp=1` means that the scale should be the same in the x and y dimensions so that our square excavation units look square on the plot. If you run these commands you will get axes and labels, but no plot. Now add the debitage counts:

```
> with(BarmoseI.grid, text(East+.5, North+.5,
  as.character(Debitage),
+    cex=.75))
+    as.character(Debitage), cex=.75))
```

This adds the debitage counts to the center of each square. This is enough to see that the highest debitage counts are in the center of the excavation block and that they decrease as we move away from the center. It would be nice to add a boundary and perhaps the individual excavation units. We can create those from the data if we assume the units are all 1 × 1 m square:

```
> mkgrid <- function(x, y) {
+    E <- c(rep(x, 2), rep(x+1, 2))
+    N <- c(y, rep(y+1, 2), y)
+    cbind(E, N)
> Units <- with(BarmoseI.grid, mapply(mkgrid, East, North,
  SIMPLIFY=FALSE))
> names(Units) <- with(BarmoseI.grid,
+    sprintf("E%02.0fN%02.0f", East, North))
> for (i in 1:107) {
+    polygon(Units[[i]], border="dark gray")
+ }
```

First, we need to create a function that takes the southwest corner of a square and adds the other three corners. The mkgrid() function does this. We define the function and its arguments and then the commands that will use the arguments are placed inside curly brackets ({ }). The last command is returned by the function. Given a coordinate, it returns a matrix with four rows and two columns containing the east and north coordinates for the square. We use the mapply() function to apply the mkgrid() function to each of the 107 units in BarmoseI.grid. It has the advantage of letting us pass two vectors to the function. By setting SIMPLIFY=FALSE we keep the function from converting the result to a single vector. We need each unit to be a separate element of a list. The results are saved as a list of 107 4×2 matrices called Units. The names(Units) line assigns a name to each member of the list using sprintf() so that we can reference them by name, for example, Units$E00N07, gives us the coordinates of the first unit. This is not necessary for the map, but it can be useful if you need to modify the coordinates of a unit or want to plot only some of the units. Finally we use a for () loop to plot each of the 107 squares using the polygon() function (see Chapter 8 for more information). This adds the squares around each of the debitage counts. Inside the parentheses, we provide a variable name (i) followed by the word "in" and then a vector. After the parentheses we provide a command or a series of commands inside curly brackets.

The plot would be less cluttered if we just plotted a boundary around the area and not the individual squares. There are several ways to get the coordinates for the boundary of the excavation unit. Later we will let R do it for us, but it is also fairly easy to do it by hand from the plot that we have already created. We need the coordinates of every corner around the outside. The following command uses the `locator()` function to get the coordinates and save them:

```
> Bounds <- locator()
```

Now click the mouse on all of the corners around the boundary. For example, start at the East 0, North 7 (the lower left corner of the box with 11 flakes) and then click every corner going clockwise. You should click on 26 points before clicking on the Stop button at the top of the graphics window. Don't worry about getting precisely on the corner since we will round the values to the nearest whole number. The object `Bounds` is a list with two vectors, *x* and *y*. Now we use it to add the outside boundary:

```
> Border <- sapply(Bounds, round)
> colnames(Border) <- c("East", "North")
> polygon(Border, border="black", lwd=2)
> save(Units, Border, file="BarmoseIMap1.RData")
```

We use `sapply()` to round off the numbers to the nearest whole value and convert the list `Bounds` to a matrix called `Border`. Then we plot the border in black using a thicker line type. Optionally, we save the `Units` and `Border` objects as `BarmoseIMap1.RData` in case we will need it later. The final map is shown in Figure 76a. If you want, you can reprint the map without the interior unit boundaries and without the axes (Figure 76b):

```
> plot(NA, xlim=box[1:2], ylim=box[3:4], axes=FALSE, xlab="",
+   ylab="", main="Debitage", type="n", asp=1)
> with(BarmoseI.grid, text(East+.5, North+.5,
+   as.character(Debitage), cex=.75))
> polygon(Border, border="black", lwd=2)
```

All of the methods we have used so far use R's S3 object oriented methods for determining what a generic function will do when we give it an object. S3 simply refers to version 3 of the S language definition that was the ancestor of R. Most of the packages in R use S3. An alternate approach was developed beginning in the mid-1990s called S4 that is used by some R packages including most of the ones for spatial

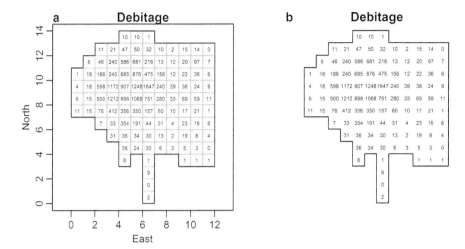

FIGURE 76 Plot of debitage counts from the Barmose I site: (a) unit boundaries and axes included; (b) block boundary only.

analysis and the structure of their objects is somewhat different. The power of these methods for spatial analysis makes it worth the effort to learn more about them.

Choropleth maps use shading to represent the count or density of some variable within a defined area on a map. We can construct these maps by simply plotting the polygons we have already created and changing the fill color or hatching to represent different densities. The process is simpler if we convert our list of polygons to a SpatialPolygons object using functions in the package sp. We need two packages, sp and maptools so you should install them. Then run the following code:

```
> library(sp)
> library(maptools)
> Polys <- lapply(Units, function(x) rbind(x, x[1,]))
> PolyList <- lapply(Polys, function(x) Polygon(x,
  hole=FALSE))
> PolysList <- lapply(seq_along(PolyList), function(x)
+   Polygons(PolyList[x] , names(Units)[x] ))
> Quads <- SpatialPolygons(PolysList, seq_along(PolysList))
> boundary <- unionSpatialPolygons(Quads, rep(1, 107))
> save(Quads, boundary, file= "BarmoseIMap2.RData")
```

First, we have to convert our list of units since the polygon() function automatically joins the last point to the first one, but a SpatialPolygons object expects the first and last points of the outline to be the same. We use the lapply() function to copy the first row to the bottom of each polygon outline. The next three lines create a Polygon list and then a Polygons list and finally a SpatialPolygons list called Quads. The complexity is necessary to allow for many kinds of maps where a country, state, or county may have multiple, discontinuous parts including offshore islands and it may have holes (e.g., lakes) inside its boundaries and islands in the lake. Our excavation grid squares have none of those complexities. Then we create a second SpatialPolygons by letting R identify the boundary of the excavation area for us. Once we have created the necessary objects, creating maps is simple. To create a choropleth map, we need to divide the debitage counts into a small number of categories using cut(). The function returns a vector with the factor levels for each square (Chapter 4). The following commands create five levels using percentiles (so the groups will be relatively equal in size):

```
> bks <- round(quantile(BarmoseI.grid$Debitage, prob=(0:5)/5))
> G.lab <- cut(BarmoseI.grid$Debitage, breaks=bks, include.
+    lowest=TRUE, dig.lab=4)
> table(G.lab)
G.lab
  [0,6]   (6,15]   (15,34]   (34,240]   (240,1647]
     24       21        20         22           20
```

The first command gets the break points (rounded to the nearest integer to make the labels easier to read. The second command cuts Debitage into five groups and uses a label to identify the boundaries of each group. A square bracket means that the adjacent value is included in that level and a parenthesis means the adjacent value is not included in the level. The first level includes 0 to 6 flakes, while the second level includes more than 6 (i.e., 7) to 15 flakes, then more than 15 to 34 flakes, and so on. Each group includes approximately 20 percent of the observations.

Then the choropleth map takes just four commands (Figure 77a):

```
> gcol <- gray(5:0/5)
> plot(Quads, col=gcol[as.integer(G.lab)])
> title("Barmose I - Debitage")
> legend("bottomleft", levels(G.lab), fill=gcol[1:5], title=
  "Flakes per unit")
```

The first command generates five grayscale levels from black to white and the next three lines produce the map, add a title, and a legend. The col=gcol[as.

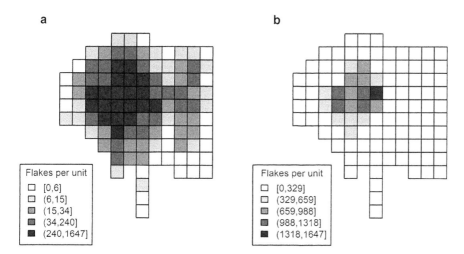

FIGURE 77 Choropleth map for Barmose I debitage: (a) equal count bins; (b) equal range bins.

integer(G.lab)] argument in the plot() command uses the numeric value of G.lab for each square to select which color to use as the fill.

You can also use color functions such as rainbow(), terrain.colors() or one of the other options instead of gray() if you want a more colorful map. Alternatively, you could use the package RColorBrewer and select one of the sequential palettes (Neuwirth, 2014). For example, run these lines to get a sequential blue palette:

```
> library(RColorBrewer)
> gcol <- brewer.pal(5, "Blues")
> plot(Quads, col=gcol[as.integer(G.lab)])
> title("Barmose I - Debitage")
> legend("bottomleft", levels(G.lab), fill=gcol[1:5], title=
  "Flakes per unit")
```

One problem with quantiles is that they may suggest a smooth transition when the differences in density are sharper. If instead of putting approximately the same number of units in each category, we divide the range of the data into equal ranges, we get a very different map (Figure 77b):

```
> bks <- round(max(BarmoseI.grid$Debitage)*(0:5)/5)
> G.lab <- cut(BarmoseI.grid$Debitage, breaks=bks, include.
+   lowest=TRUE, dig.lab=4)
```

```
> table(G.lab)
G.lab
    [0,329]   (329,659]   (659,988]   (988,1318]  (1318,1647]
         88           8           6            4            1
> gcol <- gray(5:0/5)
> plot(Quads, col=gcol[as.integer(G.lab)])
> title("Barmose I - Debitage")
> legend("bottomleft", levels(G.lab), fill=gcol[1:5], title=
  "Flakes per unit")
```

Now the first level includes squares with 0 to 329 flakes. Both maps are informative, but they are showing different aspects of the data. The second map shows strong concentration of flakes west of the center of the unit while the first map shows some of the smaller differences in density east of the main concentration.

Choropleth maps highlight differences, but they produce sharp boundaries between units that may not accurately reflect gradual changes. Dot density maps place dots randomly in each unit to reflect the density. The following commands produce a dot density map showing the debitage (Figure 78):

```
> set.seed(2)
> dots <- dotsInPolys(Quads, as.integer(BarmoseI.
  grid$Debitage/10))
> plot(Quads, lty=0)
> title("Barmose I - Debitage", xlab="Each dot represents 10
  flakes")
> points(dots, pch=20, cex=.5)
> plot(boundary, add=TRUE)
```

The set.seed(2) command ensures that your map will look like Figure 78. Also since the number of flakes in a single unit ranges from 0 to 1647, we plot one dot for every 10 flakes. Getting an informative map will involve some trial and error. Too many points and the boundaries of the square units will show up. You can change the number of dots on the map and the size of the dots. Once you have the number of dots figured out, use set.seed() and try different values. Some values may produce distinct patterns that are an artifact of that particular random sample such as a linear row of points marking an excavation unit boundary. An informative map communicates the changes in density without introducing distracting features that are artifacts of the random process. Since the points are randomly placed, there should not be any clusters or linear features within a grid square.

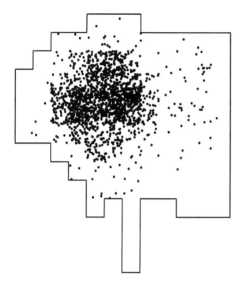

Each dot represents 10 flakes

FIGURE 78 Dot density map of the Barmose I debitage.

A third way to represent counts or densities for gridded data is to use a contour map. Constructing a contour map usually involves interpolating values between the observed values. Usually we smooth the data by using trend surface (polynomial regression), loess, splines, or kriging. We can contour the raw numbers directly although that may produce a noisy map with many small islands or peaks, but that is what we will do here to keep things simple:

```
> mat <- matrix(NA, nrow=13, ncol=15)
> indx <- with(BarmoseI.grid, cbind(East+1, North+1))
> mat[indx] <- BarmoseI.grid$Debitage
> contour(0:12, 0:14, mat, asp=1, axes=FALSE, main="Barmose
  I Debitage")
> polygon(Border, lwd=2)
```

Figure 79a shows the results. We create a matrix to hold the debitage counts that is 13 rows (for the East coordinates) by 15 columns (for the North coordinates) called mat and we extract the East and North coordinates into an object called indx. The grid starts at (0, 0), and we add 1 since the indices in the matrix start with 1. We use indx to paste the debitage counts into mat. Then we draw the contour map and add the border. The default of 10 contour intervals is enough to see that there are two areas of high debitage concentration separated by a saddle of somewhat lower density.

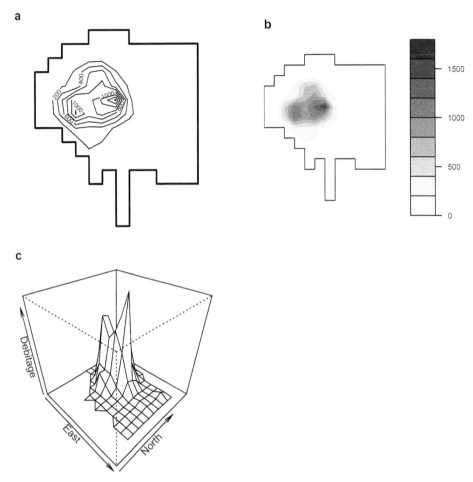

FIGURE 79 Simple contour maps of Barmose I debitage: (a) simple contour map; (b) density map; (c) 3-D perspective map.

For a filled contour map or a 3-D perspective view, try these commands (Figures 79b and 79c):

```
> filled.contour(0:12, 0:14, mat, nlevels=10, asp=1,
+    col=gray(10:0/10), main="Barmose I - Debitage",
+    plot.axes=polygon(Border), frame.plot=FALSE, lwd=2)
> persp(0:12, 0:14, mat, asp=1, xlab="East", ylab="North",
+    zlab="Debitage", main="Barmose I - Debitage",
+    theta=45, phi=35)
```

The filled contour plot shows the two high density areas and the saddle in between them very clearly. Note that we had to add the border inside the `filled.contour()` function using the `plot.axes=` argument. The perspective plot shows the dramatic difference in debitage density in the center of the site and the saddle between the two peaks, but it is not very useful otherwise.

16.3 MAPPING PIECE PLOT DATA

In addition to the data on the total debitage for each square at Barmose I, there are also piece plot data including 473 artifacts representing 11 different types. Those data are stored as a data frame called `BarmoseI.pp` in the `archdata` package. Packages `sp` (Pebesma and Bivand, 2005), `spatstat` (Baddeley and Turner, 2005) and `splancs` (Rowlingson and Diggle, 2015) provide many ways of analyzing piece plot data. To use `spatstat` we need to create a `ppp` object, which includes two-dimensional coordinates, a window, and, optionally, marks. The coordinates are just the `North` and `East` columns in `BarmoseI.pp` and we can use either the `Class` or `Label` fields as the marks. For the window, we need the excavation block coordinates created as `boundary` in the previous section. There is a small problem, however, since a polygon window in `ppp` must be in counter-clockwise order and our points are clockwise (both `Border` that we created by hand and `boundary` that we created using `unionSpatialPolygons()`. Also the polygon should not have the first point repeated at the end (`boundary`). The following commands create the `ppp` object and plot the points:

```
> data(BarmoseI.pp)
> library(spatstat)
> # bnds <- Border[26:1,] if you created Border earlier
> bnds <- boundary@polygons[[1]]@Polygons[[1]]@coords
> bnds <- bnds[nrow(bnds):2, ]
> BarmoseI.ppp <- ppp(BarmoseI.pp$East, BarmoseI.pp$North,
+    window=owin(poly=bnds, unitname=c("meter", "meters")),
+    marks=BarmoseI.pp$Label)
> summary(BarmoseI.ppp)
Marked planar point pattern:   473 points
Average intensity 4.42 points per square meter

Coordinates are given to 2 decimal places
i.e. rounded to the nearest multiple of 0.01 meters
```

```
Multitype:
                         frequency   proportion   intensity
Scrapers                        38      0.08030      0.3550
Burins                          25      0.05290      0.2340
Lanceolate Microliths           36      0.07610      0.3360
Microburins                     16      0.03380      0.1500
Flake Axes                      28      0.05920      0.2620
Core Axes                        4      0.00846      0.0374
Square Knives                  192      0.40600      1.7900
Blade/Flake Knives              18      0.03810      0.1680
Denticulated/Notched Pieces     26      0.05500      0.2430
Cores                           81      0.17100      0.7570
Core Platforms                   9      0.01900      0.0841

Window: polygonal boundary
single connected closed polygon with 26 vertices
enclosing rectangle: [0, 12] x [0, 14] meters
Window area = 107 square meters
Unit of length: 1 meter
> oldp <- par(mar=c(.5, .5, 1, .5))
> plot(BarmoseI.ppp, main="Barmose I - Artifacts", use.
  marks=FALSE, pch=20)
> par(oldp)
```

We extract the coordinates from the boundary object that we created for the quad data maps, but they are buried deep in the SpatialPolygons structure. If you created Bounds interactively, you could use the command bnds <- Border[26:1,] instead.

After creating the ppp object, we use the summary command to produce a descriptive summary. There are 473 artifacts spread over 107 square meters for an intensity (density) of 4.42 artifacts per square meter. We also get a table showing the frequency, proportion, and intensity for each of the 11 artifact types. The most common tool types are square knives and cores. Then we produce a plot showing the distribution of artifacts over the excavation block (Figure 80). Note the use of the par() function to set and then reset the plot margins so that the plot fills the window. There is clearly a concentration in the center of the block in the same area as the debitage (Figures 76–79). This plot does not show the different artifact types however. Since there are 11 types, it is very difficult to show them legibly on a single plot. Figure 81 shows one approach by combining open symbols and filled symbols to get a plot in black and white:

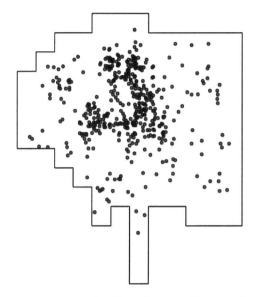

FIGURE 80 Piece plot map of Barmose I artifacts.

```
> oldp <- par(mar= c(.5, .5, 1, .5))
> plot(BarmoseI.ppp, main="Barmose I - Artifacts",
+    chars=c(1:6, 21:25), bg="gray", cex=.75,
+    legend=FALSE)
> legend("bottomleft", legend=levels(BarmoseI.ppp$marks),
+    pch= c(1:6, 21:25), pt.bg="gray", cex=.7)
> par(oldp)
```

An alternative is to use RColorBrewer to create a qualitative palette of colors and combine that with different plot symbols, but it is very different to identify the distribution of individual types. To examine the distributions side by side, we can have R produce separate tiny plots by artifact type:

```
> oldp <- par(mar=c(.5, .5, 1, .5))
> plot(split(BarmoseI.ppp), main="Barmose I - Artifacts",
+    pch=16, cex=.5, cex.main=.7)
> par(oldp)
```

The plots provide a visual indication of the abundance of each type and how it is distributed across the block, but they are too small to examine closely.

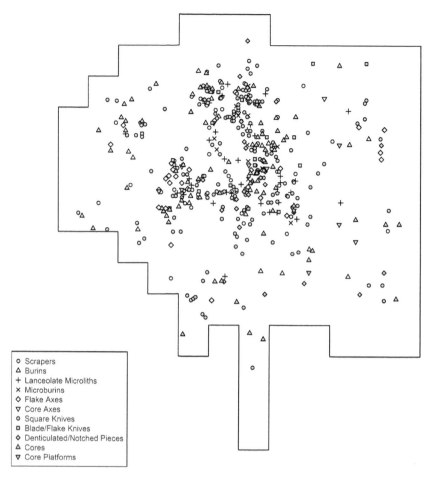

○	Scrapers
△	Burins
+	Lanceolate Microliths
×	Microburins
◇	Flake Axes
▽	Core Axes
○	Square Knives
▫	Blade/Flake Knives
◇	Denticulated/Notched Pieces
△	Cores
▽	Core Platforms

FIGURE 81 Piece plot map of Barmose I artifacts by type.

To visualize the density of artifacts, we can compute a two-dimensional kernel density plot to show the areas of concentration in the form of a contour map. The following commands produce the kernel density contour map and then overlay the excavation boundary, the artifacts, and the location of a hearth feature (Figure 82):

```
> oldp <- par(mar=c(.5, .5, 1, .5))
> plot(BarmoseI.ppp, type="n", main="Barmose I - Artifacts",
  legend=FALSE)
> contour(density(BarmoseI.ppp, bw.diggle), add=TRUE)
> points(BarmoseI.ppp, pch=20, cex=.75)
> symbols(5.5, 9.5, circles=.5, inches=FALSE, bg=gray(.5, .5),
  add=TRUE)
> par(oldp)
```

FIGURE 82 Kernel density map.

The hearth feature is simply represented as a circle, but a polygon of any shape can be added to the plot with the polygon() function. Kernel density maps can also be produced as filled contour maps for all of the points or by artifact type:

```
# Overall shaded density
> plot(density(BarmoseI.ppp, bw.diggle),
+    main="Barmose I - Artifacts", xlab= "", ylab= "")
# Shaded density by artifact type
> BarSplit.ppp <- split(BarmoseI.ppp)
> KD <- lapply(BarSplit.ppp, density, bw.diggle)
> plot(as.listof(KD), main="Barmose I", cex.main=1)
```

These plots provide multiple ways to look at the distribution of piece plot data and to identify artifact types that seem to be associated with one another.

16.4 SIMPLE SPATIAL STATISTICS

A standard question about point distributions is the degree to which they are clustered, random, or regularly spaced. At Barmose I, it is pretty clear that the data are clustered. Nearest neighbor statistics (Clark and Evans, 1954) are one way to test for complete spatial randomness (CSR). The statistic is the mean distance to the nearest neighbor divided by the expected distance if the point distribution is random. The expected distance is based on the number of points and the area of the excavation unit. If the ratio is below 1, the points are clustered and if it is above 1, they are regularly spaced. If they are approximately 1, they are randomly distributed. The expected distance can be computed from the area and the number of points in the area, but irregular areas will give misleading results because of boundary effects. In archaeology, the main problem with nearest neighbor statistics is that they are affected by the shape of the excavation area. These border effects must be controlled in order to get useful results.

We can can use functions in the spatstat package to compare the nearest neighbor distance at Barmose I against a null hypothesis that the distribution is random:

```
> clarkevans(BarmoseI.ppp)
naive  cdf
0.710 0.688
> clarkevans.test(BarmoseI.ppp, correction="cdf")

        Clark-Evans test
        CDF correction
        Monte Carlo test based on 999 simulations of CSR with
        fixed n

data:  BarmoseI.ppp
R = 0.7, p-value = 0.002
alternative hypothesis: two-sided
```

The first command computes the nearest neighbor (Clark–Evans) index. The value labeled "naïve" is the raw value that has not been adjusted for boundary effects and the value labeled "cdf" has been adjusted for those effects. The second function uses 999 random samples to test the significance of the adjusted value, which will take a few seconds. Since the p-value is less than .05, we can reject the null hypothesis that the points are randomly distributed. Since the nearest neighbor statistic is less than 1, we conclude that the points are clustered.

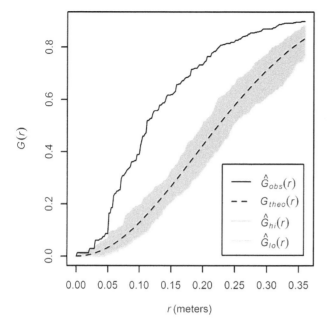

FIGURE 83 Plot of the nearest neighbor distribution function (G).

The spatstat package has a number of distribution functions for examining the degree of clustering at various scales and for examining the association between two types. Rather than looking at a single value, the mean nearest neighbor, they plot the cumulative distribution of the nearest neighbor distances and use simulation to construct significance bands using various methods to correct for border effects (Figure 83):

```
> BarmoseI.Gest <- envelope(BarmoseI.ppp, Gest,
  correction="rs", verbose=FALSE)
> plot(BarmoseI.Gest, main="Barmose I - Piece Plot",
  col="black", lwd=2)
```

On the plot, the corrected, observed distribution is shown as a solid black line and the theoretical Poisson (random) distribution is shown as a dashed line. Significance bands mark the boundaries of 99 simulations of complete spatial randomness. When the observed line is above the theoretical distribution as it is here, the points are clustered. When the observed line is below the theoretical distribution, the points are regularly spaced. The vertical axis is the proportion of the data and the horizontal axis is the distance. Looking at the plot, we can see that about 50 percent of the nearest neighbor distances (0.5 on the y-axis) are less than about 0.12 m (on the x-axis).

We could also compute nearest neighbor statistics on each of the 11 artifact types to look for differences between them:

```
> set.seed(42)
> BarmoseI.split <- split(BarmoseI.ppp)
> CEstat <- sapply(BarmoseI.split, clarkevans,
  correction="cdf")
> CEpval <- sapply(BarmoseI.split, function(x) clarkevans.
+   test(x, correction="cdf")$p.value)
> print(data.frame(stat=CEstat, p.value=CEpval, p.adjust=p.
+   adjust(CEpval)), digits=3)
                              stat     p.value     p.adjust
Scrapers                     0.667       0.008        0.030
Burins                       0.540       0.006        0.030
Lanceolate Microliths        0.450       0.002        0.018
Microburins                  0.388       0.006        0.030
Flake Axes                   0.519       0.002        0.018
Core Axes                    0.743          NA           NA
Square Knives                0.570       0.002        0.018
Blade/Flake Knives           0.673       0.118        0.118
Denticulated/Notched Pieces  0.661       0.022        0.044
Cores                        0.665       0.002        0.018
Core Platforms               0.699          NA           NA
```

After splitting the data by artifact type, we compute the nearest neighbor index for each type and then the p-value for each type and the adjusted p-value to take into account the fact that we are testing 11 null hypotheses (the 11,000 simulations will take a few minutes). There are not enough core axes or core platforms to estimate p-values. The p-value for blade/flake knives is greater than 0.05 so we cannot reject the null hypothesis of complete spatial randomness for that type, but the other types show significant clustering. Denticulated/notched pieces is close and in some simulations the adjusted p-value is not significant.

There are a number of ways to proceed with the data at this point, but we will look at only one. K-means has been a popular heuristic tool for looking at spatial distributions (Kintigh and Ammerman, 1982). We can use k-means clustering to see if there are clear spatial clusters and if those clusters have differences in the kinds of artifacts present. First, what does nbClust() suggest as the correct number of clusters for these data?

```
> library(NbClust)
> clusters <- NbClust(BarmoseI.pp[, 1:2],
  method="kmeans")$Best.nc
  . . . Output deleted . . .
> table(clusters[1,])
```

```
 0  1  2  3  4  6  7 14 15
 2  1  6  5  1  1  5  2  3
```

The top recommendations are for two, three, or seven so we will use seven as the number of clusters for this analysis. Now we can use kmeans() to form seven spatial groups:

```
> set.seed(42)
> BarmoseI.km <- kmeans(BarmoseI.pp[,1:2], 7, nstart=10)
> BarmoseI.pp$cluster <- BarmoseI.km$cluster
> plot(North~East, BarmoseI.pp, pch=as.character(cluster),
+     cex=.75,ylim=c(0, 14), xlab= "", ylab= "",
+     main="Barmose I - Clusters", axes=FALSE,
+     asp=1)
> polygon(bnds)
```

We create seven clusters and add the cluster membership to BarmoseI.pp. Then we plot the results using cluster number as the symbol for each group to see where the clusters are located. Finally, we add the excavation boundary using the bnds object we created earlier in the chapter and saved. Although the clusters are identified by number, it would be helpful to identify them further. One way to do that is to create convex hulls around each cluster. A convex hull draws lines between the outer points of a group. Adding them to the plot makes the clusters more distinct (Figure 84).

```
> KMgrp <- split(BarmoseI.pp[,2:1], BarmoseI.pp$cluster)
> CHgrp <- lapply(KMgrp, chull)
> HullPolys <- lapply(1:7, function(x) cbind(KMgrp[[x]]
  [CHgrp[[x]], 1:2]))
> for (x in seq_along(CHgrp)) {
+     polygon(HullPolys[[x]], lty=3)
+ }
```

The first command creates a list called KMgrp with seven parts containing the coordinates of the artifacts assigned to each cluster. The second command creates a list called CHgrp with seven parts containing the points in each group that define

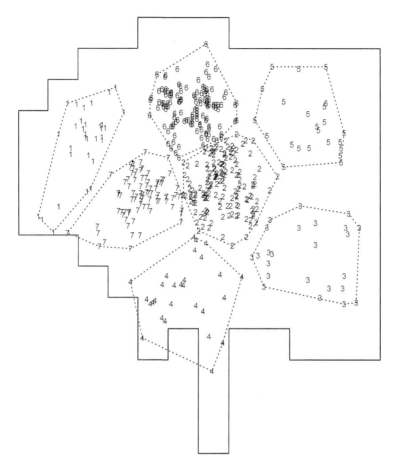

FIGURE 84 *K*-means clusters identified with convex hulls.

a convex hull for that group using the `chull()` function. So `KMgrp` contains the points in each group and `CHgrp` contains the points and the order needed to create the convex hull. The third command combines the two to create the polygons. For each group, we use `CHgrp` to select which points in `KMrgrp` to use for the polygon. Finally, we draw the polygons with a dotted line. Now the separation between the clusters is more apparent, although some of them are still close together.

Next we might explore the artifact composition of each of the to see if different activities were performed in different areas. Since we added the cluster information to the data frame we can produce a table showing which artifact types are in which cluster:

```
> BarmoseI.tbl <- xtabs(~Label+cluster, BarmoseI.pp)
```

```
> addmargins(BarmoseI.tbl)
                            cluster
Label                         1    2   3   4   5    6   7  Sum
  Scrapers                    3   13   1   1   2    8  10   38
  Burins                      2   10   2   2   2    5   2   25
  Lanceolate Microliths       1   17   1   1   1   10   5   36
  Microburins                 0    9   0   0   0    7   0   16
  Flake Axes                  2    5   0   1   4    3  13   28
  Core Axes                   0    1   0   0   1    1   1    4
  Square Knives              11   51   8  15   7   67  33  192
  Blade/Flake Knives          1    8   0   0   2    3   4   18
  Denticulated/Notched Pieces 0   11   3   2   1    7   2   26
  Cores                      12   22   6   6   2   18  15   81
  Core Platforms              0    3   3   0   1    0   2    9
  Sum                        32  150  24  28  23  129  87  473
```

It is very clear that each cluster contains a variety of artifacts. The clusters range in size from 23 to 150 artifacts. No cluster has fewer than seven types and five types are found in all seven clusters. These examples just scratch the surface of the kinds of spatial analyses that are possible using R.

Table 18 *Functions introduced in Chapter 16*

Function	Package	Description
arrows.circular	circular	Draw arrow on a circular plot
as.listof	spatstat	Used to make multiple plots for categories
brewer.pal	RColorBrewer	Create color palettes
chull	grDevices	Identify points that define a convex hull of a set of points
circular	circular	Create a circular object
clarkevans	spatstat	Clark–Evans nearest neighbor statistic
clarkevans.test	spatstat	Test significance of Clark–Evans statistic
dotsInPolys	maptools	Coordinates for randomly drawn points in a polygon
envelope	spatstat	Compute simulation envelopes of a function
filled.contour	graphics	Produce a filled contour plot
Gest	spatstat	Cumulative nearest neighbor distribution
kuiper.test	circular	Kuiper's one sample test of uniformity

Table 18 (*cont.*)

Function	Package	Description
locator	graphics	Read position of graphics cursor when mouse clicked
mapply	base	Apply function using multiple arguments
owin	spatstat	Define a window object
Polygon	sp	Create Polygon object from list of polygons
Polygons	sp	Create Polygons object from Polygon object
ppp	spatstat	Create a ppp object representing a point pattern
rainbow	grDevices	Create a vector of colors from red to violet
range.circular	circular	Compute circular range and test for uniformity
rao.spacing.test	circular	Rao's spacing test of uniformity
rao.test	circular	Rao's test for homogeneity on k groups of angular data
rayleigh.test	circular	Rayleigh test of uniformity for circular direction
rho.circular	circular	Mean resultant length of a vector of circular data
rose.diag	circular	Rose diagram for circular data
rpoint	spatstat	Generate a random point pattern within a window
seq_along	base	Create sequence of integers based on members of a list
SpatialPolygons	sp	Create Spatial Polygons object from Polygons object
sprintf	base	Format variables and text
symbols	graphics	Draw various symbols on a plot
terrain.colors	grDevices	Create a vector of terrain colors
unionSpatialPolygons	maptools	Combine polygons in spatial polygons to a single polygon
watson.test	circular	Watson's goodness of fit test

Note: Packages `base`, `datasets`, `graphics`, `grDevices`, `methods`, `stats`, and `utils` are automatically loaded when R starts.

17

Seriation

Seriation involves finding a one-dimensional ordering of multivariate data (Marquardt, 1978). In archaeology, it is usually expected that the ordering will reflect chronological change, but the methods cannot guarantee that the ordering will be chronological. Seriation has a long history in archaeology beginning with Sir Flinders Petrie (1899) who was attempting to order 900 graves chronologically. The idea provoked the interest of a number of mathematicians over the last century because it involves interesting problems in combinatorial mathematics including David Kendall (1963) and W. S. Robinson (1951). Ecologists share an interest in finding one-dimensional orderings of ecological communities that match environmental gradients although they refer to the process as ordination rather than seriation.

The usual organization of data for seriation is a data frame where the columns represent artifact types (whether present/absent, or percentages) and the rows represent assemblages (graves, houses, sites, stratigraphic layers within sites, etc.). Before the widespread use of computers, seriation involved shuffling the rows of the data set to concentrate the values in each column into as few contiguous rows as possible. Ford (1962) proposed an approach to seriation of assemblages with types represented as percentages that involved shuffling rows to form "battleship curves." In 1951, Robinson proposed an alternative approach that involved the construction of a similarity matrix. The rows and columns of the matrix are shuffled until the "best" solution is reached based on criteria that Robinson proposed. As computers became available, programs were written to implement both types of seriation. More recently, multivariate methods including multidimensional scaling, principal components, and correspondence analysis have been applied to seriation. These methods often represent the seriation as a parabola, which is referred to in the archaeological, statistical, and ecological literature as a "horseshoe" (Kendall, 1971). Kendall noted that the horseshoe results from the fact that distance measures generally have a maximum distance such that we cannot resolve the relative distances of objects beyond the maximum distance (a horizon effect). Assemblages that do not share any types are on this horizon. Unwrapping the horseshoe is necessary to produce a one-dimensional ordering.

R provides multiple approaches to seriation. The `plotrix` package (Lemon, 2006) includes a basic seriation plot, `battleship.plot()`, and package `seriation` implements a number of distance matrix ordering algorithms and indices for evaluating alternate seriations (Hahsler, Buchta, and Hornik, 2016). The package also includes the version of Hodson's Munsingen graves data set (1968) used by Kendall (1971), which is slightly different from the one used by Doran (1971) in the same publication. The existence of multiple algorithms reflects the fact that, except for small problems, seriation cannot be solved by a brute force consideration of all the possible permutations so it is necessary to use short cuts. That means that multiple seriations, just like multiple k-means clusterings, can produce different results. To ensure useful results, the procedure must be run multiple times and the orderings compared to select the best one. Using dimension reduction techniques such as principal components and correspondence analysis produce a single result, but that result is not necessarily the best possible.

How do we know which ordering is the best? Just as with the number of clusters question, there are many answers and no straightforward way of choosing one of them over others. The result should be useful to archaeologists, rather than meeting some standard set by mathematicians (Kendall, 1971: 237). Kendall goes on to suggest a number of possible answers, any of which might be more important given the particular goals of a particular analysis.

The `seriation` package has nine algorithms for analyzing distance matrices ("two-way one-mode" data because only the rows are ordered) and 13 different criteria for measuring the quality of an ordering. It also has four algorithms for analyzing the data matrix directly ("two-way, two-mode" data because both the rows and columns are ordered) with three criteria for measuring the quality of an ordering. Rectangular data can also be analyzed by principal components (Chapter 12), correspondence analysis (Chapter 13), and distance/dissimilarity data by multidimensional scaling (Chapter 14).

17.1 DISTANCE MATRIX ORDERING

We can illustrate seriation by distance matrix ordering with some data published by Nels Nelson in 1916. The data are stored in `archdata` as `Nelson`. The data consist of the counts of seven ceramic types by depth (1 foot levels) at the Pueblo San Christobal site. Nelson argued that the corrugated type did not reflect chronological change and eliminated it from his discussion. To produce a basic battleship curve, we need to eliminate the first two columns and compute row percentages:

```
> data(Nelson)
> library(plotrix)
> View(Nelson)
> Nelson.pct <- Nelson[, 3:8]/rowSums(Nelson[, 3:8])*100
> types <- gsub("_", " ", colnames(Nelson)[3:8])
> battleship.plot(Nelson.pct, mar=c(2, 5, 7, 1),
+    main="Pueblo San Christobal", xaxlab=types, col="gray")
```

After loading `Nelson` and the `plotrix` package, we look at the data and then compute percentages for the ceramic types excluding the corrugated ware (columns 3 through 8). We also create a vector of the ceramic type names using the variable names but replacing the underscore "_" with a space. Then we use `battleship.plot()` to create the plot (Figure 85). The `mar = c(2, 5, 7, 1)` argument creates a larger margin at the top of the plot to make room for the title since the variable names are relatively long. Notice that there are some modest deviations from the expected battleship shape. In particular level 3 seems too high in the plot. These probably reflect sampling issues since levels 3 through 6 are very similar.

Robinson's method involves the creation of a similarity matrix. For each pair of rows, the absolute value of the differences between the types is summed (the Manhattan distance measure) and then subtracted from 200 to create a similarity index (Chapter 14). He reordered the similarity matrix so that the highest values were along the diagonal and they decreased toward the sides. Package `seriation` uses distance instead of similarity matrices so it tries to find small values along the diagonal and increasing values toward the sides. Algorithms and criteria that focus on this goal are called "anti-Robinson" (AR) for that reason (Hahsler, Hornik, and Buchta, 2008; Hahsler and Hornik, 2016).

To create a seriation, we need to construct a distance matrix using `method="manhattan"`, randomize the order of the distance matrix, create a seriation, and then evaluate the results using several criteria.

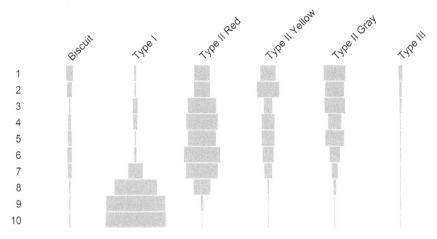

FIGURE 85 Battleship curve for Pueblo San Christobal.

```
> library(seriation)
> options(digits=3)
> Nelson.dist <- dist(Nelson.pct, method="manhattan")
> set.seed(42)
> (rnd <- sample.int(10))
 [1] 10  9  3  6  4  8  5  1  2  7
> Nelson.rnd <- permute(Nelson.dist, rnd)
> Nelson.ser <- seriate(Nelson.rnd)
> rnd[get_order(Nelson.ser)]
 [1] 10  9  8  7  6  4  3  5  1  2
> Nelson.ord <- permute(Nelson.rnd, Nelson.ser)
> Crit <- c("AR_events", "AR_deviations", "Gradient_raw",
+    "Gradient_weighted")
> Results <- list(Random=Nelson.rnd, Original=Nelson.dist,
+    Ordered=Nelson.ord)
> sapply(Results, criterion, method=Crit)
```

	Random	Original	Ordered
AR_events	87	35	18.0
AR_deviations	4362	252	77.4
Gradient_raw	66	170	204.0
Gradient_weighted	5632	13769	14295.1

After loading the seriation package, we compute the distance matrix. We use sample() and permute() to randomly shuffle the matrix before we try to seriate it. The original ordering has the row numbers in order from 1 through 10. The randomly permuted matrix has the order: 10, 9, 3, 6, 4, 8, 5, 1, 2, 7. We use `seriate()` to produce the seriation using the default method, anti-Robinson simulated annealing (ARSA; Brusco et al., 2008)) which attempts to optimize Robinson's criterion while avoiding local optima. The `seriate(Nelson.ser)` function returns an ordering that we display using `rnd[get_order()]` since the new order was based on the randomized matrix not the original data. Notice that the ordered matrix is close to the original, but reversed. Seriations are unique only as far as reversal since they find an optimal ordering, but have no way to know which end is up. The bottom five levels are in order, then three, four, and five, but mixed, and finally one and two reversed. Then we use `permute()` to shuffle the random matrix into the computed order (`Nelson.ord`). To compare the results, we bundle the three matrices into a list called Results and use `sapply()` to run the `criterion()` function on each matrix. This gives us four indices that measure the quality of the seriation. Generally you would do this several times, compare the results, and choose the best one.

`AR_events` (anti-Robinson events) is the number of times the values in a row or column fail to increase when moving away from the diagonal. In the ordered matrix, there are only 18 events. In the original matrix, there are 35 and the randomized matrix has 87. `AR_deviations` sums the size of the events (difference between adjacent values so that small deviations count less than large ones). The ordered matrix has 77.4 compared to the original matrix with 252.3 and the random matrix with 4,362. These two indices are **loss measures**, which means that smaller is better. The Gradient measures are counts over triplets of values (`Gradient_raw`) or weighted counts (`Gradient_weighted`). These are **merit measures** so larger values are better.

The criteria for the random matrix have the largest anti-Robinson measures and the smallest Gradient measures. The ordered sequence is better than the original, stratigraphic ordering, but not necessarily optimal. We do not conclude that Nelson somehow mislabeled his levels, but that the levels 1 and 2 and levels 3, 4, and 5 are temporally close and the sample sizes were not large enough in each level to reduce fluctuations that overlapped adjacent levels.

With 10 levels, we can actually implement a complete enumeration of all the possible orderings since there are `factorial(10)/2 = 1,814,400` possible orderings excluding reversals. Running the `criterion()` function on each one took a little over an hour on my desktop computer and demonstrated that the result produced by this run of `seriate()` was the best possible ordering using the anti-Robinson and Gradient measures. At this rate a complete enumeration for 11 assemblages would take about 14 hours, 12 assemblages, about a week, and 15 assemblages would take 50 years! Even with much faster computers, complete enumeration is only possible with small data sets.

We can also use the results to produce a battleship plot of the ordered matrix:

```
> roword <- rev(rnd[get_order(Nelson.ser)])
> (type.depth <- sapply(Nelson.pct[roword,], function(x)
+    weighted.mean(1:10, x)))

        Biscuit        Type_I    Type_II_Red    Type_II_Yellow
          4.14          8.66           4.83              3.39
  Type_II_Gray      Type_III
          3.43          2.30

> colord <- order(type.depth, decreasing=TRUE)
> battleship.plot(Nelson.pct[roword, colord], mar=c(2,
+    5, 7, 1), xaxlab=types[colord], col="gray",
+    main="Pueblo San Christobal - Seriation")
```

We use `rev()` to reverse the seriated order so that the battleship plot will resemble the original one and rearrange the columns so that the types that occur earlier in time are on the left and the more recent types are on the right. To do that, compute the average depth by multiplying each row number by the percentage of that type to compute a weighted mean for each type using `weighted.mean()`. For example, the average depth for type I is 8.66 so it is the deepest (oldest) type. The average depth for type III is 2.30 so it is the uppermost (youngest) type. Finally we print the battleship plot with the rows and columns re-ordered (Figure 86).

17.2 ORDERING THE DATA MATRIX DIRECTLY

The `seriate` package also operates directly on rectangular matrices (e.g., `Nelson.pct`) to order the rows and columns simultaneously. There are four algorithms available. The default is to use the first principal component as the order (PCA). Alternatively, the angle from the origin around the first two principal components can be used (PCA_angle). These methods do not involve any random component so they will always produce the same results, but they cannot guarantee the result will be the best one possible. The other two methods use a bond energy algorithm (BEA) or the bond energy algorithm with traveling salesperson problem solver (BEA_TSP) to maximize the measure of effectiveness (ME). The BEA takes a random row and then inserts rows above or below it that are most similar. ME

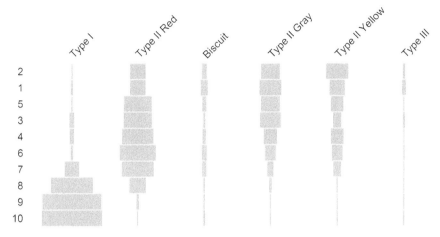

FIGURE 86 Nelson data with re-ordered rows and types.

summarizes how similar the neighboring row and column values are for each cell in the matrix. It is a merit measure so larger values indicate a better ordering.

We do not need a distance matrix since we start with matrix of percentage values, but we must convert the data frame to a matrix:

```
> Nelson.pct <- as.matrix(Nelson.pct)
> Nelson.pca <- seriate(Nelson.pct, "PCA_angle")
> get_order(Nelson.pca, 1)
 [1] 10  9  8  7  6  4  3  5  2  1
> get_order(Nelson.pca, 2)
 [1] 6 1 4 5 3 2
> criterion(Nelson.pct)
        ME  Moore_stress    Neumann_stress
     51651        361083            146258
> criterion(Nelson.pct, Nelson.pca)
        ME  Moore_stress    Neumann_stress
     53549        218317             90453
```

The value of ME is higher after using PCA_angle to seriate the rows and columns and the two stress measures are lower. For each cell, Moore stress looks at the eight neighbors (including the diagonal neighbors) and Neumann stress looks at the four neighbors. These are loss measures so smaller values indicate a better ordering. Most of the difference is due to the fact that in the original data table, the pottery types were not in chronological order, but alphabetical order. The only difference from the stratigraphic order is the position of levels 3, 4, and 5. The only difference from the seriation in the previous section is that the first two levels were reversed when we seriated the distance matrix. We have already noted that this is a reflection of how similar those levels are to one another.

As with the methods that work on distance matrices, BEA uses random numbers for the starting configuration and then tries to improve on that ordering. That means that it is subject to the same local optima problems as the matrix re-ordering methods:

```
> set.seed(42)
> Nelson.bea <- seriate(Nelson.pct, "BEA")
> get_order(Nelson.bea, 1)
 [1]  1  2  5  3  4  6  7  8 10  9
> get_order(Nelson.bea, 2)
[1] 6 1 4 5 3 2
> criterion(Nelson.pct, Nelson.bea)
        ME    Moore_stress    Neumann_stress
     53628          220206             90970
```

The measure of effectiveness is 53,628 (which is the best value based on complete enumeration), but the two stress measures have increased. The middle section of this order is identical to the matrix ordering except that 9 and 10 are switched instead of 1 and 2. This order maximizes ME while the other order minimizes AR_events. The order for the types is the same as the principal components analysis.

The optimal row and column solutions are independent so we can solve for each separately using complete enumeration. For the ME measure, row order 1-2-5-3-4-6-7-8-10-9 and column order 2-3-5-4-1-6 is the best. For Moore stress, it is row order 6-3-5-2-1-4-7-8-9-10 and column order 3-5-4-6-1-2 and for Neumann stress, it is row order 2-1-5-3-4-6-7-8-9-10 and column order 3-5-4-1-6-2. The most striking difference is that Moore stress is minimized by placing row 6 at the beginning of the sequence. This example should make it clear that there are multiple criteria available for identifying the "best" seriation and they do not always agree. In this case, the slight variations in the results suggest that we should group closely similar levels together so that from bottom to top we have six distinct stratigraphic units: (10, 9), 8, 7, 6, (5, 4, 3), (2, 1).

Hodson's Munsingen data present a greater challenge. The data set is much larger and based on presence/absence data. The data consists of 59 graves and the presence/absence of 70 artifact types. A seriation was originally published by Hodson in 1968. He sorted the matrix to produce an ordering for both the graves

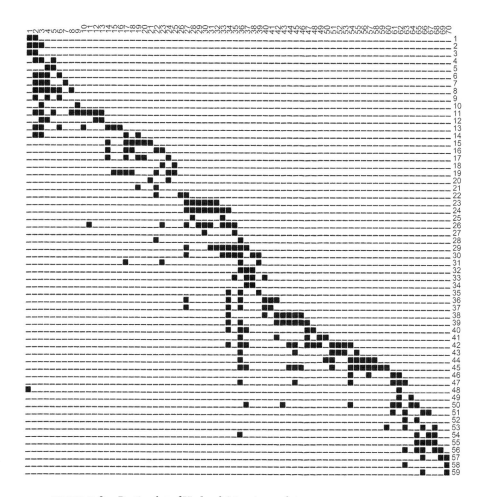

FIGURE 87 Bertin plot of Hodson's Munsingen data.

and the artifact types. The data is included in the `seriation` package and we can produce a basic plot of Hodson's original ordering in a few commands (Figure 87):

```
> library(grid)
> data(Munsingen)
> dev.new(width=10, height=8)
> bertinplot(Munsingen, options=list(reverse=TRUE, gp_
+    labels=gpar(cex=.75), mar=rep(1.5, 4)))
```

The `bertinplot()` function uses `grid` graphics so the graphics parameters are set somewhat differently and base graphics functions that add to the will not work. Instead you must use functions included in the `grid` package.

Kendall (1971) used the Munsingen data as an example of a challenging problem in seriation to see if a computer ordering could match Hodson's ordering. Kendall used a similarity measure he referred to as "common content" that measures the overlap between two assemblages. It belongs to a family of proximity measures called intersection or overlap measures (Cha, 2007). He then used multidimensional scaling, which produced a typical horseshoe curve and used programs to unbend the curve to produce three different orderings which he averaged and compared to Hodson's order. Rank order correlations between his composite curve and Hodson's order very were good (.95 for Spearman's rank correlation). The `seriate()` function has eight different permutation methods for distance matrices, but none of them give useful results on the Munsingen data if the matrix is randomized first. That is even true using the distance measure that Kendall proposed, which is implemented in the example code on the `Munsingen` manual page.

17.3 DETRENDED CORRESPONDENCE ANALYSIS

An alternative approach is to use one of the dimension reduction procedures we have already discussed: principal components, multidimensional scaling, or correspondence analysis. It is typical for any of these methods to produce a horseshoe-shaped curve in the first two dimensions for reasons discussed by Kendall (1971) and many other mathematicians, archaeologists, and ecologists. For seriation, the challenge is to unwrap the curve to produce a single dimension ordering of the data. Of the three methods, correspondence analysis often works well and there is a version of correspondence analysis, detrended correspondence analysis, that tries to automatically unwrap the curve.

Detrended correspondence analysis attempts to straighten out the curve during the analysis (Hill and Gauch, 1980). It is available in the `vegan` package (Oksanen et al., 2016) using function `decorana()`:

```
> library(vegan)
 . . . (informational messages) . . .
> Nelson.dec <- decorana(Nelson[, 3:8])
> plot(Nelson.dec, display="sites")
> roword <- order(Nelson.dec$rproj[, 1])
> roword
 [1]  2  1  5  3  4  6  7  8  9 10
> colord <- order(Nelson.dec$cproj[, 1])
> colord
[1] 6 4 5 1 3 2
> criterion(Nelson.dist, roword, method=Crit)
```

AR_events	AR_deviations	Gradient_raw	Gradient_weighted
18.0	77.4	204.0	14295.1

Note the message about the function `permute()` being masked since a function of the same name exists in the `permute` package, which package `vegan` loads. You still be able to use the one in `seriation` but you will have to specify the package name: `seriation::permute()`. Figure 88 shows that the curve is much flatter although not completely straightened. The row ordering is the same as the one produced by ordering the distance matrix using `seriate()` even though it is based on Chi-square distances instead of Manhattan distances on the percentages.

The Munsingen data provide greater challenge since the data frame is larger and provides only presence/absence values. We can compare the seven different indices for Hodson's original order and a new order based on the results of the correspondence analysis.

```
> Munsingen.dist <- dist(Munsingen, method= "manhattan")
> Munsingen.dec <- decorana(Munsingen)
> plot(Munsingen.dec, display="sites")
> Munsingen.ord <- order(Munsingen.dec$rproj[, 1])
> cor(1:59, rev(Munsingen.ord))
[1] 0.949
> data.frame(Original=criterion(Munsingen.dist, method=Crit),
+    Decorana=criterion(Munsingen.dist, Munsingen.ord,
+    method=Crit))
```

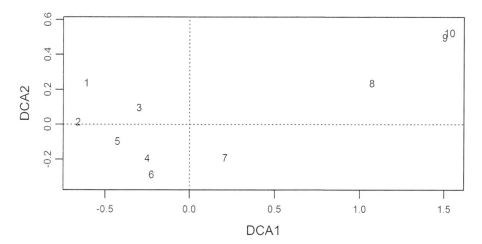

FIGURE 88 Detrended correspondence analysis of Nelson data.

```
                     Original   Decorana
AR_events               26611      24263
AR_deviations           86043      77583
Gradient_raw             3297       8041
Gradient_weighted       18558      36576
> data.frame(Original=criterion(Munsingen), Decorana=
+   criterion(Munsingen[Munsingen.ord, ]))
                     Original   Decorana
ME                        239        223
Moore_stress             2574       2766
Neumann_stress           1206       1268
```

Figure 89 is a bit difficult to read because of the point numbers but there is a clear tendency for larger numbers on the left and smaller numbers on the right. The correlation coefficient between Hodson's original ordering and the detrended correspondence analysis is .95 after we reverse the Decorana results. We compute the measures for distance matrices and the measures for rectangular matrices to compare the results. The number of AR events is 26,611 for Hodson's original ordering and 24,263 for the Decorana ordering so it is somewhat better by that criterion. Also the gradient measures are higher for the new order. But the measure of effectiveness (ME) is higher and the stress values are lower for Hodson's ordering.

17.4 PRINCIPAL CURVES

Another way to straighten the horseshoe curve is to use principal curves, a generalization of principal components that finds a curve through a set of points in two or more dimensions (Hastie and Stuetzle, 1989; De'ath, 1999). Principal curves will work with any of the three methods (principal components, correspondence analysis, and multidimensional scaling). We can illustrate the process using correspondence analysis on the Nelson data:

```
> library(seriation)
> library(ca)
> library(princurve)
> Nelson.ca <- ca(Nelson[, 3:8], nd=2)
> plot(Nelson.ca$rowcoord, pch=16)
> text(Nelson.ca$rowcoord, as.character(1:10), pos=c(rep(4,
   9), 2))
```

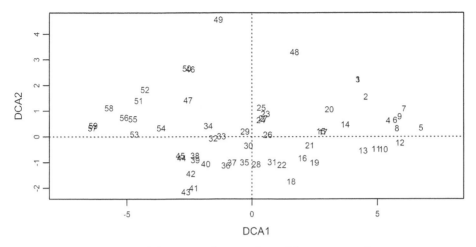

FIGURE 89 Detrended correspondence analysis of the Munsingen data.

```
> Nelson.prc <- principal.curve(Nelson.ca$rowcoord[,1:2])
> lines(Nelson.prc$s[Nelson.prc$tag,])
> segments(Nelson.ca$rowcoord[,1], Nelson.ca$rowcoord[,2],
+    Nelson.prc$s[,1], Nelson.prc$s[,2], lty=2)
```

These commands load the seriation, ca, and princurve packages and then compute a correspondence analysis on the Nelson ceramic counts. Then we plot the coordinates returned from the correspondence analysis and label them using the pos= argument so that the labels do not overlap. Figure 90a shows the points. From the upper left corner of the plot, levels 1 and 2 are together, then 3 and 5 with 4, 6, and 7 further down. Levels 8, 9, and 10 rise to the upper right of the plot.

Now we use the principal.curve() function to fit a curve though points. We can specify one of three different smoothing functions. The default is smooth. spline, which fits a spline curve through the points. The other alternatives are lowess and periodic.lowess. The last one is useful if the ends of the horseshoe are curving inward forming a circle. The bend in the curve is subtle since levels 8, 9, and 10 are separated by empty space and the principal curve misses ordering that is easily apparent to any human observer. We need to provide the function with some help in this case by specifying a starting curve with the start= argument. The easiest way to do that is to use the locator() function to sketch out the curve. In this case three points is enough.

```
> start <- do.call(cbind, locator(3))
> points(start, cex=3)
```

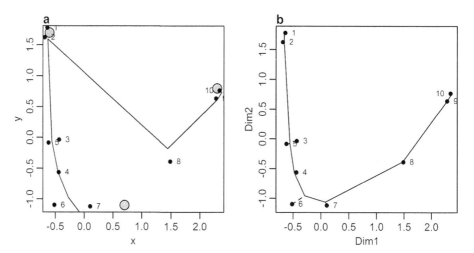

FIGURE 90 Correspondence analysis of the Nelson data with principal curve showing missed horseshoe (a) and corrected version by identifying three points (b). Gray circles show the points used to adjust the principle curve.

The first command uses the `locator()` function, which returns a list of two elements, the x and y coordinates. By using `do.call(cbind, locator(3))` we combine the list elements into a matrix with three rows and two columns, which is what `principal.curve()` needs. Then we define three points on the plot starting at the upper left, the bottom center, and then the upper right corner. The second command just plots those points on Figure 90a. More detailed plots might require more points, but they do not have to be in exactly the same places shown in the figure in order to work. Now we try again:

```
> Nelson.prc <- principal.curve(Nelson.ca$rowcoord[, 1:2],
  start=start)
> plot(Nelson.ca$rowcoord, pch=16)
> text(Nelson.ca$rowcoord, as.character(1:10), pos=c(rep(4, 9),
  2))
> lines(Nelson.prc$s[Nelson.prc$tag,])
> segments(Nelson.ca$rowcoord[,1], Nelson.ca$rowcoord[,2],
+    Nelson.prc$s[,1], Nelson.prc$s[,2], lty=2)
> Nelson.prc$tag
 [1]  1  2  3  5  4  6  7  8  9 10
> round(Nelson.prc$lambda, 2)
 [1] 0.00 0.15 1.83 2.36 1.86 2.79 3.17 4.73 6.02 6.17
```

Figure 90b shows the new principal curve. Now the principal curve traces the points very well. The object returned by `principal.curve()` includes an element called `tag`, which shows the order of the points along the curve. The order matches the stratigraphic sequence except for a single transposition of levels 4 and 5. Also included is a matrix, `s`, that gives the coordinates defining the curve. Notice that the `lines()` function plots the points defined in `s` in the order listed in `tag` to draw the line in Figure 90b. The `segments()` function draws dashed lines from the original point to its position on the principal curve. The vector, `lambda`, represents the distance of each point along the curve. You can see the transposition of levels 4 and 5 in lambda where 3 and 5 have lambda values of 1.83 and 1.86 while 4 is farther along the line at 2.36. Also included is information on the number of iterations and whether the result converged. If the fit is poor, it may reflect a lack of convergence in which case increasing the number of iterations may help.

Now we can return to the `Munsingen` data:

```
> data(Munsingen)
> Munsingen.ca <- ca(Munsingen)
> plot(Munsingen.ca$rowcoord[, 1:2], pch=20)
> Munsingen.prc <- principal.curve(Mun.ca$rowcoord[, 1:2])
> lines(Munsingen.prc$s[Munsingen.prc$tag,])
> start <- do.call(cbind, locator(3))
> points(start, pch=1, cex=3)
> # start <- cbind(x=c(-1.8, 0.3, 1.2), y=c(0.8, -1.2, 3))
```

Figure 91a shows that the `principal.curve()` function has missed the horseshoe again, in this case because of an aberrant point in the middle of the plot. This is grave 48 and as Figure 87 shows, it contains one early artifact (type 1) and one late artifact (type 62). Leaving it out of the analysis would be a reasonable approach. Instead, we leave it in and identify the horseshoe with three points as before. Then we use these three points as the start and try again:

```
> plot(Munsingen.ca$rowcoord[, 1:2], pch=20)
> Munsingen.prc <- principal.curve(Mun.ca$rowcoord[, 1:2],
  start=start)
> lines(Munsingen.prc$s[Munsingen.prc$tag,])
> segments(Munsingen.ca$rowcoord[,1],
+    Munsingen.ca$rowcoord[,2], Munsingen.prc$s[,1],
+    Munsingen.prc$s[,2], lty=2)
```

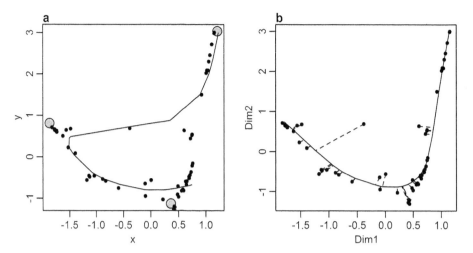

FIGURE 91 Correspondence analysis of the Munsingen data with principal curve showing missed horseshoe (a) and corrected version by identifying three points (b). Gray circles
show the points used to adjust the principle curve.

Now the fit shown in Figure 91b is very good. We can compare it to Hodson's
original order and to the Decorana results:

```
> cor(cbind(Original=1:59, Decorana=rev(Munsingen.ord),
+    PrincipalCurve=Munsingen.prc$tag))
```

	Original	Decorana	PrincipalCurve
Original	1.000	0.949	0.949
Decorana	0.949	1.000	0.917
PrincipalCurve	0.949	0.917	1.000

The correlations between each method and Hodson's order are both .95. The correlation between decorana and the principal curve is lower, .92.

```
> data.frame(Original=criterion(Munsingen.dist, method=Crit),
+    Decorana=criterion(Munsingen.dist, Munsingen.ord,
+    method=Crit), PrincipalCurve=criterion(Munsingen.dist,
+    Munsingen.prc$tag, method=Crit))
```

	Original	Decorana	PrincipalCurve
AR_events	26611	24263	25457
AR_deviations	86043	77583	83138
Gradient_raw	3297	8041	5652
Gradient_weighted	18558	36576	24858

The anti-Robinson and Gradient measures indicate the decorana has fewer AR events or deviations and that it has the higher gradient scores. The principal curve is better than Hodson's original order, but not as good as decorana by these criteria.

```
> data.frame(Original=criterion(Munsingen), Decorana=
+     criterion(Munsingen[Munsingen.ord, ]), PrincipalCurve=
+     criterion(Munsingen[Munsingen.prc$tag, ]))
```

	Original	Decorana	PrincipalCurve
ME	239	223	225
Moore_stress	2574	2766	2706
Neumann_stress	1206	1268	1260

In terms of ME and the stress measures, Hodson's original order is superior and the principal curve comes in second, but only by a small margin.

A different index was originally proposed by Kendall (1963) and implemented by Doran (1971) called the concentration principle that applies only to presence/absence data. If presence/absence data are perfectly seriated, each column should consist of a single column of 1's with zeros above or below, but not interspersed with the 1's. Doran measured this by counting the number of rows between the uppermost 1 and the lowermost 1. The minimum value is the sum of all the 1's in the matrix. We can compute the concentration principal index by creating a function called CPIndex() that computes this value and then use it to compute the index for the three orderings:

```
> (CPI.min <- sum(Munsingen))
[1] 273
> CPI <- function(x) {
+     sum(apply(x, 2, function(y) diff(range(which(y > 0)))
+     + 1))
+ }
> c(Original=CPI(Munsingen), Decorana=
+     CPI(Munsingen[Munsingen.ord, ]),
+     PrincipalCurve=CPI(Munsingen[Munsingen.prc$tag, ]))
```

Original	Decorana	PrincipalCurve
518	545	514

The first command computes the minimum possible index, which is 273. That would represent a matrix with solid strings of 1's in each column with no gaps. The next three lines create a function called CPI() that computes the index on a two-dimensional matrix containing only 1's and 0's. The function contains a single, complicated line. The `apply()` function will process each column of the matrix. For each column we use `which()` to get the index numbers (row numbers in the original matrix) that have non-zero values. For example, `which(Munsingen[, 1] > 0)` returns 1, 2, 3, and 48, the row numbers in the first column that contain 1's. Then `range()` gets the minimum and maximum row values (1 and 48) and `diff()` subtracts the first value from the second (47). We need to add 1 to this value to get 48, the number of rows from the first to the last non-zero value. The outermost `sum()` function sums the values for all of the columns.

Once the function is created, we use it on the three different orderings. Hodder's original ordering has 518 (that is 518 − 273 = 245 holes). The decorana order has 545 (272 holes), and the principal curve order has 514 (241 holes) for the best order based on this criterion.

In summary, each method can be viewed as superior depending on which criteria of success are used. More important is what the differences in the orderings tell us about blocks of potentially contemporaneous graves and the degree to which the alternative orderings can be related to independent information such as chronometric dates or location within the cemetery.

Table 19 *Functions introduced in Chapter 17*

Function	Package	Description
bertinplot	seriation	Plot data matrix of cases and variables
criterion	seriation	Compute loss and merit values for a permutation
do.call	base	Run a function on a list of arguments
get_order	seriation	Get the order information from a seriation
gpar	grid	Used to set graphical parameters with grid graphics
grid.text	grid	Draw text on a grid object
gsub	base	Replace one string with another
permute	seriation	Reorder rows and columns
principal.curve	princurve	Find principal curve through middle of the data
rev	base	Reverse the order of a vector
sample.int	base	Take a random sample of integers
seriate	seriation	Seriate objects into a linear order
weighted.mean	stats	Compute a weighted mean

Note: Packages `base`, `datasets`, `graphics`, `grDevices`, `methods`, `stats`, and `utils` are automatically loaded when R starts.

18

Assemblage Diversity

Archaeological assemblages are collections of artifacts that have been assigned to different groups. The boundaries defining an assemblage can be a whole site, the part of the site excavated, a feature within a site (e.g., pit, grave, house), or an arbitrary unit defined in terms of horizontal and vertical space (Level 7 of unit N302E200). A description of an assemblage includes how its boundaries are defined and how many of each kind of archaeological material was present within those boundaries.

One of the challenges in analyzing archaeological assemblages is that the factors that control the counts are usually not controlled by the archaeologist. The boundaries of the assemblage usually do not represent a consistent amount of time from one assemblage to another. It does not matter if time is measured in years or person-years, we cannot assume that the amount of time is the same between assemblages except in rare circumstances such as graves and shipwrecks. Artifact composition, whether the result of a geological event (obsidian) or a behavioral event (ceramics) does not include the same level of uncertainty. Artifact composition is expressed using some similar measure that standardizes abundance (e.g., percent, per mil, ppm, ppb). Artifact assemblages may be similarly standardized in terms of percentage of the whole assemblage or only those items under analysis (e.g., ceramics, but not lithics; faunal material, but not botanical material; lithic artifacts, but not lithic debitage) or in terms of density (items per volume), but usually we are not certain that volume means the same thing across the various assemblages under consideration.

This means the analysis of artifact assemblages is similar, but different from artifact composition and from species composition in ecological communities. While it makes sense to borrow from the approaches used by both, it is important to recognize the differences. In comparison with ecological communities, artifact types are less clear-cut than species. The assemblage represents an accumulation of discarded material rather than the observation of living individuals present at a particular point in time and in that sense archaeological assemblages are more similar to fossil communities. Instead of the niches occupied by biological species, artifacts occupy space defined by human interaction with the physical environment and with social networks. While fossil species vary in reproductive potential and preservation, artifacts vary in utilization, use life, and preservation.

All of this means that there are few baselines that we can use in comparing artifact assemblages because we control so few of the relevant factors. As an example of assemblages analysis, we will use data on 43 Early Stone Age (8000–4000 BC) assemblages from Norway published by Bølviken et al. (1982). Load the data frame and look at it:

```
> data(ESASites)
> View(ESASites)
> View(attr(ESASites, "Variables"))
```

Viewing the data suggests that the assemblage sizes are relatively small and that each assemblage has only a few of the 16 types. We can generate some basic descriptive statistics to see if our initial conclusions are correct:

```
> options(digits=3)
> (N <- rowSums(ESASites))
 [1]  21  11   4   5   5   6   5   2  14  10  19  45  14  19   4  12  15   7
[19]  37  29  19   6   7   2  47  65   6  11   9   8   4   7   3   3   6  10
[37]   5  12  23  75 136   8 151
> (T <- colSums(ESASites))
 TA  BA TOA  AA   M  FK  BK  NK CFS  BS  DS  Bu  Ax  Ch SAx  Pf
103  15  67  15  47 101  43   2 246  29  53 136  19  11   2  18
> ESASites.pct <- ESASites/N*100
> (Mp <- colMeans(ESASites.pct))
     TA      BA     TOA      AA       M      FK      BK      NK     CFS
 7.8380  1.1944  8.7354  3.8189  4.5351  8.3125  4.3041  0.0716 30.9468

     BS      DS      Bu      Ax      Ch     SAx      Pf
 2.3388  7.7314 13.8718  3.1165  1.2281  0.2448  1.7119
```

The first line shows us that assemblage size ranges from 2 to 151 artifacts. This range is not unusual. One question is how many artifacts does a site need to have to be useful in our analysis? The second command shows how many specimens of each type were found (T). There are only two each of NK (notched knives) and SAx (slate axes), but 246 `CFS` (core and flake scrapers). Finally we compute a percentage version of the data (`ESASites.pct`) and look at the mean percentage of each type across the assemblages (`Mp`). Nearly a third of an assemblage consists of core and flake scrapers on average. Burins (`Bu`) are the next most common type averaging almost 14 percent. All of the other types average less than 9 percent.

We would like to know how diverse the assemblages are and if differences in the number of types of artifacts is simply a result of the different assemblage sizes. One hypothesis explored by Bølviken et al. (1982) was whether the assemblages provided support for the idea that there were two different seasonal types of settlement represented: late summer-late winter settlements and spring-early summer settlements.

18.1 DIVERSITY, UBIQUITY, AND EVENNESS

Ecologists have developed a number of ways of characterizing species composition. The processes generating archaeological assemblages are different in important ways, but the ecological measures do provide useful ways of comparing one assemblage to another. We can compute a meaningful set of descriptive statistics for the Norwegian Early Stone Age assemblages using the `vegan` package:

```
> library(vegan)
> (S <- specnumber(ESASites))
 [1]  5  3  2  3  2  5  4  2  5  5 10 10  9  5  4  4  8  4  7  5  8  3  5
[24]  2  9 12  4  4  4  3  2  5  3  3  5  5  2  2  8 10 12  5 11
> (U <- specnumber(ESASites, MARGIN=2))
 TA BA TOA AA  M FK  BK  NK CFS BS DS Bu Ax Ch SAx Pf
 21  5  21  9 15 22  15   1  36 12 19 30 10  5   1  7
> (Up <- U/length(N)*100)
    TA     BA    TOA     AA      M     FK     BK     NK    CFS     BS
 48.84  11.63  48.84  20.93  34.88  51.16  34.88   2.33  83.72  27.91
    DS     Bu     Ax     Ch    SAx     Pf
 44.19 69.77 23.26  11.63   2.33  16.28
```

The simplest measure of **diversity**, **richness** is just the number of types in an assemblage (`S`). For the Norwegian Early Stone Age sites, richness ranges from two to 12 types. Higher richness values suggest that more kinds of tools were discarded on the site. That could be because many different activities were performed at the site or just that the site was occupied for a longer period of time (or that the archaeologists excavated or surface collected more of the site). As we will see shortly, richness is usually correlated with assemblage size. The transpose of richness is **ubiquity**, which is just the number of assemblages that contain a particular type (U). Notice that the ubiquity for notched knives (NK) and slate axes (SAx) is 1, but that each type was represented by two specimens. That tells us that both specimens of each of type were found at a single site. Finally, we can divide ubiquity by the number of assemblages to get a measure of the percentage of sites that have each type (Up). Core and flake scrapers (CFS) are found on 84 percent of the sites and burins (Bu) are found on 70 percent of the sites. Tanged arrows (TA), transverse and oblique arrows (TOA), and flake knives (FK) are found on about half of the sites.

Richness is one measure of diversity, but it does not indicate how the artifacts are distributed over the types. More types indicate a more diverse assemblage, but among assemblages with the same number of types, those with the same number of artifacts in each type are more diverse than assemblages having a dominant type with the remaining types having very few specimens. One approach to measuring this aspect of diversity uses information theory. Imagine that we have selected a species (or artifact) at random from a community (or assemblage). Does knowing the species or type of that individual help us to predict subsequent randomly selected individuals? If the answer is yes, then the diversity is low, most of the individuals are the same species. If the answer is no, then diversity is high. Low diversity is equivalent to low information content and high diversity to high information content.

This is the basis for the **Shannon diversity** measure (also called Shannon's information index, Shannon–Weaver, or Shannon–Wiener). The measure comes from a 1948 paper by Claude Shannon who developed information entropy as a measure of uncertainty using concepts developed by Norbert Wiener. Shannon's work was later popularized by Warren Weaver. The measure increases when there is more uncertainty in predicting what type a randomly selected artifact will be. High diversity (entropy) means that there are more types and the artifacts are spread more evenly over the types:

$$H' = -\sum_{i=1}^{S} p_i \ln p_i$$

where H' is the Shannon diversity measure and p_i is the proportion of individuals represented by the ith species and S is the number of species.

```
> (H <- diversity(ESASites))
 [1] 1.228 0.760 0.562 0.950 0.673 1.561 1.332 0.693 1.376 1.471 2.129
[12] 2.075 2.107 1.503 1.386 1.119 1.894 1.277 1.618 1.134 1.851 1.099
[23] 1.550 0.693 1.979 2.084 1.330 1.288 1.311 0.900 0.562 1.475 1.099
[34] 1.099 1.561 1.418 0.673 0.679 1.888 1.907 2.141 1.494 2.153
```

The value of the Shannon diversity index (H) varies from 0.56 to 2.15. Another common diversity index is the **Simpson index**. It gives the probability that two artifacts drawn randomly will represent different types:

$$D_1 = \sum_{i=1}^{S} p_i^2$$

where D_1 is the Simpson index and p_i is the proportion of individuals represented by the ith species and S is the number of species.

```
> (D1 <- diversity(ESASites, index="simpson"))
 [1]  0.617 0.430 0.375 0.560 0.480 0.778 0.720 0.500 0.704 0.740 0.859
[12]  0.858 0.867 0.765 0.750 0.597 0.818 0.694 0.744 0.568 0.814 0.667
[23]  0.776 0.500 0.837 0.834 0.722 0.694 0.716 0.531 0.375 0.735 0.667
[34]  0.667 0.778 0.720 0.480 0.486 0.828 0.815 0.859 0.750 0.866
```

H and D1 are usually highly correlated (for these data, .96). Part of the problem with these measures is that it is difficult to interpret the values beyond saying one sample is more diverse than another. Another approach expresses diversity in terms of the **effective number of species**. This is the number of species that if evenly distributed, would produce the same diversity index as the sample. The **inverse Simpson index** (D2) gives the effective number of species for the Simpson index (D1) and H_{max} gives the effective number of species for the Shannon diversity index (H):

```
> (D2 <- diversity(ESASites, index="invsimpson"))
 [1]  2.61 1.75 1.60 2.27 1.92 4.50 3.57 2.00 3.38 3.85 7.08 7.06 7.54 4.25
[15]  4.00 2.48 5.49 3.27 3.90 2.32 5.39 3.00 4.45 2.00 6.15 6.01 3.60 3.27
[29]  3.52 2.13 1.60 3.77 3.00 3.00 4.50 3.57 1.92 1.95 5.81 5.40 7.07 4.00
[43]  7.46
> (Hmax <- exp(H))
 [1]  3.42 2.14 1.75 2.59 1.96 4.76 3.79 2.00 3.96 4.35 8.40 7.97 8.22 4.50
[15]  4.00 3.06 6.65 3.59 5.04 3.11 6.37 3.00 4.71 2.00 7.24 8.04 3.78 3.63
[29]  3.71 2.46 1.75 4.37 3.00 3.00 4.76 4.13 1.96 1.97 6.61 6.73 8.51 4.46
[43]  8.61
```

For example, assemblage 26 has 12 types but the effective number of types is about half that (D2 = 6). So an assemblage of six types with each representing 16.7 percent should give us roughly the same values (diversity(rep(1/6, 6), "simpson") = 0.833, compared to D1[26] = 0.834). We cannot expect exact results since we have no way to compute diversity for fractional types. As you would expect, the two indices are highly correlated with one another (.99).

The last two indices attempt to measure the **evenness** of the distribution independently of richness. Both vary from 0 to 1, with larger values indicating more
even distributions. **Pielou's** J is the Shannon diversity index divided by natural log
of richness (H/log(S)). **E** and is simply the ratio of effective species to richness
(Hmax/S). A value of 1 means that Hmax=S and the sample is as even as it can be
(Buzas and Hayek, 2005; Hayek and Buzas, 2010). The correlation between the two
evenness measures is also high (.87).

```
> (J <- H/log(S))
 [1] 0.763 0.691 0.811 0.865 0.971 0.970 0.961 1.000 0.855 0.914 0.924
[12] 0.901 0.959 0.934 1.000 0.807 0.911 0.921 0.831 0.705 0.890 1.000
[23] 0.963 1.000 0.901 0.839 0.959 0.929 0.946 0.819 0.811 0.917 1.000
[34] 1.000 0.970 0.881 0.971 0.980 0.908 0.828 0.862 0.928 0.898
> (E <- Hmax/S)
 [1] 0.683 0.712 0.877 0.862 0.980 0.952 0.947 1.000 0.792 0.871 0.840
[12] 0.797 0.913 0.899 1.000 0.765 0.831 0.896 0.720 0.622 0.796 1.000
[23] 0.942 1.000 0.804 0.670 0.945 0.907 0.927 0.820 0.877 0.874 1.000
[34] 1.000 0.952 0.826 0.980 0.986 0.826 0.673 0.709 0.891 0.783
```

We can summarize the assemblage diversity in terms of Shannon diversity (H)
and Pielou's *J* (J) in order to identify high and low diversity assemblages:

```
> library(maptools)
> plot(H, J, main="Early Stone Age Site Diversity",
+     pch=ifelse(N > 10, 16, 1))
> abline(h=median(J), v=median(H), lty=2)
> pointLabel(H, J, rownames(ESASites), cex=.75)
> leg.txt <- c(as.expression(bquote(Tools <= 10)),
+     as.expression(bquote(Tools > 10)))
> legend("bottomright", leg.txt, pch=c(1, 16))
```

Figure 92 shows the assemblages plotted by Shannon diversity and Pielou's evenness. In addition, open and closed circles distinguish smaller from larger assemblages. The package maptools has a useful function called pointLabel() that
attempts to place labels on a plot so they do not overlap. The function returns the
coordinates so that you can save them and tweak them if necessary. Also the functions as.expression() and bquote() are used to create legend text that
includes the less than or equal sign.

Since H (Shannon diversity) is correlated with N (assemblage size), most of the
smaller assemblages are on the left side of the graph. The sites located in the lower left
quadrat have lower diversity and evenness while those in the upper left quadrat have

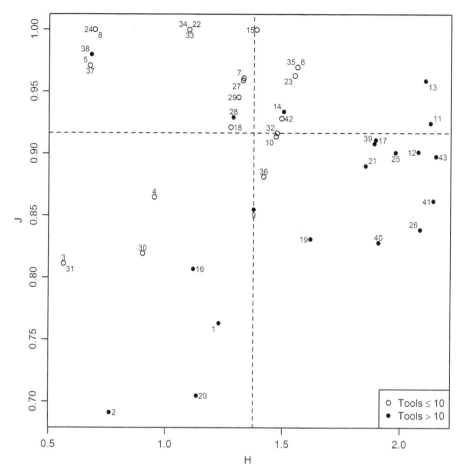

FIGURE 92 Summary of Early Stone Age site assemblage diversity: Pielou's J index of evenness by the Shannon diversity index (H).

lower diversity but higher evenness. On the right side are the sites with higher diversity and evenness. Clearly there is variability in diversity and evenness over the Early Stone Age assemblages, but the values do not tell us why. The differences could relate to behavior or formation processes. We need to look at additional lines of evidence.

18.2 SAMPLE SIZE AND RICHNESS

Generally, we expect to find more species (types) as the sample size increases. To see if that is true for the Early Stone Age sites, we plot S (richness) by N (number of artifacts):

```
> plot(S~N, ylim=c(0, 12), xaxp=c(0, 150, 6), pch=16,
+    main="Early Stone Age Sites")
> abline(h=seq(0, 12, by=2), v=seq(0, 150, by=25),
+    col="black", lty=3)
```

From Figure 93 it is clear that for sample sizes less than 50 richness is lower, but above that value they vary around 11 types. That suggests that assemblage sizes over 50 are generally comparable in the sense that higher or lower diversity is not a result of sample size. We can use regression to try to fit an equation to the points in order to estimate richness for any sample size. A linear regression would be misleading because the plot shows a curving relationship. Archaeologists have typically used three different types of nonlinear equations to fit data like these. The first two use transformations of the data so that linear regression can be used to estimate the parameters (Chapter 9). The third requires nonlinear least squares.

The logarithmic function uses linear regression after taking the log of the explanatory variable:

```
> ESASites.log <- lm(S~log(N))
> summary(ESASites.log)

Call:
lm(formula = S ~ log(N))

Residuals:
   Min      1Q   Median      3Q     Max
-3.489  -1.047    0.051   0.885   3.393

Coefficients:
             Estimate Std.  Error  t value      Pr(>|t|)
(Intercept)    -0.559  0.579    -0.97          0.34
log(N)          2.434  0.220    11.05    7.2e-14  ***
---
Signif. codes:  0 '***' 0.001 '**' 0.01 '*' 0.05 '.' 0.1 ' ' 1

Residual standard error: 1.49 on 41 degrees of freedom
Multiple R-squared:  0.749,    Adjusted R-squared:  0.743
F-statistic:  122 on 1 and 41 DF,  p-value: 7.16e-14

> deviance(ESASites.log)
[1] 90.8
> xval <- seq(1, 150, by=1)
```

```
> lines(xval, predict(ESASites.log,
+    data.frame(N=xval)), lty=1)
```

The equation is $S = 0.56 + 2.43^*\log(N)$. To compute the equation, we simply take the log of N and use it to predict S. The summary indicates that the slope value is significant with a R-squared value of .75. The deviance is the sum of the squared differences between the observed values and the fitted values so it provides a way to compare this curve with others. The line shows the resulting curve. To plot the curve we create a set of 150 N values between 1 and 150 in increments of 1 and use predict() to get the S values so that we can plot a smooth curve (Figure 93). The curve fits the points reasonably well.

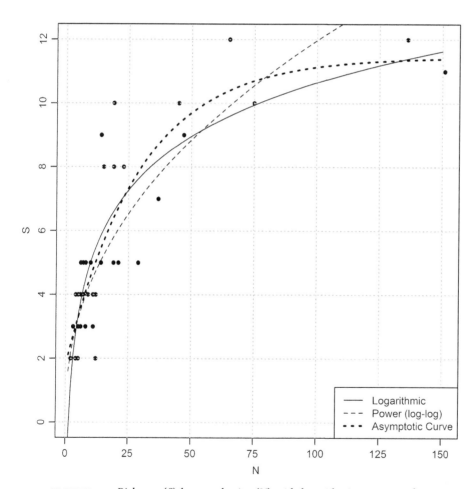

FIGURE 93 Richness (S) by sample size (N) with logarithmic, power, and asymptotic curve fits.

Another approach is to use a power function. The power function is $S = a^*N^b$. To fit the power function with linear regression, we take the logarithms of both the explanatory and the response variables to create the equation $\log(S) = \log(a) + b^*\log(N)$:

```
> ESASites.pow <- lm(log(S)~log(N))
> summary(ESASites.pow)

Call:
lm(formula = log(S) ~ log(N))

Residuals:
    Min       1Q    Median       3Q      Max
-0.8642  -0.1636   -0.0151   0.2201   0.5727

Coefficients:
              Estimate Std.   Error    t value   Pr(>|t|)
(Intercept)     0.4728   0.1194     3.96    0.00029  ***
log(N)          0.4364   0.0454     9.61    4.7e-12  ***
---
Signif. codes:  0 '***' 0.001 '**' 0.01 '*' 0.05 '.' 0.1 ' ' 1

Residual standard error: 0.307 on 41 degrees of freedom
Multiple R-squared:  0.692,    Adjusted R-squared:  0.685
F-statistic: 92.3 on 1 and 41 DF,  p-value: 4.72e-12

> sum((S-exp(fitted(ESASites.pow)))^2)
[1] 105
> lines(xval, exp(predict(ESASites.pow,
+    data.frame(N=xval))), lty=2)
```

When we use the log-log transformation, we are changing the scale of the response variable (S) and this changes the way the residuals are computed. Linear regression minimizes the squares of the deviations between the observed values and the fitted values, but since we are now working with `log(S)` values, this translates to minimizing the proportional errors since $\log(a) - \log(b)$ is the same as a/b. As a result, we cannot use the `deviance()` function to get the sum of squared deviations in terms of the original, untransformed variables. The expression `sum((S-exp(fitted(Olor.pow)))^2)` gives us the deviance in terms of S instead of $\log(S)$. The summary indicates that the power function does not fit as well as the logarithmic function. The dotted line shows the curve and it is clear that it overestimates the larger samples. The equation is $S = 1.6045 *N^{0.4364}$.

A problem with these two functions is that they continue to increase as the sample size increases whereas it seems more likely that the number of types should reach a maximum and then not increase beyond that. For the Early Stone Age sites the maximum number of types is 16 and we never reach that level in the 43 assemblages where the maximum is 12 types. The power curve predicts that we would reach 16 types at an assemblage size of 195 ($1.6045 \times 195^{.4364} = 16.02$), but the largest assemblage size is only 151. While the number of types would increase if we had sites with larger samples, it would not increase indefinitely. We need a function that takes this into account. Three possibilities are asymptotic, logistic, and Gompertz functions.

No transformation of the data will let us fit any of these functions with linear regression directly so we must use the nonlinear least squares function. To use the function, we provide an equation, data, and starting values for the parameters. The parameters are estimated iteratively and the fitting process can fail if the starting values are far away from the optimal values. To avoid this complication we can use a "self-starting" asymptotic function, `SSasymp()`, which computes the starting values for us. This is the three-parameter version used by Baxter (2003: 238). The two-parameter version used by Byrd (1997) is available as `SSasympOrig()`, but it does not fit these data quite as well. The asymptotic function is represented as `S = Asym + (R0 - Asym)*exp(-exp(lrc)*N)` where `Asym`, the asymptote or maximum value that `S` can take; `R0` is the value of `S` when `N = 0`; and `lrc` is the natural logarithm of the rate constant or how rapidly the curve reaches the asymptote. These three values are estimated by `nls()`:

```
> ESASites.nls <- nls(S ~ SSasymp(N, Asym, R0, lrc))
> summary(ESASites.nls)

Formula: S ~ SSasymp(N, Asym, R0, lrc)

Parameters:
      Estimate Std.   Error    t value    Pr(>|t|)
Asym        11.451   0.950      12.05     6.9e-15 ***
R0           1.798   0.571       3.15      0.0031 **
lrc         -3.377   0.262     -12.88     8.2e-16 ***
---
Signif. codes:  0 '***' 0.001 '**' 0.01 '*' 0.05 '.' 0.1 ' ' 1

Residual standard error: 1.47 on 40 degrees of freedom

Number of iterations to convergence: 4
```

```
Achieved convergence tolerance: 2.27e-06

> deviance(ESASites.nls)
[1] 86.6
> lines(xval, predict(ESASites.nls, data.frame(N=xval)),
  lty=3, lwd=2)
> legend("bottomright", c("Logarithmic", "Power (log-log)",
+    "Asymptotic Curve"), lty=1:3, lwd= c(1, 1, 2),
+    bg="white")
```

All three curves are shown in Figure 93. The deviance is slightly lower for the asymptotic equation than for the logarithmic function. The asymptote is 11.5, which is very close to the observed number of types in the largest assemblage, 12. The sharp bend in the curve also reflects the data more closely than the other two curves. The curve can be used to predict the expected number of artifact types for different sample sizes:

```
> est=seq(50, 200, by=25)
> P <- predict(ESASites.nls, data.frame(N=est))
> names(P) <- est
> P
    50     75    100    125    150    175    200
   9.7   10.7   11.1   11.3   11.4   11.4   11.4
attr(,"gradient")
   . . . output deleted . . .
```

An assemblage of 50 artifacts should contain about 10 types while one with 200 artifacts should contain about 11–12 types. The gradient attribute provides extra information about how the coefficients change with one another. Differences in the parameter estimates between different groups of assemblages (e.g., upland sites vs. lowland sites) may show that they vary in diversity. For these assemblages, samples with less than 50 artifacts may not accurately reflect the diversity of the whole site. Since the largest sample is 151, we don't really know what happens to richness beyond that sample size.

The other asymptotic curves can be fit using SSlogis() for the logistic curve or SSgompertz() for the Gompertz curve. For these data, they are very similar to the results given by SSasymp(), but with larger deviance values.

18.3 RAREFACTION CURVES

Another way of working with assemblages of varying size is to use rarefaction to estimate the diversity of the population at different sample sizes to adjust for the fact that rare types are less likely to occur in small samples. Package vegan has functions for **rarefaction** that we can use to illustrate the process. First, we must decide what we want to rarefy. A common choice is to combine all of the assemblages and then rarefy that aggregate to see how individual assemblages compare to the composite:

```
> xval <- seq(2, 250, by=2)
> ESASites.rar <- rarefy(T, xval, se=TRUE)
> Est <- ESASites.rar[1, ]
> Sd <- ESASites.rar[2, ]
> rare <- cbind(lower=Est-2*Sd, expected=Est, upper=Est+2*Sd)
> plot(S~N, ylim=range(rare), xlim=range(xval), pch=16,
+    main="Early Stone Age Sites - Rarefaction Curves")
> matlines(xval, rare, type="l", lty=c(2, 1, 2), col="black")
> identify(N, S, rownames(ESASites))
[1] 19 20 38 40 41 43
```

First, we create a vector, xval, containing the sample sizes that we are going to compute in order to plot a smooth curve. We could compute values to 907, the sum of all of the assemblages, but we will just go to 250, which is 100 larger than the largest assemblage. Then we use rarefy() with T, which has the abundance of each artifact type over all of the assemblages. The function returns a vector with two rows and 125 columns. The first row is the estimated richness (.S) and the second row is the standard error of the estimate (.se) computed using a hypergeometric distribution (basically sampling from the combined sample without replacement). We extract those rows as Est and Sd. Then we create a matrix called rare that has three columns: Est, Est-2*Sd, and Est+2*Sd so we can plot the estimate along with 95 percent confidence limits. Then we create a plot of S by N for the 43 assemblages and overlay the lines. Finally we use identify() to identify points outside the confidence limits interactively. Click on any point you want to label with the name of the assemblage and then click the Stop button on the upper left side of the plot window to stop identifying points. Click below, right, above, or left of the actual point to indicate where the label should go. No assemblages lie above the upper limit and a sample size of 150 should have 14 types, but no assemblage has more than 12. Based on the combined assemblage, diversity in the actual assemblages is lower than expected based on the rarefaction curves. The results are shown in Figure 94a.

But we could be interested in a slightly different question such as how different the smaller samples are from the largest one (43). We can compute rarefaction

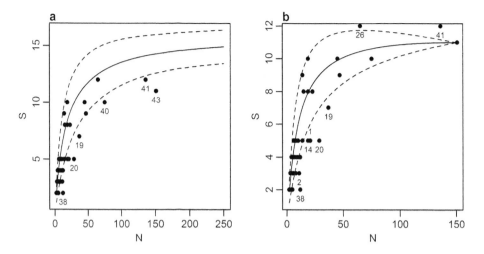

FIGURE 94 Rarefaction curves for Early Stone Age Sites based on combined (a) and largest assemblage (b).

curves for 43, indicating how many artifact types should be present at smaller sample sizes:

```
> ESASites43.rar <- rarefy(ESASites[43,], xval[1:75], se=TRUE)
> Est <- ESASites43.rar[1, ]
> Sd <- ESASites43.rar[2, ]
> rare43 <- cbind(lower=Est-2*Sd, expected=Est,
  upper=Est+2*Sd)
> plot(S~N, ylim=range(rare43), xlim=range(xval[1:75]),
+   pch=16, main="Early Stone Age Sites - Rarefaction Curve")
> matlines(xval[1:75], rare43, type="l", lty=c(2, 1, 2),
  col="black")
> identify(N, S, rownames(ESASites))
[1]   1   2 14 19 20 26 38 41
```

Figure 94b shows the results. Now we only plot expected richness for assemblages smaller than the largest one. Two assemblages have greater richness, 26 and 41 than expected in comparison to assemblage 43 and at least six sites have lower than expected diversity. Bølviken et al. (1982) were exploring a hypothesis that the assemblages represented a seasonal transhumance settlement pattern. Using correspondence analysis, they did not find clear evidence to support that hypothesis. But the lower than expected diversity of the assemblages could suggest that more than one tool kit is represented in the data so that some tool types are not found on some sites regardless of large the assemblage is.

Table 20 *Functions introduced in Chapter 18*

Function	Package	Description
as.expression	base	Create an expression object
bquote	base	Quote an argument that may contain symbols
diversity	vegan	Compute diversity indices
identify	graphics	Identify points in a scatterplot
nls	stats	Fit a nonlinear model using least squares
pointLabel	maptools	Label points without overlapping text
rarefy	vegan	Rarefy species richness
specnumber	vegan	Compute number of species and species counts
SSasymp	stats	Self-starting asymptotic regression model
SSasympOrig	stats	Self-starting asymptotic regression model through the origin
SSgompertz	stats	Self-starting Gompertz growth regression model
SSlogis	stats	Self-starting logistic regression model

Note: Packages `base`, `datasets`, `graphics`, `grDevices`, `methods`, `stats`, and `utils` are automatically loaded when R starts.

19

Conclusions

In the preceding chapters we have explored some of the ways quantitative analysis of archaeological data can help us to understand the past. In particular, we have used the R Project for Statistical Computing. Since R is a collaborative project, new packages have been added or updated as you were reading this book. By now, you should have the ability to evaluate statistical hypotheses, explore your data for new, interesting patterns, and find ways to communicate those patterns to others.

Analyzing data begins with a research design that should inform decisions about how to collect the data, how much to collect, and how to analyze the data collected. Analysis of the data involves trying many different approaches. It is not a matter of clicking on a few menus and scanning generically produced output. Do not assume that using quantitative methods on your data will be any easier than the process of excavating or analyzing the data was. Ask interesting questions of your data: where it came from, how it got there, what it was used for, what it means. Then find the methods that get you closer to answering those questions. You will need multiple methods, not one, and if they lead to conflicting conclusions, you will need to wrestle with that fact.

Quantitative methods help us make some progress in answering the big questions I posed in Chapter 1. But you may have to learn a new way to use those methods. Traditional inferential statistics encourages you to think in terms of collecting statistically significant results and to measuring your progress in those terms. In working with archaeological data, I have tried to show that engaging with data is a process and that a simple tabulation of hypothesis tests is insufficient. As soon as you have data, you should begin looking at it, checking for errors, checking for unexpected distributions and patterns, and adjusting your research accordingly. Evaluate your findings in terms of multiple lines of information. For example, shape can be compared to spatial or temporal distribution. Site distribution can be compared to assemblage variability and so on. You will rarely reach any substantive conclusions using only one line of evidence recovered from one place deposited at one time.

Many commercial statistical packages make some quantitative methods so easy that you may be tempted to limit your analyses to the ones the menus let you. Even commercial packages have many features that are not apparent from the menu structure and their explanation is usually buried in appendices. R provides a unique set of tools for wrestling with data. Because it is open source, you can always look directly at the code that performs an analysis. Nothing is hidden, or proprietary. Even if you are not familiar with programming, you can learn quickly how to write a simple function that will let you repeat an analysis many times to see how the results vary. Simple tasks that require constructing loops in other languages, including the macro languages of SPSS®, SAS®, and Excel®, can be coded in a single line. R has another advantage over commercial programs in that its programmers work for free. Thousands of people working independently and together have produced packages for R. There are so many packages that it can be a challenge to find what you need, but R provides a number of ways of searching for packages or functions within packages and general internet search engines usually work well.

Where to go from here depends on what you are interested in studying. R packages provide substantial support for many different approaches to compositional analysis, examining assemblage variability, analyzing artifact shape using geometric morphometrics, and studying spatial processes. You will find specialized books on each of these topics and many others. Archaeology thrives on new ways of finding old things and trying to understand them. The landscape of R provides lots of room for further exploration.

REFERENCES

Adler, Daniel. 2005. vioplot: Violin plot. R package version 0.2.

Agostinelli, C. and U. Lund. 2013. R package circular: Circular Statistics (version 0.4–7).

Agresti, A. 2007. *An Introduction to Categorical Data Analysis*. 2nd edition. Wiley Interscience.

Aitchison, J. 1986. *The Statistical Analysis of Compositional Data*. Chapman and Hall.

Aldenderfer, M. S. and R. K. Blashfield. 1984. *Cluster Analysis*. Sage.

Allison, P. D. 2001. *Missing Data*. Sage Publications.

Arthur, D. and S. Vassilvitskii. 2007. K-means++: The Advantages of Careful Seeding. *Proceedings of the Eighteenth Annual ACM-SIAM Symposium on Discrete Algorithms*. Society for Industrial and Applied Mathematics Philadelphia, PA, USA. pp. 1027–1035.

Baddeley, A. and R. Turnerl 2005. spatstat: An R Package for Analyzing Spatial Point Patterns. *Journal of Statistical Software* 12(6), 1–42.

Baker, T. 2006. The Acheulean Handaxe. Online article available at http://ele.net/acheulean/handaxe.htm. Accessed August 2016.

Baxter, M. J and I. C. Freestone. 2006. Log-Ratio Compositional Data Analysis in Archaeometry. *Archaeometry* 48(3): 511–531.

Baxter, M. J. 1994. *Exploratory Multivariate Analysis in Archaeology*. Edinburgh University Press.

Baxter, M. J. 2003. *Statistics in Archaeology*. Arnold.

Berry, W. D. and S. Feldman. 1985. *Multiple Regression in Practice*. Sage.

Binford, L. R. 1972. Contemporary Model Building: Paradigms and the Current State of Paleolithic Research. In *Models in Archaeology*, edited by D. L. Clarke, pp. 109–166. Methuen.

Binford, L. R. and S. Binford. 1966. A Preliminary Analysis of Functional Variability in the Mousterian of Levallois Facies. *American Anthropologist* 68: 238–295.

Bivand, R. S., E. Pebesma, and V. Gomez-Rubio, 2013. *Applied Spatial Data Analysis with R*. 2nd edition. Springer.

Blankholm. H. P. 1991. *Intrasite Spatial Analysis in Theory and Practice*. Aarhus University Press.

Bølviken, E., E. Helskog, K. Helskog, I. M. Holm-Olsen, L. Solheim, and R. Bertelsen. 1982. Correspondence Analysis: An Alternative to Principal Components. *World Archaeology* 14: 41–60.

Boots, B. N. and A. Getis. *Point Pattern Analysis*. Scientific Geography Series, No. 8. Sage.

Box, G. E. P. and Cox, D. R. (1964) An Analysis of Transformations (With Discussion). *Journal of the Royal Statistical Society B* 26, 211–252.

Brainerd, G. W. 1951. The Place of Chronological Ordering in Archaeological Analysis. *American Antiquity* 16: 301–313.

Bretz, F., T. Hothorn, and P. Westfall. 2010. *Multiple Comparisons Using R.* CRC Press.

Brusco, M., H.F. Koehn, and S. Stahl. 2008. Heuristic Implementation of Dynamic Programming for Matrix Permutation Problems in Combinatorial Data Analysis. *Psychometrika* 73(3): 503–502.

Buzas, M. A. and L. C. Hayek. 2005. On Richness and Evenness With and Between Communities. *Paleobiology* 31(2): 199–220.

Byrd, J. E. 1997. The Analysis of Diversity in Archaeological Faunal Assemblages: Complexity and Subsistence Strategies in the Southeast During the Middle Woodland Period. *Journal of Anthropological Archaeology* 16: 49–72.

Canty, A. and B. Ripley. 2016. boot: Bootstrap R (S-Plus) Functions. R package version 1.3–10.

Carlson, D. L. and G. Roth 2016. archdata: Example Datasets from Archaeological Research. R package version 1.1.

Carlson, S. B., H. B. Ensor, D. L. Carlson, E. A. Miller, and D E. Young. 1987. Archaeological Survey at Fort Hood, Texas Fiscal Year 1984. *United States Army Fort Hood. Archaeological Resource Management Series, Research Report Number* 14.

Cha, Sung-Hyuk. 2007. Comprehensive Survey on Distance/Similarity Measures between Probability Density Functions. *International Journal of Mathematical Models and Methods in Applied Sciences* 1(4): 300–307.

Charrad, M., N. Ghazzali, V. Boiteau, and A. Niknafs. 2014. NbClust: NbClust package for determining the best number of clusters. R package version 2.0.1.

Chayes, F. 1971. *Ratio Correlation: A Manual for Students of Petrology and Geochemistry.* University of Chicago Press.

Christenson, A. and D. W. Read. 1977. Numerical Taxonomy, R-Mode Factor Analysis and Archaeological Classification. *American Antiquity* 42: 163–179.

Clark, P. J. and F. C. Evans. 1954. Distance to Nearest Neighbor as a Measure of Spatial Relationships in Populations. *Ecology* 35(4): 445–453.

Clausen, S. E. 1998. *Applied Correspondence Analysis: An Introduction.* Sage.

Cleveland, W. S. 1993. *Visualizing Data.* Hobart Press.

Cleveland, W. S. 1994. *The Elements of Graphic Data.* 2nd edition. Hobart Press.

Crawley, M. J. 2007. *The R Book.* Wiley.

Dahl, D. B. 2016. xtable: Export tables to LaTeX or HTML. R package version 1.8–2.

Davison, A. C. and D. V. Hinkley, 1997. *Bootstrap Methods and Their Applications.* Cambridge University Press.

De Cáceres, M., X. Font, and F. Oliva. 2010. The Management of Vegetation Classifications with Fuzzy Clustering. *Journal of Vegetation Science* 21 (6): 1138–1151.

de Leeuw, J., P. Mair. 2009. Simple and Canonical Correspondence Analysis Using the R Package anacor. *Journal of Statistical Software* 31(5), 1–18.

De'ath, G. 1999. Principal Curves: A New Technique for Indirect and Direct Gradient Analysis. *Ecology* 80(7): 2237–2253.

Diggle, P. J. 2003. *Statistical Analysis of Spatial Point Patterns*. Arnold.

Doran, J. 1971. Computer Analysis of Data from the la Téne Cemetery at Münsingen-Rain. In *Mathematics in the Archaeological and Historical Sciences*, edited by F. R. Hodson, D. G. Kendall, and P. Tâutu, pp. 422–431. Edinburgh University Press.

Doran, J. E. and F. R. Hodson. 1975. *Mathematics and Computers in Archaeology*. Harvard University Press.

Dray, S. and A. B. Dufour. 2007. The ade4 Package: Implementing the Duality Diagram for Ecologists. *Journal of Statistical Software*. 22(4): 1–20.

Dunteman, George H. 1989. *Principal Components Analysis*. Sage.

Efron, B. and R. Tibshirani. 1993. *An Introduction to the Bootstrap*. Chapman and Hall.

Ehrenberg, A. S. C. 1977. Rudiments of Numeracy. *Journal of the Royal Statistical Society. Series A (General)*, 140(3): 277–297.

Ehrenberg, A. S. C. 1981. The Problem of Numeracy. *The American Statistician* 35(2): 67–71.

Engelstad, E. 1988. Pit Houses in Arctic Norway – An Investigation of Their Typology Using Multiple Correspondence Analysis. In *Multivariate Archaeology*, edited by T. Madsen, pp. 71–84. Aarhus University Press.

Everitt, B. S., S. Landau, M. Leese, D. Stahl. 2011. *Cluster Analysis*. 5th edition. Wiley.

Faraway, J. J. 2002. Practical Regression and Anova Using R. Web resource. http://cran.r-project.org/doc/contrib/Faraway-PRA.pdf.

Faraway, J. J. 2006. *Extending the Linear Model with R: Generalized Linear, Mixed Effects and Nonparametric Regression Models*. CRC Press.

Fienberg, S. E. 1977. *The Analysis of Cross-Classified Categorical Data*. MIT Press.

Ford, J. A. 1952. Measurements of Some Prehistoric Design Developments in the Southeastern United States. *Anthropological Papers of the American Museum of Natural History*, 44(3).

Ford, J. A. 1962. A Quantitative Method for Deriving Cultural Chronology. *Pan American Union, Technical Manual No. 1*.

Fox, J. 2005. The R Commander: A Basic Statistics Graphical User Interface to R. *Journal of Statistical Software*, 14(9): 1–42.

Fox, J. 2016. RcmdrMisc: R Commander Miscellaneous Functions. R package version 1.0–2.

Fox, J. and M. Bouchet-Valat. 2014. Getting Started With the R Commander. Online resource. http://socserv.mcmaster.ca/jfox/Misc/Rcmdr/Getting-Started-with-the-Rcmdr.pdf.

Fox, J. and S. Weisberg. 2011. *An R Companion to Applied Regression*. 2nd edition. Sage.

Fox, John. 2008. *Applied Regression Analysis and Generalized Linear Models*. 2nd edition. Sage.

Fox, W. 1969. An Analysis of the R. O. M. Collection, Lower Paleolithic Implements: Furze Platt, Maidenhead, Berkshire, England. Unpublished paper and notes in the possession of the author.

Fraley, C. and A. E. Raftery. 2002. Model-based Clustering, Discriminant Analysis and Density Estimation *Journal of the American Statistical Association* 97: 611–631.

Fraley, C., A. E. Raftery, T. B. Murphy, and L. Scrucca. 2012. mclust Version 4 for R: Normal Mixture Modeling for Model-Based Clustering, Classification, and Density Estimation. Technical Report No. 597, Department of Statistics, University of Washington.

Friendly, M. and J. Fox 2016. candisc: Visualizing Generalized Canonical Discriminant and Canonical Correlation Analysis. R package version 0.7-0.

Friendly, M. 2000. *Visualizing Categorical Data*. SAS Publishing.

Futato, E. M. 1983. Projectile Point Morphology: Steps Toward a Formal Account. In Proceedings of the Thirty-fourth Southeastern Archaeological Conference, Lafayette, Louisiana, October 27-19, 1977. *Southeastern Archaeological Conference Bulletin* 21: 38–81.

Gabriel, K. R. and C. L. Odoroff. 1990. Biplots in Biomedical Research. *Statistics in Medicine 9,* 469–485.

Gaile, G. L. and J. E. Burt. 1980. Directional Statistics. *Concepts and Techniques in Modern Geography, No. 25*. Institute of British Geographers.

Gower, J. C. 1971. A General Coefficient of Similarity and Some of Its Properties. *Biometrics* 27(4): 857–871.

Greenacre, M. 2007. *Correspondence Analysis in Practice*. 2nd edition. Chapman & Hall/CRC.

Grosjean, P. and F. Ibanez. 2014. pastecs: Package for Analysis of Space-Time Ecological Series. R package version 1.3–18.

Hahsler, M., C. Buchta, and K. Hornik 2016. Infrastructure for Seriation. R package version 1.2-1.

Hahsler, M., K. Hornik, and C. Buchta 2008, Getting Things in Order: An Introduction to the R Package seriation. *Journal of Statistical Software* 25(3): 1–34.

Harrell, F. E, Jr., with contributions from C. Dupont and many others. 2016. Hmisc: Harrell Miscellaneous. R package version 3.17–4.

Hartwig, F. and B. E. Dearing. 1979. *Exploratory Data Analysis*. Sage.

Hastie, T. and W. Stuetzle. 1989. Principal Curves. *Journal of the American Statistical Association* 84(406): 502–516.

Hayek, L. C. and M. A. Buzas. 2010. *Surveying Natural Populations: Quantitative Tools for Assessing Biodiversity*. 2nd edition. Columbia University Press.

Hill, M. O. and H. G. Gauch. 1980. Detrended Correspondence Analysis: An Improved Ordination Technique. *Vegetatio* 42, 47–58.

Hodson, F. R. 1968. *The La Téne Cemetery at Münsingen-Rain*. Acta Bernesia V. Verlag Stämpfli & Cie Ag Bern.

Hodson, F. R. 1971. Numerical Typology and Prehistoric Archaeology. In *Mathematics in the Archaeological and Historical Sciences*, edited by F. R. Hodson, D. G. Kendall, and P. Tàutu, pp. 30–45, Edinburgh University Press.

Hohorn, T., F. Bretz, and P. Westfall. 2008. Simultaneous Inference in General Parametric Models. *Biometrical Journal* 50(3): 346--363.

Holm, S. 1979. A Simple Sequentially Rejective Multiple Test Procedure. *Scandinavian Journal of Statistics* 6, 65–70.

Honaker, J., G. King, and M. Blackwell. 2011. Amelia II: A Program for Missing Data. *Journal of Statistical Software,* 45(7): 1–47.

Huberty, C. J. and S. Olejink. 2006. *Applied Manova and Discriminant Analysis*. 2nd edition. Wiley-Interscience.

Hyndman, R. J. and F. Yanan. 1996. Sample Quantiles in Statistical Packages. *The American Statistician* 50(4): 361–365.

IBM Corp. 2013. *IBM SPSS Statistics for Windows, Version 22.0*. IBM Corp.

Isaac, G. Ll. 1977. *Olorgesailie: Archeological Studies of a Middle Pleistocene Lake Basin in Kenya*. University of Chicago.

Jackson, J. E. 2003. *A User's Guide to Principal Components.* Wiley-Interscience.

James, G., D. Witten, T. Hastie, and R. Tibshirani. 2013. *An Introduction to Statistical Learning with Applications in R.* Springer.

Jammalamadaka, S. R. and A. Sengupta. 2001. *Topics in Circular Statistics.* World Scientific Publishing.

Joanes, D. N. and C. A. Gill. 1998. Comparing Measures of Sample Skewness and Kurtosis. *Journal of the Royal Statistical Society: Series D* 47: 183–189.

Jolliffe, I. T. 2002. *Principal Component Analysis.* 2nd edition. Springer.

Jungers, W. L., A. B. Falsetti, and C. E. Wall. 1995. Shape, Relative Size, and Size-Adjustments in Morphometrics. *Yearbook of Physical Anthropology* 38: 137–161.

Kampstra, P. 2008. Beanplot: A Boxplot Alternative for Visual Comparison of Distributions. *Journal of Statistical Software, Code Snippets* 28(1): 1–9.

Karp, N. A. 2014. R Commander, An Introduction. Version 2. Online resource http://cran.r-project.org/doc/contrib/Karp-Rcommander-intro2.pdf.

Kaufman, L. and P. J. Rousseeuw. 1990. *Finding Groups in Data: An Introduction to Cluster Analysis.* Wiley.

Kendall, D. G. 1963. A Statistical Approach to Flinders Petrie's Sequence Dating. *Bulletin of the International Statistics Institute* 40: 657–680.

Kendall, D. G. 1971. Seriation from Abundance Matrices. In *Mathematics in the Archaeological and Historical Sciences,* edited by F. R. Hodson, D. G. Kendall, and P. Tâutu, pp. 215–252. Edinburgh University Press.

Kim, J. and C. W. Mueller. 1978a. *Factor Analysis: Statistical Methods and Practical Issues.* Sage.

Kim, J. and C. W. Mueller. 1978b. *Introduction to Factor Analysis: What It Is and How to Do It.* Sage.

Kintigh, K. W. 1984. Measuring Archaeological Diversity by Comparison with Simulated Assemblages. *American Antiquity* 49: 44–54.

Kintigh, K. W. and A. J. Ammerman. 1982. Heuristic Approaches to Spatial Analysis in Archaeology. *American Antiquity* 47(1): 31–63.

Klecka, W. R. 1980. *Discriminant Analysis.* Sage.

Kleindienst, M. R. 1961. Variability within the Late Acheulian Assemblage in East Africa. *South African Archaeological Bulletin* 16: 35–52.

Kleindienst, M. R. 1962. Components of the East African Acheulian Assemblage: An Analytic Approach. In *Actes du IVᵉ Congrès Panafricain de Préhistoire et de l'Étude du Quaternaire,* edited by C. Mortelmans and J. Nenquin, pp. 81–105. Musee Royal de l'Afrique Centrale.

Le, S., J. Josse, and F. Husson. 2008. FactoMineR: An R Package for Multivariate Analysis. *Journal of Statistical Software* 25(1): 1–18.

Lemon, J. 2006. Plotrix: A Package in the Red Light District of R. *R-News* 6(4): 8–12.

Ligges, U. and M. Mächler. 2003. Scatterplot3d – an R Package for Visualizing Multivariate Data. *Journal of Statistical Software* 8(11): 1–20.

Maechler, M., P. Rousseeuw, A. Struyf, M. Hubert, and K. Hornik. 2014. cluster: Cluster Analysis Basics and Extensions. R package version 1.15.2.

Mardia, K. V. and P. Jupp. 2000. *Directional Statistics.* 2nd edition. Wiley.

Marquardt, W. H. 1978. Advances in Archaeological Seriation. *Advances in Archaeological Method and Theory* 1: 257–314.

McKnight, P. E., K. M. McKnight, S. Sidani, and A. J. Figueredo. 2007. *Missing Data: A Gentle Introduction*. Guilford Press.

Meyer, D., E. Dimitriadou, K. Hornik, A. Weingessel, and F. Leisch. 2015. e1071: Misc Functions of the Department of Statistics, TU Wien. R package version 1.6-7.

Mooney, Christopher Z. and Robert D. Duval. 1993. *Bootstrapping: A Nonparametric Approach to Statistical Inference*. Sage.

Mosimann, J. E.1970. Size Allometry; Size and Shape Variables with Characterizations of the Lognormal and Gamma Distributions. *Journal of the American Statistical Association* 65: 930–945.

Murrell, P. 2011. *R Graphics*. 2nd edition. CRC Press.

Nenadic, O. and M. Greenacre. 2007. Correspondence Analysis in R, with Two- and Three-Dimensional Graphics: The ca Package. *Journal of Statistical Software* 20(3):1–13.

Neuwirth, E. 2014. RColorBrewer: ColorBrewer Palettes. R package version 1.1-2.

Oksanen, J., F. G. Blanchet, R. Kindt, P. Legendre, P. R. Minchin, R. B. O'Hara, G. L. Simpson, P. Solymos, M. H. H. Stevens, and H. Wagner. 2016. vegan: Community Ecology Package. R package version 2.4.

Pebesma, E.J., R.S. Bivand. 2005. Classes and Methods for Spatial Data in R. *R News* 5(2): 9–13.

Petrie, W. M. F. 1899. Sequences in Prehistoric Remains. *The Journal of the Anthropological Institute of Great Britain and Ireland* 29(3/4): 295–301.

Potts, R. 2011. Olorgesailie – Retrospective and Current Synthesis. In *Casting the Net Wide: Papers in Honor of Glynn Isaac and His Approach to Human Origins Research*, edited by J. Sept and D. Pilbeam, pp. 1–20. American School of Prehistoric Research Monographs in Archaeology and Paleoanthropology.

R Core Team. 2016. R: A Language and Environment for Statistical Computing. R Foundation for Statistical Computing, Vienna, Austria. URL www.R-project.org/.

Racine, Jeffrey S. 2012. RStudio: A Platform-Independent IDE for R and Sweave. *Journal of Applied Econometrics*. 27: 167–172.

Read, D. W. 1974. Some Comments on Typologies in Archaeology and an Outline of a Methodology. *American Antiquity* 39: 216–242.

Read, D. W. 2007. *Artifact Classification: A Conceptual and Methodological Approach*. Left Coast Press.

Rencher, A. C. and W. F. Christensen. 2012. *Methods of Multivariate Analysis*. 3rd edition. Wiley.

Revelle, W. 2016. psych: Procedures for Personality and Psychological Research, Northwestern University, Version = 1.6.6.

Reynolds, H. T. 1984. *Analysis of Nominal Data*. 2nd edition. Sage.

Ripley, B. D. 1981. *Spatial Statistics*. John Wiley & Sons.

Robinson, W. S. 1951. A Method for Chronologically Ordering Archaeological Deposits. *American Antiquity* 16: 293–301.

Roe, D. A. 1964. The British Lower and Middle Paleolithic: Some Problems, Methods of Study and Preliminary Results. *Proceedings of the Prehistoric Society* 30: 245–267.

Roe, D. A. 1968. British Lower and Middle Paleolithic Handaxe Groups. *Proceedings of the Prehistoric Society* 34: 1–82.

Roe, D. A. 1981. *The Lower and Middle Palaeolithic Periods in Britain*. Routledge & Kegan Paul.

Rowlingson, B. and P. Diggle 2015. splancs: Spatial and Space-Time Point Pattern Analysis. R package version 2.01–38.

Sackett, J. 1966. Quantitative Analysis of Upper Paleolithic Stone Tools. *American Anthropologist* 68: 356–394.

Sarkar, D. 2008. *Lattice: Multivariate Data Visualization with R*. Springer.

Schafer, J. L. 1997a. *Analysis of Incomplete Multivariate Data*. Chapman & Hall.

Schafer, J. L. 1997b. Imputation of Missing Covariates under a General Linear Mixed Model. Vignette included with R. package pan, https://cran.r-project.org/web/packages/pan/vignettes/pan-tr.pdf.

Schafer, J. L. 1999. Multiple Imputation: A Primer. *Statistical Methods in Medical Research* 8: 3–15.

Shannon, C. 1948. A Mathematical Theory of Communication. *Bell System Technical Journal* 27 (July and October): pp. 379–423, 623–656.

Sheather, S. J. and Jones, M. C. 1991. A Reliable Data-Based Bandwidth Selection Method for Kernel Density Estimation. *Journal of the Royal Statistical Society Series B*, 53, 683–690.

Shennan, S. 1997. *Quantifying Archaeology*. Iowa University Press.

Signorell, A., et al. 2016. DescTools: Tools for descriptive statistics. R package version 0.99.17.

Simpson, G. L. 2009. cocorresp: Co-correspondence analysis ordination methods. R package version 0.3-0.

Spaulding, A. C. 1953. Statistical Techniques for the Discovery of Artifact Types. *American Antiquity* 18: 305–313.

Spaulding, A. C. 1960. The Dimensions of Archaeology. In *Essays in the Science of Culture*, edited by G. E. Dole and R. L. Carneiro, pp. 437–456. Crowell.

Spaulding, A. C. 1976. Multifactor Analysis of Association: An Application to Owasco Ceramics. In *Cultural Change and Continuity: Essays in Honor of James Bennett Griffin*, edited by C. E. Cleland, pp. 59–68. Academic Press.

Su, Y.-S., A. Gelman, J. Hill, and M. Yajima. 2011. Multiple Imputation with Diagnostics (mi) in R: Opening Windows into the Black Box. *Journal of Statistical Software* 45(2): 1–31.

Tabachnick, B. G. and L. S. Fidell. 2007. *Using Multivariate Statistics*. 5th edition. Allyn and Bacon.

Templ, M., A. Alfons, A. Kowarik, and B. Prantner. 2016. VIM: Visualization and Imputation of Missing Values. R package version 4.5.0.

Thomas, D. H. 1978. The Awful Truth about Statistics in Archaeology. *American Antiquity* 43(2): 231–244.

Tubb, A., A. J. Parker, and G. Nickless. 1980. The Analysis of Romano-British Pottery by Atomic Absorption Spectrophotometry. *Archaeometry*, 22: 153–171.

Tufte, E. 1983. *The Visual Display of Quantitative Information*. Graphics Press.

Tufte, E. 1990. *Envisioning Information*. Graphics Press.

Tukey, J. 1977. *Exploratory Data Analysis*. Pearson.

Turner, E. S. and T. R. Hester. 1993. *A Field Guide to Stone Artifacts of Texas Indians.* 2nd edition. Gulf Publishing Co.

van Buuren, S. and K. Groothuis-Oudshoorn. 2011. mice: Multivariate Imputation by Chained Equations in R. *Journal of Statistical Software* 45(3), 1–67.

van den Boogaart, K. G. 2008. Using the R package compositions. Included with R package compositions.

van den Boogaart, K. G. and R. Tolosana-Delgado. 2008. compositions: A Unified R Package to Analyze Compositional Data. *Computers & Geosciences* 34: 320–338.

van den Boogaart, K. G., R. Tolosana, and M. Bren. 2014. compositions: Compositional Data Analysis. R package version 1.40-1.

Venables, W. N. and Ripley, B. D. 2002. *Modern Applied Statistics with S*, 4th edition. Springer, New York.

Venables, W. N. and B. D. Ripley. 2002. Chapter 7. Generalized Linear Models. In *Modern Applied Statistics with S*, pp. 183–210. Springer.

Walters, E. J., C. H. Morrell, and R. E. Auer. 2006. An Investigation of the Median-Median Method of Linear Regression. *Journal of Statistics Education* 14(2).

Warton, David I, Ian J. Wright, Daniel S. Falster, and Mark Westoby. 2006. Bivariate Line-Fitting Methods for Allometry. *Biological Reviews* 81: 259–291.

Wickham, H. 2009. *ggplot2: Elegant Graphics for Data Analysis.* Springer.

Williams, G. J. 2011. *Data Mining with Rattle and R: The Art of Excavating Data for Knowledge Discovery, Use R!* Springer.

INDEX